The Developer's Reference Guide to Microsoft® Small Basic

© Philip Conrod & Lou Tylee, 2010

http://www.computerscienceforkids.com
http://www.kidwaresoftware.com

Copyright © 2010 by Philip Conrod & Lou Tylee. All rights reserved

Kidware Software, LLC.
PO Box 701
Maple Valley, Washington 98038
1.425.413.1185
www.kidwaresoftware.com
www.computerscienceforkids.com
www.biblebytebooks.com

All Rights Reserved. No part of the contents of this book may be reproduced or transmitted in any form or by any means without the written permission of the publisher.

Printed in the United States of America

ISBN-13: 978-1-937161-24-8

Cover Illustrator & Copy Editor: Stephanie Conrod

This copy of the Developer's Reference Guide To Microsoft Small Basic and the associated software is licensed to a single user. Copies of the course are not to be distributed or provided to any other user. Multiple copy licenses are available for educational institutions. Please contact Kidware Software for school site license information.

This guide is not intended to be a complete reference to the Small Basic language. Please consult the Microsoft website for detailed reference information.

This guide refers to several software and hardware products by their trade names. These references are for informational purposes only and all trademarks are the property of their respective companies and owners.

Microsoft, Visual Studio, Small Basic, Visual Basic, Visual J#, and Visual C#, IntelliSense, Word, Excel, MSDN, and Windows are all trademark products of the Microsoft Corporation.

The example companies, organizations, products, domain names, e-mail addresses, logos, people, places, and events depicted are fictitious. No association with any real company, organization, product, domain name, e-mail address, logo, person, place, or event is intended or should be inferred.

This book expresses the author's views and opinions. The information in this book is distributed on an "as is" basis, without and expresses, statutory, or implied warranties.

Neither the author(s) nor Kidware Software shall have any liability to any person or entity with respect to any loss nor damage caused or alleged to be caused directly or indirectly by the information contained in this book.

ABOUT THE AUTHORS

Philip Conrod has been programming computers since 1978. Since then, he has authored, co-authored and edited many beginning computer programming tutorials and books for kids, teens and adults. Philip also holds a BS in Computer Information Systems and a Master's certificate in the Essentials of Business Development from Regis University. Philip has also held various Information Technology leadership roles in companies like Sundstrand Aerospace, Safeco Insurance Companies, FamilyLife, Kenworth Truck Company, and PACCAR. Today, Philip serves as the Chief Information Officer for a large manufacturing company based in Seattle, Washington. In his spare time, Philip serves as the President of Kidware Software, LLC. He makes his home with his lovely wife and three beautiful and "techie" daughters in Maple Valley, Washington.

Lou Tylee holds BS and MS degrees in Mechanical Engineering and a PhD in Electrical Engineering. Lou has been programming computers since 1969 when he took his first Fortran course in college. He has written software to control suspensions for high speed ground vehicles, monitor nuclear power plants, lower noise levels in commercial jetliners, compute takeoff speeds for jetliners, locate and identify air and ground traffic and to let kids count bunnies, learn how to spell and do math problems. He has written several on-line texts teaching Visual Basic, Visual C# and Java to thousands of people. He taught a beginning Visual Basic course for over 15 years at a major university. Currently, Lou works as an engineer at a major Seattle aerospace firm. He is the proud father of five children and proud husband of his special wife. Lou and his family live in Seattle, Washington.

Acknowledgements

I would like to thank my beautiful wife, Tiffany, for sacrificing so many nights and weekends so I could finish and publish this book. I also want to thank my three wonderful daughters - Stephanie, Jessica and Chloe, who helped with various aspects of the book publishing process including software testing, book editing, creative design and many other more tedious tasks like finding bugs. I could not have accomplished this without all your hard work, love and support.

Last but definitely not least, I want to thank my multi-talented co-author, Lou Tylee, for doing all the real hard work necessary to develop, test, debug, and keep current all the examples found in this book. Lou is by far one of the best application developers and tutorial writers I have ever worked with.   Thanks Lou for collaborating with me on this book project.

Contents

1. Introducing Small Basic

Preview 1-1
Introducing The Developer's Reference Guide to Small Basic 1-2
Requirements for The Developer's Reference Guide to Small Basic 1-3
Introducing Small Basic 1-4
Starting Small Basic 1-5
Running a Small Basic Program 1-7
Chapter Review 1-11

2. Overview of Small Basic Programming

Preview 2-1
A Brief History of BASIC 2-2
Variables 2-3
Small Basic Data Types 2-4
Arrays 2-5
Intellisense Feature 2-6
Small Basic Statements and Expressions 2-7
Small Basic Arithmetic Operators 2-8
Comparison and Logical Operators 2-9
Concatenation Operator 2-10
Math Functions 2-11
Random Numbers 2-13
Small Basic Decisions - If Statements 2-14
Small Basic Looping 2-17
Small Basic Counting 2-21
Small Basic Subroutines 2-23
Small Basic Objects 2-25
Chapter Review 2-27

Small Basic Objects

3. Program Object

Preview 3-1
Program Object 3-2
    Program Properties 3-2
    Program Methods 3-2
Example 3-1. Program Directory 3-3
Example 3-2. Program Delay 3-4
Program End Method 3-5
Example 3-3. Program End 3-6
Chapter Review 3-7

4. TextWindow Object

Preview 4-1
TextWindow Object 4-2
    TextWindow Properties 4-2
    TextWindow Methods 4-3
TextWindow Features 4-4
Example 4-1. TextWindow Properties 4-6
TextWindow Input 4-7
Example 4-2. TextWindow Input 4-8
TextWindow Output 4-11
Example 4-3. Dice Rolling (TextWindow Output) 4-12
Chapter Review 4-14

5. GraphicsWindow Object

Preview 5-1
GraphicsWindow Object 5-2
    GraphicsWindow Coordinates 5-2
    GraphicsWindow Properties 5-3
    GraphicsWindow Methods 5-5
    GraphicsWindow Events 5-7
GraphicsWindow Features 5-8
GraphicsWindow Colors 5-10
GraphicsWindow Font 5-11
Example 5-1. GraphicsWindow Properties 5-12
Example 5-2. SetPixel Method 5-13
Example 5-3. DrawLine Method 5-14
Example 5-4. Drawing Rectangles 5-16
Example 5-5. Drawing Ellipses 5-17
Example 5-6. Drawing Triangles 5-18
Chapter Review 5-19

6. Controls Object

Preview 6-1
Graphic User Interface (GUI) 6-2
Button Control 6-4
    Button Properties 6-4
    Button Methods 6-4
    Button Events 6-4
Example 6-1. Change Window Color 6-6
Example 6-2. Change Button Caption 6-8
Example 6-3. Hide/Show Buttons 6-10
TextBox Control 6-12
    TextBox Properties 6-12
    TextBox Methods 6-12
    TextBox Events 6-13
Example 6-4. Random Numbers 6-14
Example 6-5. Guess the Number 6-16
Example 6-6. Tray Problem 6-19
Chapter Review 6-22

7. Clock Object

Preview 7-1
Clock Object 7-2
   Clock Properties 7-2
Example 7-1. System Time/Date 7-3
Example 7-2. Stopwatch 7-5
Chapter Review 7-7

8. Text Object

Preview 8-1
Text Object 8-2
   Text Methods 8-2
Using Text Methods 8-4
KeyDown Event 8-7
Example 8-1. Character Codes 8-10
Example 8-2. Encode/Decode 8-12
Chapter Review 8-14

9. ImageList Object

Preview 9-1
ImageList Object 9-2
   ImageList Methods 9-2
Loading Image Files 9-3
Displaying Images 9-4
Example 9-1. Image Display 9-5
Example 9-2. Resized Image Display 9-10
MouseDown Event 9-15
Example 9-3. MouseDown Event 9-16
Example 9-4. Find the Burger Game 9-18
Example 9-5. Tic-Tac-Toe Game 9-21
Chapter Review 9-28

10. Shapes Object

Preview 10-1
Shapes Object 10-2
   Shapes Methods 10-2
Lines 10-4
Example 10-1. Line 10-5
Rectangles, Ellipses, Triangles 10-6
Example 10-2. Rectangle, Ellipse, Triangle 10-7
Text 10-9
Example 10-3. Text... 10-11
Images 10-13
Example 10-4. Image 10-14
Move Method... 10-16
Example 10-5. Random Burger... 10-17
Rotate Method 10-19
Example 10-6. Random, Rotating Burger................................... 10-22
Animate Method 10-24
Example 10-7. Stacking Boxes 10-25
Chapter Review 10-28

11. Mouse Object

Preview 11-1
Mouse Object 11-2
   Mouse Properties..11-2
   Mouse Methods 11-2
Use of Mouse Object 11-3
MouseDown Event..11-4
Example 11-1. MouseDown Example 11-5
MouseMove Event 11-7
Example 11-2. MouseMove Example 11-8
MouseUp Event 11-10
Example 11-3. MouseUp Example 11-11
Example 11-4. Drawing Program 11-13
Chapter Review 11-16

12. Timer Object

Preview 12-1
Timer Object 12-2
   Timer Properties 12-2
   Timer Methods 12-2
   Timer Events 12-2
Use of Timer Object 12-3
Example 12-1. Timer Example 12-4
Example 12-2. Ellipse Example 12-6
Example 12-3. Calendar Display 12-9
Example 12-4. Dice Rolling 12-11
Timer Object for Delays 12-14
Example 12-5. Display Delay 12-15
Example 12-6. Animated Find the Burger Game 12-19
Chapter Review 12-24

13. Sound Object

Preview 13-1
Sound Object 13-2
   Sound Methods 13-2
Built-In Sounds 13-3
Example 13-1. Built-In Sounds 13-4
Playing Other Sounds 13-6
Example 13-2. Playing Sounds 13-7
Chapter Review 13-9

14. File Object

Preview	14-1
File Object	14-2
File Properties	14-2
File Methods	14-2
Sequential Files	14-4
Sequential File Output	14-6
Example 14-1. Sequential File Output	14-7
Sequential File Input	14-6
Example 14-2. Sequential File Input	14-7
CSV (Comma Separated Values) Files	14-12
Example 14-3. CSV Data Files	14-14
Writing and Reading Text Using Sequential Files	14-19
Configuration Files	14-21
Example 14-4. Configuration Files	14-23
File Directory	14-26
Example 14-5. File Directory	14-27
Locating Files	14-30
Example 14-6. Locating Files	14-31
Chapter Review	14-33

Other Topics

15. Debugging a Small Basic Program

Preview 15-1

16. Input Validation

Preview 16-1
Text Box Input Validation 16-2
Date Validation 16-4
Example 16-1. Date Validation 16-5
Numeric Validation 16-10
Example 16-2. Numeric Validation 16-11
Chapter Review 16-15

17. Date Arithmetic

Preview 17-1
Subtracting Dates 17-2
Example 17-1. Subtracting Dates 17-5
Chapter Review 17-10

18. Shuffling Integers

Preview 18-1
Shuffling Integers 18-2
Example 18-1. Shuffling Integers 18-4
Displaying Playing Cards 18-6
Example 18-2. Displaying Playing Cards 18-9
Example 18-3. Video Poker 18-11
Chapter Review 18-17

19. Line, Bar and Pie Charts

Preview 19-1
Line Charts and Bar Charts 19-2
Coordinate Conversions 19-5
Drawing a Line Chart 19-8
Example 19-1. Mariners Attendance Line Chart 19-10
Axis Labeling 19-13
Example 19-2. Y Axis Labeling 19-17
Example 19-3. X Axis Labeling 19-19
Plot Labeling 19-22
Example 19-4. Plot Labeling 19-23
Drawing a Bar Chart 19-29
Example 19-5. Mariners Attendance Bar Chart 19-31
Bar Chart X Axis Labeling 19-37
Example 19-6. Bar Chart X Axis Labeling 19-37
Example 19-7. Seattle Rainfall Bar Chart 19-41
Pie Charts 19-44
Example 19-8. Drawing a Pie Segment 19-47
Drawing a Pie Chart 19-49
Example 19-9. Seattle Rainfall Pie Chart 19-50
Pie Chart Labeling 19-53
Example 19-10. Pie Chart Labeling 19-54
Chapter Review 19-58

20. Animation

Preview 20-1
Animation with Small Basic 20-2
Example 20-1. Dropping Ball 20-4
Border Crossing...20-7
Example 20-2. Scrolling Ball 20-9
Border Intersection 20-11
Example 20-3. Bouncing Ball 20-12
Example 20-4. Bouncing Ball with Sound............................... 20-16
Example 20-5. Two Bouncing Balls.. 20-18
Collision Detection... 20-22
Example 20-6. Two Colliding Balls 20-25
Example 20-7. Bouncing Ball with Paddle.............................. 20-29
Example 20-8. The Original Video Game – Pong! 20-34
Chapter Review 20-40

21. Check Box and Radio Button Controls

Preview 21-1
Check Box Controls 21-2
Example 21-1. Create Check Box Group 21-5
Clicking a Check Box 21-7
Example 21-2. Clicking Check Boxes.......................................21-9
Radio Button Controls.. 21-12
Example 21-3. Create Radio Button Group 21-16
Clicking a Radio Button 21-18
Example 21-4. Clicking Radio Buttons 21-19
Example 21-5. Pizza Ordering 21-22
Chapter Review 21-27

22. Turtle Graphics

Preview 22-1
Turtle Object 22-2
Turtle Properties..22-2
Turtle Methods 22-3
Example 22-1. Draw a Square..22-4
Example 22-2. Draw a Polygon 22-6
Example 22-3. Draw Multi-Colored Circles............................. 22-10
Other Turtle Graphics 22-12
Example 22-4. Draw a Flower... 22-13
Example 22-5. Draw a Pinwheel.. 22-16
Example 22-6. Draw a Spiral Effect 22-18
Chapter Review 22-20

23. Flickr Photos

Preview 23-1
Flickr Class 23-2
Flickr Methods 23-2
Example 23-1. Picture of the Moment....................................23-3
Example 23-2. Tagged Picture 23-6
Chapter Review 23-10

24. Dictionary

Preview 24-1
Dictionary Class 24-2
Dictionary Methods 24-2
Example 24-1. Word Definition 24-3
Chapter Review 24-5

25. Sharing a Small Basic Program

Preview 25-1
Sharing a Program 25-2
Publishing a Program 25-5
Importing a Program 25-9
Chapter Review 25-10

Appendix I. Small Basic Colors

This page intentionally not left blank.

Introduction

The Developer's Guide to Microsoft Small Basic provides an extensive overview of the Small Basic programming environment. The guide consists of 25 chapters explaining (in simple, easy to follow terms) how to use Small Basic to build programs. You learn about each Small Basic object. You learn about button and text box controls, using the mouse, graphics, shapes, images, timers, sounds and sequential file access. Both text window and graphics window applications are discussed.

Nearly 100 programming examples are included. We discuss input validation, date arithmetic, integer shuffling, simple animation, line, bar, and pie charts, programming check box and radio button controls, turtle graphics, and ways to share your program. **The Developer's Guide to Microsoft Small Basic** is presented using a combination of over 500 pages of notes and includes the code for all examples.

Prerequisites:

To use **The Developer's Guide to Microsoft Small Basic**, you should be comfortable working within the Windows (or other operating system) environment, knowing how to find files, move windows, resize windows, etc. No programming experience is needed. You will also need the ability to view and print documents saved in Microsoft Word format. This can be accomplished in one of two ways. The first, and easiest, is that you already have Microsoft Word (or a compatible equivalent) on your computer. The second way is that you can download the Microsoft Word Viewer. This is a free Microsoft product that allows viewing and printing Word documents - it is available for download at all the major shareware internet sites and from our website.

Finally, and most obvious, you need to have Small Basic. This is a FREE product that can be downloaded from the Microsoft website. The website is:

> http://www.smallbasic.com

This site contains complete downloading and installation instructions for the latest version of Small Basic.

Installing The Developer's Guide to Microsoft Small Basic:

The notes and code for **The Developer's Guide to Microsoft Small Basic** are included in one or more ZIP files. Use your favorite 'unzipping' application to write all files to your computer. (If you've received the course on CD-ROM, the files are not zipped and no unzipping is needed.) The product is included in the folder entitled **The Developer's Guide to Microsoft Small Basic**. This folder contains two other folders: **Guide** and **Programs**.

The **Guide** folder includes all the notes needed for the guide. Each file in this folder has a DOC extension and is in Microsoft Word format. The files are:

StartHere.doc	This file in Word format
Contents.doc	Table of Contents
Chapter 1.doc	Chapter 1. Introducing Small Basic
Chapter 2.doc	Chapter 2. Overview of Small Basic Programming
Chapter 3.doc	Chapter 3. Program Object
Chapter 4.doc	Chapter 4. TextWindow Object
Chapter 5.doc	Chapter 5. GraphicsWindow Object
Chapter 6.doc	Chapter 6. Controls Object
Chapter 7.doc	Chapter 7. Clock Object
Chapter 8.doc	Chapter 8. Text Object
Chapter 9.doc	Chapter 9. ImageList Object
Chapter 10.doc	Chapter 10. Shapes Object
Chapter 11.doc	Chapter 11. Mouse Object
Chapter 12.doc	Chapter 12. Timer Object
Chapter 13.doc	Chapter 13. Sound Object
Chapter 14.doc	Chapter 14. File Object
Chapter 15.doc	Chapter 15. Debugging a Small Basic Program
Chapter 16.doc	Chapter 16. Input Validation
Chapter 17.doc	Chapter 17. Date Arithmetic
Chapter 18.doc	Chapter 18. Shuffling Integers
Chapter 19.doc	Chapter 19. Line, Bar and Pie Charts
Chapter 20.doc	Chapter 20. Animation
Chapter 21.doc	Chapter 21. Check Box and Radio Button Controls
Chapter 22.doc	Chapter 22. Turtle Graphics
Chapter 23.doc	Chapter 23. Flickr Photos
Chapter 24.doc	Chapter 24. Dictionary
Chapter 25.doc	Chapter 25. Sharing a Small Basic Program
Appendix I.doc	Appendix I. Small Basic Colors

The **Programs** folder includes all the Small Basic programs developed in the guide.

The Developer's Reference Guide to Small Basic

1. Introducing Small Basic

Preview

In this first chapter, we will do an overview of how to write a program using Small Basic. You'll get a brief history of Small Basic and look into use of the Small Basic development environment.

Introducing Guide to Small Basic

In these notes, we provide a thorough overview of the Microsoft Small Basic programming environment. We review the language of Small Basic and the objects used by Small Basic. We also cover many advanced topics. Along the way, we will build many Small Basic example programs to illustrate the skills learned. You can use many of these code "snippets" in programs and applications you build. All Small Basic code is included with the notes.

As a first step to this overview, we will review Small Basic and its development environment in the remainder of this chapter. Then, we provide a review of the Small Basic programming language in Chapter 2. Beginning with Chapter 3, we cover many of the objects included as part of Small Basic. With each chapter, objects will be summarized and several example programs will be built to show how Small Basic can be used. The notes end with chapters on advanced topics such as debugging, graphics, animation, sharing programs on the Internet, graduating programs to Microsoft Visual Basic and building libraries you can use in Small Basic.

Requirements for Guide to Small Basic

Before starting, let's examine what you need to successfully build the programs included with **The Developer's Reference Guide to Small Basic**. As far as computer skills, you should be comfortable working within the Windows environment. You should know how to run programs, find and create folders, and move and resize windows.

As far as programming skills, we assume you have had some exposure to computer programming using some language. If that language is **Small Basic**, great!! We offer two beginning Small Basic tutorials that could help you gain that exposure (see our website for details). But, if you've ever programmed in any language (Visual Basic, C, C++, C#, Java, J#, Ada, even FORTRAN), you should be able to follow what's going on.

Regarding software requirements, to use Small Basic, you must be using Windows 7, Windows XP, or Windows Vista. These notes and all programs are developed using Windows Vista and Version 0.9 of Small Basic. And, of course, you need to have the Small Basic product installed on your computer. It is available for free download from Microsoft. Follow this link for complete instructions for downloading and installing Small Basic on your computer:

http://www.smallbasic.com

Introducing Small Basic

In the late 1970's and early 1980's, it seems there were computers everywhere with names like Commodore 64, Texas Instruments 99/4A, Atari 400, Coleco Adam, Timex Sinclair and the IBM PC-Jr. Stores like Sears, JC Penneys and even K Mart sold computers. One thing these machines had in common was that they were all programmed in some version of Microsoft's BASIC. Each computer had its own fans and own magazines. Users would wait each month for the next issue of a magazine with BASIC programs you could type into your computer and try at home.

This was a fun and exciting time for the beginning programmer, but the fun times ended with the introduction of the IBM-PC in the early 1980's. Bigger and faster computers brought forth bigger languages and bigger development environments. These new languages were expensive to acquire and difficult for the beginning programmer to grasp.

Which brings us to **Small Basic**, which I would call a relative of the early, original BASIC language. The development of Small Basic is an attempt to rekindle the exciting days when just about anyone could sit down at a computer and write a simple program using the BASIC language. Those of you who wrote programs on those old "toy" computers will recognize the simplicity of the Small Basic language and the ease of its use. And, you will also notice Small Basic is a great environment for writing and testing code, something missing in the early 1980's. For those of you new to programming, I hope you can feel the excitement we old timers once had. For the old timers, I hope you rekindle your programming skills with this new product.

Small Basic possesses many features of more powerful (and more expensive) programming languages:

- Easy-to-use, Integrated Development Environment (IDE)
- Response to mouse and keyboard actions
- Button and text box controls
- Full array of mathematical, string handling, and graphics functions
- Can easily work with arrays
- Sequential file support

Starting Small Basic

We assume you have Small Basic installed and operational on your computer. Once installed, to start Small Basic:

- ➢ Click on the **Start** button on the Windows task bar
- ➢ Select **Programs**, then **Small Basic**
- ➢ Click on **Microsoft Small Basic**

(Some of the headings given here may differ slightly on your computer, but you should have no trouble finding the correct ones.) The Small Basic program should start.

After installation and trying to start, you may see an error message that announces Small Basic cannot be started. If this occurs, try downloading and installing the latest version of the Microsoft .NET framework at:

http://msdn.microsoft.com/en-us/netframework/aa569263.aspx

This contains some files that Small Basic needs to operate and such files may not be on your computer.

Upon starting, my screen shows:

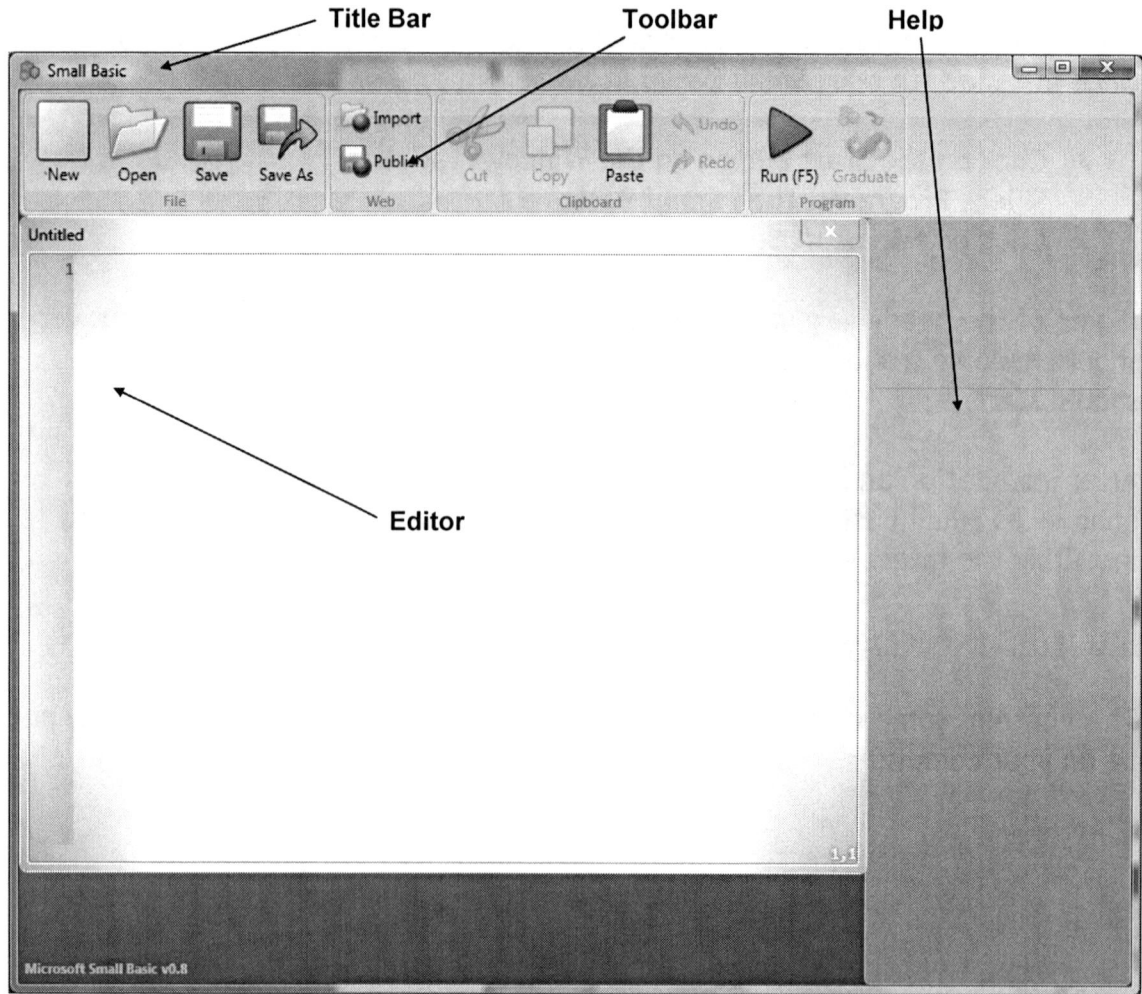

This window displays the **Small Basic Development Environment**. There are many areas of interest on the screen. At the top of the window is the **Title Bar**. The title bar gives us information about what program we're using and what Small Basic program we are working with. Below the title bar is a **Toolbar**. Here, little buttons with pictures allow us to control Small Basic.

In the middle of the screen is the **Editor**. This is where we will write our Small Basic programs. To the right is a **Help** area. Small Basic has great help features when writing programs. This area will display hints and tips while we write code.

Running a Small Basic Program

Let's write our first Small Basic program. When you start, a new editor window appears. You can also get a new editor window by clicking the **New** toolbar button. Type these two lines in the editor window:

```
TextWindow.Title = "Hello Program"
TextWindow.WriteLine("This is the first line of the program.")
```

The editor window should look like this:

```
Untitled *
  1 TextWindow.Title = "Hello Program"
  2 TextWindow.WriteLine("This is the first line of the program.")
  3
  4
```

Notice as you started typing the first line, this popped-up:

Small Basic has "intellisense" and uses this to make typing suggestions. You can just keep typing or accept its suggestion by scrolling through the pop-up list and pressing the **Enter** key.

Also, notice this appeared in the help area:

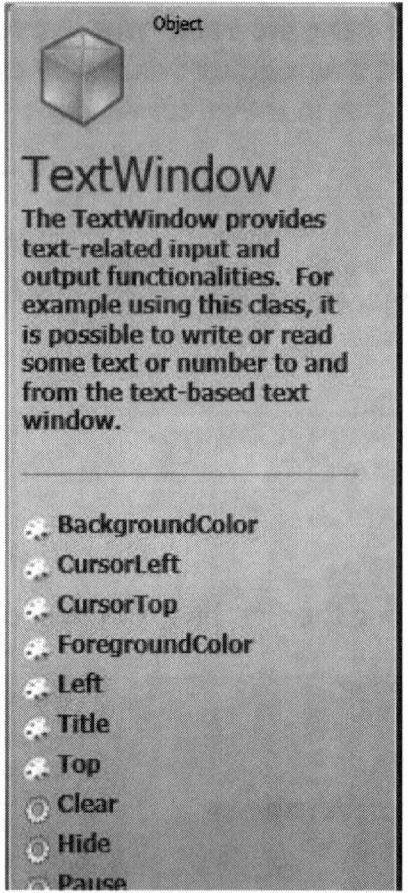

Once you typed **TextWindow**, the help feature displayed all it knows about the **TextWindow** to help you in your programming.

The **TextWindow** is a Small Basic **object**. It displays text output. The object has **properties, methods** and **events**. There are many objects in Small Basic. They will be covered in detail in individual chapters of these notes.

Introducing Small Basic 1-9

Let's **Run** the program. Simply click the **Run** button on the toolbar to see:

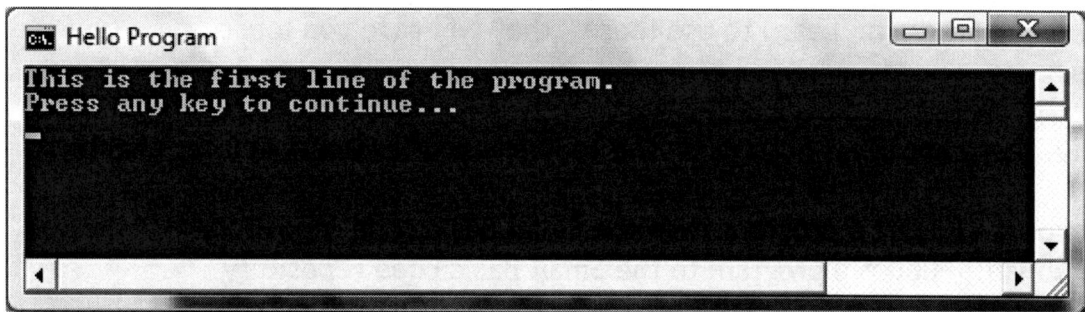

This is the text window displaying the program output. I have resized the window. To stop the program, click the **X** in the upper right corner of the window.

That's all there is to writing a Small Basic program. Type the code in the editor window. Click the **Run** button to run the code. We will learn how to use a lot of Small Basic code as we work through these notes. Chapter 2 reviews most elements of the Small Basic language.

Other useful toolbar buttons are:

   Open - Open a previously saved Small Basic program
   Save - Save a Small Basic program
   Save As - Save a Small Basic program with a different name

We suggest saving each Small Basic program in its own folder.

When you **Save** and **Run** a Small Basic program, four files are created. If you name your program **MyProgram**, the corresponding files in the program folder are:

MyProgram.sb	The code that appears in the editor of Small Basic
MyProgram.exe	A 'compiled' version of the code.
MyProgram.pdb	A database file with information needed by your program
SmallBasicLibrary.dll	The Small Basic run-time library. It contains files that help your program run.

Do not modify any of these files outside the Small Basic environment.

There are also the **Cut, Copy, Paste, Undo,** and **Redo** buttons for common editing tasks. They work just like the corresponding buttons in a word processing program. Learn to use these – they will save you lots of time typing code.

Lastly, there are other buttons on the toolbar we will discuss in later chapters:

    Import – Import a program from the Small Basic code repository
    Publish – Publish a program to the Small Basic code repository
    Graduate – Convert a Small Basic program to Visual Basic Express

Chapter Review

This completes our overview of the Small Basic environment and a brief demonstration of how to write a Small Basic program. If you've used Small Basic before, this material should be familiar. If you've programmed with other languages, you should have a fairly clear understanding of what's going on.

After completing this chapter, you should understand:

- A little of the history of Small Basic.
- The various parts of the Small Basic integrated development environment.
- The utility of "intellisense" and the Small Basic help panel.
- How to write code using the code editor.
- How to run a Small Basic program.

Next, let's review the language of Small Basic.

This page intentionally not left blank.

2. Overview of Small Basic Programming

Preview

In this chapter, we are concerned with writing code for our programs. We will provide an overview of many of the elements of the language used in Small Basic. This chapter is essentially a self-contained guide to the Small Basic language. This will give us the foundation needed to begin learning about Small Basic objects and writing more detailed programs.

A Brief History of BASIC

The BASIC language was developed in the early 1960's at Dartmouth College as a device for teaching programming to "ordinary" people. There is a reason it's called BASIC:

B (eginner's)
A (All-Purpose)
S (Symbolic)
I (Instruction)
C (Code)

When timesharing systems were introduced in the 1960's, BASIC was the language of choice. Many of the first computer simulation games (Star Trek, for example) were written in timeshare BASIC. In the mid-1970's, two college students decided that the new Altair microcomputer needed a BASIC language interpreter. They sold their product on cassette tape for a cost of $350. You may have heard of these entrepreneurs: Bill Gates and Paul Allen!

Every BASIC written since then has been based on that early version. Examples include: GW-Basic, QBasic, QuickBasic, Visual Basic. All the toy computers of the early 80's (anyone remember TI99/4A, Commodore 64, Timex, Atari 400?) used BASIC for programming. Small Basic continues the tradition of BASIC programming. It uses the simple concepts of the early BASIC language with a modern development environment.

This chapter provides an overview of the BASIC language used in the Small Basic environment. If you've ever used another programming language (or some version of BASIC), you will see equivalent structures in the language of Small Basic.

Variables

Variables are used by Small Basic to hold information needed by an application. Variables must be properly named. Rules used in naming variables:

- No more than 40 characters
- They may include letters, numbers, and underscore (_)
- The first character must be a letter
- You cannot use a reserved word (keywords used by Small Basic)

Use meaningful variable names that help you (or other programmers) understand the purpose of the information stored by the variable.

Examples of acceptable variable names:

StartingTime	Interest_Value	Letter05
JohnsAge	Number_of_Days	TimeOfDay

Small Basic Data Types

Each variable is used to store information of a particular **type**. Small Basic uses three types of data: **numeric, string** (or text) and **Boolean** variables. You must always know the type of information stored in a particular variable.

Numeric variables can store integer or decimal numbers. They can be positive or negative.

A **string** variable is just that – one that stores a string (list) of various characters. A string can be a name, a string of numbers, a sentence, a paragraph, any characters at all. And, many times, a string will contain no characters at all (an empty string). We will use lots of strings in Small Basic, so it's something you should become familiar with. Strings are always enclosed in quotes ("). Examples of strings:

"I am a Small Basic programmer"   "012345"   "Title   Author"

Boolean variables can have one of two different string values: **"true"** or **"false"**. The quotes are need to indicate these are string values. Boolean variables are helpful in making decisions.

With all the different variable types, we need to be careful not to improperly mix types. We can only do mathematical operations on numbers (integer and decimal types). String types must only work with other string types. Boolean types are used for decisions.

Small Basic has no requirements (or capabilities) for declaring variables before they are used. They are essentially declared the first time they are used.

Arrays

Small Basic has facilities for handling arrays, which provide a way to store a large number of variables under the same name. Each variable, called an element, in an array must have the same data type, and they are distinguished from each other by an array index which is enclosed in brackets **[]**.

Arrays are used in a manner identical to that of regular variables. For example, the ninth element of an array named **Item** is:

```
Item[9]
```

The index on an array variable begins at 0 and ends at the highest value used. Hence, the **Item** array in the above example actually has **ten** elements, ranging from Item[0] to Item[9]. This is different than other languages. You use array variables just like any other variable - just remember to include its name and its index. Many times, the 0 index is ignored and we just start with item 1. But sometimes the 0th element cannot be ignored. You will see examples of both 0-based and 1-based arrays in the course examples.

You can have multi-dimensional arrays. A two-dimensional array element is written as:

```
AnotherArray[2][7]
```

This refers to the element in the 2nd row and 7th column of the array **AnotherArray**.

Intellisense Feature

Working within the code editor window is easy. You will see that typing code is just like using any word processor. The usual navigation and editing features are all there.

One feature that you will become comfortable with and amazed with is called **Intellisense**. As you type code, the Intellisense feature will, at times, provide assistance in completing lines of code. For example, once you type an object name and a dot (.), a drop-down list of possible properties and methods will appear.

Intellisense is a very useful part of Small Basic. You should become acquainted with its use and how to select suggested values. We tell you about now so you won't be surprised when little boxes start popping up as you type code.

Small Basic Statements and Expressions

The simplest (and most common) statement in Small Basic is the **assignment** statement. It consists of a variable name, followed by the assignment operator (=), followed by some sort of **expression**. The expression on the right hand side is evaluated, then the variable (or property) on the left hand side of the assignment operator is **replaced** by that value of the expression.

Examples:

```
StartTime = Now
ExplorerName = "Captain Spaulding"
TextWindow.Title = "My Program"
BitCount = ByteCount * 8
Energy = Mass * LightSpeed * LightSpeed
NetWorth = Assets - Liabilities
```

The assignment statement stores information.

Comment statements begin with a single quote ('). For example:

```
' This is a comment
x = 2 * y  ' another way to write a comment
```

You, as a programmer, should decide how much to comment your code. Consider such factors as reuse, your audience, and the legacy of your code. In our notes and examples, we try to insert comment statements when necessary to explain some detail.

Small Basic Arithmetic Operators

Operators modify values of variables. The simplest **operators** carry out **arithmetic** operations. There are four **arithmetic operators** in Small Basic.

Addition is done using the plus (+) sign and **subtraction** is done using the minus (-) sign. Simple examples are:

Operation	Example	Result
Addition	7 + 2	9
Addition	3.4 + 8.1	11.5
Subtraction	6 - 4	2
Subtraction	11.1 - 7.6	3.5

Multiplication is done using the asterisk (*) and **division** is done using the slash (/). Simple examples are:

Operation	Example	Result
Multiplication	8 * 4	32
Multiplication	2.3 * 12.2	28.06
Division	12 / 2	6
Division	45.26 / 6.2	7.3

The mathematical operators have the following **precedence** indicating the order they are evaluated without specific groupings:

1. Multiplication (*) and division (/)
2. Addition (+) and subtraction (-)

If multiplications and divisions or additions and subtractions are in the same expression, they are performed in left-to-right order. **Parentheses** around expressions are used to force some desired precedence.

Comparison and Logical Operators

There are six **comparison** operators in Small Basic used to compare the value of two expressions (the expressions must be of the same data type). These are the basis for making decisions:

Operator	Comparison
>	Greater than
<	Less than
>=	Greater than or equal to
<=	Less than or equal to
=	Equal to
<>	Not equal to

It should be obvious that the result of a comparison operation is a Boolean value (**"true"** or **"false"**). Examples:

A = 9.6, B = 8.1, A > B returns "true"
A = 14, B = 14, A < B returns "false"
A = 14, B = 14, A >= B returns "true"
A = 7, B = 11, A <= B returns "true"
A = "Small", B="Small", A = B returns "true"
A = "Basic", B = "Basic", A <> B returns "false"

Logical operators operate on Boolean data types, providing a Boolean result. They are also used in decision making. We will use two **logical** operators

Operator	Operation
And	Logical And
Or	Logical Or

The **And** operator checks to see if two different Boolean data types are both "true". If both are "true", the operator returns a "true". Otherwise, it returns a "false" value. Examples:

    A = "true", B = "true", then A **And** B = "true"
    A = "true", B = "false", then A **And** B = "false"
    A = "false", B = "true", then A **And** B = "false"
    A = "false", B = "false", then A **And** B = "false"

The **Or** operator checks to see if either of two Boolean data types is "true". If either is "true", the operator returns a "true". Otherwise, it returns a "false" value. Examples:

    A = "true", B = "true", then A **Or** B = "true"
    A = "true", B = "false", then A **Or** B = "true"
    A = "false", B = "true", then A **Or** B = "true"
    A = "false", B = "false", then A **Or** B = "false"

Logical operators follow arithmetic operators in precedence. Use of these operators will become obvious as we delve further into coding.

Concatenation Operator

To **concatentate** two string data types (tie them together), use the + symbol, the string concatenation operators:

```
CurrentTime = "The current time is " + TimeNow
SampleText = "Hook this " + "to this"
```

Math Functions

Small Basic provides a set of methods (or functions) that perform tasks such as square roots, trigonometric relationships, and exponential functions. Yes, some programming does involve math!

Each of the Small Basic math functions comes from the **Math** class. All this means is that each function name must be preceded by **Math.** (say Math-dot) to work properly. The functions and the returned values are listed below.

Math Functions:

`Math.Abs(x)`
Returns the absolute value of x.

`Math.ArcCos(x)`
Returns the angle in radians, given the cosine value x.

`Math.ArcSin(x)`
Returns the angle in radians, given the sine value x.

`Math.ArcTan(x)`
Returns the angle in radians, given the tangent value x.

`Math.Ceiling(x)`
Gets an integer that is greater than or equal to x. For example, 32.233 will return 33.

`Math.Cos(x)`
Returns a value containing the cosine of the specified angle (x) in radians.

`Math.Floor(x)`
Gets an integer that is less than or equal to x. For example, 32.233 will return 32.

`Math.GetDegrees(x)`
Converts a given angle (x) in radians to degrees.

`Math.GetRadians(x)`
Converts a given angle (x) in degrees to radians.

`Math.GetRandomNumber(x)`
Gets a random number between 1 and x (inclusive).

`Math.Log(x)`
Gets the logarithm (base 10) value of the given number x.

`Math.Max(x,y)`
Returns the larger of two numbers x and y.

`Math.Min(x,y)`
Returns the smaller of two numbers x and y.

`Math.NaturalLog(x)`
Gets the natural logarithm value of the given number x.

`Math.Pi()`
A constant that specifies the ratio of the circumference of a circle to its diameter (3.14159265359...).

`Math.Power(x,y)`
Raises a number (x) to a specified power (y(.

`Math.Remainder(x,y)`
Divides the first number (x) by the second (y) and returns the remainder.

`Math.Round(x,y)`
Rounds x to the nearest integer. For example 32.233 will be rounded to 32.0 while 32.566 will be rounded to 33.

`Math.Sin(x)`
Returns a value containing the sine of the specified angle (x) in radians.

`Math.SquareRoot(x)`
Returns a value specifying the square root of a number x.

`Math.Tan(x)`
Returns a value containing the tangent of an angle (x)in radians.

Examples:

```
Math.Abs(-5.4)  returns the absolute value of -5.4 (returns 5.4)
Math.Cos(2.3)  returns the cosine of an angle of 2.3 radians
Math.Max(7, 10)  returns the larger of the two numbers (returns 10)
Math.Power(2, 4)  returns 2 raised to the fourth power (16)
Math.SquareRoot(4.5)  returns the square root of 4.5
```

Overview of Small Basic Programming

Random Numbers

We single out one math method for its importance. In writing games and learning software, we use a random number generator to introduce unpredictability. The **Math.GetRandomNumber** method is used in Small Basic for random numbers.

Whenever you need a random whole number (integer) value, use this method:

```
Math.GetRandomNumber(Limit)
```

This statement generates a random integer value that is between 1 and **Limit**. For example, the method:

```
Math.GetRandomNumber(5)
```

will generate random numbers from 1 to 5. The possible values will be 1, 2, 3, 4 and 5.

A roll of a die can produce a number from 1 to 6. To use **GetRandomNumber** to roll a die, we would write:

```
DieNumber = Math.GetRandomNumber(6)
```

For a deck of cards, the random integers would range from 1 to 52 since there are 52 cards in a standard playing deck. Code to do this:

```
CardNumber = Math.GetRandomNumber(52)
```

If we want a number between -100 and 100, we would use:

```
YourNumber = 101 - Math.GetRandomNumber(201)
```

Check the examples above to make sure you see how the random number generator produces the desired range of integers.

Small Basic Decisions - If Statements

The concept of an **If** statement for making a decision is very simple. We check to see if a particular condition is "true". If so, we take a certain action. If not, we do something else. **If** statements are also called **branching** statements. **Branching** statements are used to cause certain actions within a program if a certain condition is met.

The simplest branching statement is:

```
If (Condition) Then
    [process this code]
EndIf
```

Here, if **Condition** is "true", the code bounded by the **If/EndIf** is executed. If **Condition** is "false", nothing happens and code execution continues after the **EndIf** statement.

Example:

```
If (Balance - Check < 0) Then
   Trouble = "true"
   CheckingStatus = "Red"
EndIf
```

In this case, if **Balance - Check** is less than zero, two lines of information are processed: **Trouble** is set to "true" and the **CheckingStatus** has a value of "Red". Notice the indentation of the code between the **If** and **EndIf** lines. The Small Basic Intellisense feature will automatically do this indentation. It makes understanding (and debugging) your code much easier.

Overview of Small Basic Programming 2-15

What if you want to do one thing if a condition is "true" and another if it is "false"? Use an **If/Then/Else/EndIf** block:

```
If (Condition) Then
    [process this code]
Else
    [process this code]
EndIf
```

In this block, if **Condition** is "true", the code between the **If** and **Else** lines is executed. If **Condition** is "false", the code between the **Else** and **EndIf** statements is processed.

Example:

```
If (Balance - Check < 0) Then
  Trouble = "true"
  CheckingStatus = "Red"
Else
  Trouble = "false"
  CheckingStatus = "Black"
EndIf
```

Here, the same two lines are executed if you are overdrawn (**Balance - Check < 0**), but if you are not overdrawn (**Else**), the **Trouble** flag is turned off and your **CheckingStatus** is "Black".

Finally, we can test multiple conditions by adding the **ElseIf** statement:

```
If (Condition1) Then
    [process this code]
ElseIf (Condition2) Then
    [process this code]
ElseIf (Condition3) Then
    [process this code]
Else
    [process this code]
EndIf
```

In this block, if **Condition1** is "true", the code between the **If** and first **ElseIf** line is executed. If **Condition1** is "false", **Condition2** is checked. If **Condition2** is "true", the indicated code is executed. If **Condition2** is not true, **Condition3** is checked. Each subsequent condition in the structure is checked until a "true" condition is found, a **Else** statement is reached or the **EndIf** is reached.

Example:

```
If (Balance - Check < 0) Then
   Trouble = "true"
   CheckingStatus = "Red"
ElseIf (Balance - Check = 0) Then
   Trouble = "false"
   CheckingStatus = "Yellow"
Else
   Trouble = "false"
   CheckingStatus = "Black"
EndIf
```

Now, one more condition is added. If your **Balance** equals the **Check** amount (**ElseIf Balance - Check = 0**), you're still not in trouble and the **CheckingStatus** is "Yellow".

In using branching statements, make sure you consider all viable possibilities in the **If/Else/EndIf** structure. Also, be aware that each **If** and **ElseIf** in a block is tested sequentially. The first time an **If** test is met, the code associated with that condition is executed and the **If** block is exited. If a later condition is also "true", it will never be considered.

Small Basic Looping

Many applications require repetition of certain code segments. For example, you may want to roll a die (simulated die of course) until it shows a six. Or, you might generate financial results until a certain sum of returns has been achieved. This idea of repeating code is called iteration or **looping**.

In Small Basic, one way of looping is with the **While** loop:

```
While (Condition)
  ' Small Basic code block to repeat while Condition is true
EndWhile
```

In this structure, all code between **While** and **EndWhile** is repeated while the given logical **Condition** is "true".

Note a **While** loop structure will not execute even once if **Condition** is "false" the first time through. If we do enter the loop (**Condition** is "true"), it is assumed at some point **Condition** will become false to allow exiting. Once this happens, code execution continues at the statement following the **EndWhile** statement. This brings up a very important point about loops - if you get in one, make sure you get out at some point. In the **While** loop, if **Condition** is always "true", you will loop forever - something called an infinite loop.

Example:

```
Counter = 1
While (Counter <= 1000)
  Counter = Counter + 1
EndWhile
```

This loop repeats as long as (**While**) the variable **Counter** is less than or equal to 1000.

Another Example:

```
Rolls = 0
Counter = 0
While (Counter < 10)
  ' Roll a simulated die
  Rolls = Rolls + 1
  If (Math.GetRandomNumber(6) = 6) Then
    Counter = Counter + 1
  EndIf
EndWhile
```

This loop repeats while the **Counter** variable remains less than 10. The **Counter** variable is incremented (increased by one) each time a simulated die rolls a 6 (the **GetRandomNumber** function used here returns a random value from 1 to 6). The **Rolls** variable tells you how many rolls of the die were needed to roll 10 sixes. Theoretically, it should take 60 rolls since there is a 1 in 6 chance of rolling a six.

As mentioned, if the logical condition used by a **While** loop is "false" the first time the loop is encountered, the code block in the **While** loop will not be executed. This may be acceptable behavior – it may not be.

We can build a loop that will always be executed at least once. To do this we need to introduce the Small Basic **Goto** statement. A **Goto** allows you to transfer code execution to anywhere in your code. A **Goto** requires a **label**. A label is like a bookmark – it can be named anything you want. A label name is always followed by a colon. An example is:

```
MyLabel:
```

Anytime we want to transfer program execution to this label statement, we use a **Goto**:

```
Goto MyLabel
```

You do not write the colon in the **Goto** statement.

Overview of Small Basic Programming   2-19

Using these new concepts in a loop, we have what we'll call a **Goto loop**:

```
MyLabel:
  ' Small Basic code block to process
If (Condition) Then
  Goto MyLabel
EndIf
```

The code block repeats as long as **Condition** is "true". Unlike the **While** loop, this loop is always executed at least once. Somewhere in the loop, **Condition** should be changed to "false" to allow exiting.

Let's look at examples of the **Goto** loop. What if we want to keep adding three to a **Sum** until the value exceeds 50. This loop will do it:

```
Sum = 0
SumLoop:
  Sum = Sum + 3
If (Sum <= 50) Then
  Goto SumLoop
EndIf
```

Another Dice Example:

```
Sum = 0
Rolls = 0
SumLoop:
  ' Roll a simulated die
  Die = Math.GetRandomNumber(6)
  Sum = Sum + Die
  Rolls = Rolls + 1
If (Sum <= 30) Then
  Goto SumLoop
EndIf
```

This loop rolls a simulated die (**Die**) while the **Sum** of the rolls does not exceed 30. It also keeps track of the number of rolls (**Rolls**) needed to achieve this sum.

You need to decide which of the loop structures (**While**, **Goto**) fits your program. Recall the major difference is that a **Goto** loop is always executed at least once; a **While** loop may never be executed.

And, make sure you can always get out of a loop. In both looping structures, this means that, at some point, the checking logical condition must become "false" to allow exiting the loop. When you exit a **While** loop, processing continues at the next Small Basic statement after the **EndWhile**. In a **Goto** loop, processing continues at the Small Basic statement after the **If** structure checking whether the loop should repeat.

If, at some point in the code block of a loop, you decide you need to immediately leave the loop or move to another point in the code, a **Goto** statement can also do this. You just need a label statement at the appropriate place. When the **Goto** statement is encountered, processing is immediately transferred to the labeled statement.

Small Basic Counting

With **While** loop structures, we usually didn't know, ahead of time, how many times we execute a loop or iterate. If you know how many times you need to iterate on some code, you want to use Small Basic **counting**. Counting is useful for adding items to a list or perhaps summing a known number of values to find an average.

Small Basic counting is accomplished using the **For** loop:

```
For Variable = Start To End Step Increment
  ' Small Basic code to execute goes here
EndFor
```

In this loop, **Variable** is the counter (doesn't necessarily need to be a whole number). The first time through the loop, **Variable** is initialized at **Start**. Each time the corresponding **EndFor** statement is reached, **Variable** is incremented by an amount **Increment**. If the **Step** value is omitted, a default increment value of one is used. Negative increments are also possible. The counting repeats until **Variable** equals or exceeds the final value **End**.

Example:

```
For Degrees = 0 To 360 Step 10
  'convert to radians
  R = Degrees * Math.PI / 180
  A = Math.Sin(R)
  B = Math.Cos(R)
  C = Math.Tan(R)
EndFor
```

In this example, we compute trigonometric functions for angles from 0 to 360 degrees in increments (steps) of 10 degrees.

Another Example:

```
For Countdown = 10 To 0 Step -1
   TextWindow.WriteLine(Countdown + " Seconds")
EndFor
```

NASA called and asked us to countdown from 10 to 0. The loop above accomplishes the task.

And, Another Example:

```
Sum = 0
For I = 1 to 100
   Sum = Sum + MyValues[I]
EndFor
Average = Sum / 100
```

This code finds the average value of 100 numbers stored in the array **MyValues**. It first sums each of the values in a **For** loop. That sum is then divided by the number of terms (100) to yield the average.

You may exit a **For** loop early using an **Goto** statement. This will transfer program control to the corresponding labeled statement, usually the line after the **EndFor**.

Overview of Small Basic Programming 2-23

Small Basic Subroutines

In the looping discussion, we saw how code in one particular block could be repeated until some desired condition was met. Many times in Small Basic programs, we might have a need to repeat a certain block of code at several different points in the program. Why would you want to do this?

Say we had a game that requires us to roll 5 dice and add up their individual values to yield a sum. What if we needed to do this at 10 different places in our program? We could write the code, then copy and paste it to the 10 different places. I think you can see problems already. What if you need to change the code? You would need to change it in 10 different places. What if you needed to put the code in another place in your program? You would need to do another 'copy and paste' operation. There's a better way. And that way is to use a Small Basic **subroutine**.

A subroutine allows you to write the code to perform certain tasks just once. Then, whenever you need to access the code in your program, you can "call it," providing any information it might need to do its tasks. Subroutines are the building blocks of a Small Basic program. Using subroutines in your Small Basic programs can help divide a complex application into more manageable units of code. Just think of a subroutine as a code block you can access from anywhere in a Small Basic program. When you call the subroutine, program control goes to that subroutine, performs the assigned tasks and returns to the calling program. It's that easy.

Let's see how to create and call a subroutine. Subroutines go at the end of your **'main'** program code. A subroutine named **MySubroutine** would have the form (starts with a **Sub** keyword and ends with **EndSub**):

```
Sub MySubroutine
    ' Code to be executed in the subroutine
EndSub
```

You execute, or call, this subroutine using:

```
MySubroutine()
```

The parentheses are needed to tell the computer you are executing a subroutine. When the subroutine is called, the corresponding code is executed until the **EndSub** line is reached. At this point, program execution returns to the line of code immediately <u>after</u> the line that called the subroutine.

A subroutine can access and use any variable you use in your program. Likewise, your program can use any variables defined in your subroutines. In computer talk, we say all variables in a Small Basic program have **global scope**.

Let's try to make this clearer by looking at a subroutine example. We'll do the dice example of rolling five dice and computing their sum. The subroutine that accomplishes this task is:

```
Sub RollDice
  Die1 = Math.GetRandomNumber(6)
  Die2 = Math.GetRandomNumber(6)
  Die3 = Math.GetRandomNumber(6)
  Die4 = Math.GetRandomNumber(6)
  Die5 = Math.GetRandomNumber(6)
  SumDice = Die1 + Die2 + Die3 + Die4 + Die5
EndSub
```

This subroutine is named **RollDice** and the variable **SumDice** has the resulting sum.

Using this subroutine, any time you need the sum of five dice in your program, you would use:

```
RollDice()
A = SumDice
```

After this code is executed, the variable **A** will have sum of five dice.

As you progress in your Small Basic programming education, you will become more comfortable with using subroutines and see how useful they are. In the remainder of this course, we will use subroutines for much of the code. Study each example to help learn how to build and use subroutines.

Small Basic Objects

Objects are used by the Small Basic language to help build programs. An object can have **properties**, **methods** and/or **events**.

A **property** describes something about the object. In Chapter 1, we had this simple line of code:

```
TextWindow.Title = "Hello Program"
```

Here **TextWindow** is the object, **Title** is the property (the information that appears in the window title bar) and **"Hello Program"** is the value of the property. So, in general, to set the **Property** of an **Object**, you use this "dot-notation":

```
Object.Property = Value
```

A **method** does something to an object. Again, in Chapter 1, we had this line:

```
TextWindow.WriteLine("This is the first line of the program.")
```

Here, **WriteLine** is the method (it writes information in the text window) and the item in the parentheses is called the method argument. The argument (or sometimes arguments) provides information needed by the method to do its job. To apply a **Method** to an **Object**, use:

```
Object.Method(Arguments)
```

Sometimes, the method may compute and return a value. In this case, that **Value** is found using:

```
Value = Object.Method(Arguments)
```

Lastly, an **event** is something that happens to an object. Example events are clicking a button control, pressing a mouse button or pressing a key on the keyboard. To respond to an event, the event must be assigned a **subroutine** that is called if the event occurs. To assign the subroutine **EventSub** to the **Event** for **Object**, use:

    Object.Event = EventSub

In the next several chapters, we look at objects and how to use them. For each object, we review the properties, methods and events (if any).

Chapter Review

After completing this chapter, you should understand:

- How to properly use variables.
- Small Basic statements.
- The assignment operator, mathematics operators, comparison and logic operators and concatenation operators.
- The wide variety of built-in Small Basic methods, especially string methods and mathematics methods.
- How to use graphics methods to draw in the graphics window.
- The **If/Then/ElseIf/Else/EndIf** structure used for branching and decisions.
- How the **While** loop and **Goto** loop work.
- How the **For** loop is used for counting.
- The importance of subroutines in Small Basic programs.
- Properties, methods and events, as related to Small Basic objects.

We now have the foundation needed to start writing some programs. To do this, we will cover many of the Small Basic objects, starting with the **Program** object.

This page intentionally not left blank.

3. Program Object

Preview

In this chapter, we begin our overview of objects used to build the Small Basic programs. For each object, we summarize the properties, methods and events. Then, we build several example programs illustrating use of the object. We begin with the Small Basic **Program** object.

Program Object

The **Program** object (or more properly class) helps with program execution. We use it identify what folder your program is saved in, implement delays and stop the program.

Program Properties:

```
Directory
```
Gets the executing program's directory.

Program Methods:

```
Delay(milliseconds)
```
Delays program execution by the specified amount of **milliseconds**.

```
End()
```
Ends the program.

Example 3-1. Program Directory

Write a program that displays the directory (folder) your program is stored in.

Small Basic Code:

```
' Guide to Small Basic, Example 3-1
TextWindow.Title = "Example 3-1"
TextWindow.WriteLine("Directory: " + Program.Directory)
```

Saved as **Example 3-1** in **Guide to Small Basic\Programs\Chapter 3** folder.

Save and **Run** the program. The program directory will be written in the text window:

```
Example 3-1
Directory: C:\Guide to Small Basic\Programs\Chapter 3
Press any key to continue...
```

Your directory will be different, assuming you saved your program in a folder of a different name.

Example 3-2. Program Delay

Write a program that writes a line, delays a second, writes another line, then delays two seconds, before ending.

Small Basic Code:

```
' Guide to Small Basic, Example 3-2
TextWindow.Title = "Example 3-2"
TextWindow.WriteLine("Line 1")
Program.Delay(1000)
TextWindow.WriteLine("Line 2")
Program.Delay(2000)
```

Saved as **Example 3-2** in **Guide to Small Basic\Programs\Chapter 3** folder.

Save and **Run** the program. In the text window, you will see **Line 1** display, a delay of 1 second (1000 milliseconds), **Line 2** display, then a 2 second delay before the program ends:

Program End Method

In the short text window programs we have written, they end with this statement:

Press any key to continue...

This allows us to see the contents of the window before the program closes.

If you end a program with:

```
Program.End()
```

The "Press any key to continue..." statement will not be seen and the text window will close.

Example 3-3. Program End

Repeat **Example 3-2**, but add an **End** statement. That is, write a program that writes a line, delays a second, writes another line, then delays two seconds, before ending with an **End** statement.

Small Basic Code:

```
' Guide to Small Basic, Example 3-3
TextWindow.Title = "Example 3-3"
TextWindow.WriteLine("Line 1")
Program.Delay(1000)
TextWindow.WriteLine("Line 2")
Program.Delay(2000)
Program.End()
```

Saved as **Example 3-3** in **Guide to Small Basic\Programs\Chapter 3** folder.

Save and **Run** the program. In the text window, you will see **Line 1** display, a delay of 1 second (1000 milliseconds), **Line 2** display, then a 2 second delay, then the text window will disappear.

Chapter Review

After completing this chapter, you should understand:

- Use of the **Property** object.
- How to identify your program directory.
- How to implement a program delay.
- How to stop a program and make the text window disappear.

Next, we look in more detail at the **TextWindow** object we have been using.

This page intentionally not left blank.

4. TextWindow Object

Preview

In this chapter, we look at the Small Basic **TextWindow** object. It is used to work with text input and output.

TextWindow Object

The **TextWindow** is an object where we can receive text input and write text output. In Small Basic, text windows are usually used for simple programs with no graphic elements. We used the text window in the examples in Chapter 3.

TextWindow Properties:

`BackgroundColor`
Gets or sets the background color of the text to be output in the text window.

`CursorLeft`
Gets or sets the cursor's column position in the text window.

`CursorTop`
Gets or sets the cursor's row position in the text window.

`ForegroundColor`
Gets or sets the foreground color of the text to be output in the text window.

`Left`
Gets or sets the left position of text window on your computer screen.

`Title`
Gets or sets the title for the text window.

`Top`
Gets or sets the top position of text window on your computer screen.

TextWindow Methods:

`Clear()`
Clears the text window.

`Hide()`
Hides the text window.

`Pause()`
Waits for user input before returning.

`PauseIfVisible()`
Waits for user input only when the text window is open.

`PauseWithoutMessage()`
Waits for user input before returning (but there is no 'Press Any Key' message).

`Read()`
Reads a line of text from the text window. This method will not return until the user presses **Enter**. Returns entered text.

`ReadKey()`
Reads a key press from the text window. Returns the pressed key.

`ReadNumber()`
Reads a number from the text window. This method will not return until the user presses **Enter**. Returns entered number.

`Show()`
Shows the text window.

`Write(data)`
Writes text or number (**data**) to the text window. Unlike **WriteLine**, this will not append a new line character, which means, anything written to the text window after this call will be on the same line.

`WriteLine(data)`
Writes text or number (**data**) to the text window. A new line character will be appended to the output, so that the next time something is written to the text window, it will go in a new line.

TextWindow Features

By default, the text window displays white text on a black background:

```
C:\Users\Lou\AppData\Local\Temp\tmp99BB.tmp.exe
Press any key to continue...
```

The default window has 25 rows (**CursorTop** values from 0 to 24) and 80 columns (**CursorLeft** values from 0 to 79)

To change the background color for the entire window, set the **TextWindow.BackgroundColor** property followed by a **Clear** method. The **ForegroundColor** property sets the text color.

The text window is located on your computer screen as follows:

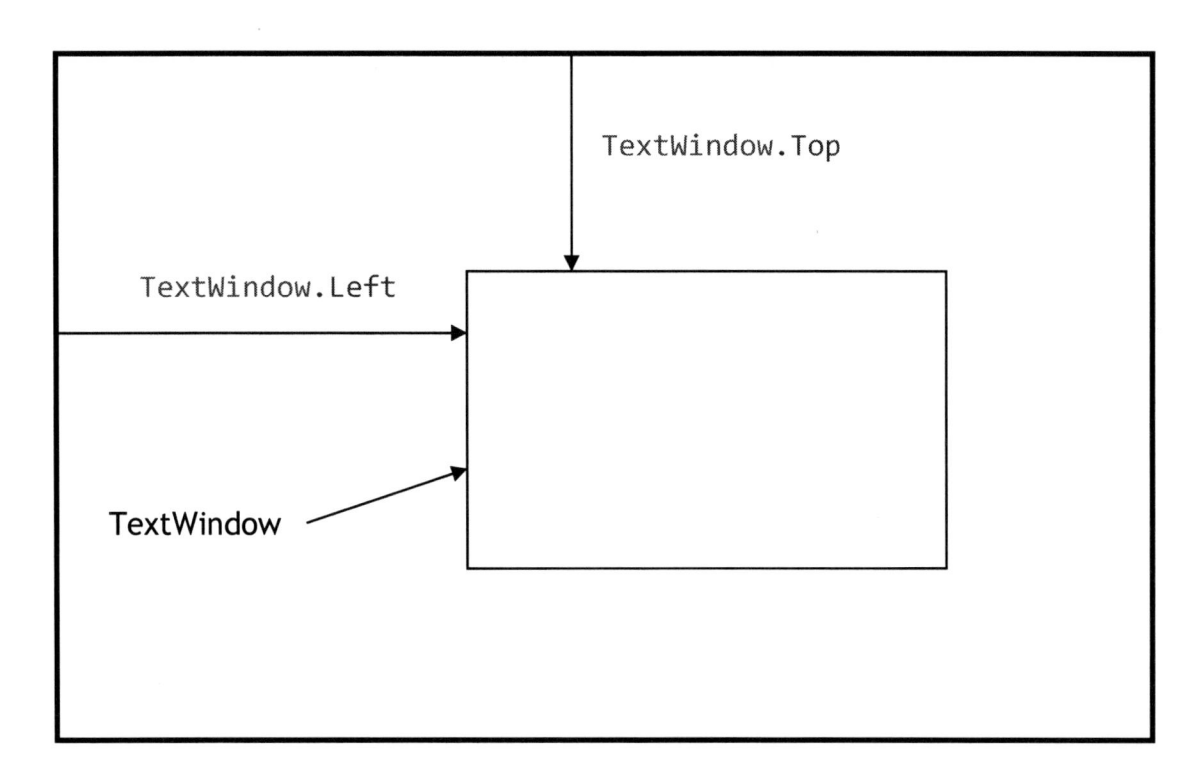

```
                    TextWindow.Top
                         ↓
  TextWindow.Left  →  ┌─────────┐
                      │         │
  TextWindow      →   │         │
                      └─────────┘
```

Example 4-1. TextWindow Properties

Write a program that writes blue text on a yellow background. Write a line of text near the middle of the window.

Small Basic Code:

```
' Guide to Small Basic, Example 4-1
TextWindow.Title = "Example 4-1"
TextWindow.BackgroundColor = "Yellow"
TextWindow.ForegroundColor = "Blue"
TextWindow.Clear()
TextWindow.Left = 200
TextWindow.Top = 100
TextWindow.CursorLeft = 30
TextWindow.CursorTop = 10
TextWindow.WriteLine("This is Example 4-1")
```

Saved as **Example 4-1** in **Guide to Small Basic\Programs\Chapter 4** folder.

This program illustrates use of all the properties of the **TextWindow** object. The **Title** property is set as are **BackgroundColor** and **ForegroundColor**. We use the **WriteLine** method (preceded by **CursorLeft** and **CursorTop**) to position the text in the window. **Left** and **Top** position the window on your screen.

Save and **Run** the program to see the results:

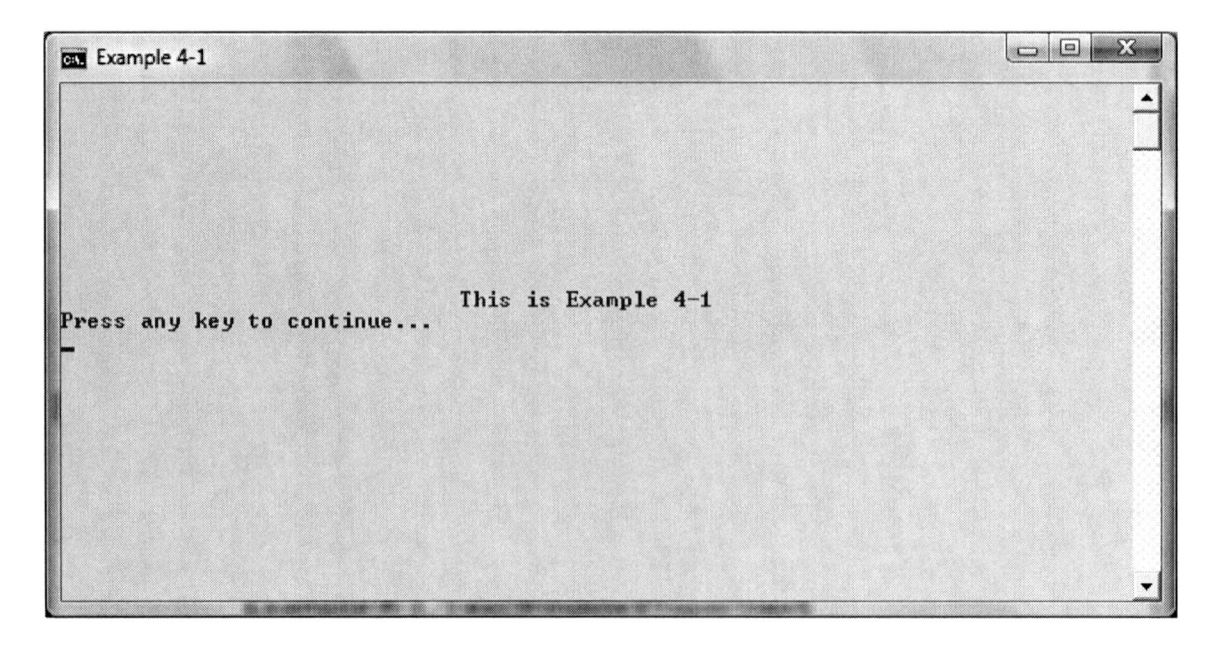

TextWindow Input

There are three methods used to get user input in the text window. The **Read** method is used to obtain text information. The <**Enter**> key is pressed to complete the input. Similarly, the **ReadNumber** method is used to obtain numeric information. With **ReadNumber**, non-numeric keystrokes are ignored. Lastly, the **ReadKey** method obtains individual keystrokes with no need to press <**Enter**>.

Example 4-2. TextWindow Input

Write a program where the user first inputs a line of text then a numeric value. Lastly, intercept keystrokes typed by the user.

Small Basic Code:

```
' Guide to Small Basic, Example 4-2
TextWindow.Title = "Example 4-2"
A = TextWindow.Read()
TextWindow.WriteLine(A)
B = TextWindow.ReadNumber()
TextWindow.WriteLine(B)
GetKeystroke:
C = TextWindow.ReadKey()
TextWindow.WriteLine(C)
Goto GetKeystroke
```

Saved as **Example 4-2** in **Guide to Small Basic\Programs\Chapter 4** folder.

Save and **Run** the program. First, you see a flashing cursor waiting for you to type a line of text, then press <**Enter**>:

Type something in and press <**Enter**>. Here's what I see now:

Example 4-2
This is a line of text
This is a line of text

You see the line I input and the line written back out with **WriteLine**. The program is now waiting for a numeric input. Type such an input and press <**Enter**>. You will only be able to type numeric characters (0, 1, 2, 3, 4, 5, 6, 7, 8, 9, single decimal point, single negative sign to start input). Try non-numeric characters – they won't appear. Here's what I have now (my input and it's written value):

Example 4-2
This is a line of text
This is a line of text
-3.14159265359
-3.14159265359

Now, the program is waiting for individual keystrokes. Type some. Notice there is no need to press <Enter> after the keystrokes. With each keystroke, the program will write out what you typed:

```
Example 4-2
This is a line of text
This is a line of text
-3.14159265359
-3.14159265359
a
b
c
d
e
f
g
h
i
j
k
l
m
n
o
p
q
r
s
t
u
```

To stop the program, click the X in the upper right corner of the window.

TextWindow Output

There are two methods used to write information in the text window. We have used the **WriteLine** method. It writes the information to the window and appends a new line character. Any subsequent output methods start on a new line. **WriteLine** can also be used to write a blank line using:

    TextWindow.WriteLine("")

An alternate to **WriteLine** is the **Write** method. It writes information to the window, but does not append a new line character. Subsequent output methods start at the end of the information written by the **Write** method. The **Write** method is useful for providing prompts prior to a **Read**, **ReadNumber** or **ReadKey** method.

Output using both **WriteLine** and **Write** can be positioned anywhere in the text window by setting the **CursorLeft** and **CursorTop** properties prior to using the output method. By default, each output method uses a **CursorLeft** value of 0. **CursorTop** is incremented by one with each **WriteLine** method.

Example 4-3. Dice Rolling (TextWindow Output)

Write a program that rolls a dice until an input number of sixes is rolled (we showed this code when discussing **While** loops in Chapter 2). Once the rolls are complete, write out how many rolls it took to achieve the input value.

Small Basic Code:

```
' Guide to Small Basic, Example 4-3
TextWindow.Title = "Example 4-3"
TextWindow.BackgroundColor = "White"
TextWindow.ForegroundColor = "Black"
TextWindow.Clear()
GetNumberSixes:
TextWindow.Write("How many sixes must be rolled? ")
Number = TextWindow.ReadNumber()
Rolls = 0
Counter = 0
While (Counter < Number)
  ' Roll a simulated die
  Rolls = Rolls + 1
  If (Math.GetRandomNumber(6) = 6) Then
    Counter = Counter + 1
  EndIf
EndWhile
TextWindow.WriteLine("It took " + Rolls + " rolls to get " + Number + " sixes.")
TextWindow.WriteLine("")
Goto GetNumberSixes
```

Saved as **Example 4-3** in **Guide to Small Basic\Programs\Chapter 4** folder.

Save and **Run** the program. The **Write** statement is used to prompt the user for the needed input (notice no new line is started – the flashing cursor is to the right of the question mark):

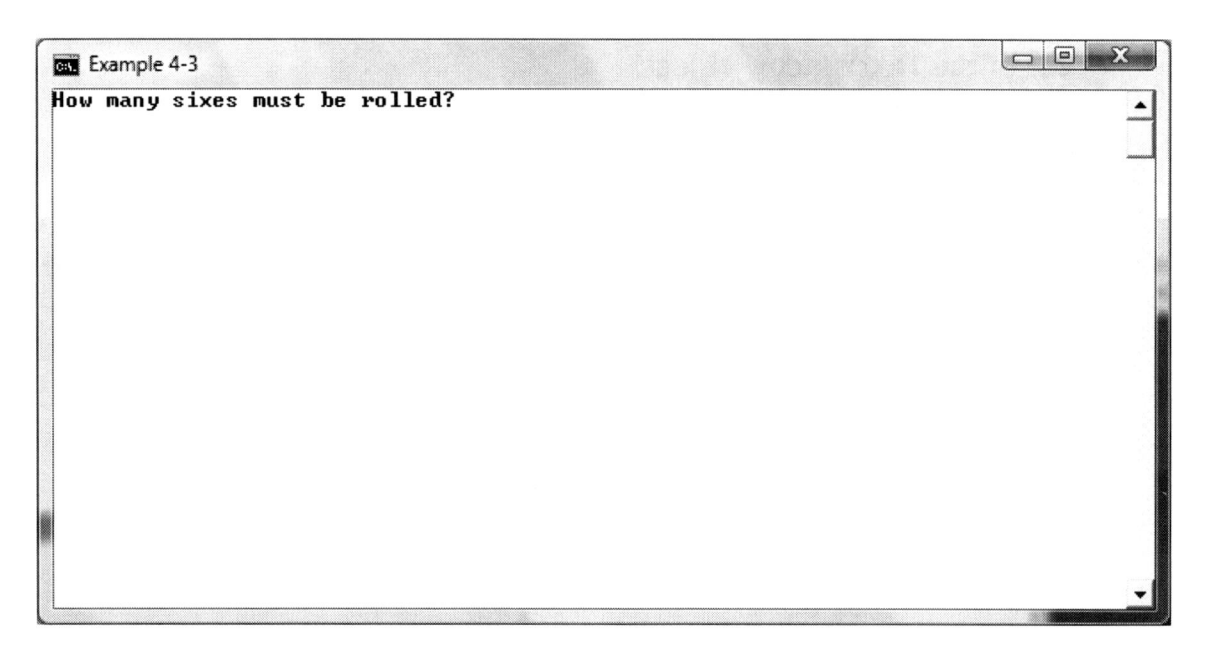

```
Example 4-3
How many sixes must be rolled?
```

I picked 10 and see that it took 53 rolls to achieve 10 sixes:

```
Example 4-3
How many sixes must be rolled? 10
It took 53 rolls to get 10 sixes.
How many sixes must be rolled? _
```

Theoretically, it should take 60 rolls (since each roll has a 1 in 6 chance of rolling a six). At this point, I can type in another value. Try several values. Stop the program when you are done.

Chapter Review

After completing this chapter, you should understand:

> - Use of the **TextWindow** object.
> - Setting **TextWindow** properties.
> - Difference between **Read**, **ReadNumber** and **ReadKey** methods.
> - Difference between **WriteLine** and **Write** methods.

The **TextWindow** object can only accept and output text information. Next, we look at the **GraphicsWindow** object which allows graphical elements.

5. GraphicsWindow Object

Preview

We saw the text window is useful for input and output of text based information. In this chapter, we look at the object used to host most Small Basic programs – the **GraphicsWindow**. With this object, we can build very power applications.

GraphicsWindow Object

GraphicsWindow Coordinates:

The **GraphicsWindow** object is a cornerstone of Small Basic programming. In the graphics window, we can draw lines, shapes, and text in many colors. We can host controls (buttons and text boxes). We can receive mouse and keyboard input from a user. The coordinate system used by the graphics window is:

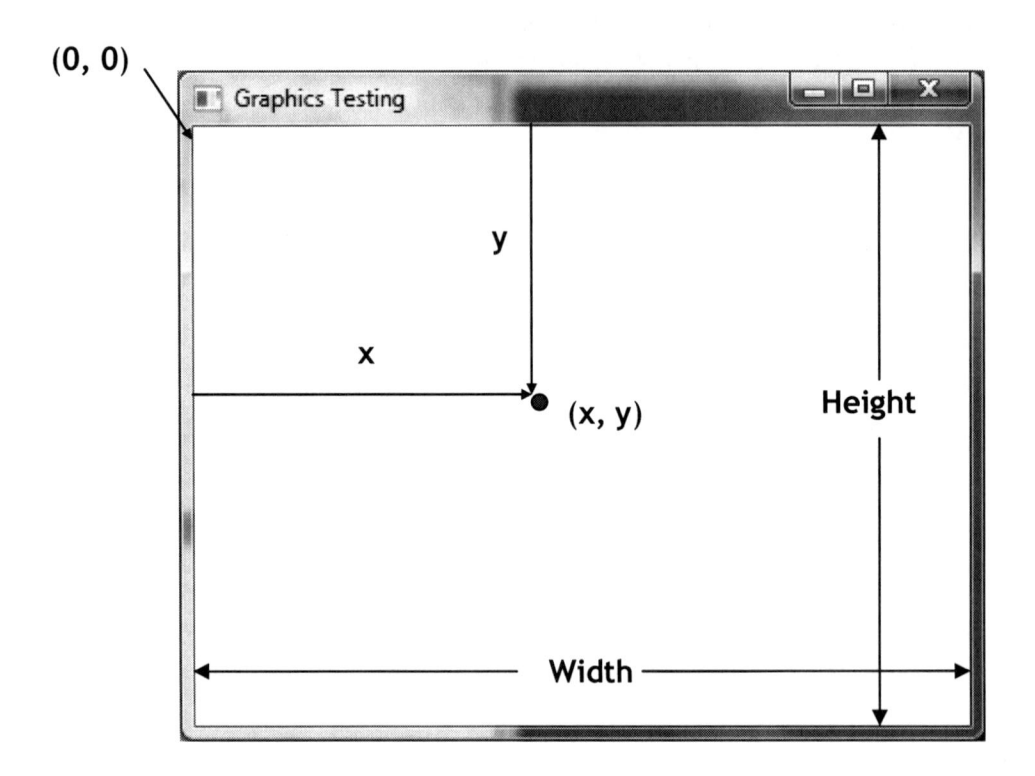

The window is **Width** pixels wide and **Height** pixels high. We use two values (coordinates) to identify a single pixel in the window. The **x** (horizontal) coordinate increases from left to right, starting at **0**. The **y** (vertical) coordinate increases from top to bottom, also starting at **0**. Points in the region are referred to by the two coordinates enclosed in parentheses, or **(x, y)**.

GraphicsWindow Object

GraphicsWindow Properties:

`BackgroundColor`
Gets or sets the background color of the graphics window.

`BrushColor`
Gets or sets the brush color to be used to fill shapes drawn on the graphics window.

`CanResize`
Specifies whether or not the graphics window can be resized by the user. Can be "true" or "false".

`FontBold`
Gets or sets whether or not the font to be used when drawing text on the graphics window, is bold.

`FontItalic`
Gets or sets whether or not the font to be used when drawing text on the graphics window, is italic.

`FontName`
Gets or sets the font name when drawing text on the graphics window.

`FontSize`
Gets or sets the font size to be used when drawing text on the graphics window.

`Height`
Gets or sets the height of the graphics window.

`LastKey`
Gets the last key that was pressed or released.

`LastText`
Gets the last text that was entered on the graphics window.

`Left`
Gets or sets the left position of the graphics window.

`MouseX`
Gets the x-position of the mouse relative to the graphics window.

`MouseY`
Gets the y-position of the mouse relative to the graphics window.

`PenColor`
Gets or sets the color of the pen used to draw shapes on the graphics window.

`PenWidth`
Gets or sets the width of the pen used to draw shapes on the graphics window.

`Title`
Gets or sets the title for the graphics window.

`Top`
Gets or sets the top position of the graphics window.

`Width`
Gets or sets the width of the graphics window.

GraphicsWindow Methods:

```
Clear()
```
Clears the window.

```
DrawBoundText(x, y, text, w, h)
```
Draws a line of **text** on the screen at the specified location (**x, y**) within a region bounded by width **w** and height **h**. Helps define when text should wrap. Uses current brush and font properties.

```
DrawEllipse(x, y, w, h)
```
Draws an ellipse (width **w**, height **h**) at (**x, y**) on the screen using the current pen.

```
DrawImage(image, x, y)
```
Draws the specified **image** from memory on to the screen at (**x, y**).

```
DrawLine(x1, y1, x2, y2)
```
Draws a line from one point (**x1, y1**) to another (**x2, y2**). Uses current pen.

```
DrawRectangle(x, y, w, h)
```
Draws a rectangle (width **w**, height **h**) on the screen at (**x, y**) using the current pen.

```
DrawResizedImage(image, x, y, w, h)
```
Draws the specified **image** from memory on to the screen at (**x, y**), in the specified size (width **w**, height **h**).

```
DrawText(x, y, text)
```
Draws a line of **text** on the screen at the specified location (**x, y**). Uses current brush and font properties.

```
DrawTriangle(x1, y1, x2, y2, x3, y3)
```
Draws a triangle connecting the three input points on the screen using the current pen.

`FillEllipse(x, y, w, h)`
Fills an ellipse (width **w**, height **h**) on the screen at (**x, y**) using the current brush.

`FillRectangle(x, y, w, h)`
Fills a rectangle (width **w**, height **h**) on the screen at (**x, y**) using the current brush.

`FillTriangle(x1, y1, x2, y2, x3, y3)`
Fills a triangle connecting the three input points on the screen using the current brush.

`GetColorFromRGB(red, green, blue)`
Constructs a color give the **red**, **green**, **blue** values (0-255). Returns the color.

`GetRandomColor()`
Gets a valid random color. Returns the color.

`Hide()`
Hides the graphics window.

`SetPixel(x, y, c)`
Draws the pixel specified by (**x, y**) in the color **c**.

`Show()`
Shows the graphics window to enable interactions with it.

`ShowMessage(text, title)`
Displays a message box (with message **text** and **title**) to the user.

GraphicsWindow Events:

KeyDown
Raises an event when a key is pressed down on the keyboard.

KeyUp
Raises an event when a key is released on the keyboard.

MouseDown
Raises an event when the mouse button is clicked down.

MouseMove
Raises an event when the mouse is moved around.

MouseUp
Raises an event when the mouse button is released.

TextInput
Raises an event when text is entered on the graphics window.

GraphicsWindow Features

By default, the graphics window has a white background:

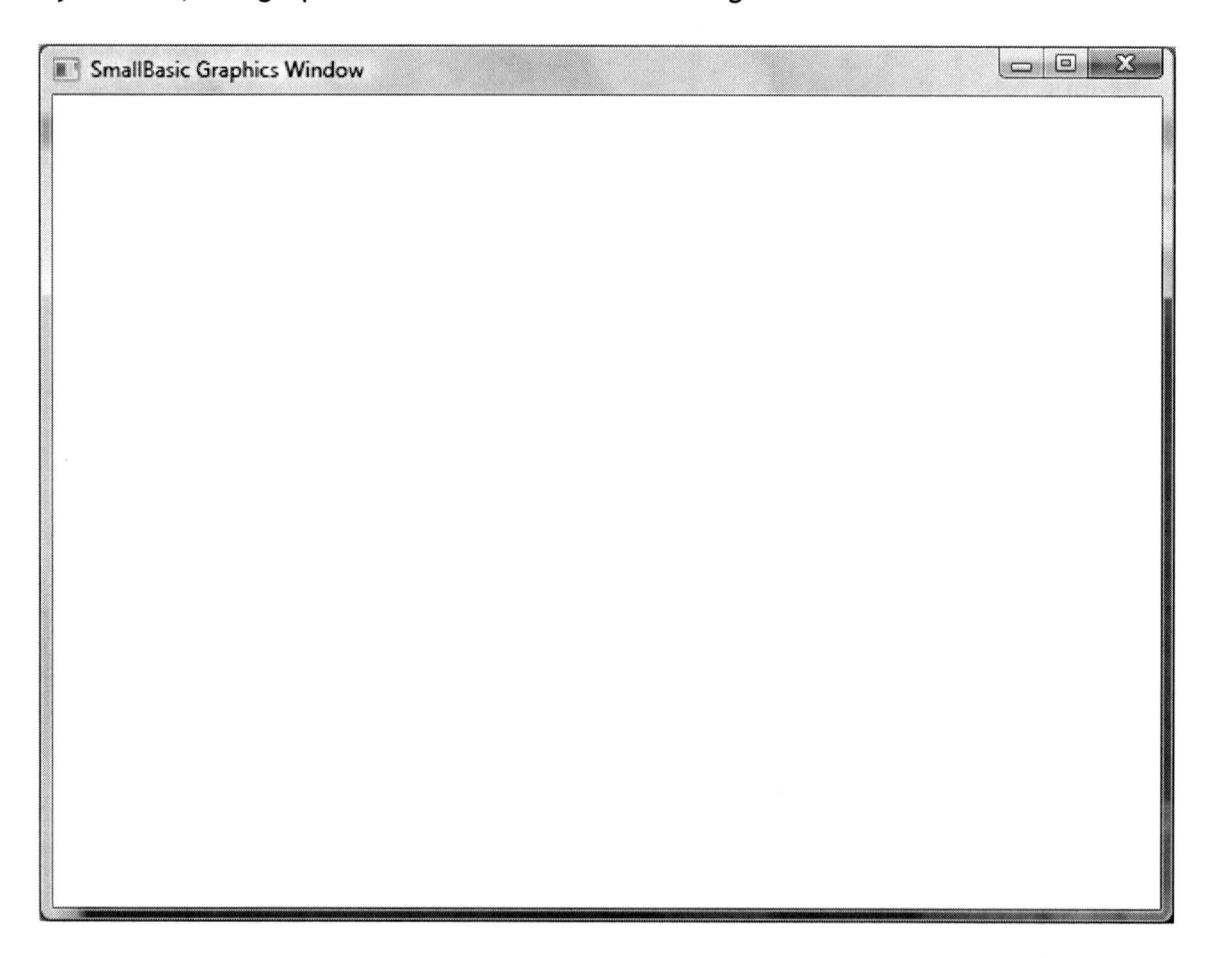

The default window is 624 pixels wide (**Width**) by 444 pixels high (**Height**).

To change the background color for the entire window, set the **GraphicsWindow.BackgroundColor**.

GraphicsWindow Object

Similar to the text window, the graphics window is located on your computer screen as follows:

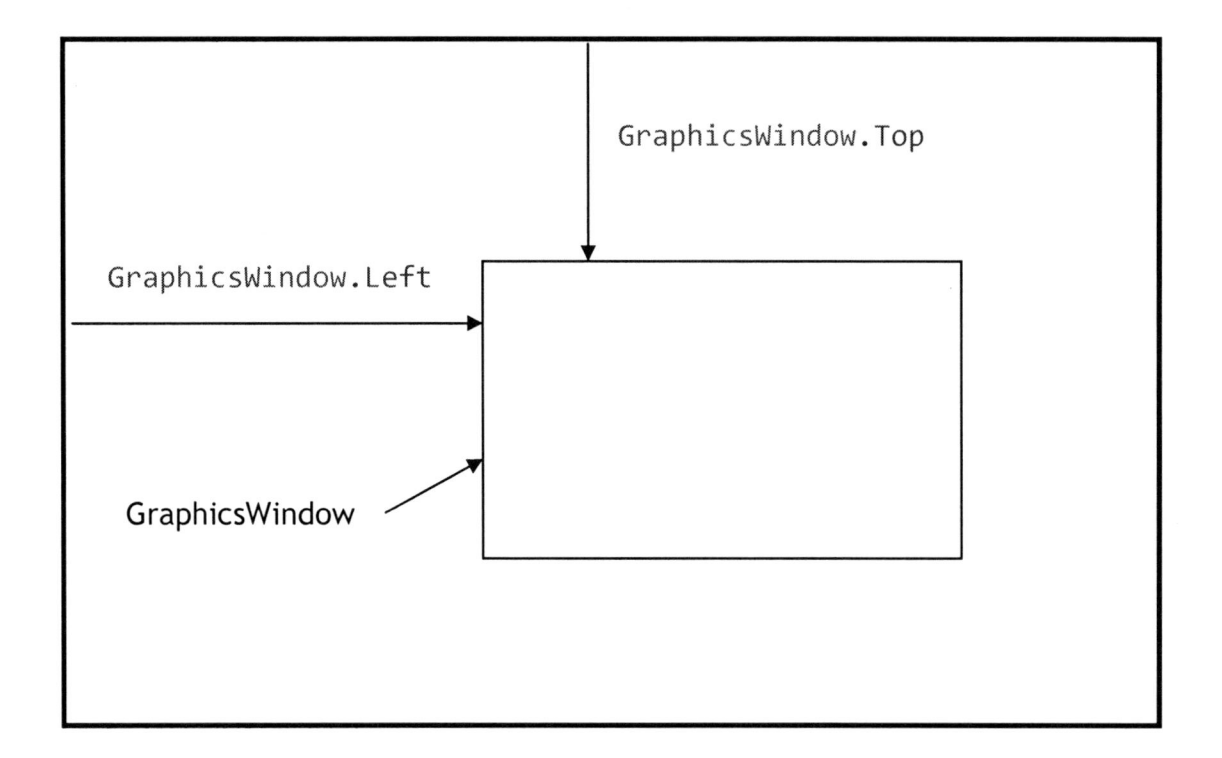

To center the graphics window on your computer screen, use these relations:

```
GraphicsWindow.Left = 0.5 * (Desktop.Width - GraphicsWindow.Width)

GraphicsWindow.Top = 0.5 * (Desktop.Height - GraphicsWindow.Height)
```

GraphicsWindow Colors

The graphics window (and also the text window) uses colors for various program elements. Colors are specified by color names. The color names used by Small Basic are listed in Appendix I to this guide. There are two other ways to get colors in Small Basic. The **GetRandomColor** method:

```
GraphicsWindow.GetRandomColor()
```

will return a random color. It is fun to use for display and games. The **GetColorFromRGB** method:

```
GraphicsWindow.GetColorFromRGB(Red, Green, Blue)
```

builds a color based on three specified components: **Red, Green, Blue**, each of which range from 0 to 255.

The graphics window background color is set by:

```
GraphicsWindow.BackgroundColor
```

And, as mentioned, the default value for this color is "White".

Lines and shapes in Small Basic are drawn using a "pen." The color and width of the pen is specified by:

```
GraphicsWindow.PenColor
GraphicsWindow.PenWidth
```

The default value for **PenColor** is "Black" and the default **PenWidth** is 2.

Shapes and text (yes, text) are filled (painted) using a "brush." The color of the brush is specified by:

```
GraphicsWindow.BrushColor
```

The default value for **BrushColor** is "SlateBlue".

GraphicsWindow Font

The font used to draw text in the graphics window is specified by four different properties:

```
GraphicsWindow.FontName
GraphicsWindow.FontSize
GraphicsWindow.FontBold
GraphicsWindow.FontItalic
```

The **FontName** property is the name of the font. The default value is "Tahoma". Other font names can be found by opening a word processor and selecting the change font option.

The **FontSize** property sets the size of the current font. The default value is 12. **FontBold** can have one of two values. If "true", the font will be bold. If "false", it will not be bold. The default value is "true". Similarly, **FontItalic** indicates if a font is italicized. The default value is "false" – no italics.

Example 5-1. GraphicsWindow Properties

Write a program that writes "Graphics Window" in a large, bold, italic font in the middle of a yellow graphics window. Set window size to 400 by 150 pixels.

Small Basic Code:

```
'Guide to Small Basic, Example 5-1
GraphicsWindow.Show()
GraphicsWindow.Title = "Example 5-1"
GraphicsWindow.Width = 400
GraphicsWindow.Height = 150
GraphicsWindow.BackgroundColor = "Yellow"
GraphicsWindow.FontSize = 36
GraphicsWindow.FontBold = "true"
GraphicsWindow.FontItalic = "true"
GraphicsWindow.BrushColor = "Black"
GraphicsWindow.DrawText(20, 40, "Graphics Window")
```

Saved as **Example 5-1** in **Guide to Small Basic\Programs\Chapter 5** folder.

Save and **Run** the program to see the results:

Example 5-2. SetPixel Method

Write a program that fills a graphics window with randomly colored pixels.

Small Basic Code:

```
'Guide to Small Basic, Example 5-2
GraphicsWindow.Show()
GraphicsWindow.Title = "Example 5-2"
GraphicsWindow.Width = 300
GraphicsWindow.Height = 200
For X = 0 To 299
  For Y = 0 To 199
    GraphicsWindow.SetPixel(X, Y, GraphicsWindow.GetRandomColor())
  EndFor
EndFor
```

Saved as **Example 5-2** in **Guide to Small Basic\Programs\Chapter 5** folder. This code just "marches" through all the pixels and assigns a random color to each.

Save and **Run** the program to see the results (it takes a while for the window to fill):

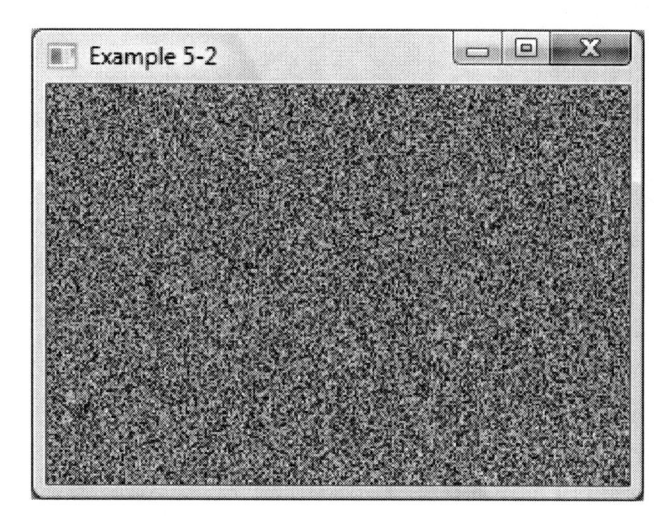

Example 5-3. DrawLine Method

Write a program that draws randomly colored lines from the center of a graphics window out to some random point in the window.

Small Basic Code:

```
'Guide to Small Basic, Example 5-3
GraphicsWindow.Show()
GraphicsWindow.Title = "Example 5-3"
GraphicsWindow.Width = 600
GraphicsWindow.Height = 400
GraphicsWindow.PenWidth = 1
For I = 1 To 200
  GraphicsWindow.PenColor = GraphicsWindow.GetRandomColor()
  X = Math.GetRandomNumber(600) - 1
  Y = Math.GetRandomNumber(400) - 1
  GraphicsWindow.DrawLine(300, 200, X, Y)
EndFor
```

Saved as **Example 5-3** in **Guide to Small Basic\Programs\Chapter 5** folder. Each line has the same starting point (the center of the window). Then, lines are drawn to the random point (X, Y).

Save and **Run** the program to see the results. Look at all the pretty lines:

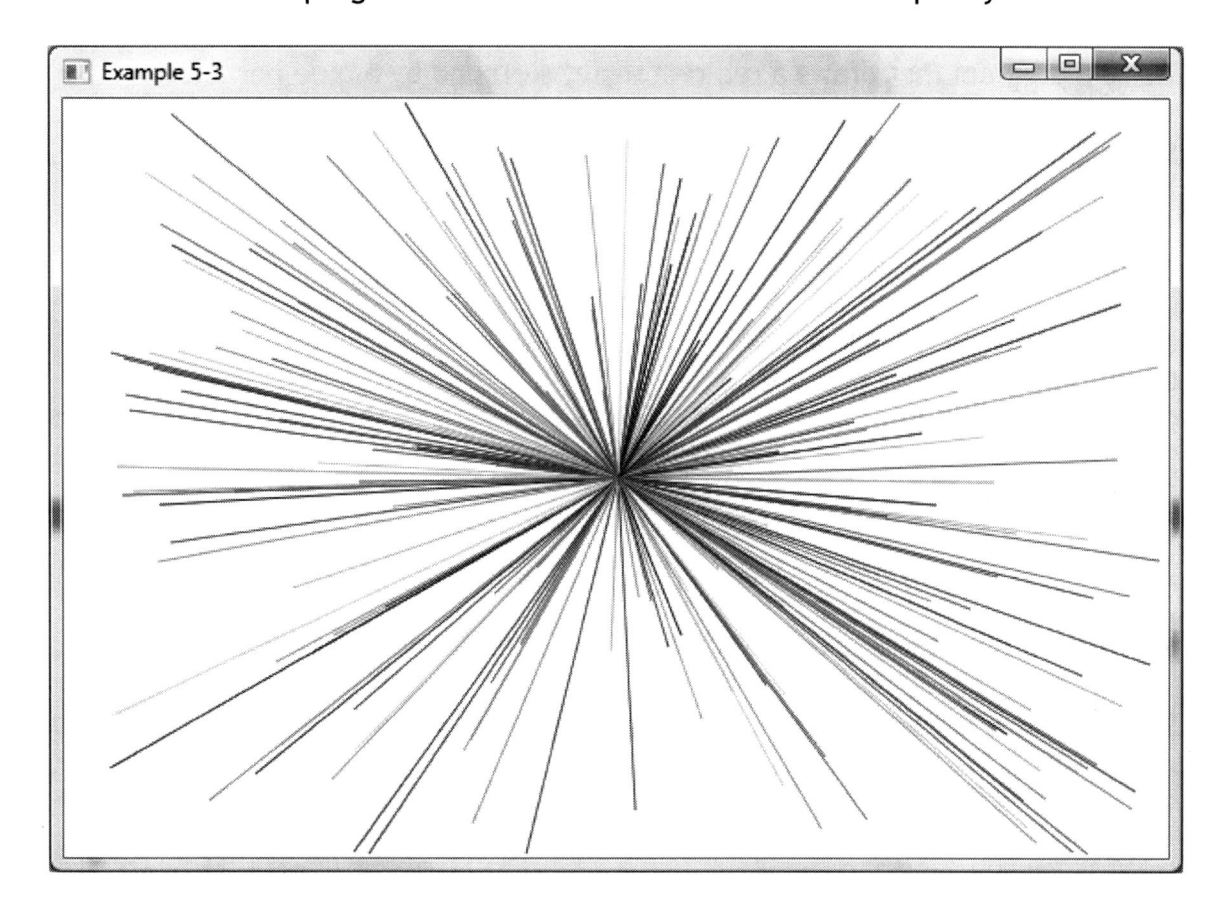

Example 5-4. Drawing Rectangles

Write a program that draws a red rectangle, surround by a blue border.

Small Basic Code:

```
'Guide to Small Basic, Example 5-4
GraphicsWindow.Show()
GraphicsWindow.Title = "Example 5-4"
GraphicsWindow.Width = 400
GraphicsWindow.Height = 300
GraphicsWindow.BrushColor = "Red"
GraphicsWindow.FillRectangle(50, 50, 300, 200)
GraphicsWindow.PenColor = "Blue"
GraphicsWindow.PenWidth = 5
GraphicsWindow.DrawRectangle(50, 50, 300, 200)
```

Saved as **Example 5-4** in **Guide to Small Basic\Programs\Chapter 5** folder.

Save and **Run** the program to see the rectangle:

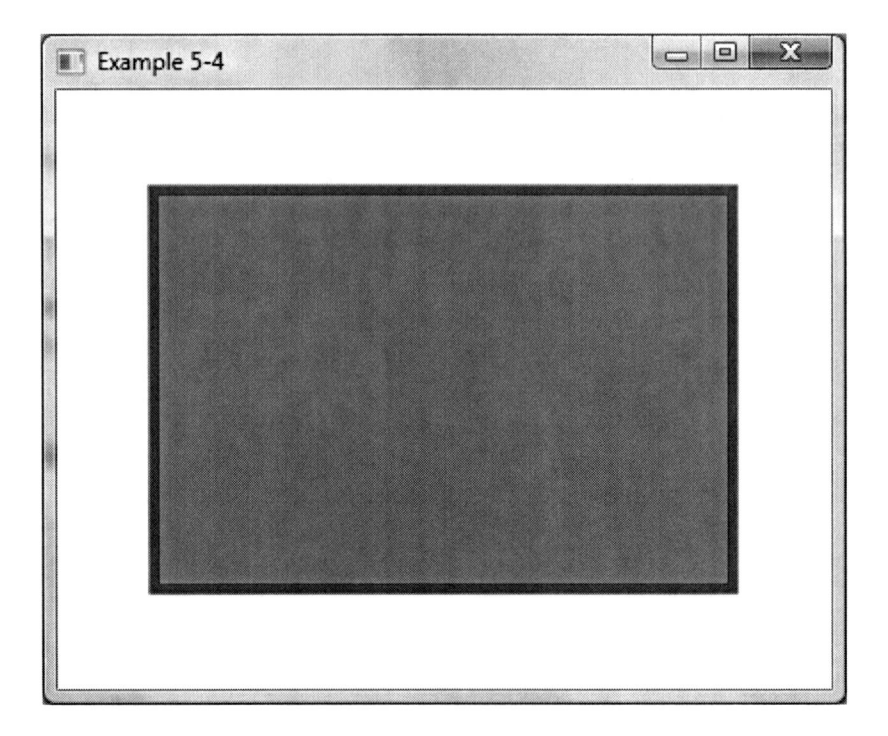

We fill the rectangle first, then draw. This insures the border is not erased by the fill operation.

Example 5-5. Drawing Ellipses

Write a program that draws a yellow ellipse, surround by a red border.

Small Basic Code:

```
'Guide to Small Basic, Example 5-5
GraphicsWindow.Show()
GraphicsWindow.Title = "Example 5-5"
GraphicsWindow.Width = 400
GraphicsWindow.Height = 340
GraphicsWindow.BrushColor = "Yellow"
GraphicsWindow.FillEllipse(100, 20, 200, 300)
GraphicsWindow.PenColor = "Red"
GraphicsWindow.PenWidth = 5
GraphicsWindow.DrawEllipse(100, 20, 200, 300)
```

Saved as **Example 5-5** in **Guide to Small Basic\Programs\Chapter 5** folder.

Save and **Run** the program to see the ellipse:

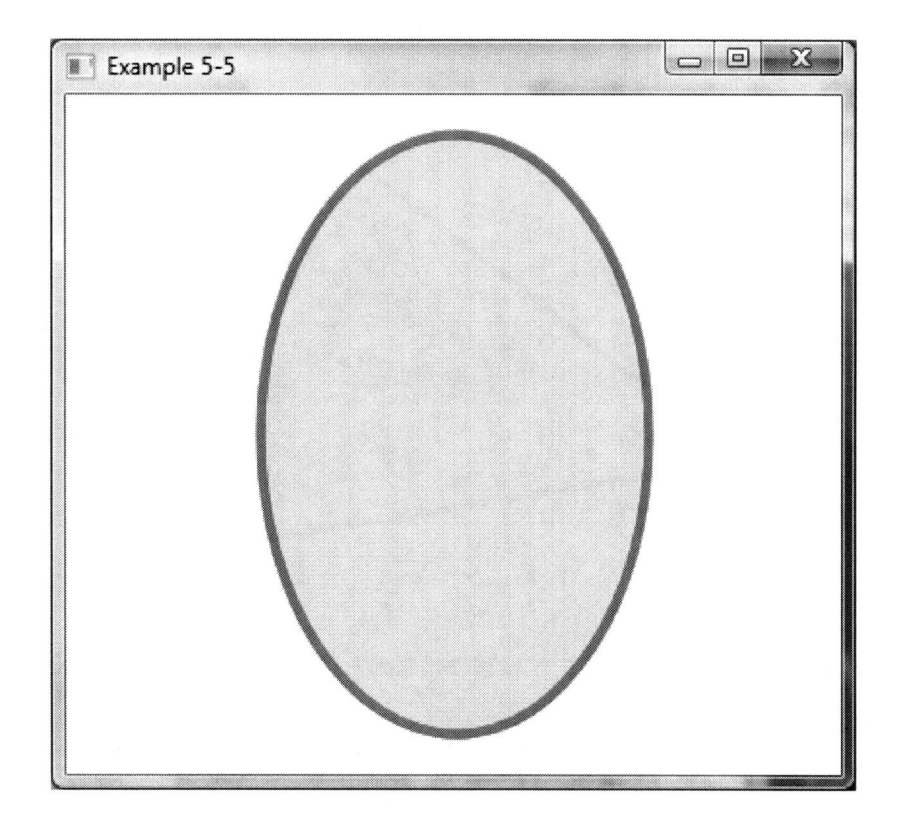

Again, fill then draw to see the full border.

Example 5-6. Drawing Triangles

Write a program that draws a green-bordered triangle that connects these three points (250, 50), (50, 200), (350, 250).

Small Basic Code:

```
'Guide to Small Basic, Example 5-6
GraphicsWindow.Show()
GraphicsWindow.Title = "Example 5-6"
GraphicsWindow.Width = 400
GraphicsWindow.Height = 300
GraphicsWindow.PenWidth = 3
GraphicsWindow.PenColor = "Green"
GraphicsWindow.DrawTriangle(250, 50, 50, 200, 350, 250)
```

Saved as **Example 5-6** in **Guide to Small Basic\Programs\Chapter 5** folder.

Save and **Run** the program to see the triangle (identify the three points):

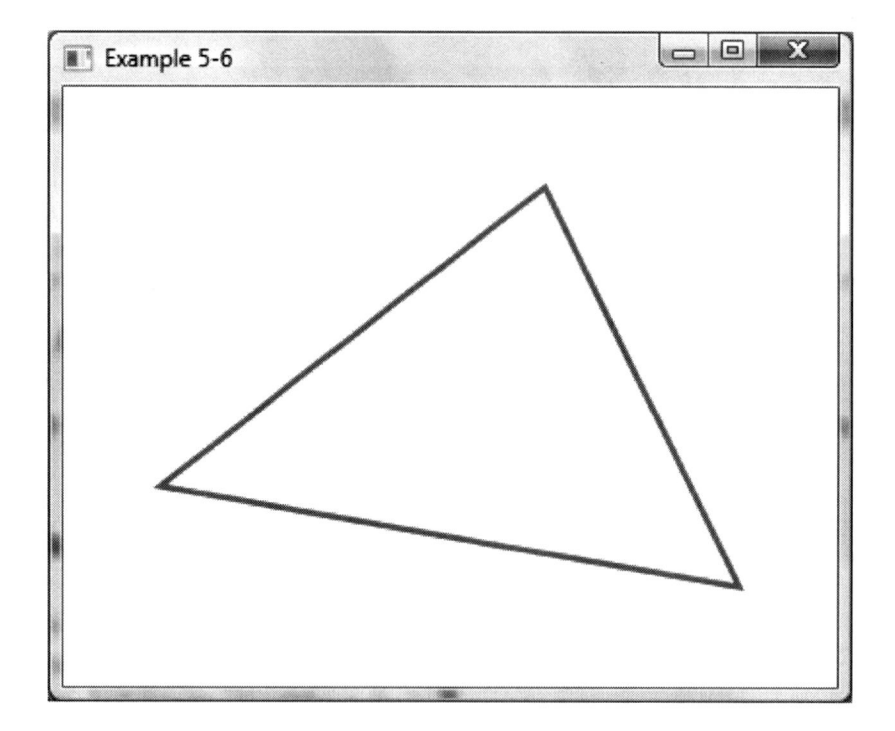

Chapter Review

After completing this chapter, you should understand:

- ➢ Use of the **GraphicsWindow.**
- ➢ How colors and fonts are used in the graphics windows.
- ➢ Drawing with **DrawText, DrawPixel, DrawLine** methods.
- ➢ Drawing and filling rectangles, ellipses, triangles.

We will do a lot more with the graphics window as we learn more about Small Basic. In particular, we will learn about using the graphics window events to recognize key presses and mouse clicks.

Next, we learn about some of the controls associated with Small Basic and the idea of event-driven programming.

This page intentionally not left blank.

6. Controls Object

Preview

In this chapter, we continue working with the **GraphicsWindow** object. We look at how to use the **Controls** object within the graphics window. This object allows us to use clickable **buttons** and **text boxes** for input and output. Inherent with using these controls is understanding the idea of a graphic user interface (GUI) and event-driven programming.

Graphic User Interface (GUI)

All the Small Basic programs built thus far have been very simple. We set up some conditions, run the program where statements are processed sequentially and the program stops after producing the desired results. Such little programs are a good way to learn the Small Basic programming language. But, let's move on.

Most computer programs today feature what is called a **graphic user interface**. This is abbreviated **GUI** and pronounced **"gooey."** In GUI applications, the user interacts with the program using the mouse and keyboard to inform the computer (and the underlying program) what steps to take. One way of interacting is via **controls**, such as buttons and text boxes. If you've used a computer, you have used GUI applications. Examples include video games, spreadsheet programs, word processors, Internet browsers, the Windows operating system itself. The Small Basic environment is a GUI application. In each of these applications, you would be helpless without your mouse to make choices!

Running (and building) a GUI application is different than a simple sequential program that runs to completion. In a GUI application, the computer sits and waits until the user does something – clicks on some area of the window, clicks a button control, types in a text box. We say the application is waiting for an **event** to occur. For this reason, GUI applications are called **event-driven**. When a particular event occurs, the application processes a series of statements (Small Basic statements in our applications) associated with that event. That series of statements is called an **event subroutine**.

Here's how it works:

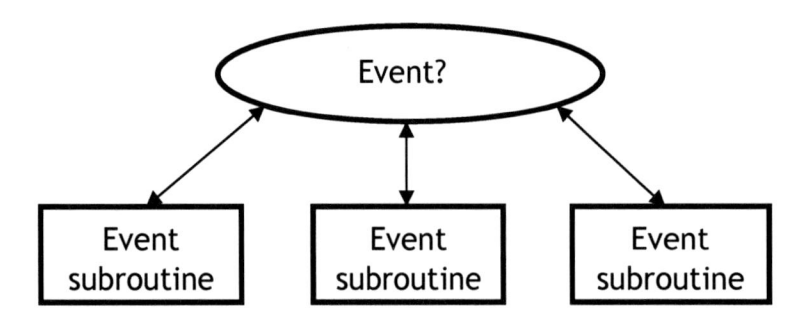

In this diagram, the program waits for an **event** to occur. Once an event is detected, program control transfers to the corresponding **event subroutine**. Once that subroutine is executed, the program waits for the next event to occur. Each event subroutine is a set of Small Basic code with instructions on what to do if the particular event occurs. So, in GUI programming, we spend most of our time writing event subroutines.

How does Small Basic know which subroutine to process if a particular event occurs? Let's do an example. Recall, we saw that the **GraphicsWindow** had an event called **MouseDown**. This event occurs whenever the user clicks a mouse button in the graphics window. If we want the code in **MouseDownSub** to be processed when a **MouseDown** event occurs, we just use the line:

```
GraphicsWindow.MouseDown = MouseDownSub
```

This statement goes in the program initialization area. And, we need to add the **MouseDownSub** to our code. Its form is:

```
Sub MouseDownSub
    'code to process for MouseDown event
EndSub
```

All programs (except little examples) we write from now on will be GUI applications. We will start with simple programs. As we cover more material, the programs will get more detailed. You will find they are actually relatively easy to write. Everything goes in subroutines that can be tested in stages. Each program will have an "initialization" subroutine (we will call it **InitializeProgram**). In this subroutine, we will set values for variables, draw the needed user interface elements in the graphics window and assign event subroutines. The remainder of the program will be event subroutines and other subroutines we need to complete our task. Look at each example closely to see just how straightforward GUI programming is.

We start our study of GUI applications by looking at the most used graphic interface element – the button control. It is part of the Small Basic **Controls** object.

Button Control

The button control is used to begin, interrupt, or end a particular process. The **Controls** object properties, methods and events associated with the button control are listed below.

Button Properties:

```
LastClickedButton
```
Gets the last button that was clicked on the graphics window.

Button Methods:

```
AddButton(caption, x, y)
```
Adds a button with **caption** to the graphics window at (**x, y**). Returns the added button.

```
GetCaption(button)
```
Gets the current caption of the specified **button**. Returns the caption.

```
HideControl(button)
```
Hides an already added **button**.

```
Move(button, x, y)
```
Moves the **button** with the specified name to a new position (**x, y**).

```
Remove(button)
```
Removes a **button** from the graphics window.

```
SetButtonCaption(button, caption)
```
Sets the **caption** of the specified **button**.

```
SetSize(button, w, h)
```
Sets the size (width **w**, height **h**) of the **button**.

```
ShowControl(button)
```
Shows a previously hidden **button**.

Button Events:

```
ButtonClicked
```
Raises an event when any button control is clicked.

Typical use of **Button** control:

- Create the button using **AddButton** method, positioning it in the desired position in the graphics window.
- Write code for the button in **ButtonClicked** event subroutine.

Some features of the **Button** control:

- The background is gray in color.
- The text color is the value of **GraphicsWindow.BrushColor** when the button is created.
- The text font assumes the values of **GraphicsWindow FontName, FontSize, FontBold** and **FontItalic** properties when the button is created.
- The button width and height will automatically adjust to the selected caption and font size. Many times, though, you might adjust these values (use **SetSize** method) if you have multiple buttons you want to be the same size.

Example 6-1. Change Window Color

Write a program that changes the background color of the graphics window every time a button control is clicked.

Small Basic Code:

```
'Guide to Small Basic, Example 6-1
InitializeProgram()

Sub InitializeProgram
  GraphicsWindow.Show()
  GraphicsWindow.Title = "Example 6-1"
  GraphicsWindow.Width = 400
  GraphicsWindow.Height = 200
  'button
  GraphicsWindow.BrushColor = "Black"
  GraphicsWindow.FontSize = 24
  GraphicsWindow.FontBold = "false"
  ColorButton = Controls.AddButton("Change Color", 70, 70)
  Controls.ButtonClicked = ButtonClickedSub
EndSub

Sub ButtonClickedSub
  GraphicsWindow.BackgroundColor = GraphicsWindow.GetRandomColor()
EndSub
```

Saved as **Example 6-1** in **Guide to Small Basic\Programs\Chapter 6** folder.

Since this is the first button example (and first GUI example), let's spend a little time explaining it. The "main" part of the program is just a single line calling the subroutine **InitializeProgram**. In that subroutine, we set up the window and button control. We create the button **ColorButton** with caption **Change Color**. Notice it will have black, non-bold, size 24 font (the default Tahoma font).

The **ButtonClicked** event is assigned to a subroutine **ButtonClickedSub**. Hence, when a user clicks on **ColorButton**, the program calls **ButtonClickedSub**, which assigns a random color to the **GraphicsWindow BackgroundColor**.

Save and **Run** the program to see:

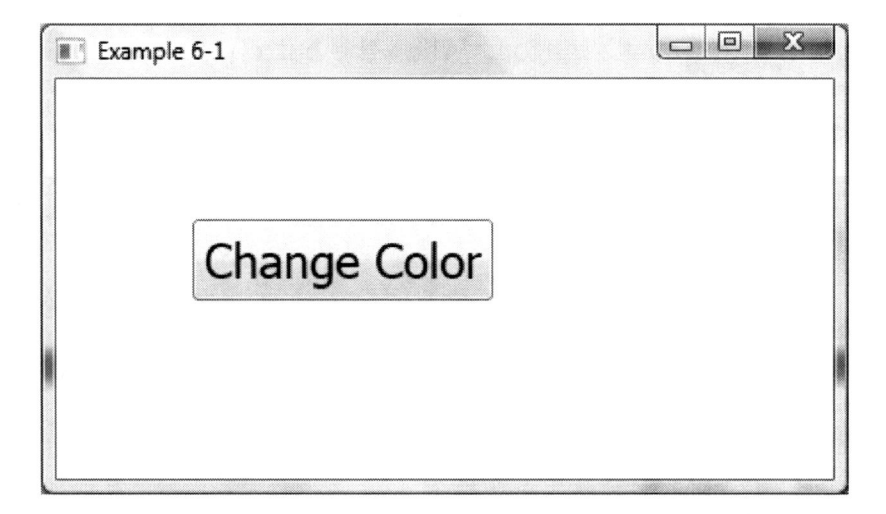

The program is waiting for an event to occur. Click **Change Color**. This causes a **ButtonClick** event and the window will change color:

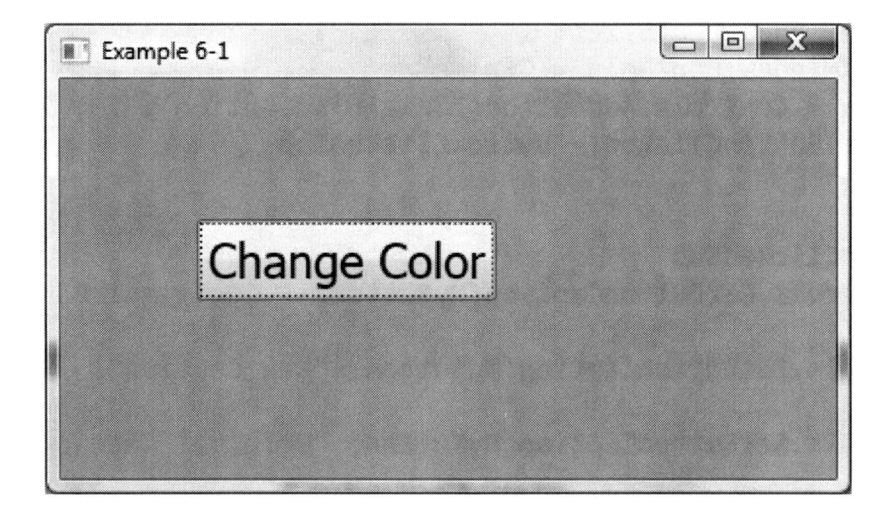

Change the color as many times as you like. To stop the program, click the X in the upper right corner of the window.

Example 6-2. Change Button Caption

Write a program with a single button. When the button is clicked, change the button's **caption** value. This allows a button to be used for multiple purposes. If you click the button again, have the original caption appear.

Small Basic Code:

```
'Guide to Small Basic, Example 6-2
InitializeProgram()

Sub InitializeProgram
  GraphicsWindow.Show()
  GraphicsWindow.Title = "Example 6-2"
  GraphicsWindow.Width = 400
  GraphicsWindow.Height = 200
  'button
  GraphicsWindow.BrushColor = "Black"
  GraphicsWindow.FontSize = 24
  GraphicsWindow.FontBold = "false"
  MyButton = Controls.AddButton("Original Caption", 70, 70)
  Controls.ButtonClicked = ButtonClickedSub
EndSub

Sub ButtonClickedSub
  If (Controls.GetButtonCaption(MyButton) = "Original Caption") Then
    Controls.SetButtonCaption(MyButton, "New Caption")
  Else
    Controls.SetButtonCaption(MyButton, "Original Caption")
  EndIf
EndSub
```

Saved as **Example 6-2** in **Guide to Small Basic\Programs\Chapter 6** folder. Notice use of the **GetButtonCaption** and **SetButtonCaption** methods in **ButtonClickedSub**.

Save and **Run** the program to see the initial button caption:

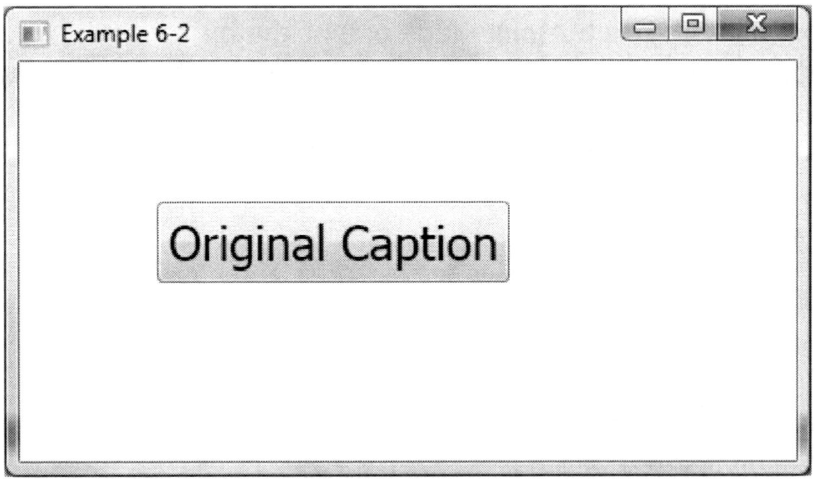
Example 6-2
Original Caption

Click the button to see the next caption (the button will be light blue indicating it was clicked):

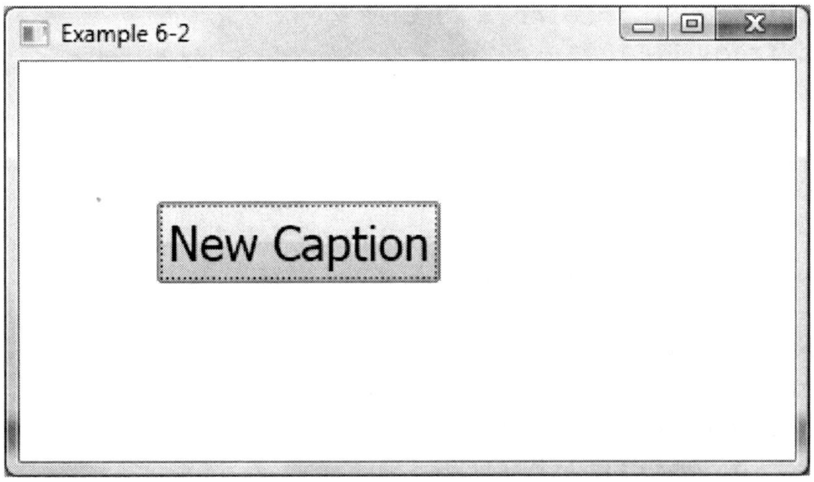
Example 6-2
New Caption

If you click it again, the original caption appears. Notice, too, that the button sizes changes as the caption changes. If you don't like this behavior, set the button to a fixed size using the **SetSize** method. You may have to try a few width/height values to get the desired result.

Example 6-3. Hide/Show Buttons

Build an program with two buttons – hide one of the buttons initially. When you click the button that is showing, hide it and make the other button appear. Reverse the process when you click the second button. This is useful when a particular button's function is not available at some time.

Small Basic Code:

```
'Guide to Small Basic, Example 6-3
InitializeProgram()

Sub InitializeProgram
  GraphicsWindow.Show()
  GraphicsWindow.Title = "Example 6-3"
  GraphicsWindow.Width = 400
  GraphicsWindow.Height = 200
  'button
  GraphicsWindow.BrushColor = "Black"
  GraphicsWindow.FontSize = 16
  GraphicsWindow.FontBold = "false"
  Button1 = Controls.AddButton("Button 1", 70, 30)
  Button2 = Controls.AddButton("Button 2", 70, 70)
  Controls.HideControl(Button2)
  Controls.ButtonClicked = ButtonClickedSub
EndSub

Sub ButtonClickedSub
  If (Controls.LastClickedButton = Button1) Then
    Controls.HideControl(Button1)
    Controls.ShowControl(Button2)
  Else
    Controls.ShowControl(Button1)
    Controls.HideControl(Button2)
  EndIf
EndSub
```

Saved as **Example 6-3** in **Guide to Small Basic\Programs\Chapter 6** folder. Notice since we have two buttons, we need to see which button is clicked in **ButtonClickedSub** (using **Controls.LastButtonClicked**).

Save and **Run** the program to see one button (**Button1**; **Button2** is hidden):

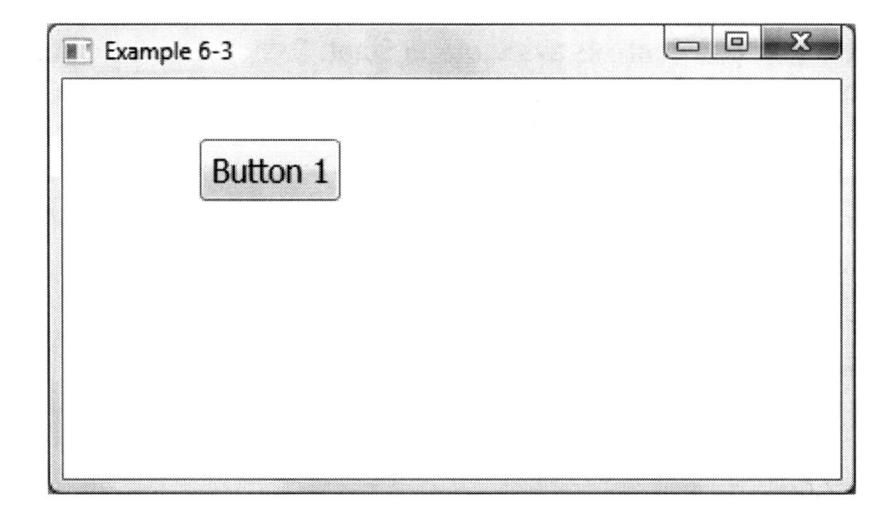

Click the button. It will disappear and **Button2** will appear:

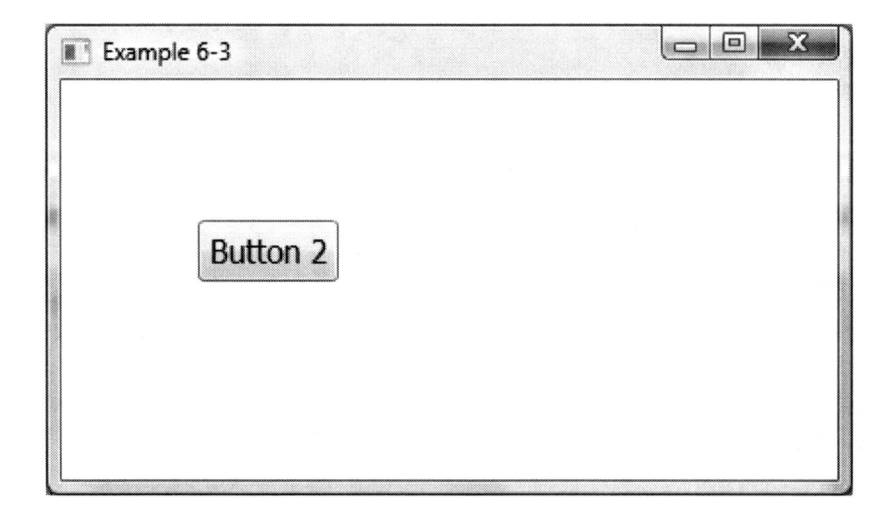

Click **Button2** and it will disappear and **Button1** will return. Try it as many times as you like. Stop the program.

TextBox Control

There are two text box controls available in Small Basic. The **TextBox** (single line) and **MultiLineTextBox** (multiple lines) are used to both receive input from a user and, optionally, to provide information to a user. The **Controls** object properties, methods and events associated with the text box controls are listed below.

TextBox Properties:

```
LastTypedTextBox
```
Gets the last text box that text was typed into.

TextBox Methods:

```
AddMultiLineTextBox(x, y)
```
Adds a multi-line text box to the graphics window at (**x, y**). Returns the added text box.

```
AddTextBox(x, y)
```
Adds a single line text box to the graphics window at (**x, y**). Returns the added text box.

```
GetTextBoxText(textbox)
```
Gets the current text of the specified **textbox**. Returns the text.

```
HideControl(textbox)
```
Hides an already added **textbox**.

```
Move(textbox, x, y)
```
Moves the **textbox** with the specified name to a new position (**x, y**).

```
Remove(textbox)
```
Removes a **textbox** from the graphics window.

```
SetTextboxText(textbox, text)
```
Sets the **text** of the specified **textbox**.

```
SetSize(textbox, w, h)
```
Sets the size (width **w**, height **h**) of the **textbox**.

```
ShowControl(textbox)
```
Shows a previously hidden **textbox**.

TextBox Events:

```
TextTyped
```
Raises an event when text is typed into any textbox.

Typical use of **TextBox** control for display:

- ➢ Create the textbox using **AddTextBox** or **AddMultiLineTextBox** (if displaying more than one line) method, positioning it in the desired position in the graphics window.
- ➢ Initialize **text** to desired string.
- ➢ Set **text** in code where needed.
- ➢ Write code for the **TextTyped** event (optional).

Typical use of **TextBox** control as input device:

- ➢ Create the textbox using **AddTextBox** or **AddMultiLineTextBox** (if displaying more than one line) method, positioning it in the desired position in the graphics window.
- ➢ Initialize **text** to desired string.
- ➢ Read **text** in code where needed.
- ➢ Write code for the **TextTyped** event (optional).

Some features of the **TextBox** and **MultiLineTextBox** controls:

- ➢ The background is white in color.
- ➢ The text color is the value of **GraphicsWindow.BrushColor** when the text box is created.
- ➢ The text font assumes the values of **GraphicsWindow FontName, FontSize, FontBold** and **FontItalic** properties when the button is created.
- ➢ Default width is 160 pixels for the **TextBox**, 200 pixels for the **MultiLineTextBox**. This width be changed using the **SetSize** method.
- ➢ The **TextBox** height will automatically adjust to the selected font size.
- ➢ A scroll bar will be automatically added to the **MultiLineTextBox** when needed.

Example 6-4. Random Numbers

Build a program where each time a button is clicked, a random number from 1 to 100 is displayed in a text box control.

Small Basic Code:

```
'Guide to Small Basic, Example 6-4
InitializeProgram()

Sub InitializeProgram
  GraphicsWindow.Show()
  GraphicsWindow.Title = "Example 6-4"
  GraphicsWindow.BackgroundColor = "LightYellow"
  GraphicsWindow.Width = 400
  GraphicsWindow.Height = 200
  'text box
  GraphicsWindow.BrushColor = "Black"
  GraphicsWindow.FontSize = 16
  GraphicsWindow.FontBold = "false"
  NumberTextBox = Controls.AddTextBox(70, 30)
  NumberButton = Controls.AddButton("Random Number", 70, 60)
  Controls.ButtonClicked = ButtonClickedSub
EndSub

Sub ButtonClickedSub
  Controls.SetTextBoxText(NumberTextBox, Math.GetRandomNumber(100))
EndSub
```

Saved as **Example 6-4** in **Guide to Small Basic\Programs\Chapter 6** folder.

Save and **Run** the program to see the text box with a button underneath:

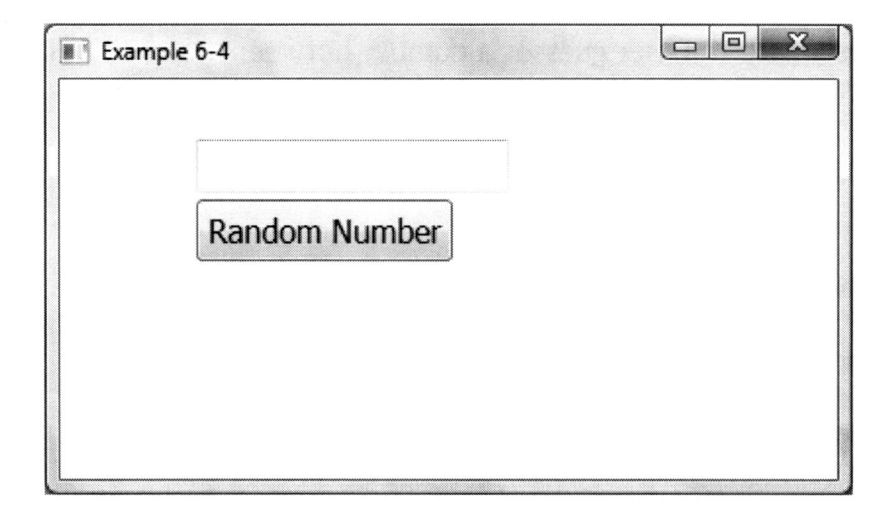

Click **RandomNumber** to see a number from 1 to 100 displayed:

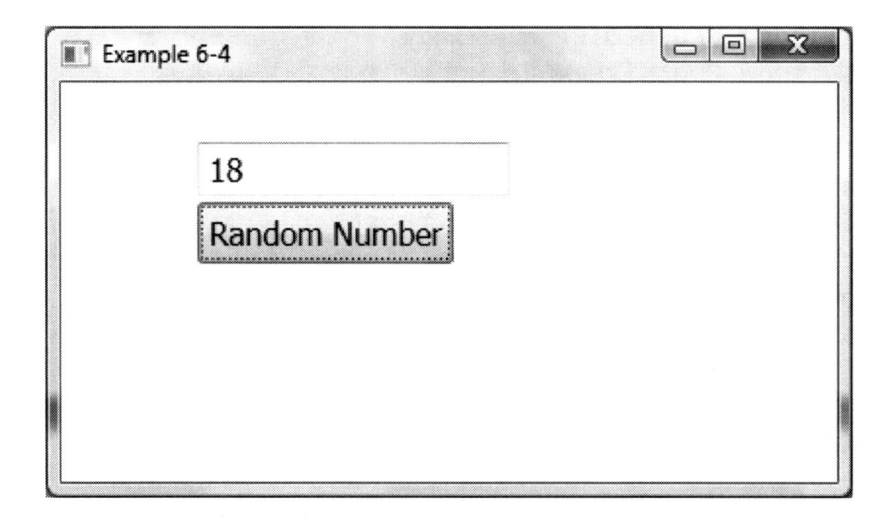

Click the button as many times as you want.

Example 6-5. Guess the Number

Build a game where the user guesses a number between 1 and 100. Clicking a button tells the user if the guess is too high or too low (or correct).

Small Basic Code:

```
'Guide to Small Basic, Example 6-5
InitializeProgram()

Sub InitializeProgram
  GraphicsWindow.Show()
  GraphicsWindow.Title = "Example 6-5"
  GraphicsWindow.BackgroundColor = "LightYellow"
  GraphicsWindow.Width = 400
  GraphicsWindow.Height = 200
  'text boxes/button
  GraphicsWindow.BrushColor = "Black"
  GraphicsWindow.FontSize = 16
  GraphicsWindow.FontBold = "false"
  GraphicsWindow.DrawText(20, 30, "Your Guess:")
  GuessTextBox = Controls.AddTextBox(110, 30)
  MessageTextBox = Controls.AddTextBox(110, 70)
  CheckButton = Controls.AddButton("Check Guess", 130, 110)
  NumberToGuess = Math.GetRandomNumber(100)
  Controls.ButtonClicked = ButtonClickedSub
EndSub

Sub ButtonClickedSub
  'check guess
  YourGuess = Controls.GetTextBoxText(GuessTextBox)
  If (YourGuess = NumberToGuess) Then
    Controls.SetTextBoxText(MessageTextBox, "That's It!!")
  ElseIf (YourGuess > NumberToGuess) Then
    Controls.SetTextBoxText(MessageTextBox, "Too high ...")
  Else
    Controls.SetTextBoxText(MessageTextBox, "Too low ...")
  EndIf
EndSub
```

Saved as **Example 6-5** in **Guide to Small Basic\Programs\Chapter 6** folder.

Save and **Run** the program. Notice how we used **DrawText** to label the text box for entering your guess:

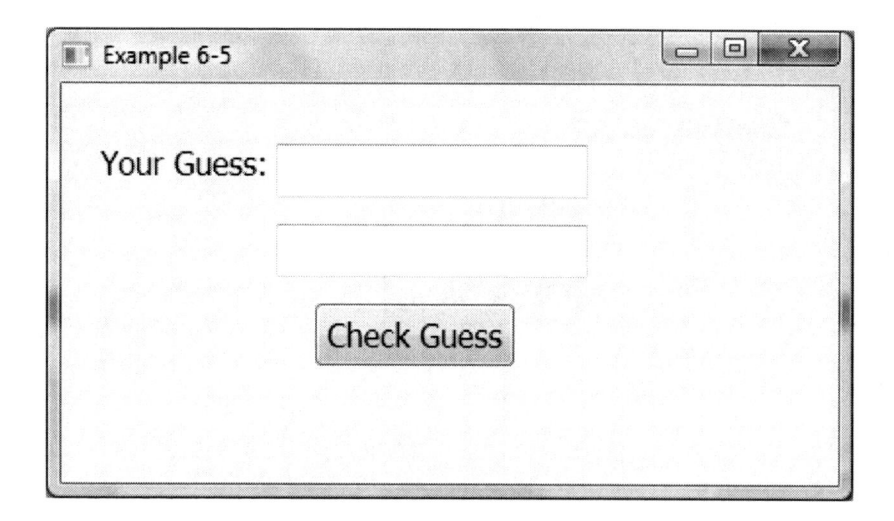

Try a guess and click **Check Guess** - you will be told if you are too high or too low:

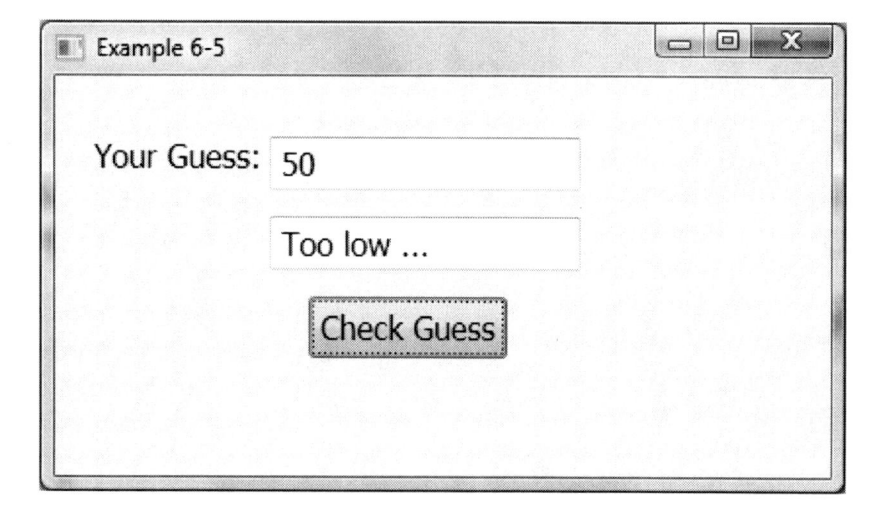

Keep adjusting your guess until you see:

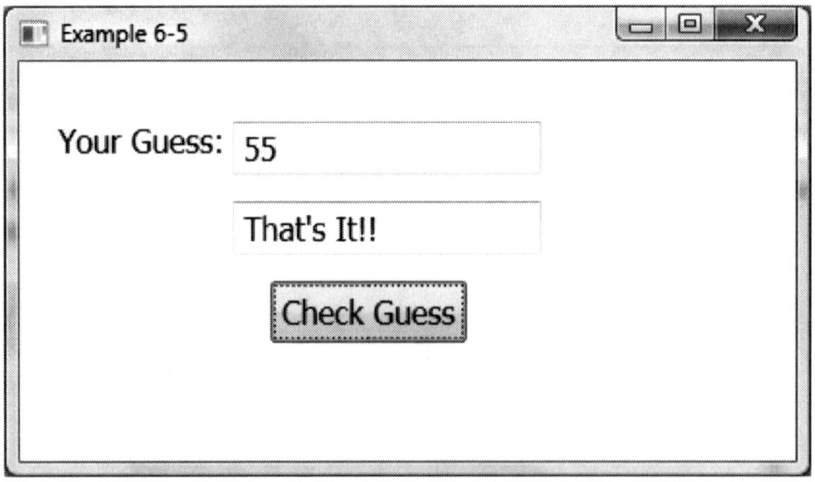
Example 6-5
Your Guess:
55
That's It!!
Check Guess

Example 6-6. Tray Problem

Here's a sheet of cardboard (**L** units long and **W** units wide). A square cut **X** units long is made in each corner:

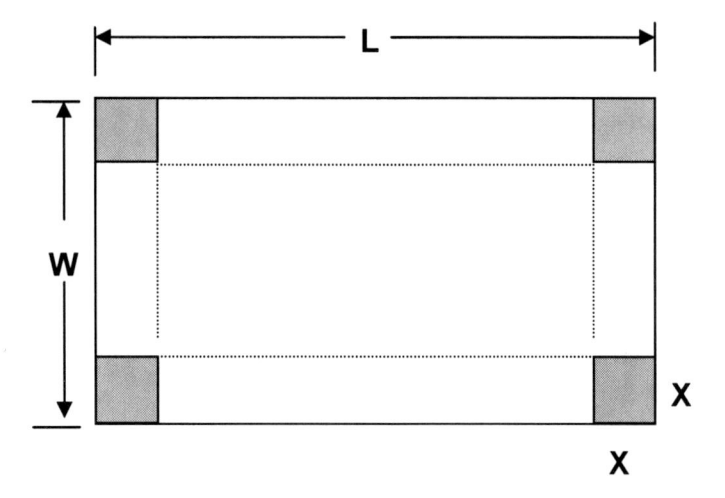

If you cut out the four shaded corners and fold the resulting sides up along the dotted lines, a tray is formed. Build a program that lets a user input the length (L) and width (W). Have the program decide what value X should be such that the tray has the largest volume possible.

Small Basic Code:

```
'Guide to Small Basic, Example 6-6
InitializeProgram()

Sub InitializeProgram
  GraphicsWindow.Show()
  GraphicsWindow.Title = "Example 6-6"
  GraphicsWindow.BackgroundColor = "LightGreen"
  GraphicsWindow.Width = 300
  GraphicsWindow.Height = 200
  'text boxes/button
  GraphicsWindow.BrushColor = "Black"
  GraphicsWindow.FontSize = 16
  GraphicsWindow.FontBold = "false"
  GraphicsWindow.DrawText(10, 10, "Length:")
  LengthTextBox = Controls.AddTextBox(90, 10)
  GraphicsWindow.DrawText(10, 40, "Width:")
  WidthTextBox = Controls.AddTextBox(90, 40)
  GraphicsWindow.DrawText(10, 110, "Cut Size:")
  CutSizeTextBox = Controls.AddTextBox(90, 110)
```

```
    GraphicsWindow.DrawText(10, 140, "Volume:")
    VolumeTextBox = Controls.AddTextBox(90, 140)
    ComputeButton = Controls.AddButton("Compute Cut Size", 90, 70)
    Controls.ButtonClicked = ButtonClickedSub
EndSub

Sub ButtonClickedSub
  'Read L and W
  L = Controls.GetTextBoxText(LengthTextBox)
  W = Controls.GetTextBoxText(WidthTextBox)
  If (L <= 0 Or W <= 0) Then
    GraphicsWindow.ShowMessage("L and W must both be positive", "Invalid values")
  Else
    'Largest cut is one-half of smallest side
    If (L > W) Then
      XMax = W / 2
    Else
      XMax = L / 2
    EndIf
    'Go through 1000 possible cuts from 0 to XMax
    'Find largest volume
    VolMax = 0
    For X = 0 To XMax Step XMax / 1000
      Volume = X * (L - 2 * X) * (W - 2 * X)
      If (Volume > VolMax) Then
        XBest = X
        VolMax = Volume
      EndIf
    EndFor
    'Display best values
    Controls.SetTextBoxText(CutSizeTextBox, XBest)
    Controls.SetTextBoxText(VolumeTextBox, VolMax)
  EndIf
EndSub
```

Saved as **Example 6-6** in **Guide to Small Basic\Programs\Chapter 6** folder.

Save and **Run** the program:

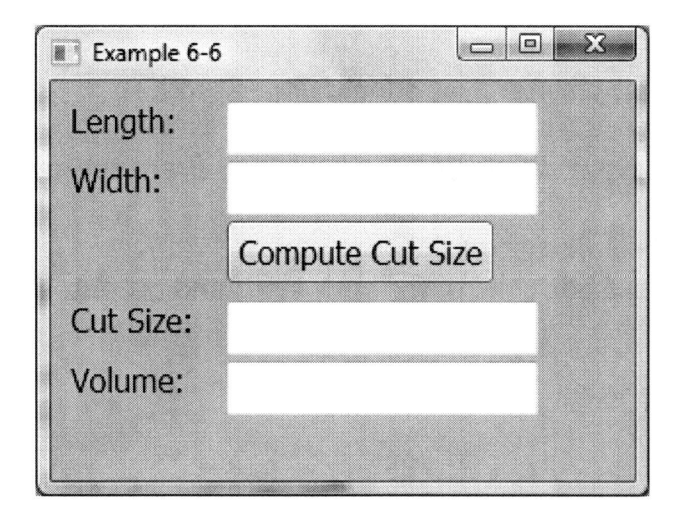

Enter a value for **Length** and **Width**, then click **Compute Cut Size**. Here's what I got for an 8.5 x 11 piece of paper.

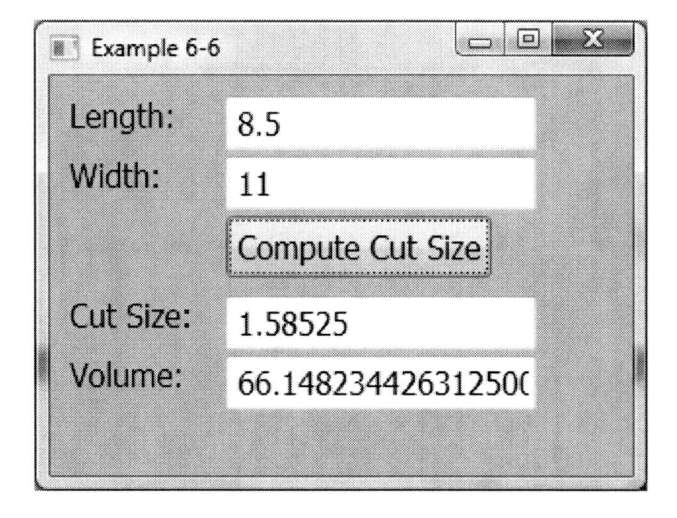

Look through the code to understand how these values were computed.

Chapter Review

After completing this chapter, you should understand:

- ➢ The idea of event driven programming and event subroutines in Small Basic.
- ➢ Use of the button control.
- ➢ Use of the text box control for both input and output.

7. Clock Object

Preview

In this chapter, we take a quick look at the Small Basic **Clock** object. This object provides date and time information and can be used to obtain elapsed times.

Clock Object

The **Clock** object (or more properly class) gives us access to date and time information we can use in our programs. The object only has properties - no methods or events.

Clock Properties:

```
Date
```
Gets the current system date.

```
Day
```
Gets the current day of the month.

```
ElapsedMilliseconds
```
Gets the number of milliseconds that elapsed since 1900.

```
Hour
```
Gets the current hour.

```
Millisecond
```
Gets the current millisecond.

```
Minute
```
Gets the current minute.

```
Month
```
Gets the current month (1-12).

```
Second
```
Gets the current second.

```
Time
```
Gets the current system time.

```
Weekday
```
Gets the current day of the week (1-7).

```
Year
```
Gets the current year.

Example 7-1. System Time/Date

Build a program with two text boxes and a button. When the button is clicked, have the computer display the current time and date in the text boxes.

Small Basic Code:

```
'Guide to Small Basic, Example 7-1
InitializeProgram()

Sub InitializeProgram
  GraphicsWindow.Show()
  GraphicsWindow.Title = "Example 7-1"
  GraphicsWindow.BackgroundColor = "LightBlue"
  GraphicsWindow.Width = 300
  GraphicsWindow.Height = 120
  'text boxes/button
  GraphicsWindow.BrushColor = "Black"
  GraphicsWindow.FontSize = 16
  GraphicsWindow.FontBold = "false"
  GraphicsWindow.DrawText(10, 10, "Time:")
  TimeTextBox = Controls.AddTextBox(90, 10)
  GraphicsWindow.DrawText(10, 40, "Date:")
  DateTextBox = Controls.AddTextBox(90, 40)
  DisplayButton = Controls.AddButton("Display Time/Date", 90, 70)
  Controls.ButtonClicked = ButtonClickedSub
EndSub

Sub ButtonClickedSub
    'Display values
    Controls.SetTextBoxText(TimeTextBox, Clock.Time)
    Controls.SetTextBoxText(DateTextBox, Clock.Date)
EndSub
```

Saved as **Example 7-1** in **Guide to Small Basic\Programs\Chapter 7** folder.

Save and **Run** the program. Click the button to see the time and date:

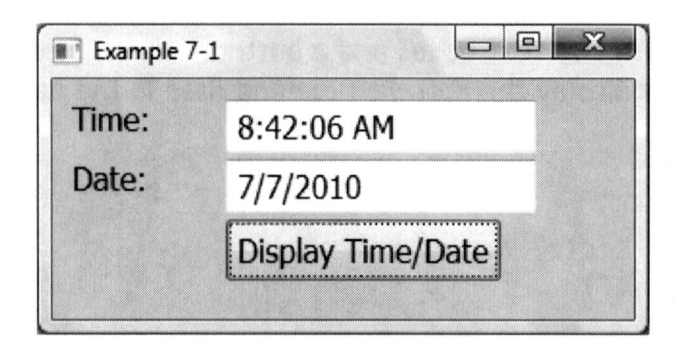

Example 7-2. Stopwatch

Build a program with that tracks elapsed time in seconds. Have a **Start/Stop** button.

Small Basic Code:

```
'Guide to Small Basic, Example 7-2
InitializeProgram()

Sub InitializeProgram
  GraphicsWindow.Show()
  GraphicsWindow.Title = "Example 7-2"
  GraphicsWindow.BackgroundColor = "LightBlue"
  GraphicsWindow.Width = 300
  GraphicsWindow.Height = 100
  'text box/buttons
  GraphicsWindow.BrushColor = "Black"
  GraphicsWindow.FontSize = 16
  GraphicsWindow.FontBold = "false"
  GraphicsWindow.DrawText(10, 10, "Elapsed Time:")
  ElapsedTimeTextBox = Controls.AddTextBox(120, 10)
  Controls.SetTextBoxText(ElapsedTimeTextBox, "0.0")
  StartStopButton = Controls.AddButton("Start", 90, 50)
  Controls.ButtonClicked = ButtonClickedSub
EndSub

Sub ButtonClickedSub
  If (Controls.GetButtonCaption(StartStopButton) = "Start") Then
    StartTime = Clock.ElapsedMilliseconds
    Controls.SetTextBoxText(ElapsedTimeTextBox, "Timing ...")
    Controls.SetButtonCaption(StartStopButton, "Stop")
  Else
    Controls.SetTextBoxText(ElapsedTimeTextBox,
(Clock.ElapsedMilliseconds - StartTime) / 1000)
    Controls.SetButtonCaption(StartStopButton, "Start")
  EndIf
EndSub
```

Saved as **Example 7-2** in **Guide to Small Basic\Programs\Chapter 7** folder. Notice how we check the caption of **StartStopButton** to decide whether to start or stop the timing process.

Save and **Run** the program. The stopwatch appears as:

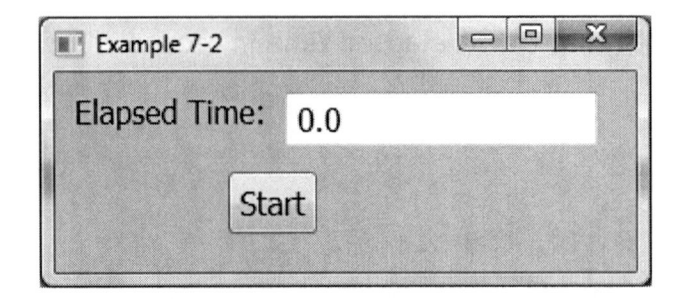

Click **Start** to see the timing start:

Notice how the button caption changes. At some point, click **Stop** to see the elapsed time (in seconds – we divided milliseconds by 1000):

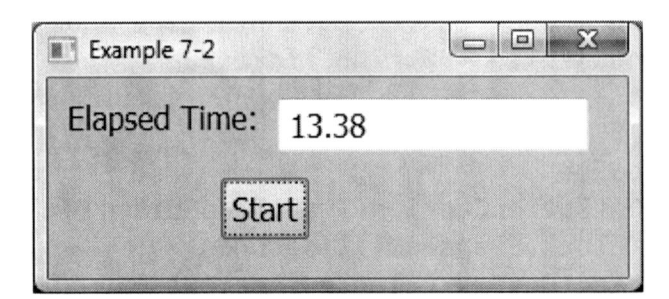

You can **Start** again at this point if you choose.

Chapter Review

After completing this chapter, you should understand:

- Use of the **Clock** object.
- The many properties available with the **Clock** object.
- How to determine elapsed time.

This page intentionally not left blank.

8. Text Object

Preview

In this chapter, we look at the **Text** object. This object is useful when working with strings.

Text Object

The **Text** object provides helpful operations when working with strings of text.

Text Methods:

`Append(text1, text2)`
Appends two text inputs (**text1**, **text2**) and returns the result as another text. This operation is particularly useful when dealing with unknown text in variables which could accidentally be treated as numbers and get added, instead of getting appended.

`ConvertToLowerCase(text)`
Converts the given **text** to lower case. Returns the converted text.

`ConvertToUpperCase(text)`
Converts the given **text** to upper case. Returns the converted text.

`EndsWith(text, subtext)`
Returns "true" if **subtext** is found at end of **text**. Otherwise, returns "false".

`GetCharacter(code)`
Given Unicode character **code**, returns corresponding text character.

`GetCharacterCode(character)`
Given **character**, returns the corresponding Unicode value.

`GetIndexOf(text, subtext)`
Finds position where **subtext** appears in **text**. Returns 0 if subtext not found.

`GetLength(text)`
Gets the length of the given **text**. Returns the length (number of characters).

`GetSubText(text, start, length)`
Gets a subtext from the given **text**. Returns the text starting at **start** and **length** characters long.

`GetSubTextToEnd(text, start)`
Gets a subtext from the given **text** from a specified position (**start**) to the end.

`IsSubText(text,subtext)`
Gets whether or not a given **subtext** is a subset of the larger **text**. Returns "true" if subtext is found in text.

`StartsWith(text, subtext)`
Returns "true" if **subtext** is found at start of **text**. Otherwise, returns "false".

Using Text Methods

Let's look at several examples of how to use some of the **Text** methods. Others will be used in future examples.

To determine the number of characters in (or length of) a string variable, we use the **GetLength** method. Using **MyString** as example:

```
MyString = "Small Basic is fun!"
LenString = Text.GetLength(MyString)
```

LenString will have a value of **19**. Characters in the string variable start at index 1 and end at 19.

You can extract substrings of characters. The **GetSubText** method is used for this task. You specify the string, the starting position and the number of characters to extract. This example starts at character 2 and extracts 6 characters:

```
MyString = "Small Basic is fun!"
SubString = Text.GetSubText(MyString, 2, 6)
```

The **SubString** variable is equal to **"mall B"** Notice you can use this to extract from 1 to as many characters as you wish.

Perhaps, you just want a far left portion of a string. Use the **GetSubText** method with a starting position of 1. This example extracts the 3 left-most characters from a string:

```
MyString = "Small Basic is fun!"
LeftString = Text.GetSubText(MyString, 1, 3)
```

The **LeftString** variable is equal to **"Sma"**

To get the far right portion of a string, use the **GetSubTextToEnd** method. Specify the character to start with and the right portion of the string is returned. To get 6 characters at the end of our example, you would use:

```
MyString = "Small Basic is fun!"
RightString = Text.GetSubTextToEnd(MyString, 14)
```

The **RightString** variable is equal to **"s fun!"**

To locate a substring within a string, use the **GetIndexOf** method. Two pieces of information are needed: **String1** (the string to search) and **String2** (the substring to find). The method will work left-to-right and return the location of the first character of the substring (it will return 0 if the substring is not found). For our example:

```
MyString = "Small Basic is fun!"
Location = Text.GetIndexOf(MyString, "sic")
```

This says find the substring **"sic"** in **MyString**. The returned **Location** will have a value of **9**.

Many times, you want to convert letters to upper case or vice versa. Small Basic provides two methods for this purpose: **ConvertToUpperCase** and **ConvertToLowerCase**. The **ConvertToUpperCase** method will convert all letters in a string variable to upper case, while the **ConvertToLowerCase** method will convert all letters to lower case. Any non-alphabetic characters are ignored in the conversion. And, if a letter is already in the desired case, it is left unmodified. For our example (modified a bit):

```
MyString = "Read About Small Basic in 2010!"
A = Text.ConvertToUpperCase(MyString)
B = Text.ConvertToLowerCase(MyString)
```

The first conversion using **ConvertToUpperCase** will result in:

```
A = "READ ABOUT SMALL BASIC IN 2010!"
```

And the second conversion using **ConvertToLowerCase** will yield:

```
B = "read about small basic in 2010!"
```

Another useful pair of functions are the **GetCharacterCode** and **GetCharacter** methods. These work with individual characters (strings of length one). Every 'typeable' character has a numeric representation called a Unicode. The **GetCharacterCode** method returns the Unicode for an individual character. For example:

```
Text.GetCharacterCode("A")
```

returns the Unicode for the upper case A (65, by the way). The **GetCharacter** method returns the character represented by a Unicode. For example:

```
Text.GetCharacter(49)
```

returns the character represented by a Unicode value of 49 (a "1"). The **GetCharacterCode** and **GetCharacter** methods are used often in determining what a user is typing in conjunction with the **GraphicsWindow KeyDown** event.

KeyDown Event

The **KeyDown** event has the ability to detect the pressing of a key on the computer keyboard. Among others, it can detect:

- Letter and number keys
- Numeric keypad keys (it can distinguish these numbers from those on the top row of the keyboard)
- Cursor control keys

The **KeyDown** event is triggered whenever a key is pressed. If the subroutine to be executed in case of such an event is **KeyDownSub**, we add this event to our program using:

```
GraphicsWindow.KeyDown = KeyDownSub
```

The corresponding subroutine is added to the program in the usual manner and has the form:

```
Sub KeyDownSub
  ' Small Basic code for KeyDown event
EndSub
```

To determine which key was pressed, use the **LastKey** method of the graphics window:

```
KeyPressed = GraphicsWindow.LastKey
```

KeyPressed returns a string representation of the pressed key.

Here are returned values for some of the keys on a standard keyboard.

Letter and Number Keys

Key	Value	Key	Value	Key	Value	Key	Value
A	"A"	J	"J"	S	"S"	1	"D1"
B	"B"	K	"K"	T	"T"	2	"D2"
C	"C"	L	"L"	U	"U"	3	"D3"
D	"D"	M	"M"	V	"V"	4	"D4"
E	"E"	N	"N"	W	"W"	5	"D5"
F	"F"	O	"O"	X	"X"	6	"D6"
G	"G"	P	"P"	Y	"Y"	7	"D7"
H	"H"	Q	"Q"	Z	"Z"	8	"D8"
I	"I"	R	"R"	0	"D0"	9	"D9"

Numeric Keypad Keys

Key	Value	Key	Value
0	"NumPad0"	8	"NumPad8"
1	"NumPad1"	9	"NumPad9"
2	"NumPad2"	/	"Divide"
3	"NumPad3"	*	"Multiply"
4	"NumPad4"	-	"Subtract"
5	"NumPad5"	+	"Add"
6	"NumPad6"	Enter	"Return"
7	"NumPad7"	.	"Decimal"

Cursor Control Keys

Key	Value	Key	Value
Left arrow	"Left"	Delete	"Delete"
Right arrow	"Right"	Home	"Home"
Up arrow	"Up"	End	"End"
Down arrow	"Down"	Page Up	"PageUp"
Insert	"Insert"	Page Down	"Next"

Using the **KeyDown** event is not necessarily easy. There is a lot of work involved in interpreting the information provided in the **KeyDown** event and **LastKey** method. For example, the **KeyDown** event cannot distinguish between an upper and lower case letter and many symbols (!, @, #, ...) cannot be easily recognized. You usually use an **If** structure to determine which key was pressed. For example, to see if the left cursor arrow is pressed, we would write code like this:

```
If (GraphicsWindow.LastKey = "Left") Then
   ' code to execute if left arrow is pressed
EndIf
```

Notice you must enclose the desired key value in quotes since it is a string value. Let's see how to use **KeyDown** to recognize some keys and get their corresponding Unicode value.

Example 8-1. Character Codes

Build a program with a single text box. When you press a letter or number key, display the key and the corresponding Unicode for the key.

Small Basic Code:

```
'Guide to Small Basic, Example 8-1
InitializeProgram()

Sub InitializeProgram
  GraphicsWindow.Show()
  GraphicsWindow.Title = "Example 8-1"
  GraphicsWindow.BackgroundColor = "Blue"
  GraphicsWindow.Width = 200
  GraphicsWindow.Height = 100
  'text box
  GraphicsWindow.BrushColor = "Black"
  GraphicsWindow.FontSize = 24
  GraphicsWindow.FontBold = "false"
  TypedTextBox = Controls.AddTextBox(10, 10)
  GraphicsWindow.KeyDown = KeyDownSub
EndSub

Sub KeyDownSub
  KeyPressed = Text.GetSubTextToEnd(GraphicsWindow.LastKey, 
Text.GetLength(GraphicsWindow.LastKey))
  KeyCode = Text.GetCharacterCode(KeyPressed)
  Controls.SetTextBoxText(TypedTextBox, KeyPressed + " - " + 
KeyCode)
EndSub
```

Saved as **Example 8-1** in **Guide to Small Basic\Programs\Chapter 8** folder. Note we are looking for the **KeyDown** event.

The code is a little tricky. There are different **LastKey** values for numbers pressed on the top row of the keyboard and the numeric keypad (for example, a 0 can be **D0** or **NumPad0**). Here, we find the last character in **LastKey** (using **GetSubTextToEnd**). If a numeric key is pressed, this last character will be the number. If it is a letter, the last character (only character) is that letter.

Save and **Run** the program. Press any letter or number key to see the key and its Unicode value. Here's the letter A:

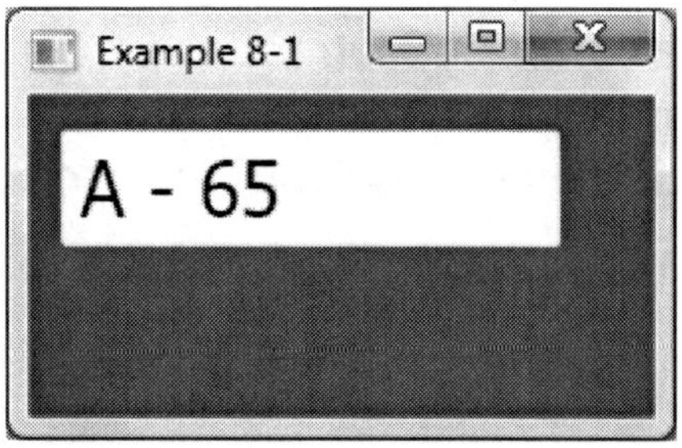
Example 8-1
A - 65

And, here's the number 1 (typed from the top row of the keyboard):

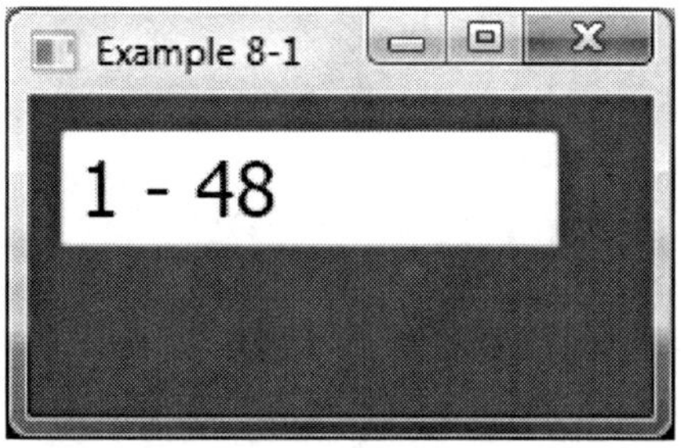
Example 8-1
1 - 48

And the 1 from the keypad (the same result):

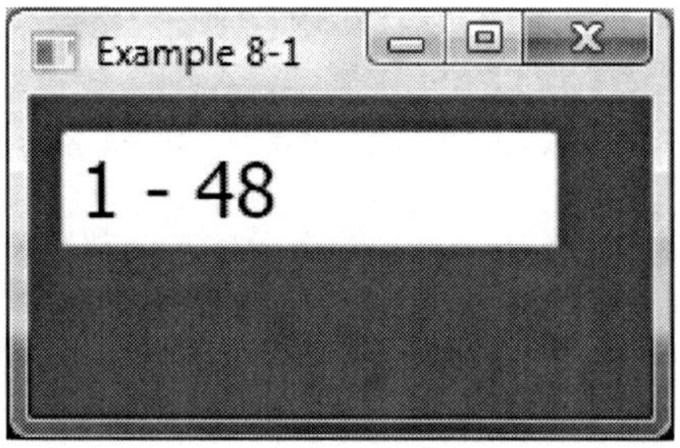
Example 8-1
1 - 48

Try as many keys as you like. You'll get some weird results if you press anything other than numbers or letters.

8-12   The Developer's Reference Guide to Small Basic

Example 8-2. Encode/Decode

Build an program with a text box and two buttons. Type a word or words in the text box. Click one of the buttons. Subtract one from the Unicode value of each character in the typed word(s), then redisplay it. This is a simple encoding technique. When you click the other button, reverse the process to decode the word.

Small Basic Code:

```
'Guide to Small Basic, Example 8-2
InitializeProgram()

Sub InitializeProgram
  GraphicsWindow.Show()
  GraphicsWindow.Title = "Example 8-2"
  GraphicsWindow.BackgroundColor = "Pink"
  GraphicsWindow.Width = 320
  GraphicsWindow.Height = 100
  'text box/buttons
  GraphicsWindow.BrushColor = "Black"
  GraphicsWindow.FontSize = 16
  GraphicsWindow.FontBold = "false"
  WordTextBox = Controls.AddTextBox(10, 10)
  Controls.SetSize(WordTextBox, 300, 30)
  EncodeButton = Controls.AddButton("Encode", 10, 50)
  DecodeButton = Controls.AddButton("Decode", 90, 50)
  Controls.ButtonClicked = ButtonClickedSub
EndSub

Sub ButtonClickedSub
  If (Controls.LastClickedButton = EncodeButton) Then
    CodeChange = -1
  ElseIf (Controls.LastClickedButton = DecodeButton) Then
    CodeChange = 1
  EndIf
  Word1 = Controls.GetTextBoxText(WordTextBox)
  Word2 = ""
  'Find Unicode representation for each character and apply Codechanges
  For I = 1 To Text.GetLength(Word1)
    Character = Text.GetSubText(Word1, I, 1)
    Code = Text.GetCharacterCode(Character) + CodeChange
    NewCharacter = Text.GetCharacter(Code)
    Word2 = Text.Append(Word2, NewCharacter)
```

```
  EndFor
  'Display newly formed word
  Controls.SetTextBoxText(WordTextBox, Word2)
EndSub
```

Saved as **Example 8-2** in **Guide to Small Basic\Programs\Chapter 8** folder.

Save and **Run** the program. Type something in the text box. I tried this:

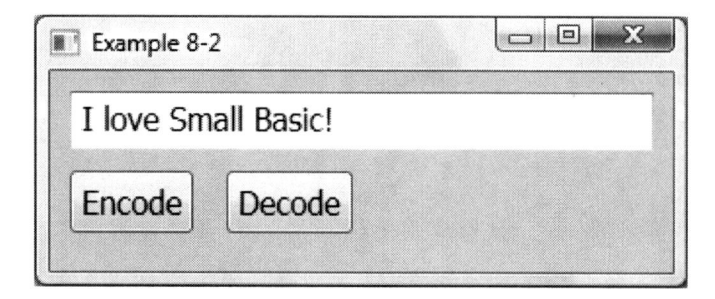

Clicking **Encode**, I see:

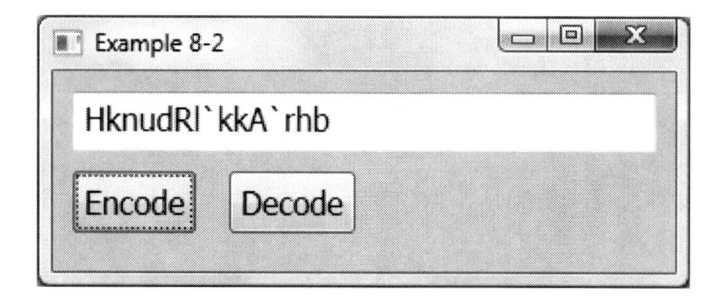

Clicking **Decode** gets my original sentence back!

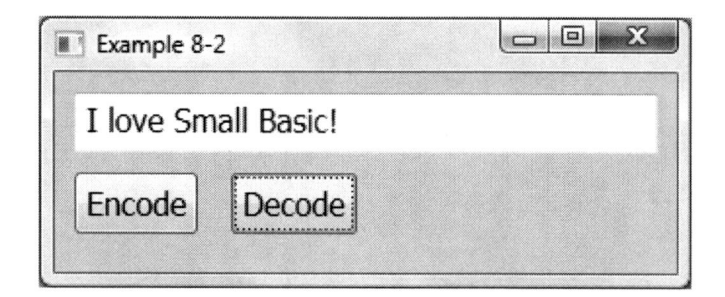

Chapter Review

After completing this chapter, you should understand:

- Use of the **Text** object.
- Working with strings using the text object methods.
- Recognizing key presses using the graphics window **KeyDown** event.

9. ImageList Object

Preview

In this chapter, we look at the **ImageList** object. It is used to load graphics files and make them available for display in the graphics window.

ImageList Object

The **ImageList** object (or more properly class) helps to load and store images in variables. These images can be displayed on the graphics window or in **Shapes** object.

ImageList Methods:

`GetHeightOfImage(image)`
Gets the height of the stored **image**. Returns the height.

`GetWidthOfImage(image)`
Gets the width of the stored **image**. Returns the width.

`LoadImage(filename)`
Loads an image from a file or the internet into memory (**filename** can be a local file or a URL). Returns the name of the image that was loaded.

ImageList Object 9-3

Loading Image Files

The **LoadImage** method is used to load a graphic file into a Small Basic variable. Any image to be loaded from your computer should be in the same folder as your Small Basic program (designated by **Program.Directory**).

To load **MyFile** into a variable **MyImage**, you use:

```
MyImage = ImageList.LoadImage(Program.Directory + "\MyFile")
```

Once loaded the image (**MyImage**) can be displayed in the graphics window or used in a **Shapes** object (studied in the next chapter).

Four types of graphics files that can be loaded using **LoadImage**:

File Type	Description
Icon	A small graphic 32 pixels by 32 pixels in size. Icon filenames have an **.ico** extension. Icons are used to represent Windows applications.
Bitmap	An image represented by pixels and stored as a collection of bits in which each bit corresponds to one pixel. This is the format commonly used by scanners and paintbrush programs. Bitmap filenames have a **.bmp** extension.
JPEG	JPEG (Joint Photographic Experts Group) is a compressed bitmap format which supports 8 and 24 bit color. It is popular on the Internet and is the most common format for digital cameras. JPEG filenames have a **.jpg** extension.
GIF	GIF (Graphic Interchange Format) is a compressed bitmap format originally developed by CompuServe. It supports up to 256 colors and is also popular on the Internet. GIF filenames have a **.gif** extension.

Displaying Images

An image can be displayed in the graphics window using one of two methods. The first is **DrawImage**:

```
GraphicsWindow.DrawImage(image, x, y)
```

This method will draw an **image** at location (**x, y**) in the graphics window. It will be displayed in its original-size. If the graphics window is larger than **image**, there will be blank space. If the graphics window is smaller than **image**, **image** will be cropped. The dimensions of **image** can be obtained using:

```
ImageList.GetHeightOfImage(image)
ImageList.GetWidthOfImage(image)
```

To display the **image** with a specified width (**w**) and height (**h**), you use the **DrawResizedImage** method:

```
GraphicsWindow.DrawResizedImage(image, x, y, w, h)
```

With this method, **image** will 'fill' the defined rectangle at (**x, y**) and w wide, h high. If **image** is smaller than the rectangle, it will expand. If **image** is larger than the rectangle, it will scale down. Bitmap and icon files do not scale nicely. JPEG and GIF files do scale nicely.

To completely fill a graphic window with **image**, you would use:

```
GraphicsWindow.DrawResizedImage(image, 0, 0,
GraphicsWindow.Width, GraphicsWindow.Height)
```

Example 9-1. Image Display

Write a program that displays images using the **DrawImage** method.

Small Basic Code:

```
'Guide to Small Basic, Example 9-1
GraphicsWindow.Show()
GraphicsWindow.Title = "Example 9-1"
GraphicsWindow.Width = 300
GraphicsWindow.Height = 200
GraphicsFile = "cdrom.ico"
ImageToDraw = ImageList.LoadImage(Program.Directory + "\" + GraphicsFile)
GraphicsWindow.DrawImage(ImageToDraw, 0, 0)
```

Saved as **Example 9-1** in **Guide to Small Basic\Programs\Chapter 9** folder. The variable **GraphicsFile** is set to the name of the file you want to display (do not include the directory structure - it is appended when loading the image). See the example line above for **cdrom.ico**:

```
GraphicsFile = "cdrom.ico"
```

When you want to view a different image, change the file name in this line of code

Save the program. If you have some graphics files you would like to view, copy them to your program folder. If you don't have any, you can use the four examples we have included in the **Guide to Small Basic\Programs\Chapter 9** folder.

We have included one of each file type that can be displayed. There is an icon file of a CD-ROM (**cdrom.ico**), a bitmap sketch of my hometown Seattle (**seattle.bmp**), a Queen of Hearts playing card (**queen.gif**) and a photo from my Mexico vacation (**mexico.jpg**).

Let's look at the examples (make sure you copied them to your program folder). Set the file to **cdrom.ico** with:

```
GraphicsFile = "cdrom.ico"
```

Run the program to see:

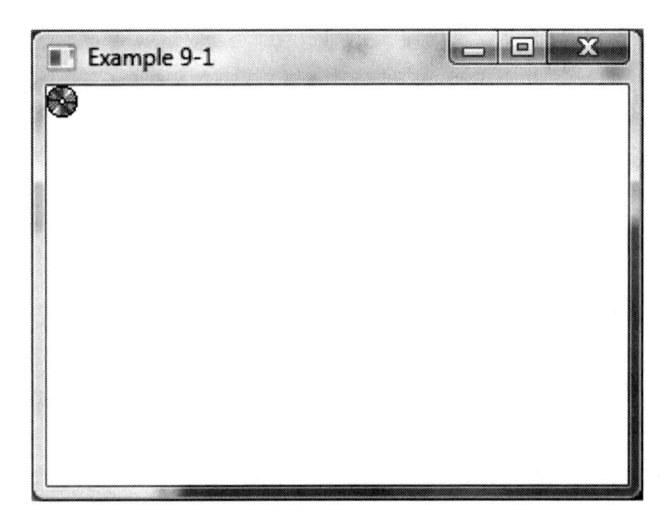

The image is in the upper left hand corner of the graphics window. It appears in full-size. Stop the program.

Set the file to **seattle.bmp** with:

```
GraphicsFile = "seattle.bmp"
```

Run the program to see:

In this example, the graphics window is smaller than the bitmap file (which appears in full size), so the display is "cropped" in both width and height.

Set the file to **queen.gif** with:

    GraphicsFile = "queen.gif"

Run the program to see:

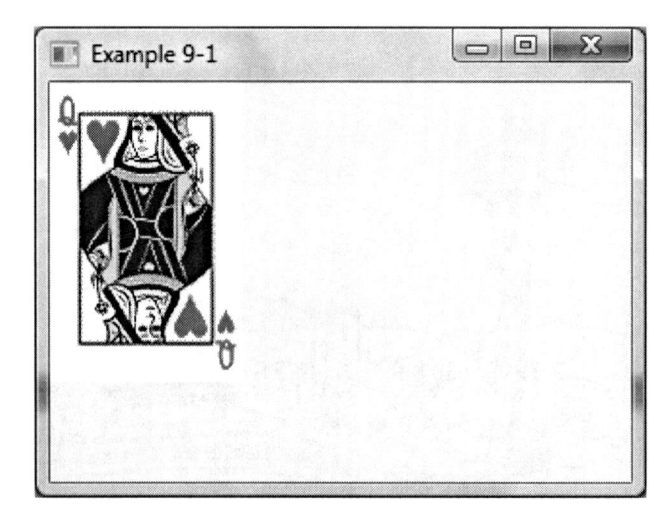

In this example, the graphics window is larger than the gif file. The graphic appears in the upper left corner – much of the window is blank.

Set the file to **queen.gif** with:

    GraphicsFile = "mexico.jpg"

Run the program to see:

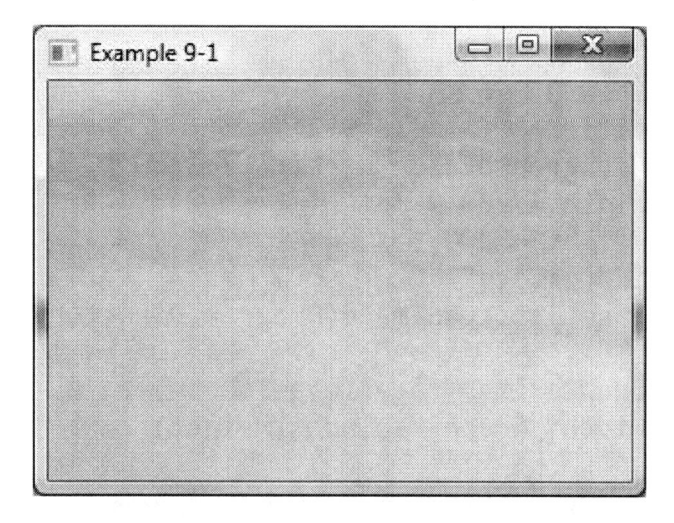

There's not much to see here. The graphics window is smaller than the photo, so only the sky is seen. The picture appears in full-size and is seriously cropped.

Using the **DrawImage** method, we see that the icon file and GIF file seem to display satisfactorily, since they are smaller than the graphics window. The bitmap and JPEG a files had cropping problems though. Next, we look at the **DrawResizedImage** method where we can have the image fill the space we give it.

Example 9-2. Resized Image Display

Write a program that displays images using the **DrawResizedImage** method.

Small Basic Code:

```
'Guide to Small Basic, Example 9-2
GraphicsWindow.Show()
GraphicsWindow.Title = "Example 9-2"
GraphicsWindow.BackgroundColor = "LightYellow"
GraphicsWindow.Width = 300
GraphicsWindow.Height = 200
GraphicsFile = "cdrom.ico"
ImageToDraw = ImageList.LoadImage(Program.Directory + "\" + GraphicsFile)
GraphicsWindow.DrawResizedImage(ImageToDraw, 0, 0, GraphicsWindow.Width, GraphicsWindow.Height)
```

Saved as **Example 9-2** in **Guide to Small Basic\Programs\Chapter 9** folder. This code is identical to that of **Example 9-1**, with the **DrawImage** method replaced by **DrawResizedImage**. We have set the width and height of the resized image to the dimensions of the graphics window.

Let's look at the example files again. **Save** and **Run** the program using:

```
GraphicsFile = "cdrom.ico"
```

You will see:

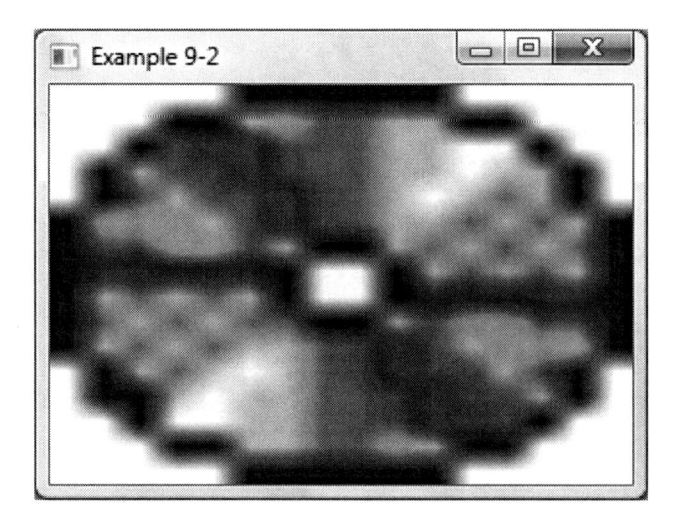

Not real pretty - we only use icon files in full size.

Run the program using:

```
GraphicsFile = "seattle.bmp"
```

You will see:

The entire graphics is visible (as opposed to the cropping we saw using **DrawImage**). That's Mount Rainier in the background.

Run the program using:

```
GraphicsFile = "queen.gif"
```

You will see:

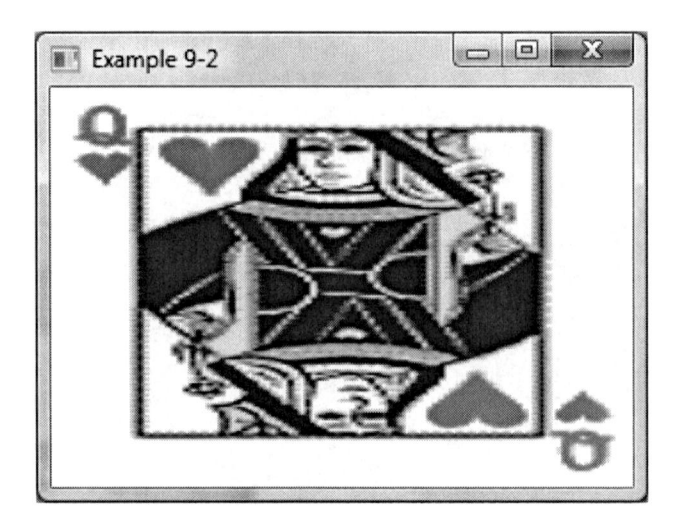

There is no longer any blank space in the window (as seen using **DrawImage**), but the card is distorted, being much wider than it needs to be. When images are enlarged using **DrawResizedImage**, it is suggested you maintain the original width to height ratio. This value can be determined by adding these two lines of code:

```
TextWindow.WriteLine(ImageList.GetWidthOfImage(ImageToDraw))
TextWindow.WriteLine(ImageList.GetHeightOfImage(ImageToDraw))
```

Run the program. The width and height of the image will write in the text window. If I do this for the card, I find it is 100 pixels wide by 150 pixels high. The image has a width to height ratio of 2/3.

The current graphics window has a width to height ratio of 3/2 (300/200). Let's keep the height the same (200 pixels) and change the width to match the width to height ratio of the card. Multiply 200 by 2/3 or get an adjusted width of 167 pixels. Change the graphics window width to this value and rerun the program to see:

The card now looks very nice. Before leaving this example, change the graphics window width back to 300.

Lastly, **Run** the program using:

```
GraphicsFile = "mexico.jpg"
```

You will see:

Recall when we used **DrawImage** for this photo, we only saw sky - it was severely cropped. Now, we see the entire picture. It is not distorted because, coincidentally, the graphics window width to height ratio (3/2) is the same as the ratio for a standard photo that is 6 inches wide by 4 inches high.

MouseDown Event

In the previous chapter, we studied the **KeyDown** event which recognized pressing keys on the keyboard. Now that we have the ability to display images, it would be fun to build a couple of little games where you use the mouse to make choices. To do this, we need to briefly study the **MouseDown** event. We will look at this event in more detail in a later chapter on the **Mouse** object.

The **MouseDown** event is triggered whenever a mouse button is pressed while the mouse cursor is over the graphics window. If the subroutine to be executed in case of such an event is **MouseDownSub**, we add this event to our program using:

```
GraphicsWindow.MouseDown = MouseDownSub
```

The corresponding subroutine is added to the program in the usual manner and has the form:

```
Sub MouseDownSub
  ' Small Basic code for MouseDown event
EndSub
```

Every time the user clicks the mouse, a **MouseDown** event occurs and the subroutine (**MouseDownSub**) is called automatically. In this subroutine, we usually check to see where the window was clicked and process code accordingly. The (X, Y) point clicked in the graphics window is given by two **GraphicsWindow** properties:

```
GraphicsWindow.MouseX
```
x coordinate of mouse cursor in graphics window when mouse is pressed

```
GraphicsWindow.MouseY
```
y coordinate of mouse cursor in graphics window when mouse is pressed

Example 9-3. MouseDown Event

Write a program that prints the coordinates of a point clicked in the graphics window using the mouse.

Small Basic Code:

```
'Guide to Small Basic, Example 9-3
InitializeProgram()

Sub InitializeProgram
  GraphicsWindow.Show()
  GraphicsWindow.Title = "Example 9-3"
  GraphicsWindow.Width = 600
  GraphicsWindow.Height = 400
  GraphicsWindow.MouseDown = MouseDownSub
EndSub

Sub MouseDownSub
  TextWindow.WriteLine("Clicked X = " + GraphicsWindow.MouseX + ", Y = " + GraphicsWindow.MouseY)
EndSub
```

Saved as **Example 9-3** in **Guide to Small Basic\Programs\Chapter 9** folder.

Save and **Run** the program. Click the graphics window and a text window will appear telling you the click coordinate. Here's my results when I clicked near the middle of the graphics window:

```
C:\Guide to Small Basic\Programs\Chapter 9\Example 9-3.exe
Clicked X = 290, Y = 193
```

Move the graphics window and text window (resize it if you like; I did in the above window) so you can see both windows. Click various spots in the window and see how the coordinates change. Notice you cannot detect mouse clicks in the title bar area. Play with this example until you are comfortable with how the **MouseDown** event works and what the coordinates mean. Stop the program.

Example 9-4. Find the Burger Game

Build a game where a burger is hidden behind one of three boxes. You click on the boxes trying to find the burger. A burger graphic, **burger.gif**, is included in the **Guide to Small Basic\Programs\Chapter 9** folder:

Small Basic Code:

```
'Guide to Small Basic, Example 9-4
InitializeProgram()

Sub InitializeProgram
  GraphicsWindow.Show()
  GraphicsWindow.Title = "Example 9-4"
  GraphicsWindow.Width = 380
  GraphicsWindow.Height = 180
  'burger
  BurgerImage = ImageList.LoadImage(Program.Directory +
"\burger.gif")
  'box locations
  BoxX[1] = 20
  BoxX[2] = 140
  BoxX[3] = 260
  'button
  GraphicsWindow.BrushColor = "Black"
  GraphicsWindow.FontSize = 16
  GraphicsWindow.FontBold = "false"
  NewGameButton = Controls.AddButton("New Game", 140, 140)
  Controls.ButtonClicked = ButtonClickedSub
  GraphicsWindow.MouseDown = MouseDownSub
EndSub

Sub ButtonClickedSub
  'hide button, display boxes, pick burger location
  Controls.HideControl(NewGameButton)
  GraphicsWindow.BrushColor = "Blue"
  For I = 1 To 3
    GraphicsWindow.FillRectangle(BoxX[I], 20, 100, 100)
```

```
    EndFor
    BurgerLocation = Math.GetRandomNumber(3)
EndSub

Sub MouseDownSub
    'find clicked box
    X = GraphicsWindow.MouseX
    Y = GraphicsWindow.MouseY
    ClickedBox = 0
    If (Y > 20 And Y < 120) Then
        For I = 1 To 3
            If (X > BoxX[I] And X < BoxX[I] + 100) Then
                ClickedBox = I
            EndIf
        EndFor
    EndIf
    'clear box, see if burger is there
    GraphicsWindow.BrushColor = GraphicsWindow.BackgroundColor
    GraphicsWindow.FillRectangle(BoxX[ClickedBox], 20, 100, 100)
    If (ClickedBox = BurgerLocation) Then
        GraphicsWindow.DrawResizedImage(BurgerImage, BoxX[ClickedBox], 20, 100, 100)
        Controls.ShowControl(NewGameButton)
    EndIf
EndSub
```

Saved as **Example 9-4** in **Guide to Small Basic\Programs\Chapter 9** folder.

The programs are getting longer. In the **InitializeProgram** subroutine, we set up the interface and load the burger image (**BurgerImage**). Make sure you copy burger.gif in your program folder.

When the user clicks **New Game**, the boxes are drawn and a position for the burger selected. Notice how we find which of the three boxes is clicked by the mouse by examining values of X and Y (the clicked position).

Save and **Run** the program. Click **New Game**. The three boxes will be shown. Click on boxes trying to find the burger. If the burger graphics does not appear behind any of the boxes, make sure you copied the graphics file to your program folder. Here's a run I made, where I found the burger on my second try:

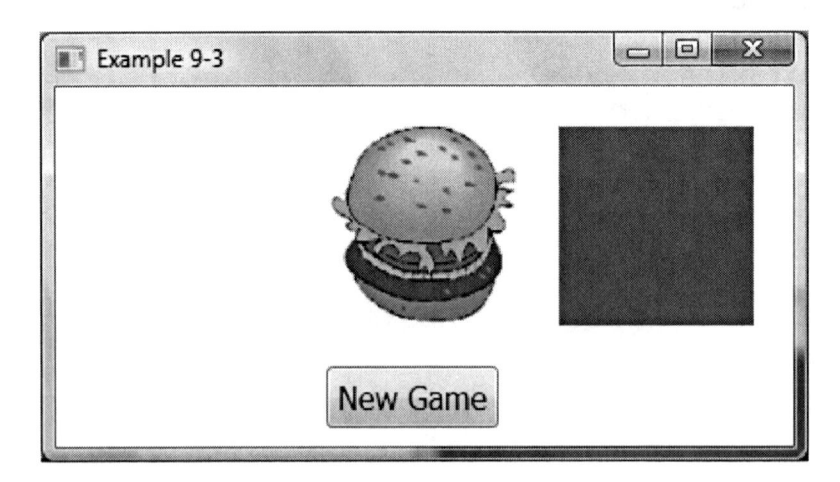

As written, you just randomly guess burger location. In the chapter where we discuss the **Timer** object, we'll add a cool feature to the program. We will show you what box the burger is behind and then shuffle the boxes. A keen eye is needed to follow the moving burger.

Example 9-5. Tic-Tac-Toe Game

Build a simple Tic-Tac-Toe game. Use different images to distinguish player markers. Click the Tic-Tac-Toe grid to add the markers. Two sample marker files (**apple.jpg** and **banana.jpg**) are included in the **Guide to Small Basic\Programs\Chapter 9** folder:

Small Basic Code:

```
'Guide to Small Basic, Example 9-5
InitializeProgram()

Sub InitializeProgram
  GraphicsWindow.Show()
  GraphicsWindow.Title = "Example 9-5"
  GraphicsWindow.Width = 380
  GraphicsWindow.Height = 420
  'images
  XImage = ImageList.LoadImage(Program.Directory + "\apple.jpg")
  OImage = ImageList.LoadImage(Program.Directory + "\banana.jpg")
  'grid
  GraphicsWindow.PenColor = "Black"
  GraphicsWindow.PenWidth = 5
  GraphicsWindow.DrawLine(10, 130, 370, 130)
  GraphicsWindow.DrawLine(10, 250, 370, 250)
  GraphicsWindow.DrawLine(130, 10, 130, 370)
  GraphicsWindow.DrawLine(250, 10, 250, 370)
  'grid locations
  BoxX[1] = 20
  BoxY[1] = 20
  BoxX[2] = 140
  BoxY[2] = 20
  BoxX[3] = 260
  BoxY[3] = 20
  BoxX[4] = 20
  BoxY[4] = 140
  BoxX[5] = 140
```

```
      BoxY[5] = 140
      BoxX[6] = 260
      BoxY[6] = 140
      BoxX[7] = 20
      BoxY[7] = 260
      BoxX[8] = 140
      BoxY[8] = 260
      BoxX[9] = 260
      BoxY[9] = 260
      'button
      GraphicsWindow.BrushColor = "Black"
      GraphicsWindow.FontSize = 16
      GraphicsWindow.FontBold = "false"
      NewGameButton = Controls.AddButton("New Game", 140, 380)
      Controls.ButtonClicked = ButtonClickedSub
      GraphicsWindow.MouseDown = MouseDownSub
      CanClick = "false"
EndSub

Sub ButtonClickedSub
    'hide button, clear boxes
    Controls.HideControl(NewGameButton)
    GraphicsWindow.BrushColor = GraphicsWindow.BackgroundColor
    For I = 1 To 9
      GraphicsWindow.FillRectangle(BoxX[I], BoxY[I], 100, 100)
      BoxValue[I] = 0
    EndFor
    CanClick = "true"
    XTurn = "true"
    NumberClicks = 0
EndSub

Sub MouseDownSub
    'find clicked box
    If (CanClick) Then
      X = GraphicsWindow.MouseX
      Y = GraphicsWindow.MouseY
      ClickedBox = 0
      For I = 1 To 9
        If (Y > BoxY[I] And Y < BoxY[I] + 100) Then
          If (X > BoxX[I] And X < BoxX[I] + 100) Then
            ClickedBox = I
          EndIf
        EndIf
      EndFor
      If (ClickedBox <> 0 And BoxValue[ClickedBox] = 0) Then
```

```smallbasic
      'hasn't been selected yet
      If (XTurn) Then
        'show apple
        BoxValue[ClickedBox] = 1
        GraphicsWindow.DrawResizedImage(XImage, BoxX[ClickedBox],
BoxY[ClickedBox], 100, 100)
        XTurn = "false"
      Else
        'show orange
        BoxValue[ClickedBox] = 2
        GraphicsWindow.DrawResizedImage(OImage, BoxX[ClickedBox],
BoxY[ClickedBox], 100, 100)
        XTurn = "true"
      EndIf
      NumberClicks = NumberClicks + 1
      If (NumberClicks = 9) Then
        CanClick = "false"
        Controls.ShowControl(NewGameButton)
      EndIf
    EndIf
  EndIf
EndSub
```

Saved as **Example 9-5** in **Guide to Small Basic\Programs\Chapter 9** folder.

Even for this simple version of the class game, there is quite a bit of code. In the **InitializeGame** subroutine, we load the graphics to be used as markers (an apple and a banana) and set up the grid structure for the game. We number the different grid locations as:

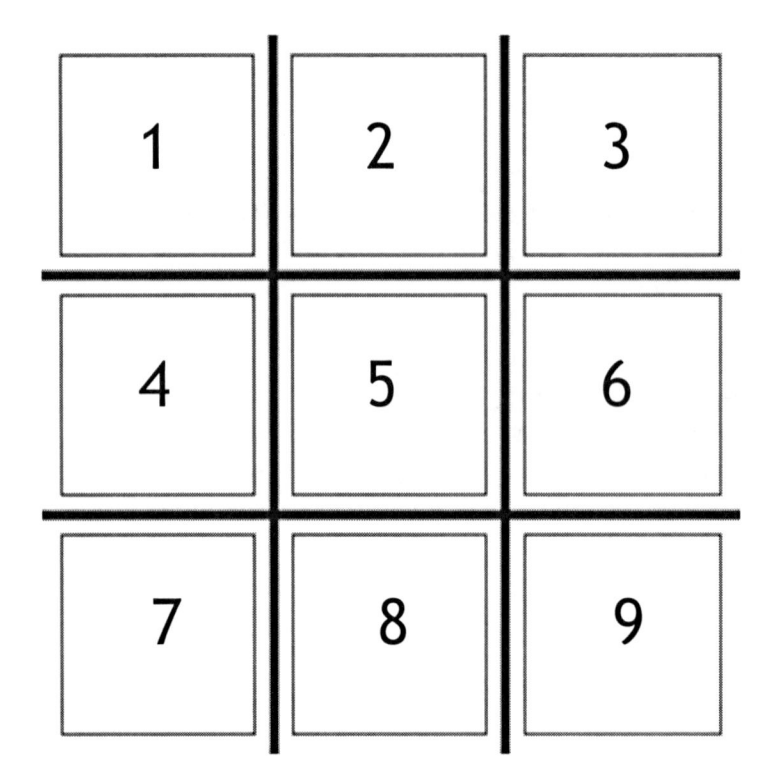

1	2	3
4	5	6
7	8	9

Each image is 100 pixels wide by 100 pixels high. There is a margin of 10 pixels around each image. The arrays **BoxX** and **BoxY** hold the locations of each of the clickable regions. The variable **CanClick** controls whether the grid can be clicked.

The game starts by clicking the **New Game** button. Turns alternate between X (the apple, **XTurn** is "true") and O (the banana, **XTurn** is "false"). The array **BoxValue** keeps track of whether a particular box holds an apple (value 1), a banana (2) or nothing (0). Game play continues until the game grid is full (**NumberClicks = 9**).

Save and **Run** the program. An empty grid appears.

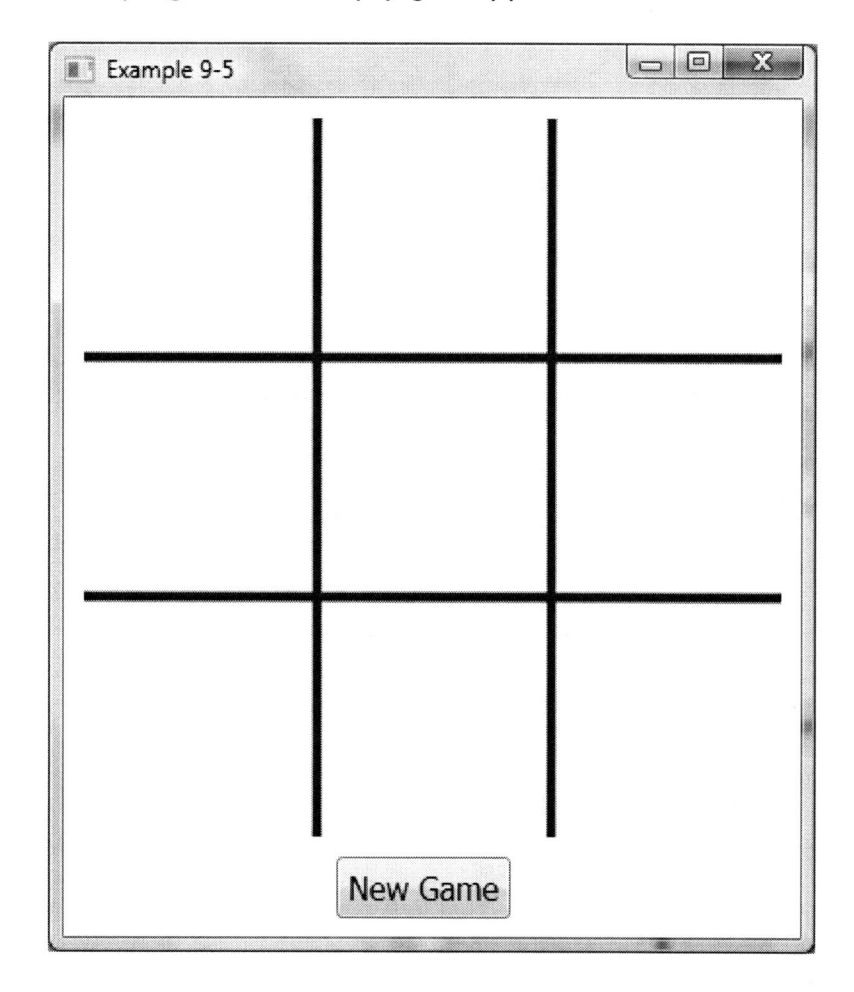

Click **New Game** to start playing.

The first player (the apple) makes a selection by clicking a grid location. I chose the middle square:

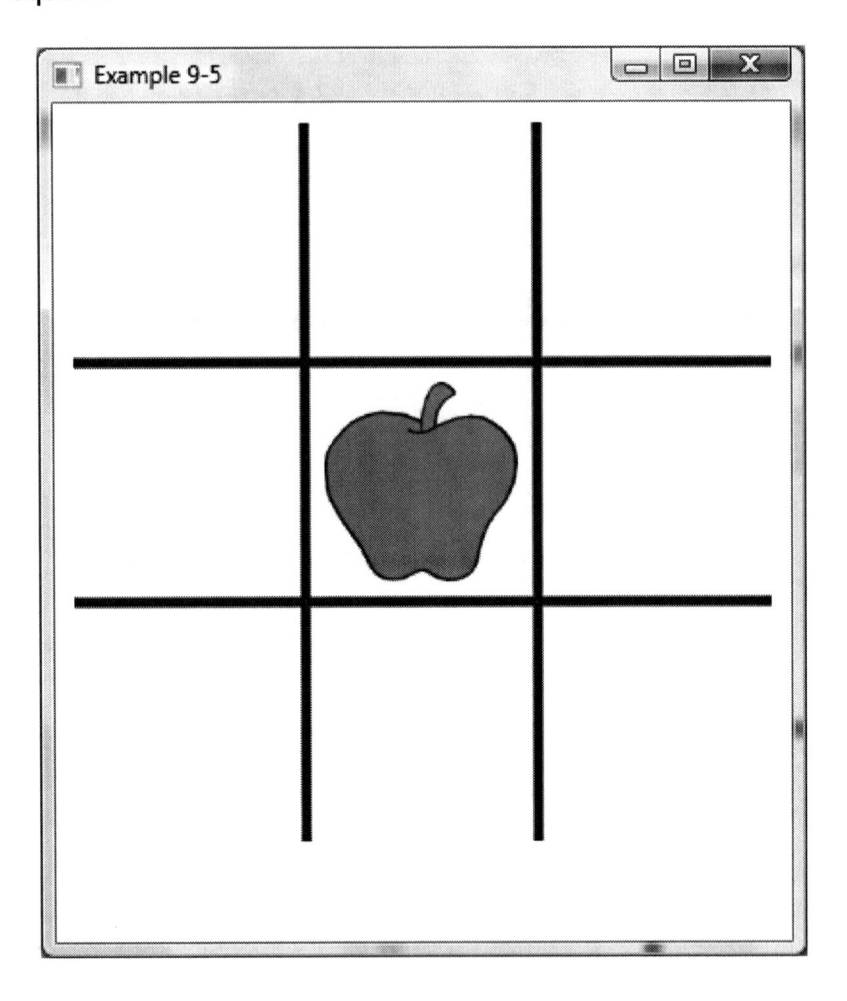

Alternate turns until the grid is full. Here's a game I played to completion:

It's a draw. At this point, clicking New Game will clear the grid for another game.

As mentioned, there is no logic to detect a win. Perhaps you could add such logic using the **BoxValue** array. Or, if you are really ambitious, can you write code that allows you to play against the computer?

Chapter Review

After completing this chapter, you should understand:

- Use of the **ImageList.**
- How to load images from files.
- The types of files that can be loaded.
- Displaying files with the graphics window **DrawImage** and **DrawResizedImage** methods.
- Recognizing mouse clicks with the graphics window **MouseDown** event.

10. Shapes Object

Preview

In this chapter, we look at the Small Basic **Shapes** object. The shapes seen are similar to many of the graphics window elements (lines, rectangles, ellipses, triangles, text, images) we have seen previously, but have additional methods to allow easy movement within the window.

Shapes Object

The **Shapes** object allows you to add, move and rotate shapes to the graphics window. They are key elements to doing animation with Small Basic.

You will see many of the **Shapes** methods are very similar to the graphics window methods for drawing shapes and text. The big difference here is that the shapes are named as variables. This allows us to do the mentioned movement, rotation and animation.

Shapes Methods:

```
AddEllipse(w, h)
```
Adds an ellipse shape with the specified width **w** and height **h**. Returns the ellipse.

```
AddImage(image)
```
Adds an **image** as a shape that can be moved, animated or rotated. Returns the image.

```
AddLine(x1, y1, x2, y2)
```
Adds a line between the specified points (**x1, y1**) and (**x2, y2**). Returns the line.

```
AddRectangle(w, h)
```
Adds a rectangle shape with the specified width **w** and height **h**. Returns the rectangle.

```
AddText(text)
```
Adds **text** as a shape that can be moved, animated or rotated. Returns the text shape.

```
AddTriangle(x1, y1, x2, y2, x3, y3)
```
Adds a triangle shape represented by the specified points. Returns the triangle.

```
Animate(shape, x, y, duration)
```
Animates a **shape** with the specified name to a new position (**x, y**). The animation lasts **duration** milliseconds.

GetLeft(shape)
Gets the left coordinate of the specified **shape**. Returns the left coordinate.

GetOpacity(shape)
Gets opacity of **shape**. Returns opacity value, a number between 0 and 100 (0 is completely transparent, 100 is completely opaque).

GetTop(shape)
Gets the top coordinate of the specified **shape**. Returns the top coordinate.

HideShape(shape)
Hides a previously added **shape**.

Move(shape, x, y)
Moves the **shape** with the specified name to a new position (**x, y**).

Remove(shape)
Removes **shape** from the graphics window.

Rotate(shape, angle)
Rotates the **shape** with the specified name to the specified **angle** (in degrees).

SetOpacity(shape, value)
Sets opacity of **shape** to **value**. The **value** is a number between 0 and 100 (0 is completely transparent, 100 is completely opaque).

SetText(shape, text)
Sets **text** of already added text **shape**.

ShowShape(shape)
Shows a previously hidden **shape**.

Zoom(shape, scalex, scaley)
Scales **shape** using specified zoom levels (**scalex, scaley**). Minimum zoom is 0.1; maximum zoom is 20.

Lines

A line is the simplest geometric **Shapes** object. It is created using:

    Shapes.AddLine(x1, y1, x2, y2)

This method creates a **Shapes** object that is a line between (**x1, y1**) and (**x2, y2**).

A **Shapes** object that is a **line** is drawn using the value of **GraphicsWindow.PenColor** and **GraphicsWindow.PenWidth** when the line object is created.

Example 10-1. Line

Write a program that creates a **Shapes** object that is a blue line, with width 10.

Small Basic Code:

```
'Guide to Small Basic, Example 10-1
GraphicsWindow.Show()
GraphicsWindow.Title = "Example 10-1"
GraphicsWindow.Width = 300
GraphicsWindow.Height = 200
GraphicsWindow.PenColor = "Blue"
GraphicsWindow.PenWidth = 5
ExampleLine = Shapes.AddLine(30, 30, 100, 100)
```

Saved as **Example 10-1** in **Guide to Small Basic\Programs\Chapter 10** folder.

Save and **Run** the program to see the blue line segment (**ExampleLine**):

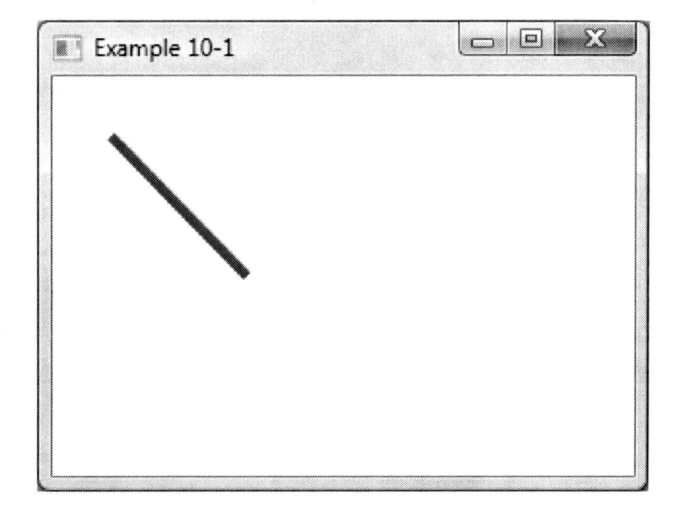

Rectangles, Ellipses, Triangles

Rectangles, ellipses and triangles can be used in games you might design. They can represent game paddles, bouncing balls, and flying spaceships. The methods to create these objects are, respectively:

```
Shapes.AddRectangle(w, h)
Shapes.AddEllipse(w, h)
Shapes.AddTriangle(x1, y1, x2, y2, x3, y3)
```

Rectangles and ellipses will be **w** pixels wide and **h** pixels high. The triangle connects (**x1, y1**), (**x2, y2**), (**x3, y3**).

Other features of **Shapes** objects that are **rectangles**, **ellipses** or **triangles**:

- Each figure will be drawn filled and bordered.
- The current pen color (**GraphicsWindow.PenColor**) and pen width (**GraphicsWindow.PenWidth**) establishes the object border.
- The current brush color (**GraphicsWindow.BrushColor**) establishes the fill color.
- By default, rectangles and ellipses will be put in the upper left corner of the graphics window.

Since rectangles and ellipses are placed in the upper left corner of the graphics window, you usually do one of two things once an object is created. You either hide the object (using the **HideShape** method) or move the object (using **Move**) to a desired position. If you hide the object for later display, don't forget to show the object (using **ShowShape**) once it is in its desired position.

Example 10-2. Rectangle, Ellipse and Triangle

Write a program that creates three **Shapes** objects: a rectangle, an ellipse and a triangle. Choose border color and width and fill color. Position the shapes within the graphics window.

Small Basic Code:

```
'Guide to Small Basic, Example 10-2
GraphicsWindow.Show()
GraphicsWindow.Title = "Example 10-2"
GraphicsWindow.Width = 400
GraphicsWindow.Height = 200
GraphicsWindow.PenColor = "Blue"
GraphicsWindow.PenWidth = 5
GraphicsWindow.BrushColor = "Yellow"
ExampleRectangle = Shapes.AddRectangle(50, 100)
Shapes.Move(ExampleRectangle, 20, 20)
GraphicsWindow.PenColor = "Black"
GraphicsWindow.PenWidth = 2
GraphicsWindow.BrushColor = "LightBlue"
ExampleEllipse = Shapes.AddEllipse(150, 75)
Shapes.Move(ExampleEllipse, 80, 20)
GraphicsWindow.PenColor = "Red"
GraphicsWindow.PenWidth = 2
GraphicsWindow.BrushColor = "PeachPuff"
ExampleTriangle = Shapes.AddTriangle(300, 40, 350, 160, 200, 150)
```

Saved as **Example 10-2** in **Guide to Small Basic\Programs\Chapter 10** folder. Notice we need to move the rectangle object (**ExampleRectangle**) and ellipse object (**ExampleEllipse**) away from the upper left corner (default position). There is no need to move the triangle object (**ExampleTriangle**). It is positioned when added.

Save and Run the program to see the three Shapes objects:

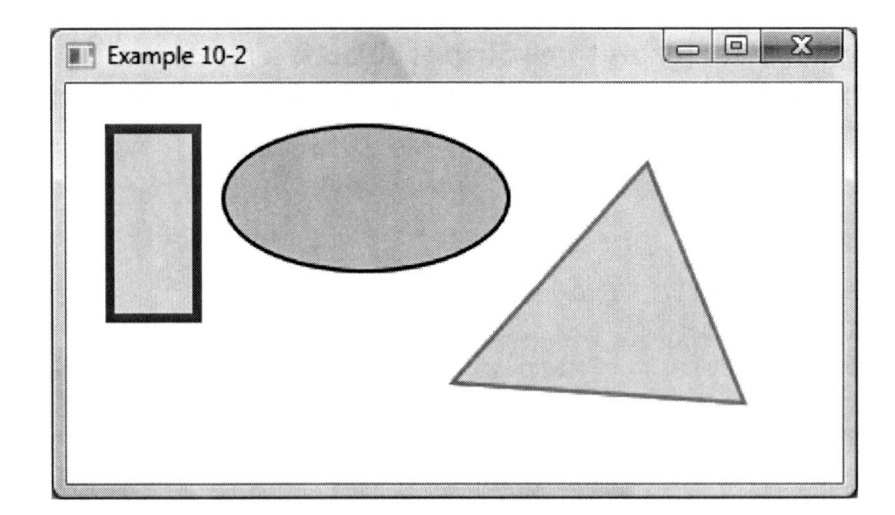

Look back at the code to see how we set border line width and line color and fill color.

Text

A text **Shapes** object displays text you specify. You might be asking what good is a **Shapes** object that just holds text? Why not just draw the text to the graphics window (**DrawText**) or put the text in a text box control?

Text Shapes objects are very useful for providing text information that needs to be updated periodically. For example, they areused for game scores, players names or calculation results. They are easier to use than the **DrawText** method where you must erase any displayed text before updating it. Such objects can be rotated (**Rotate** method) providing nice labeling information. And, they are have a big advantage over text box controls – the displayed information cannot be altered by a user. Such an object holding the string **text** is created using:

    GraphicsWindow.AddText(text)

Features of the **Shapes text** object:

- ➤ The text font assumes the values of **GraphicsWindow FontName, FontSize, FontBold** and **FontItalic** properties when the object is created.
- ➤ The text color is set by the current brush color, **GraphicsWindow.BrushColor**.
- ➤ The object 'background' is transparent – anything behind the object will be seen. We usually place the object over a colored rectangle.
- ➤ The object width and height will automatically adjust to hold the specified **text**.
- ➤ By default, the object will be put in the upper left corner of the graphics window.

Like the rectangle and ellipse **Shapes** object, the object is initially placed in the upper left corner of the graphics window. So, you usually do one of two things once an object is created. You either hide the object (using the **HideShape** method) or move the object (using **Move**) to a desired position. If you hide the object for later display, don't forget to show the object (using **ShowShape**) once it is in its desired position.

The usual steps in using a text **Shapes** object are:

- Determine and specify font characteristics and text color.
- Decide on a background color (if other than the graphics window background). Draw a rectangle of that color at desired text object location. Make sure the rectangle is as large as the longest text string to be displayed by the object.
- Create the text **Shapes** object with initial text and **Move** it within the colored rectangle.
- When a new text value is available, change it using the **SetText** method.

Example 10-3. Text

Write a program that creates a text **Shapes** object with blue text on a yellow background. Periodically update the displayed text.

Small Basic Code:

```
'Guide to Small Basic, Example 10-3
GraphicsWindow.Show()
GraphicsWindow.Title = "Example 10-3"
GraphicsWindow.Width = 300
GraphicsWindow.Height = 100
GraphicsWindow.BackgroundColor = "LightBlue"
'draw background
GraphicsWindow.BrushColor = "Yellow"
GraphicsWindow.FillRectangle(20, 20, 260, 60)
'shapes object
GraphicsWindow.FontSize = 36
GraphicsWindow.FontBold = "false"
GraphicsWindow.BrushColor = "Blue"
Display = Shapes.AddText("100")
Shapes.Move(Display, 120, 25)
For I = 100 To 0 Step -1
  Shapes.SetText(Display, I)
  Program.Delay(500)
EndFor
```

Saved as **Example 10-3** in **Guide to Small Basic\Programs\Chapter 10** folder. This code first creates a yellow rectangle for the background. A **Shapes** object (**Display**, with large 36 size font) is created with an initial display of **100**. We immediately move **Display** into the yellow rectangle. The **(x, y)** values used in the **Move** method were found by trial and error to give a nice display. The displayed value counts down from 100 to 0 with a 0.5 second delay between each update.

Save and Run the program to see the countdown. Here's the middle of my run:

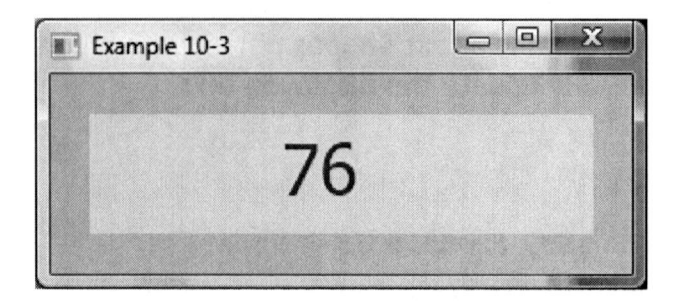

[Example 10-3 window showing: 76]

Images

Using images as **Shapes** objects is nearly identical to use with the graphics window. We need two steps. First, we must load the image, then create the shape. Assume you have an image file named **MyImage**. The file with this image must be in the same folder as your Small Basic program. The image is loaded using the **LoadImage** method of the **ImageList** object:

```
MyImage = ImageList.LoadImage(Program.Directory + "\MyImage")
```

Then the image shape (**MyImageShape**) is created using:

```
MyImageShape = Shapes.AddImage(MyImage)
```

The shape will be placed in the upper left corner of the graphics window, so either move it (**Move** method) or hide it (**HideShape** method) once it is created.

The created **Shapes** object will display the image in full-size. If this is not desired, the object size can be changed using the **Zoom** method:

```
Shapes.Zoom(MyImageShape, scalex, scaley)
```

The scaling factors **scalex** and **scaley** can range from 0.1 to 20. Values less than one reduce the image size, while values greater than 1 increase the size. Notice you can independently zoom the image in the x (horizontal) and y (vertical) directions. The **Zoom** method can be used on any shape, not just images.

Example 10-4. Image

Write a program that creates **Shapes** object holding an image. Shrink and grow the image to see how the **Zoom** method works. We will use the burger image from Chapter 9 (**burger.gif**, located in **Guide to Small Basic\Programs\Chapter 9** folder):

Copy this file to your program folder. I put a copy in **Guide to Small Basic\Programs\Chapter 10** folder.

Small Basic Code:

```
'Guide to Small Basic, Example 10-4
GraphicsWindow.Show()
GraphicsWindow.Title = "Example 10-4"
GraphicsWindow.Width = 500
GraphicsWindow.Height = 250
'load image
Burger = ImageList.LoadImage(Program.Directory + "\burger.gif")
'create shape and move it
RegularBurger = Shapes.AddImage(Burger)
Shapes.Move(RegularBurger, 0, 20)
'tiny burger
TinyBurger = Shapes.AddImage(Burger)
Shapes.Move(TinyBurger, 120, 20)
Shapes.Zoom(TinyBurger, 0.5, 0.5)
'giant burger
GiantBurger = Shapes.AddImage(Burger)
Shapes.Move(GiantBurger, 300, 50)
Shapes.Zoom(GiantBurger, 1.5, 1.5)
```

Saved as **Example 10-4** in **Guide to Small Basic\Programs\Chapter 10** folder. Three **Shapes** objects (**RegularBurger**, **TinyBurger** and **GiantBurger**) are created and displayed.

Save and **Run** the program to see the different burger displays:

Move Method

We have used the **Move** method to position Shapes objects once they are created. The **Move** method can also be used to give the appearance of motion or animation.

Moving **Shapes** objects in a graphics window is easy to do. It is a simple two step process: use some rule to determine a new position, then redraw it in this new position using the **Shapes** object **Move** method. If you have a shape object named **MyShape** and you want to move it to (**NewX**, **NewY**), the code is:

    Shapes.Move(MyShape, NewX, NewY)

This code will 'erase' **MyShape** at its current position, then 'redraw' it at the newly specified position. Successive transfers (or moves) gives the impression of motion, or animation.

Example 10-5. Random Burger

Write a program that randomly moves the burger image from Example 10-4 within the graphics window. Make sure the burger graphics file is in your program folder.

Small Basic Code:

```
'Guide to Small Basic, Example 10-5
GraphicsWindow.Show()
GraphicsWindow.Title = "Example 10-5"
GraphicsWindow.Width = 500
GraphicsWindow.Height = 300
'load image
Burger = ImageList.LoadImage(Program.Directory + "\burger.gif")
BurgerWidth = ImageList.GetWidthOfImage(Burger)
BurgerHeight = ImageList.GetHeightOfImage(Burger)
'create shape
RegularBurger = Shapes.AddImage(Burger)
'randomly position the burger 25 times
For I = 1 To 25
  X = Math.GetRandomNumber(GraphicsWindow.Width - BurgerWidth)
  Y = Math.GetRandomNumber(GraphicsWindow.Height - BurgerHeight)
  Shapes.Move(RegularBurger, X, Y)
  Program.Delay(500)
EndFor
```

Saved as **Example 10-5** in **Guide to Small Basic\Programs\Chapter 10** folder. Notice how we choose a random location for the burger (**X, Y**). The chosen random values insure the entire burger will be displayed.

10-18   The Developer's Reference Guide to Small Basic

Save and **Run** the program to watch the burger bounce around. Here's where mine ended up:

Rotate Method

The **Shapes Rotate** method takes an existing object and rotates it through a specified number of degrees. It can be used for some fun effects. To rotate an object **MyShape** through **D** degrees, use:

```
Shapes.Rotate(MyShape, D)
```

The rotation angle **D** is measured in a clockwise direction. Values can range from 0 (no rotation) to 360 (complete rotation). Hence a value of 180 would turn an object upside down. Rotation is done about the **Shapes** object center point.

Recall one of the advantages of using a text **Shapes** object is the ability to rotate the text for some neat labeling effects. Let's rotate some text to see some examples. Here is an 'unrotated' string of text:

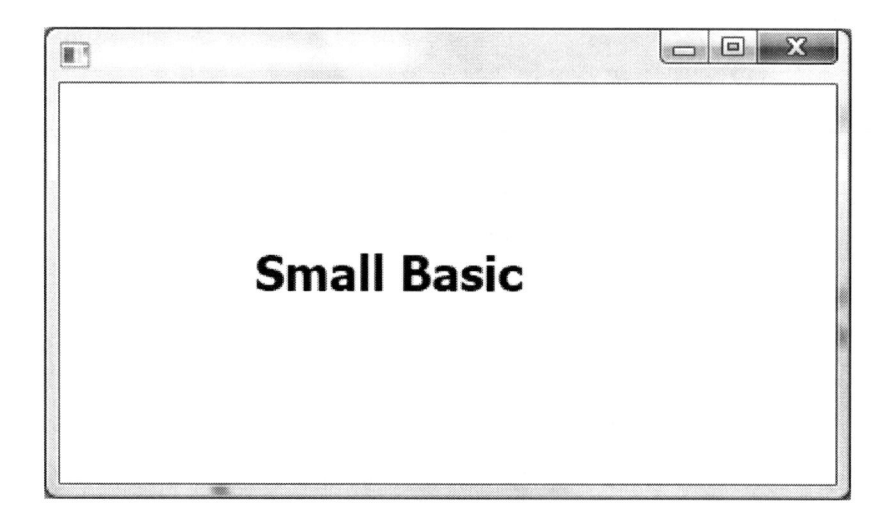

Small Basic

The same string rotated 45 degrees (D = 45):

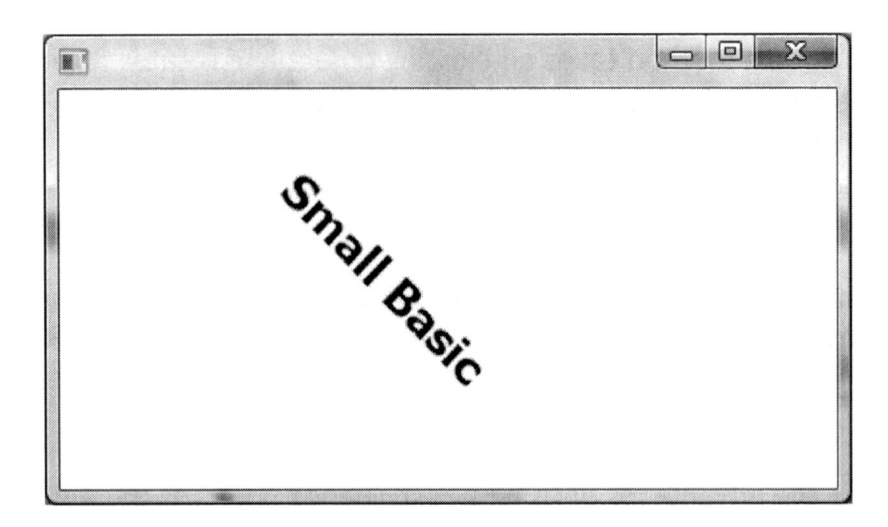

Vertical text (D = 90):

Upside down text (**D = 180**):

More vertical text (**D = 270**):

Example 10-6. Random, Rotating Burger

Modify **Example 10-5** so that, in addition to random motion, the burger randomly rotates.

Small Basic Code (changes are shaded):

```
'Guide to Small Basic, Example 10-6
GraphicsWindow.Show()
GraphicsWindow.Title = "Example 10-6"
GraphicsWindow.Width = 500
GraphicsWindow.Height = 300
'load image
Burger = ImageList.LoadImage(Program.Directory + "\burger.gif")
BurgerWidth = ImageList.GetWidthOfImage(Burger)
BurgerHeight = ImageList.GetHeightOfImage(Burger)
'create shape
RegularBurger = Shapes.AddImage(Burger)
'randomly position the burger 25 times
For I = 1 To 25
  X = Math.GetRandomNumber(GraphicsWindow.Width - BurgerWidth)
  Y = Math.GetRandomNumber(GraphicsWindow.Height - BurgerHeight)
  Shapes.Move(RegularBurger, X, Y)
  A = Math.GetRandomNumber(360)
  Shapes.Rotate(RegularBurger, A)
  Program.Delay(500)
EndFor
```

Saved as **Example 10-6** in **Guide to Small Basic\Programs\Chapter 10** folder. This code is identical to **Example 10-5** with the addition of the shaded lines to randomly rotate the graphic to an angle **A**.

Save and **Run** the program to watch the burger bounce around and rotate. Here's where mine ended up:

Animate Method

Like the **Rotate** method, the **Shapes Animate** method allows for some cool graphic effects. Here's how it works. Say you have a shape **MyShape** currently displayed in the graphics window. Provide the **Animate** method with a new location (**X, Y**) and a time duration (**T**, in milliseconds). The method will smoothly move the shape from its current location to (**X, Y**) in **T** milliseconds. The corresponding method is:

```
Shapes.Animate(MyShape, X, Y, T)
```

Before looking at a couple of examples, you might wonder why we even bothered talking about animation using the **Move** method if we have this great **Animate** method available? Recall most of our programs will be event driven applications where the program waits for user input to do its job. The problem with the **Animate** method is nothing can happen in a program until the method completes its task. It we want to stop something from moving by making a choice by clicking on something or pressing a key, we can't. If we want to see if two moving things collide (a ball with a paddle, for example), we can't. So there are limitations to using the **Animate** method.

In a later chapter where we discuss animation in detail, we will see how to stop things from moving or see if two things collide. In these discussions, we will use the **Move** method in conjunction with another object still to be studied, the **Timer** object.

Example 10-7. Stacking Boxes

Write a program that animates a stacking of boxes.

Small Basic Code:

```
'Guide to Small Basic, Example 10-7
GraphicsWindow.Show()
GraphicsWindow.Title = "Example 10-7"
GraphicsWindow.Width = 500
GraphicsWindow.Height = 400
'create and stack boxes
GraphicsWindow.PenColor = "Black"
GraphicsWindow.PenWidth = 1
X = 450
Y = 370
For I = 1 To 100
  GraphicsWindow.BrushColor = GraphicsWindow.GetRandomColor()
  Box[I] = Shapes.AddRectangle(50, 30)
  Shapes.Animate(Box[I], X, Y, 250)
  Program.Delay(200)
  X = X - 50
  If (X < 0) Then
    X = 450
    Y = Y - 30
  EndIf
EndFor
```

Saved as **Example 10-7** in **Guide to Small Basic\Programs\Chapter 10** folder.

In this code, we stack 100 randomly colored boxes (rectangle **Shapes** objects 50 pixels wide by 30 pixels high), 10 boxes in each row. The code is straightforward. We compute a location for each box (**X, Y**) and move it there from the default (**0, 0**) location with the **Animate** method. A little delay after each movement adds a nice effect.

Save and **Run** the program and the stacking begins. Here's the middle of the process:

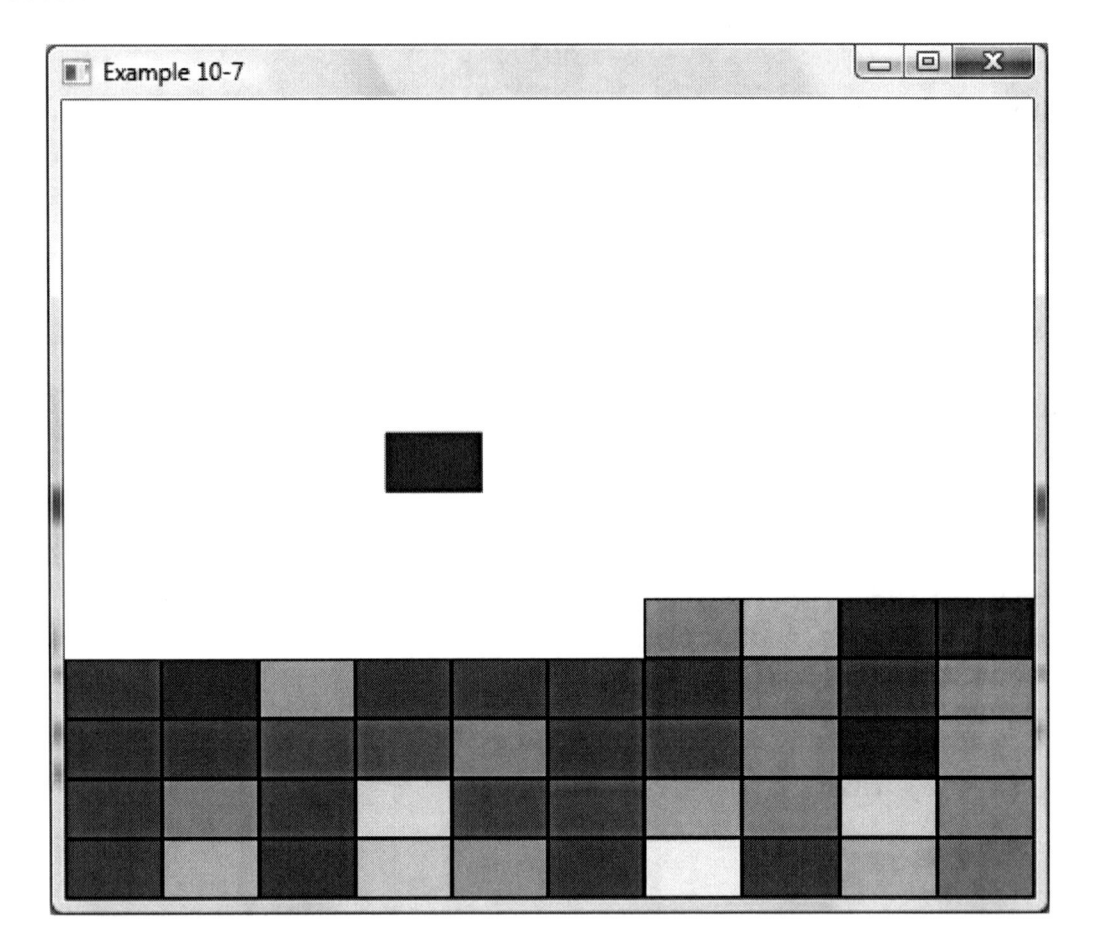

And here's the final stacked up boxes:

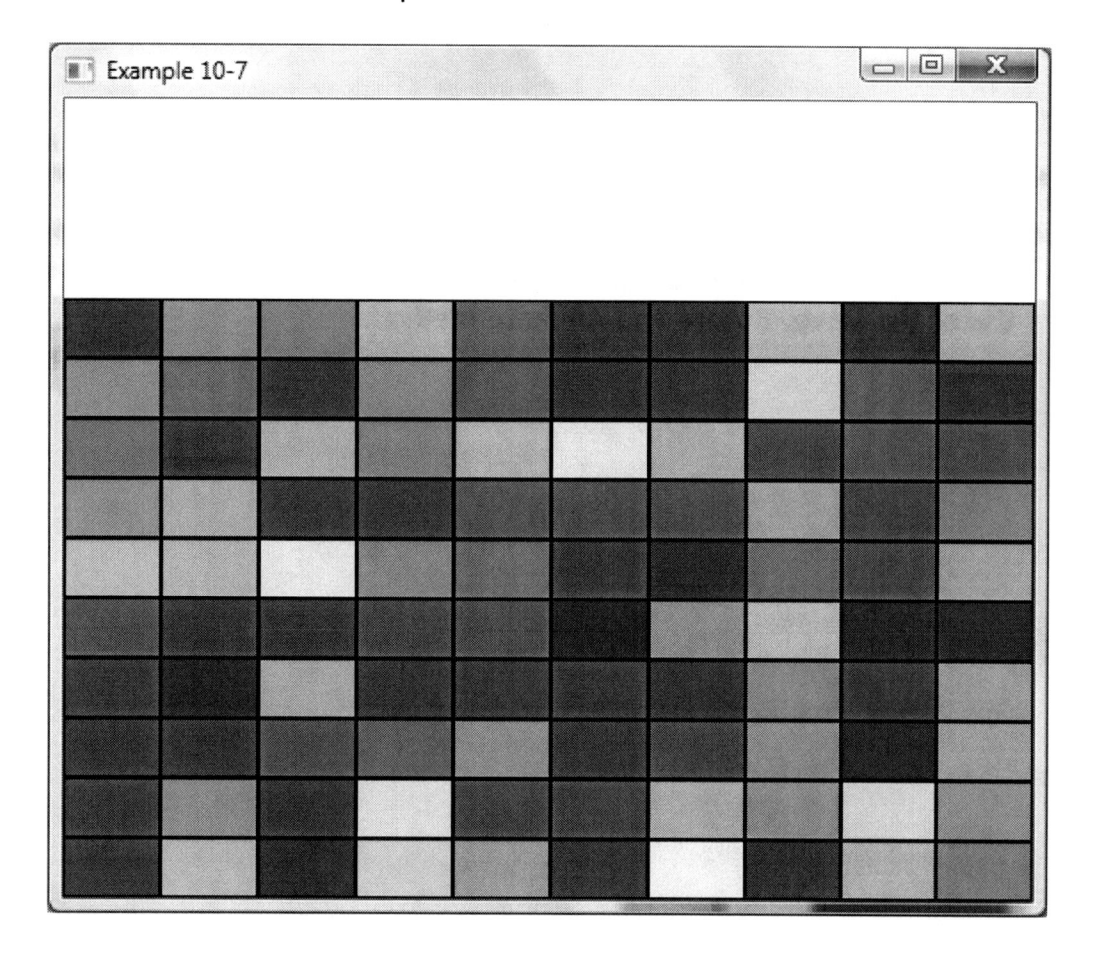

Chapter Review

After completing this chapter, you should understand:

- The various **Shapes** objects.
- Use of the text **Shapes** object for labeling.
- How to use images with **Shapes** objects.
- Use of the **Move, Rotate** and **Animate** methods.

11. Mouse Object

Preview

In this chapter, we look at the **Mouse** object. With this, we can detect which mouse buttons are being clicked (if any). In conjunction with the graphics windows mouse events, we build a little drawing program.

Mouse Object

The **Mouse** object (or more properly class) helps decide if the mouse is being used.

Mouse Properties:

IsLeftButtonDown
Gets whether or not the left button is pressed. Is "true" if left button is pressed.

IsRightButtonDown
Gets whether or not the right button is pressed. Is "true" if right button is pressed.

MouseX
Gets or sets the mouse cursor's x coordinate (relative to top right corner of your computer screen).

MouseY
Gets or sets the mouse cursor's y coordinate (relative to top right corner of your computer screen).

Mouse Methods:

HideCursor()
Hides the mouse cursor on the screen.

ShowCursor()
Shows the mouse cursor on the screen.

Use of Mouse Object

The **Mouse** object is usually used to determine if a particular mouse button is pressed. For all other mouse operations, we use the graphics window **MouseX** and **MouseY** properties, and the graphics window **MouseDown**, **MouseMove** and **MouseUp** events.

We don't use the **Mouse** object **MouseX** and **MouseY** properties because they are relative to your computer screen, not the graphics window (like the corresponding **GraphicsWindow** properties). Let's see what this means:

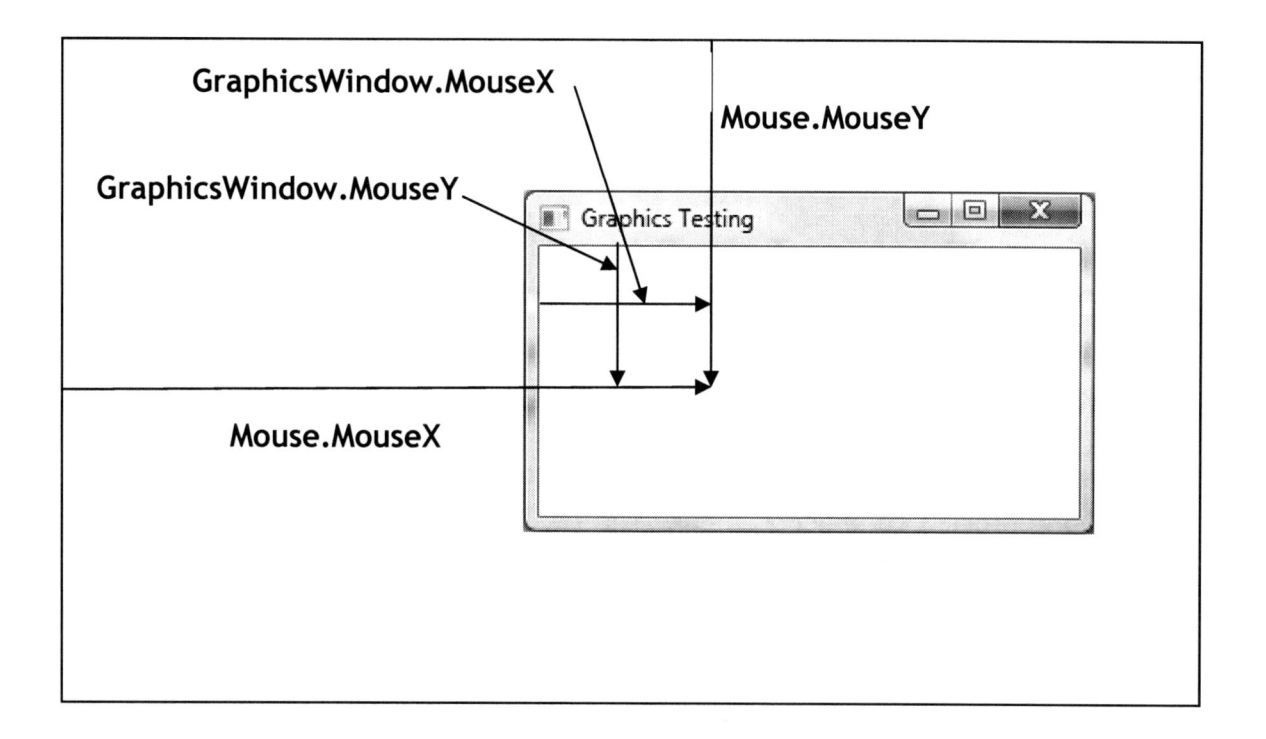

The value of **Mouse.MouseX** and **Mouse.MouseY** depend on the position of the graphics window on your screen. **GraphicsWindow.MouseX** and **GraphicsWindow.MouseY** are not. Using the **Mouse** object properties would give us different results if a user moves the window. This can really mess up your code. We only use the **GraphicsWindow** location properties.

MouseDown Event

The graphics window supports three mouse events: **MouseDown**, **MouseMove** and **MouseUp**. We will study each method. We looked at the **MouseDown** event briefly in the **ImageList** chapter. We repeat our description of that event here and look at an example.

The graphics window **MouseDown** event is triggered whenever a mouse button is pressed while the mouse cursor is over the graphics window. If the subroutine to be executed in case of such an event is **MouseDownSub**, we add this event to our program using:

```
GraphicsWindow.MouseDown = MouseDownSub
```

The corresponding subroutine is added to the program in the usual manner and has the form:

```
Sub MouseDownSub
  ' Small Basic code for MouseDown event
EndSub
```

Every time the user clicks the mouse, a **MouseDown** event occurs and the subroutine (**MouseDownSub**) is called automatically. In this subroutine, we usually check to see what mouse button was clicked, where the window was clicked and process code accordingly. The (**X, Y**) point clicked in the graphics window is given by two **GraphicsWindow** properties, **GraphicsWindow.MouseX** and **GraphicsWindow.MouseY**.

Example 11-1. MouseDown Example

Write a program that detects mouse clicks. When the graphics window is clicked, print out which button was clicked and the corresponding **MouseX** and **MouseY** values (for both the **GraphicsWindow** object and **Mouse** object).

Small Basic Code:

```
'Guide to Small Basic, Example 11-1
InitializeProgram()

Sub InitializeProgram
  GraphicsWindow.Show()
  GraphicsWindow.Title = "Example 11-1"
  GraphicsWindow.Width = 400
  GraphicsWindow.Height = 300
  GraphicsWindow.MouseDown = MouseDownSub
EndSub

Sub MouseDownSub
  If (Mouse.IsLeftButtonDown) Then
    TextWindow.WriteLine("Clicked Left Mouse Button")
  ElseIf (Mouse.IsRightButtonDown) Then
    TextWindow.WriteLine("Clicked Right Mouse Button")
  EndIf
  TextWindow.WriteLine("Mouse Object, X = " + Mouse.MouseX + "  Y = " + Mouse.MouseY)
  TextWindow.WriteLine("GraphicsWindow Object, X = " + GraphicsWindow.MouseX + "  Y = " + GraphicsWindow.MouseY)
EndSub
```

Saved as **Example 11-1** in **Guide to Small Basic\Programs\Chapter 11** folder.

Save and **Run** the program. Click the graphics window and a text window will appear telling you what button was clicked and the click coordinates.

Here's my results when I clicked near the center of the window:

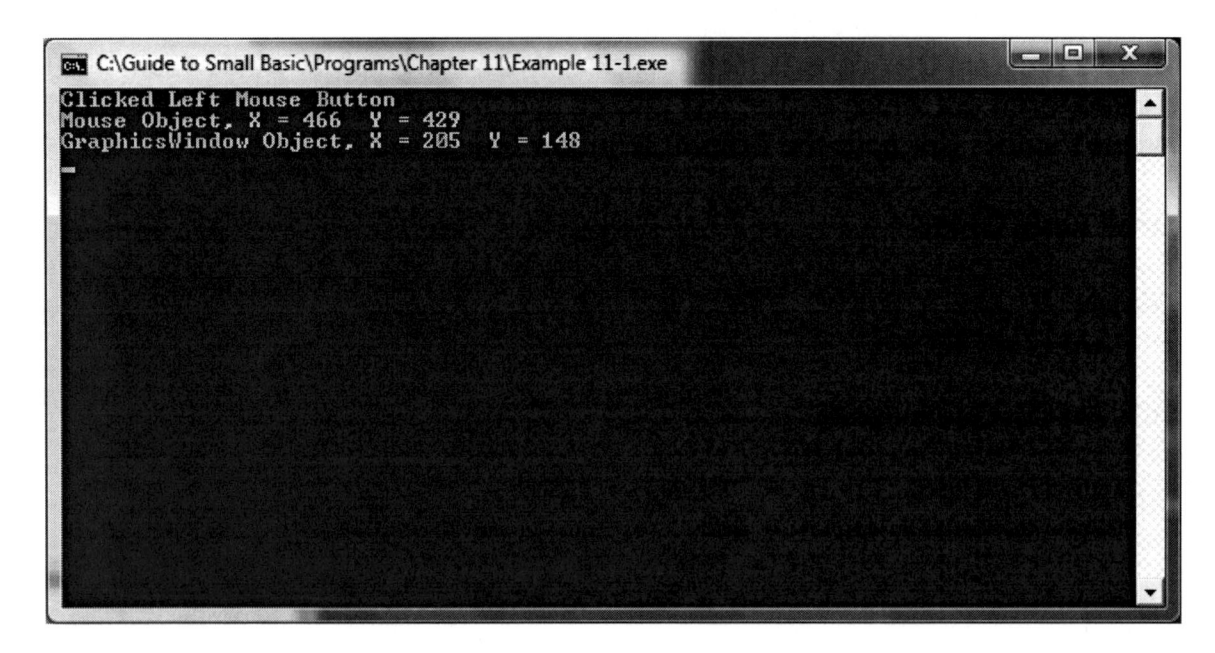

```
Clicked Left Mouse Button
Mouse Object, X = 466   Y = 429
GraphicsWindow Object, X = 205   Y = 148
```

The **Mouse** object coordinates will always be larger than the corresponding **GraphicsWindow** coordinates.

Click various spots in the window and see how the coordinates change. Try both mouse buttons. Notice you cannot detect mouse clicks in the title bar area. Play with this example until you are comfortable with how the **MouseDown** event works and what the coordinates mean. Move the graphics window around to see that the **Mouse** object coordinates can change dramatically.

MouseMove Event

The graphics window **MouseMove** event is continuously triggered whenever the mouse is being moved. If the subroutine to be executed in case of such an event is **MouseMoveSub**, we add this event to our program using:

```
GraphicsWindow.MouseMove = MouseMoveEvent
```

The corresponding subroutine is added to the program in the usual manner and has the form:

```
Sub MouseMoveSub
  ' Small Basic code for MouseMove event
EndSub
```

Whenever a user moves the mouse, a **MouseMove** event occurs and the subroutine (**MouseMoveSub**) is called automatically.

Example 11-2. MouseMove Example

Modify **Example 11-1** so it only displays the **GraphicsWindow** coordinates. Also, print out the coordinates if the mouse is moved while a mouse button is being held down.

Small Basic Code:

```
'Guide to Small Basic, Example 11-2
InitializeProgram()

Sub InitializeProgram
  GraphicsWindow.Show()
  GraphicsWindow.Title = "Example 11-2"
  GraphicsWindow.Width = 400
  GraphicsWindow.Height = 300
  GraphicsWindow.MouseDown = MouseDownSub
  GraphicsWindow.MouseMove = MouseMoveSub
EndSub

Sub MouseDownSub
  If (Mouse.IsLeftButtonDown) Then
    TextWindow.WriteLine("Clicked Left Mouse Button")
  ElseIf (Mouse.IsRightButtonDown) Then
    TextWindow.WriteLine("Clicked Right Mouse Button")
  EndIf
  TextWindow.WriteLine("Clicked at X = " + GraphicsWindow.MouseX +
"  Y = " + GraphicsWindow.MouseY)
EndSub

Sub MouseMoveSub
  If (Mouse.IsLeftButtonDown Or Mouse.IsRightButtonDown) Then
    TextWindow.WriteLine("Moved to X = " + GraphicsWindow.MouseX +
"  Y = " + GraphicsWindow.MouseY)
  EndIf
EndSub
```

Saved as **Example 11-2** in **Guide to Small Basic\Programs\Chapter 11** folder. The modifications to **Example 11-1** are shaded. The primary change is that we added a **MouseMove** event and in the corresponding subroutine (**MouseMoveEvent**), we use a **WriteLine** statement to specify the x and y coordinate the mouse has been moved to.

Save and **Run** the program. Move the cursor into the graphics window and click the window. A text window will appear showing you the clicked location. Move the mouse around the window while holding a mouse button down. Notice the coordinates (x, y) continuously change as the mouse is moving. Here's the text window from one of my runs:

```
C:\Guide to Small Basic\Programs\Chapter 11\Example 11-2.exe
Moved to X = 186    Y = 96
Moved to X = 187    Y = 96
Moved to X = 188    Y = 97
Moved to X = 189    Y = 98
Moved to X = 190    Y = 99
Moved to X = 191    Y = 99
Moved to X = 192    Y = 101
Moved to X = 195    Y = 102
Moved to X = 196    Y = 103
Moved to X = 197    Y = 104
Moved to X = 198    Y = 104
Clicked Right Mouse Button
Clicked at X = 198    Y = 104
Moved to X = 198    Y = 105
Moved to X = 198    Y = 106
Moved to X = 198    Y = 107
Moved to X = 199    Y = 108
Moved to X = 200    Y = 110
Moved to X = 200    Y = 111
Moved to X = 201    Y = 113
Moved to X = 202    Y = 114
Moved to X = 202    Y = 115
Moved to X = 202    Y = 116
Moved to X = 202    Y = 117
```

MouseUp Event

The graphics window **MouseUp** event is triggered whenever a previously pressed mouse button is released while the mouse cursor is over the graphics window. If the subroutine to be executed in case of such an event is **MouseUpSub**, we add this event to our program using:

```
GraphicsWindow.MouseUp = MouseUpSub
```

The corresponding subroutine is added to the program in the usual manner and has the form:

```
Sub MouseUpSub
  ' Small Basic code for MouseDown event
EndSub
```

Every time the user clicks the mouse and then release a mouse button, a **MouseUp** event occurs and the subroutine (**MouseUpSub**) is called automatically. To determine which mouse button was released, you need to keep track of the last clicked button in your code (using a variable).

Example 11-3. MouseUp Example

Modify **Example 11-2** so it also tells you when a mouse button has been released.

Small Basic Code:

```
'Guide to Small Basic, Example 11-3
InitializeProgram()

Sub InitializeProgram
  GraphicsWindow.Show()
  GraphicsWindow.Title = "Example 11-3"
  GraphicsWindow.Width = 400
  GraphicsWindow.Height = 300
  GraphicsWindow.MouseDown = MouseDownSub
  GraphicsWindow.MouseMove = MouseMoveSub
GraphicsWindow.MouseUp = MouseUpSub
EndSub

Sub MouseDownSub
  If (Mouse.IsLeftButtonDown) Then
    TextWindow.WriteLine("Clicked Left Mouse Button")
    ClickedButton = "Left"
  ElseIf (Mouse.IsRightButtonDown) Then
    TextWindow.WriteLine("Clicked Right Mouse Button")
    ClickedButton = "Right"
  EndIf
  TextWindow.WriteLine("Clicked at X = " + GraphicsWindow.MouseX + " Y = " + GraphicsWindow.MouseY)
EndSub

Sub MouseMoveSub
  If (Mouse.IsLeftButtonDown Or Mouse.IsRightButtonDown) Then
    TextWindow.WriteLine("Moved to X = " + GraphicsWindow.MouseX + " Y = " + GraphicsWindow.MouseY)
  EndIf
EndSub

Sub MouseUpSub
  TextWindow.WriteLine("Released " + ClickedButton + " Button")
EndSub
```

Saved as **Example 11-3** in **Guide to Small Basic\Programs\Chapter 11** folder. The modifications to **Example 11-2** are shaded. The primary change is that we added a **MouseUp** event and in the corresponding subroutine (**MouseUpEvent**). The variable **ClickedButton** tells us which button is clicked.

Save and **Run** the program. Click the graphics window, move the mouse and release the button. You should now see how all three mouse events work. Here's a run I made:

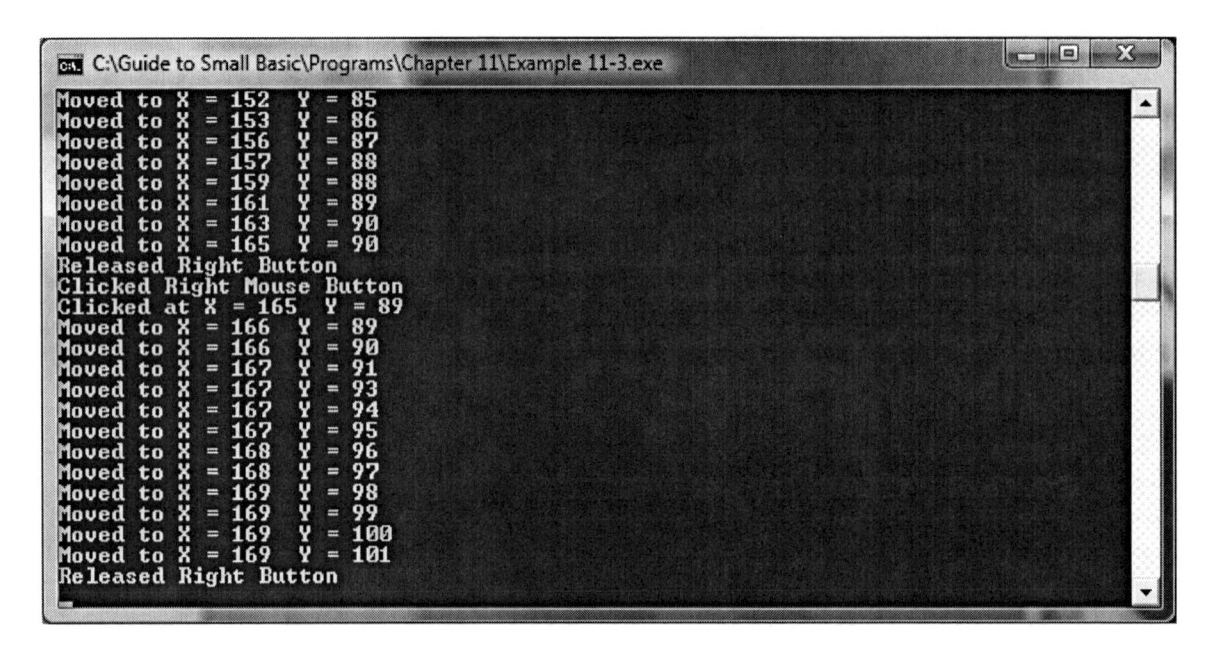

```
C:\Guide to Small Basic\Programs\Chapter 11\Example 11-3.exe
Moved to X = 152  Y = 85
Moved to X = 153  Y = 86
Moved to X = 156  Y = 87
Moved to X = 157  Y = 88
Moved to X = 159  Y = 88
Moved to X = 161  Y = 89
Moved to X = 163  Y = 90
Moved to X = 165  Y = 90
Released Right Button
Clicked Right Mouse Button
Clicked at X = 165  Y = 89
Moved to X = 166  Y = 89
Moved to X = 166  Y = 90
Moved to X = 167  Y = 91
Moved to X = 167  Y = 93
Moved to X = 167  Y = 94
Moved to X = 167  Y = 95
Moved to X = 168  Y = 96
Moved to X = 168  Y = 97
Moved to X = 169  Y = 98
Moved to X = 169  Y = 99
Moved to X = 169  Y = 100
Moved to X = 169  Y = 101
Released Right Button
```

Example 11-4. Drawing Program

Write a program that draws red lines when you click and move the left mouse button, blue lines when you click and move the right mouse button.

Small Basic Code:

```
'Guide to Small Basic, Example 11-4
InitializeProgram()

Sub InitializeProgram
  GraphicsWindow.Show()
  GraphicsWindow.Title = "Example 11-4"
  GraphicsWindow.Width = 600
  GraphicsWindow.Height = 400
  GraphicsWindow.MouseDown = MouseDownSub
  GraphicsWindow.MouseMove = MouseMoveSub
EndSub

Sub MouseDownSub
  X = GraphicsWindow.MouseX
  Y = GraphicsWindow.MouseY
  GraphicsWindow.PenWidth = 3
  If (Mouse.IsLeftButtonDown) Then
    GraphicsWindow.PenColor = "Red"
  ElseIf (Mouse.IsRightButtonDown) Then
    GraphicsWindow.PenColor = "Blue"
  EndIf
EndSub

Sub MouseMoveSub
  If (Mouse.IsLeftButtonDown Or Mouse.IsRightButtonDown) Then
    XNew = GraphicsWindow.MouseX
    YNew = GraphicsWindow.MouseY
    GraphicsWindow.DrawLine(X, Y, XNew, YNew)
    X = XNew
    Y = YNew
  EndIf
EndSub
```

Saved as **Example 11-4** in **Guide to Small Basic\Programs\Chapter 11** folder. Drawing is initiated in **MouseDownSub** and pen color is defined. Drawing continues in **MouseMoveSub**, connecting the previous point (**X, Y**) to the new point (**XNew, YNew**). Notice we only draw a line if a mouse button is down.

Save and **Run** the program. Click the graphics window with the left and right mouse buttons and draw away. Here's my sketch:

I am not an artist.

Try this change. Comment out these lines in **MouseMoveSub**:

    X = XNew
    Y = YNew

Run the program again. Click with the left or right mouse button and move around. You will see you can draw a fan effect (the program just connects the first clicked point with all the points you move to). It's kind of cool. Here's one I drew:

Remember to 'uncomment' out the lines you commented out.

Chapter Review

After completing this chapter, you should understand:

- Use of the **Mouse** object.
- The difference between **MouseX** and **MouseY** from the **Mouse** and **GraphicsWindow** objects.
- Use of the mouse events.

12. Timer Object

Preview

In this chapter, we study the Small Basic **Timer** object. This is an object that generate periodic events without interaction from a user. It is an essential component of animation.

Timer Object

The Small Basic **Timer object** has an interesting feature. It can generate events (called **Tick** events) without any input from the user. **Timer** objects work in your program's background, generating events at time intervals you specify. This event generation feature comes in handy for graphics animation (or any other task) where screen displays need to be updated at regular intervals.

Timer Properties:

```
Interval
```
Gets or sets the interval (in milliseconds) specifying how often the timer should raise the **Tick** event.

Timer Methods:

```
Pause()
```
Pauses the timer. Tick events will not be raised.

```
Resume()
```
Resumes the timer from a paused state. Tick events will now be raised.

Timer Events:

```
Tick
```
Raises an event when the timer ticks.

Use of Timer Object

A few examples should clarify how the **Timer** object works. It's very simple and very powerful. To review, here's what happens. When a timer is running, every **Interval** milliseconds, Small Basic will generate an event and execute the corresponding **Tick** event subroutine. No user interaction is needed. The **Tick** event subroutine (here **TickSub**) is assigned using:

```
Timer.Tick = TickSub
```

There are two methods we need to monitor status. To start a timer and begin event processing, use:

```
Timer.Resume()
```

To stop the timer and stop event processing, use:

```
Timer.Pause()
```

Note: By default, the timer is "turned on" meaning event processing will immediately begin when starting a program with a timer object. We usually turn off the timer initially and let some user interaction start it.

The **Interval** property is important. This property is set to the number of milliseconds between timer events. A millisecond is 1/1000th of a second, or there are 1,000 milliseconds in a second. If you want to generate N events per second, set the **Interval** to 1000 / N. For example, if you want a timer event to occur 4 times per second, use a delay of 250. About the lowest practical value for **Interval** is 50 and values that differ by 5, 10, or even 20 are likely to produce similar results. It all depends on your particular computer. Now, let's try some examples.

Example 12-1. Timer Example

Write a program with a single button control that starts and stops a **Timer** object. Have the program change the window color every second.

Small Basic Code:

```
'Guide to Small Basic, Example 12-1
InitializeProgram()

Sub InitializeProgram
  GraphicsWindow.Show()
  GraphicsWindow.Title = "Example 12-1"
  GraphicsWindow.Width = 400
  GraphicsWindow.Height = 200
  'button
  GraphicsWindow.BrushColor = "Black"
  GraphicsWindow.FontSize = 24
  GraphicsWindow.FontBold = "false"
  TimerButton = Controls.AddButton("Start", 70, 70)
  Controls.ButtonClicked = ButtonClickedSub
  Timer.Interval = 1000
  Timer.Tick = TickSub
  Timer.Pause()
EndSub

Sub ButtonClickedSub
  If (Controls.GetButtonCaption(TimerButton) = "Start") Then
    Controls.SetButtonCaption(TimerButton, "Stop")
    Timer.Resume()
  Else
    Controls.SetButtonCaption(TimerButton, "Start")
    Timer.Pause()
  EndIf
EndSub

Sub TickSub
  GraphicsWindow.BackgroundColor = GraphicsWindow.GetRandomColor()
EndSub
```

Saved as **Example 12-1** in **Guide to Small Basic\Programs\Chapter 12** folder.

The **InitializeProgram** subroutine establishes the button control (**TimerButton**) and its event subroutine (**ButtonClickedSub**). The **Timer** object **Interval** is set to 1000 (one second) and the event subroutine established (**TickSub**). The timer is turned off initially. The timer is 'toggled' between off and on in the **ButtonClickedSub**. In **TickSub**, the color is randomly changed.

Save and **Run** the program. You will see:

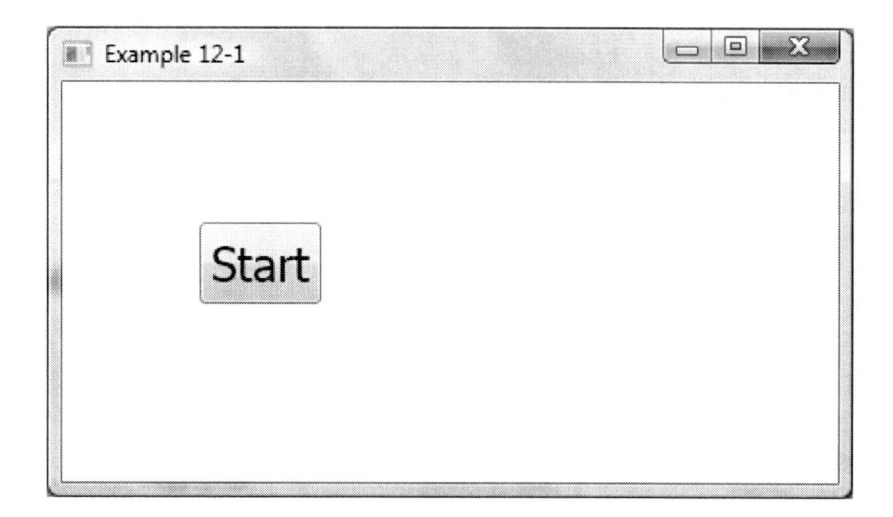

Click **Start** and the screen will change color every second:

If you then click **Stop**, the color changing (in **TickSub**) stops. **Start** and **Stop** the timer as much as you'd like.

Example 12-2. Ellipse Example

Write a program with a single button control that starts and stops a **Timer** object. Have the program draw a smaller, randomly colored ellipse with each **Tick** event.

Small Basic Code:

```
'Guide to Small Basic, Example 12-2
InitializeProgram()

Sub InitializeProgram
  GraphicsWindow.Show()
  GraphicsWindow.Title = "Example 12-2"
  GraphicsWindow.Width = 400
  GraphicsWindow.Height = 350
  'button
  GraphicsWindow.BrushColor = "Black"
  GraphicsWindow.FontSize = 16
  GraphicsWindow.FontBold = "false"
  TimerButton = Controls.AddButton("Start", 170, 310)
  Controls.ButtonClicked = ButtonClickedSub
  Timer.Interval = 100
  Timer.Tick = TickSub
  Timer.Pause()
  Delta = 0
  GraphicsWindow.PenWidth = 2
EndSub

Sub ButtonClickedSub
  If (Controls.GetButtonCaption(TimerButton) = "Start") Then
    Controls.SetButtonCaption(TimerButton, "Stop")
    Timer.Resume()
  Else
    Controls.SetButtonCaption(TimerButton, "Start")
    Timer.Pause()
  EndIf
EndSub

Sub TickSub
  GraphicsWindow.PenColor = GraphicsWindow.GetRandomColor()
  GraphicsWindow.DrawEllipse(Delta, Delta, GraphicsWindow.Width - 2 * Delta, 300 - 2 * Delta)
  Delta = Delta + GraphicsWindow.PenWidth
  If (Delta > 150) Then
```

```
    Delta = 0
    GraphicsWindow.BrushColor = GraphicsWindow.BackgroundColor
    GraphicsWindow.FillRectangle(0, 0, GraphicsWindow.Width, 350)
  EndIf
EndSub
```

Saved as **Example 12-2** in **Guide to Small Basic\Programs\Chapter 12** folder.

The **InitializeProgram** code is nearly identical to **Example 12-1** (the **Timer Interval** was lowered to 100). In **TickSub**, you should see the **DrawEllipse** method draws the first ellipse in a rectangle the width of the graphics window and 300 pixels high. The surrounding rectangle moves "in" an amount **Delta** (in each direction) with each **Tick** event, resulting in a smaller rectangle (the width and height are decreased by both **2*Delta**). Once **Delta** (incremented by the pen width in each step) exceeds half of the original ellipse height (300/2 = 150), it is reset to 0, the rectangle is cleared and the process starts all over.

Save and **Run** the program. Click the **Start** button. Are you hypnotized? Here's a sample of a run I made:

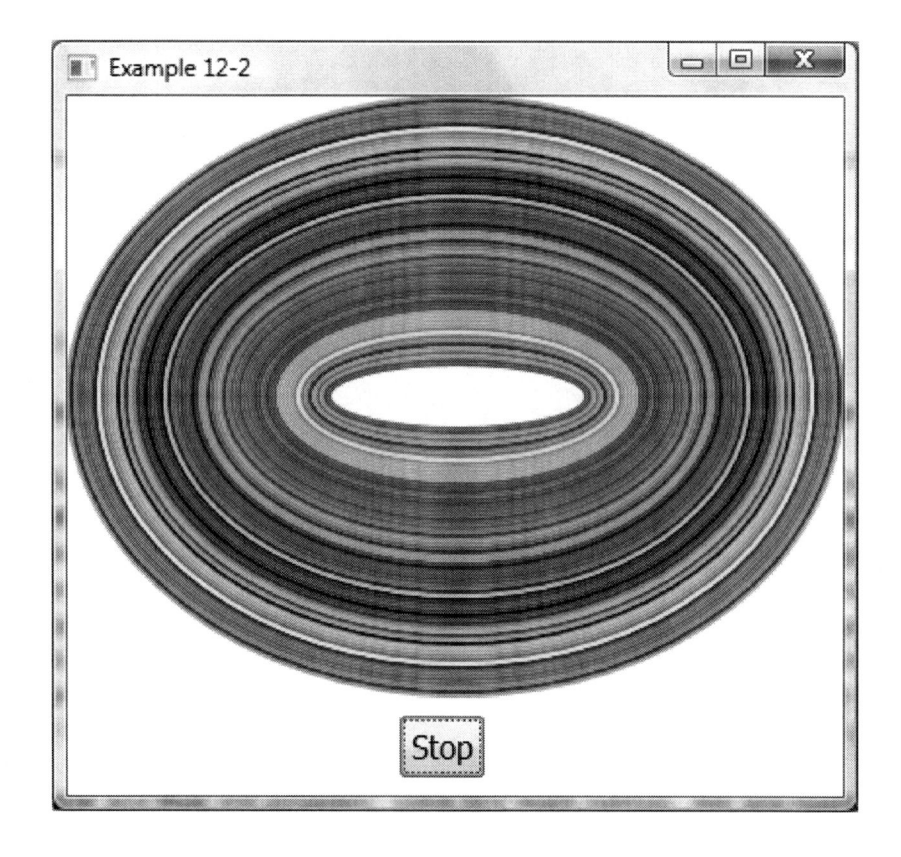

In this example, the periodic (every 0.1 seconds) changing of the display, imparted by the **Timer** object, gives the appearance of motion – the ellipses seem to be moving inward. This is the basic concept behind a very powerful graphics technique - **animation**. In animation, we have a sequence of pictures, each a little different from the previous one. With the ellipse example, in each picture, we add a new ellipse. By displaying this sequence over time, we can trick the viewer into thinking things are moving. It all has to do with how fast the human eye and brain can process information. That's how cartoons work - 24 different pictures are displayed every second - it makes things look like they are moving, or animated. Obviously, the **Timer** object is a key element to animation, as well as for other Small Basic timing tasks. In a later chapter, we will look at how to do simple animations and some other things.

Example 12-3. Calendar Display

Write a program that displays the current month, day, and year. Also, display the current time, updating it every second.

Small Basic Code:

```
'Guide to Small Basic, Example 12-3
InitializeProgram()

Sub InitializeProgram
  GraphicsWindow.Show()
  GraphicsWindow.Title = "Example 12-3"
  GraphicsWindow.Width = 250
  GraphicsWindow.Height = 150
  'shapes to hold displays - initialize with current values
  GraphicsWindow.BrushColor = "Black"
  GraphicsWindow.FontSize = 36
  GraphicsWindow.FontBold = "false"
  DateShape = Shapes.AddText(Clock.Date)
  Shapes.Move(DateShape, 20, 20)
  TimeShape = Shapes.AddText(Clock.Time)
  Shapes.Move(TimeShape, 20, 80)
  Timer.Interval = 1000
  Timer.Tick = TickSub
EndSub

Sub TickSub
  'update displays
  Shapes.SetText(DateShape, Clock.Date)
  Shapes.SetText(TimeShape, Clock.Time)
EndSub
```

Saved as **Example 12-3** in **Guide to Small Basic\Programs\Chapter 12** folder. The date and time are displayed in **Shapes** objects. Notice the timer is on by default so we don't have to do anything to start it.

Save and **Run** the program. You will see the current date and time (updating every second):

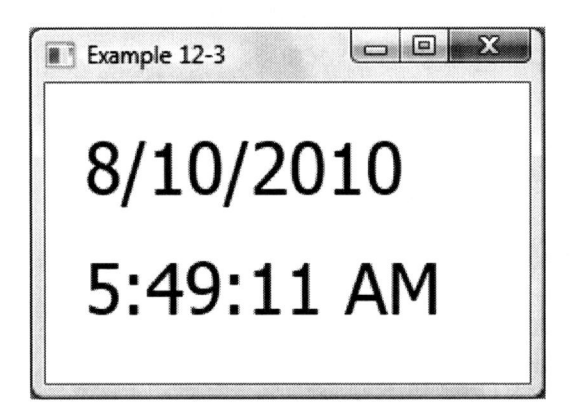

Example 12-3

8/10/2010

5:49:11 AM

Example 12-4. Dice Rolling

Build a program that rolls two dice and displays the results. Display a random die every 0.2 seconds for a random time period. Graphics of the six die faces are included in the **Guide to Small Basic\Programs\Chapter 12** folder:

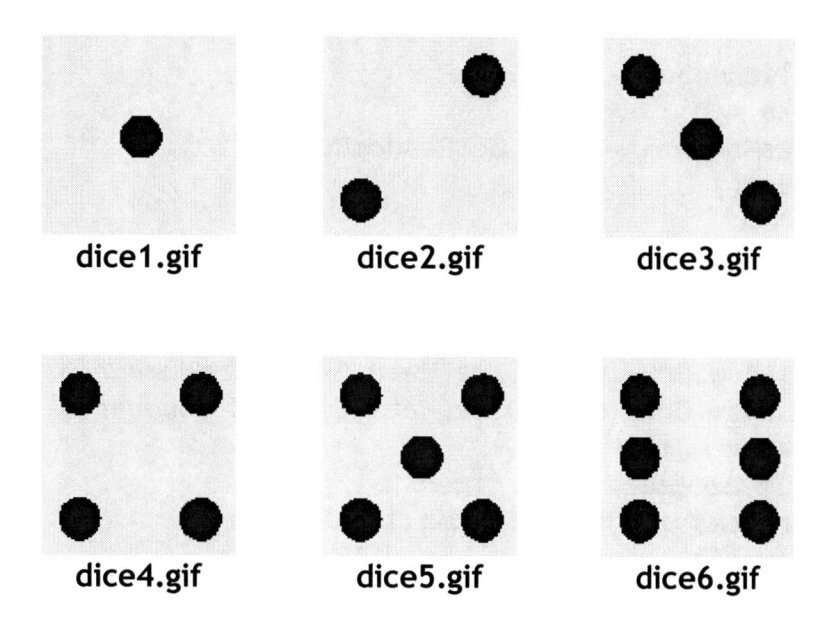

dice1.gif **dice2.gif** **dice3.gif**

dice4.gif **dice5.gif** **dice6.gif**

Copy each of these files to your program folder.

Small Basic Code:

```
'Guide to Small Basic, Example 12-4
InitializeProgram()

Sub InitializeProgram
  GraphicsWindow.Show()
  GraphicsWindow.Title = "Example 12-4"
  GraphicsWindow.Width = 230
  GraphicsWindow.Height = 200
  'images
  Dice[1] = ImageList.LoadImage(Program.Directory + "\dice1.gif")
  Dice[2] = ImageList.LoadImage(Program.Directory + "\dice2.gif")
  Dice[3] = ImageList.LoadImage(Program.Directory + "\dice3.gif")
  Dice[4] = ImageList.LoadImage(Program.Directory + "\dice4.gif")
  Dice[5] = ImageList.LoadImage(Program.Directory + "\dice5.gif")
  Dice[6] = ImageList.LoadImage(Program.Directory + "\dice6.gif")
  'button
  GraphicsWindow.BrushColor = "Black"
  GraphicsWindow.FontSize = 16
  GraphicsWindow.FontBold = "false"
```

```
  TimerButton = Controls.AddButton("Roll the Dice", 10, 160)
  Controls.ButtonClicked = ButtonClickedSub
  Timer.Interval = 200
  Timer.Tick = TickSub
  Timer.Pause()
EndSub

Sub ButtonClickedSub
  NumberTicks = 0
  NumberTicksMax = 5 + Math.GetRandomNumber(20)
  Timer.Resume()
EndSub

Sub TickSub
  'draw two random dice
  GraphicsWindow.DrawImage(Dice[Math.GetRandomNumber(6)], 10, 30)
  GraphicsWindow.DrawImage(Dice[Math.GetRandomNumber(6)], 120, 30)
  NumberTicks = NumberTicks + 1
  'if maximum exceeded stop timer
  If (NumberTicks > NumberTicksMax) Then
    Timer.Pause()
  EndIf
EndSub
```

Saved as **Example 12-4** in **Guide to Small Basic\Programs\Chapter 12** folder.

The program is actually quite simple. We choose a value for how many times we want the dice to flash (**NumberTicksMax**). The timer starts when you click **Roll the Dice**. Random dice are displayed until **NumberTicks** exceeds **NumberTicksMax**. When this happens, the timer is turned off (using **Pause** method).

Save and **Run** the program. Click **Roll the Dice**. The dice will flash eventually stopping at some values. Here's a roll I made:

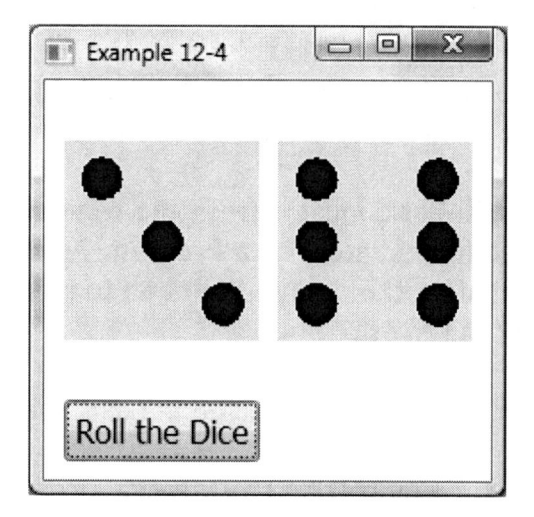

Timer Object for Delays

The **Timer** object can also be used to implement delays in a Small Basic program. You might be asking, why do this when the **Program** object has a **Delay** method. The problem with this particular method is that it doesn't always work as you want. It is particularly problematic when working with images.

In displaying images, Small Basic must refresh the window occasionally. If you draw an image, followed immediately by a **Program Delay** method, you often do not see the display until after the delay. We need to slow down the program a bit to allow the window to refresh.

We use the **Timer** object. The steps involved in using the **Timer** for a delay are:

- Establish a delay time by setting the **Interval** property.
- Establish a subroutine to call when the **Timer Tick** event occurs. Put the code to be processed following the delay in this subroutine.
- Turn the timer off initially.
- When a delay is needed, turn on the timer.
- Once the code in the **Tick** subroutine is processed, turn off the timer.

Example 12-5. Display Delay

Write a program that displays an image for two seconds, then clears the burger. First, try the program using the **Delay** method, then using a **Timer** object. We will use the burger graphic (**burger.gif**) from **Example 9-4**:

Copy this file to your program folder. We have put a copy in **Guide to Small Basic\Programs\Chapter 12**.

Small Basic Code (using **Delay** method):

```
'Guide to Small Basic, Example 12-5
InitializeProgram()

Sub InitializeProgram
  GraphicsWindow.Show()
  GraphicsWindow.Title = "Example 12-5"
  GraphicsWindow.Width = 200
  GraphicsWindow.Height = 300
  'button
  GraphicsWindow.BrushColor = "Black"
  GraphicsWindow.FontSize = 16
  GraphicsWindow.FontBold = "false"
  ShowButton = Controls.AddButton("Show Burger", 40, 200)
  Controls.ButtonClicked = ButtonClickedSub
  'image
  Burger = ImageList.LoadImage(Program.Directory + "\burger.gif")
EndSub

Sub ButtonClickedSub
  'display/delay/clear
  GraphicsWindow.DrawResizedImage(Burger, 25, 25, 150, 150)
  Program.Delay(2000)
  GraphicsWindow.BrushColor = GraphicsWindow.BackgroundColor
  GraphicsWindow.FillRectangle(25, 25, 150, 150)
EndSub
```

In this version, when the button is clicked, we draw the burger image, delay 1000 milliseconds, then erase the image.

Save and **Run** the program. You will see an empty window with a button:

Click **Show Burger** – my guess is you won't see anything or it may flash briefly. The burger is not able to draw before the **Delay** method "locks" the processor. To prove it will draw without the delay, comment out these lines of code:

```
Program.Delay(1000)
GraphicsWindow.BrushColor = GraphicsWindow.BackgroundColor
GraphicsWindow.FillRectangle(25, 25, 150, 150)
```

Timer Object   12-17

Save and Run again. Click Show Burger to see:

Leave these lines commented out and make the shaded changes (including the commented out lines) to the code:

```
'Guide to Small Basic, Example 12-5
InitializeProgram()

Sub InitializeProgram
  GraphicsWindow.Show()
  GraphicsWindow.Title = "Example 12-5"
  GraphicsWindow.Width = 200
  GraphicsWindow.Height = 300
  'button
  GraphicsWindow.BrushColor = "Black"
  GraphicsWindow.FontSize = 16
  GraphicsWindow.FontBold = "false"
  ShowButton = Controls.AddButton("Show Burger", 40, 200)
  Controls.ButtonClicked = ButtonClickedSub
  'image
  Burger = ImageList.LoadImage(Program.Directory + "\burger.gif")
  Timer.Interval = 2000
  Timer.Tick = TickSub
  Timer.Pause()
EndSub
```

```
Sub ButtonClickedSub
  'display/delay/clear
  GraphicsWindow.DrawResizedImage(Burger, 25, 25, 150, 150)
  Timer.Resume()
  'Program.Delay(2000)
  'GraphicsWindow.BrushColor = GraphicsWindow.BackgroundColor
  'GraphicsWindow.FillRectangle(25, 25, 150, 150)
EndSub

Sub TickSub
  GraphicsWindow.BrushColor = GraphicsWindow.BackgroundColor
  GraphicsWindow.FillRectangle(25, 25, 150, 150)
  Timer.Pause()
EndSub
```

This version is saved as **Example 12-5** in **Guide to Small Basic\Programs\Chapter 12** folder. We now have implemented the same delay using a **Timer** object. When the button is clicked, we draw the image and start the timer. After a delay of two seconds, the code in **TickSub** to clear the image is processed.

Save and **Run** the program. Click **Show Burger**. You should immediately see the burger display:

And two seconds later, it's gone. You can repeat this process as many times as you'd like.

Example 12-6. Animated Find the Burger Game

Recall the **Find the Burger** game we built in Chapter 9 (**Example 9-4**). A burger was hidden behind one of three boxes - you needed to find it. There was no real skill involved in the game, just pure guesswork. Modify the **Find the Burger** game as follows: draw the three boxes, show what box the burger is behind, then cover it (use a **Timer** object for delay). Next, shuffle the boxes using the **Shapes Animate** method. A keen eye is needed to follow the moving burger. Make sure the burger graphic (**burger.gif**) is in your program folder.

Small Basic Code:

```
'Guide to Small Basic, Example 12-6
InitializeProgram()

Sub InitializeProgram
  GraphicsWindow.Show()
  GraphicsWindow.Title = "Example 12-6"
  GraphicsWindow.Width = 380
  GraphicsWindow.Height = 180
  'burger
  BurgerImage = ImageList.LoadImage(Program.Directory + "\burger.gif")
  'box locations/boxes
  BoxX[1] = 20
  BoxX[2] = 140
  BoxX[3] = 260
  GraphicsWindow.PenColor = "Blue"
  GraphicsWindow.BrushColor = "Blue"
  For I = 1 To 3
    Box[I] = Shapes.AddRectangle(100, 100)
    Shapes.HideShape(Box[I])
  EndFor
  'button
  GraphicsWindow.BrushColor = "Black"
  GraphicsWindow.FontSize = 16
  GraphicsWindow.FontBold = "false"
  NewGameButton = Controls.AddButton("New Game", 140, 140)
  Controls.ButtonClicked = ButtonClickedSub
  GraphicsWindow.MouseDown = MouseDownSub
  Timer.Interval = 1000
  Timer.Tick = TickSub
  Timer.Pause()
EndSub
```

```
Sub ButtonClickedSub
  'hide button
  Controls.HideControl(NewGameButton)
  'clear screen, determine burger location
  GraphicsWindow.BrushColor = GraphicsWindow.BackgroundColor
  For I = 1 To 3
    GraphicsWindow.FillRectangle(BoxX[I], 20, 100, 100)
    Shapes.Move(Box[I], BoxX[I], 20)
    Shapes.HideShape(Box[I])
    BoxOrder[I] = I
  EndFor
  BurgerLocation = Math.GetRandomNumber(3)
  'display burger for brief time, then draw boxes
  GraphicsWindow.DrawResizedImage(BurgerImage,
BoxX[BurgerLocation], 20, 100, 100)
  Timer.Resume()
EndSub

Sub TickSub
  Timer.Pause()
  'erase burger and show boxes
  GraphicsWindow.BrushColor = GraphicsWindow.BackgroundColor
  For I = 1 To 3
    GraphicsWindow.FillRectangle(BoxX[I], 20, 100, 100)
    Shapes.ShowShape(Box[I])
  EndFor
  'animate the boxes
  NumberSwaps = 5 + Math.GetRandomNumber(10)
  For I = 1 To NumberSwaps
    J = Math.GetRandomNumber(3)
    If (J = 1) Then
      'swap 1 and 2
      FromBox = 1
      ToBox = 2
    ElseIf (J = 2) Then
      'swap 1 and 3
      FromBox = 1
      ToBox = 3
    Else
      'swap 2 and 3
      FromBox = 2
      ToBox = 3
    EndIf
    If (Math.GetRandomNumber(2) = 1) Then
      'do from first
```

```
            Shapes.Animate(Box[BoxOrder[FromBox]], BoxX[ToBox], 20,
1500)
            Program.Delay(500)
            Shapes.Animate(Box[BoxOrder[ToBox]], BoxX[FromBox], 20,
1500)
            Program.Delay(1500)
        Else
            'do to first
            Shapes.Animate(Box[BoxOrder[ToBox]], BoxX[FromBox], 20,
1500)
            Program.Delay(500)
            Shapes.Animate(Box[BoxOrder[FromBox]], BoxX[ToBox], 20,
1500)
            Program.Delay(1500)
        EndIf
        Temp = BoxOrder[FromBox]
        BoxOrder[FromBox] = BoxOrder[ToBox]
        BoxOrder[ToBox] = Temp
    EndFor
EndSub


Sub MouseDownSub
    'find clicked box
    X = GraphicsWindow.MouseX
    Y = GraphicsWindow.MouseY
    ClickedBox = 0
    If (Y > 20 And Y < 120) Then
        For I = 1 To 3
            If (X > BoxX[I] And X < BoxX[I] + 100) Then
                ClickedBox = I
            EndIf
        EndFor
    EndIf
    'clear box, see if burger is there
    Shapes.HideShape(Box[BoxOrder[ClickedBox]])
    If (BoxOrder[ClickedBox] = BurgerLocation) Then
        GraphicsWindow.DrawResizedImage(BurgerImage, BoxX[ClickedBox],
20, 100, 100)
        Controls.ShowControl(NewGameButton)
    EndIf
EndSub
```

Saved as **Example 12-6** in **Guide to Small Basic\Programs\Chapter 12** folder.

This is our longest program yet. Let's see how we modified the original program. First, we now use **Shapes** objects for the boxes (**Box** array) so they can be animated. When **New Game** is clicked, the burger is shown in its hiding position then, after a delay implemented by the **Timer** object, the burger is erased and replaced by three blue boxes. The shuffling begins. This is the biggest addition to the program.

The shuffling occurs in the **TickSub** subroutine after the burger is hidden. There are three positions on the screen: 1, 2, 3, left to right. Before shuffling **Box[1]** is in position 1, **Box[2]** is in position 2 and **Box[3]** is in position 3. The array **BoxOrder** keeps track of which box is in each position after each shuffle. With each shuffle, we either swap location 1 and 2, 1 and 3 or 2 and 3 in either order. The boxes in the selected positions are swapped using the **Animate** method. Delays are used after each swap to see the animation results. The **Delay** method works fine here (we don't have any images). The swaps are a little subtle especially as the boxes overlap.

Save and **Run** the program. Click **New Game**. Here's the middle of a swap process:

Once done, the screen is:

Pick the box you think the burger is behind. I found it in one try:

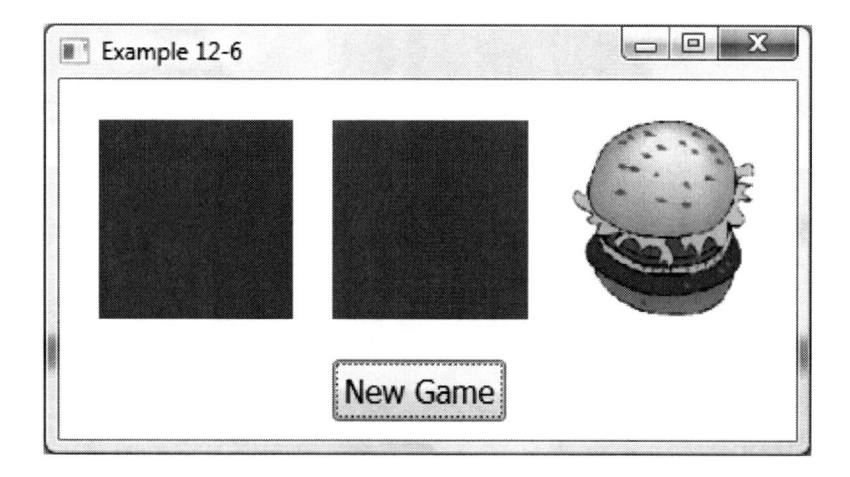

I can play again now.

Chapter Review

After completing this chapter, you should understand:

- ➢ Meaning of **Timer Interval** property.
- ➢ Starting and stopping timer.
- ➢ Updating displays using timer.
- ➢ Using **Timer** object for delays.

13. Sound Object

Preview

In this chapter, we look at the **Sound** object. This lets us add any sound to our program.

Sound Object

And exciting and fun feature of many programs are sounds. The **Sound** object provides operations that allow the playback of sounds. Some simple sounds are built into Small Basic.

Sound Methods:

```
Pause(file)
```
Pauses playback of an audio **file**. If the file was not already playing, this operation will not do anything.

```
Play(file)
```
Plays an audio **file**. If the file was already paused, this operation will resume from the position where the playback was paused.

```
PlayAndWait(file)
```
Plays an audio **file** and waits until it is finished playing. If the file was already paused, this operation will resume from the position where the playback was paused.

```
PlayBellRing()
```
Plays the bell ring sound.

```
PlayBellRingAndWait()
```
Plays the bell ring sound and waits for it to finish.

```
PlayChime()
```
Plays the chime sound.

```
PlayChimeAndWait()
```
Plays the chime sound and waits for it to finish.

```
PlayChimes()
```
Plays the chimes sound.

```
PlayChimesAndWait()
```
Plays the chimes sound and waits for it to finish.

`PlayClick()`
Plays the click sound.

`PlayClickAndWait()`
Plays the click sound and waits for it to finish.

`PlayMusic(notes)`
Plays a set of notes. The format of the notes is a subset of the Music Markup Language originally used in QBasic.

`Stop(file)`
Stops playback of an audio **file**. If the file was not already playing, this operation will not do anything.

Built-In Sounds

There are four built-in sounds you can play: **BellRing, Chime, Chimes, Click**. The statements to play each of these sounds are:

```
Sound.PlayBellRing()
Sound.PlayBellRingAndWait()
Sound.PlayChime()
Sound.PlayChimeAndWait()
Sound.PlayChimes()
Sound.PlayChimesAndWait()
Sound.PlayClick()
Sound.PlayClickAndWait()
```

When you play a sound <u>without</u> the "**AndWait**" suffix, the sound will start playing and code processing will continue immediately. When you play a sound with the "**AndWait**" suffix, code processing does not continue until the sound has finished. This adds delay (sometimes desired) to a program, especially for long playing sounds.

Example 13-1. Built-In Sounds

Write a program that with each click in the window, a random built-in sound plays.

Small Basic Code:

```
'Guide to Small Basic, Example 13-1
InitializeProgram()

Sub InitializeProgram
  GraphicsWindow.Show()
  GraphicsWindow.Title = "Example 13-1"
  GraphicsWindow.Width = 300
  GraphicsWindow.Height = 100
  GraphicsWindow.MouseDown = MouseDownSub
EndSub

Sub MouseDownSub
  'play one of four sounds
  GraphicsWindow.Clear()
  GraphicsWindow.FontSize = 16
  J = Math.GetRandomNumber(4)
  If (J = 1) Then
    GraphicsWindow.DrawText(10, 10, "Bell Ring")
    Sound.PlayBellRing()
  ElseIf (J = 2) Then
    GraphicsWindow.DrawText(10, 10, "Chime")
    Sound.PlayChime()
  ElseIf (J = 3) Then
    GraphicsWindow.DrawText(10, 10, "Chimes")
    Sound.PlayChimes()
  ElseIf (J = 4) Then
    GraphicsWindow.DrawText(10, 10, "Click")
    Sound.PlayClick()
  EndIf
EndSub
```

Saved as **Example 13-1** in **Guide to Small Basic\Programs\Chapter 13** folder.

Save and **Run** the program. You will see a blank window. Click the window. A sound will play and the name of the sound will display. Keep clicking until you hear all four sounds.

Playing Other Sounds

The Small Basic built in sounds are kind of boring. Games and other program feature elaborate sounds that take advantage of stereo sound cards. By using the Small Basic **Sound** object, we can add such sounds to our programs.

The **Sound** object is used to play one particular type of sound, those represented by **wav** files (files with wav extensions). Most sounds you hear played in Windows applications are saved as **wav** files. These are the files formed when you record using one of the many sound recorder programs available. In the **Guide to Small Basic\Programs\Chapter 13** folder are four example **wav** files we've used in game programming before:

throw.wav	throwing sound
splat.wav	splat sound
ouch.wav	screaming sound
gameover.wav	little tune when game is over

You can play each of these sounds in your computer's media player if you want.

There are two ways to play a sound file. To play the sound (represented by **SoundFile**) to completion before executing any more code (delaying the program), use the single line:

```
Sound.PlayAndWait(SoundFile)
```

To start playing a sound and immediately continue executing code:

```
Sound.Stop(SoundFile)
Sound.Play(SoundFile)
```

We execute a **Stop** before playing a sound, just in case it's still playing from a previous call. In each of the above methods, **SoundFile** is a complete path (including directory) to the needed file.

It is normal practice to include any sound files an application uses in the same folder as the program. This makes them easily accessible (use the **Program.Directory** parameter).

Example 13-2. Playing Sounds

Write a program that with each click in the window, one of the four sample sounds plays. Copy the sample files (**throw.wav, splat.wav, ouch.wav, gameover.wav**) to your program folder.

Small Basic Code:

```
'Guide to Small Basic, Example 13-2
InitializeProgram()

Sub InitializeProgram
  GraphicsWindow.Show()
  GraphicsWindow.Title = "Example 13-2"
  GraphicsWindow.Width = 300
  GraphicsWindow.Height = 100
  GraphicsWindow.MouseDown = MouseDownSub
EndSub

Sub MouseDownSub
  'play one of four sounds
  GraphicsWindow.Clear()
  GraphicsWindow.FontSize = 16
  J = Math.GetRandomNumber(4)
  If (J = 1) Then
    GraphicsWindow.DrawText(10, 10, "Throw")
    Sound.Stop(Program.Directory + "\throw.wav")
    Sound.Play(Program.Directory + "\throw.wav")
  ElseIf (J = 2) Then
    GraphicsWindow.DrawText(10, 10, "Splat")
    Sound.Stop(Program.Directory + "\splat.wav")
    Sound.Play(Program.Directory + "\splat.wav")
  ElseIf (J = 3) Then
    GraphicsWindow.DrawText(10, 10, "Ouch")
    Sound.Stop(Program.Directory + "\ouch.wav")
    Sound.Play(Program.Directory + "\ouch.wav")
  ElseIf (J = 4) Then
    GraphicsWindow.DrawText(10, 10, "Game Over")
    Sound.Stop(Program.Directory + "\gameover.wav")
    Sound.Play(Program.Directory + "\gameover.wav")
  EndIf
EndSub
```

Saved as **Example 13-2** in **Guide to Small Basic\Programs\Chapter 13** folder.

Save and **Run** the program. Click the blank window. A sound will play and the name of the sound will display. Keep clicking until you hear all four sounds.

Chapter Review

After completing this chapter, you should understand:

- Use of the **Sound** object.
- Playing any of the four built-in sounds.
- Playing sounds represented by **wav** files.

This page intentionally not left blank.

14. File Object

Preview

In this final chapter on Small Basic objects, we study the **File** object. It provides read/write access to sequential files and allows locating, creating and deleting files and directories.

File Object

The **File** object provides methods to access, read and write information from and to a file on disk. You provide the complete path to the file.

File Properties:

```
LastError
```
Gets or set the last encountered file operation based on error message.

File Methods:

```
AppendContents(file, contents)
```
Opens the specified **file** and appends the **contents** to the end of the file. Returns "**SUCCESS**" if successful, otherwise returns "**FAILED**".

```
CopyFile(sourcefile, destinationfile)
```
Copies **sourcefile** to **destinationfile**. Existing files will be overwritten. Returns "**SUCCESS**" if successful, otherwise returns "**FAILED**".

```
CreateDirectory(directory)
```
Creates the specified **directory**. Returns "**SUCCESS**" if successful, otherwise returns "**FAILED**".

```
DeleteDirectory(directory)
```
Deletes the specified **directory**. Returns "**SUCCESS**" if successful, otherwise returns "**FAILED**".

```
GetDirectories(directory)
```
Gets all subdirectories in **directory**. Returns subdirectories as an array if successful, otherwise returns "**FAILED**".

```
GetFiles(directory)
```
Gets all files in **directory**. Returns files as an array if successful, otherwise returns "**FAILED**".

```
InsertLine(file, linenumber, contents)
```
Opens the specified **file** and inserts the **contents** at the specified **linenumber**. This operation will not overwrite any existing content at the specified line. Returns "**SUCCESS**" if successful, otherwise returns "**FAILED**".

`ReadContents(file)`
Opens a **file** and reads the entire file's contents. Returns the contents of the file.

`ReadLine(file, linenumber)`
Opens the specified **file** and reads the contents at the specified **linenumber**. Returns the text at the specified line.

`WriteContents(file, contents)`
Opens a **file** and writes the specified **contents** into it, replacing the original contents with the new content. Returns "**SUCCESS**" if successful, otherwise returns "**FAILED**".

`WriteLine(file, linenumber, contents)`
Opens the specified **file** and write the **contents** at the specified **linenumber**. This operation will overwrite any existing content at the specified line. Returns "**SUCCESS**" if successful, otherwise returns "**FAILED**".

Sequential Files

The read and write methods of Small Basic work with sequential files A sequential file is a line-by-line list of data that can be viewed with any text editor. Sequential access easily works with files that have lines with mixed information of different lengths. Hence, sequential files can include both variables and text data. When using sequential files, it is helpful, but not necessary, to know the order data was written to the file to allow easy retrieval.

The ability to read and generate sequential files is a very powerful capability of Small Basic. This single capability is the genesis of many applications I've developed. Let's examine a few possible applications where we could use such files. One possibility is to use sequential files to provide initialization information for a project. Such a file is called a **configuration** or **initialization file** and almost all applications use such files. Here is the idea:

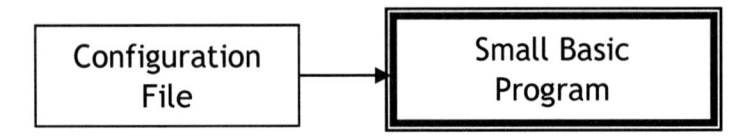

Configuration File → Small Basic Program

In this diagram, the configuration file (a sequential file) contains information that can be used to initialize different parameters (control properties, variable values) within the Small Basic program. The file is opened when the application begins, the file values are read and the various parameters established.

Similarly, when we exit a program, we could have it write out current parameter values to an output configuration file:

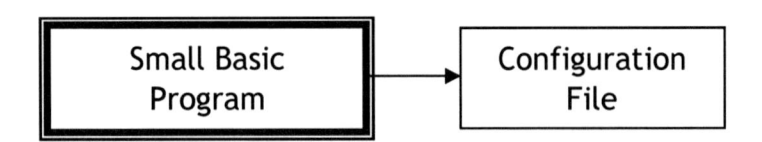

Small Basic Program → Configuration File

This output file could then become an input file the next time the program is executed. We will look at how to implement such a configuration file in a Small Basic application.

Many data-intensive, or not-so intensive, Windows applications provide file export capabilities. For example, you can save data from a Microsoft Excel spreadsheet to an external file. The usual format for such an exported data file is a **CSV** (comma separated variables) sequential file. You can write a Small Basic program that reads this exported file and performs some kind of analysis or further processing of the data:

```
[Windows Application] → [Exported Data File] → [Small Basic Program]
```

In the above example, the results of the Small Basic program could be displayed using objects (text boxes, shapes, images) or the program could also write another sequential file that could be used by some other application (say Microsoft Access or Microsoft Word). This task is actually more common than you might think. Many applications support exporting data. And, many applications support importing data from other sources. A big problem is that the output file from one application might not be an acceptable input file to another application. Small Basic to the rescue:

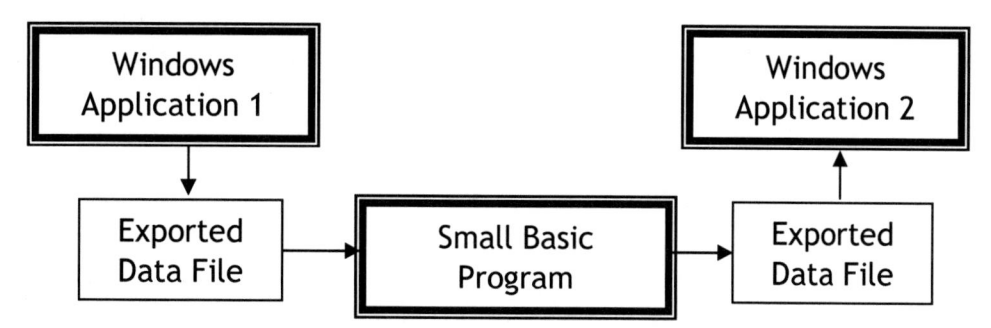

```
[Windows Application 1] → [Exported Data File] → [Small Basic Program] → [Exported Data File] → [Windows Application 2]
```

In this diagram, Application 1 writes an exported data file that is read by the Small Basic program. This program writes a data file in an input format required by Application 2.

You will find that you can use Small Basic to read a sequential file in any format and, likewise, write a file in any format. As we said, the ability to read and generate sequential files is a very powerful capability of Small Basic.

Sequential File Output

We will first look at **writing** to sequential files. You need to know the complete path to the file (**filename**), the line of information you want to write (**contents**) and the line number in the file where the contents goes (**linenumber**). With this information, the write procedure is:

    File.WriteLine(filename, linenumber, contents)

If there is already information at **linenumber**, it will be overwritten. To insert a new line in a file and not overwrite existing information, use:

    File.InsertLine(filename, linenumber, contents)

All lines below **linenumber** will be shifted down one position.

The content written to the file can be any information you desire: a single variable, a line of text, a list of variables separated by commas. You choose the format to fit your programming needs - you control what goes on each line of the file. For example, if you are writing a file for input to another program, you can have your file match that needed format. Small Basic provides that flexibility.

Example 14-1. Sequential File Output

Write a program that writes the 12 months and number of days in each to a sequential file. For each, write the month name on a line, then the number of days on a separated line. Write the file to your program folder.

Small Basic Code:

```
'Guide to Small Basic, Example 14-1
'month arrays
MonthName[1] = "January"
MonthName[2] = "February"
MonthName[3] = "March"
MonthName[4] = "April"
MonthName[5] = "May"
MonthName[6] = "June"
MonthName[7] = "July"
MonthName[8] = "August"
MonthName[9] = "September"
MonthName[10] = "October"
MonthName[11] = "November"
MonthName[12] = "December"
MonthDays[1] = 31
MonthDays[2] = 28
MonthDays[3] = 31
MonthDays[4] = 30
MonthDays[5] = 31
MonthDays[6] = 30
MonthDays[7] = 31
MonthDays[8] = 31
MonthDays[9] = 30
MonthDays[10] = 31
MonthDays[11] = 30
MonthDays[12] = 31
'write to file
For I = 1 To 12
  File.WriteLine(Program.Directory + "\months.txt", I * 2 - 1, MonthName[I])
  File.WriteLine(Program.Directory + "\months.txt", I * 2, MonthDays[I])
EndFor
```

Saved as **Example 14-1** in **Guide to Small Basic\Programs\Chapter 14** folder.

The program doesn't even need a window. Values are stored in arrays then written to the file (**months.txt**) a the **For** loop. Notice how the **For** index **I** is used to determine file line numbers – there will be 24 lines in the file.

Save and **Run** the program. You will not see a window – the program will run and return to the code editor. Go to your program folder (mine is **Guide to Small Basic\Programs\Chapter 14**). Open the file **months.txt** using Windows Notepad and you will see:

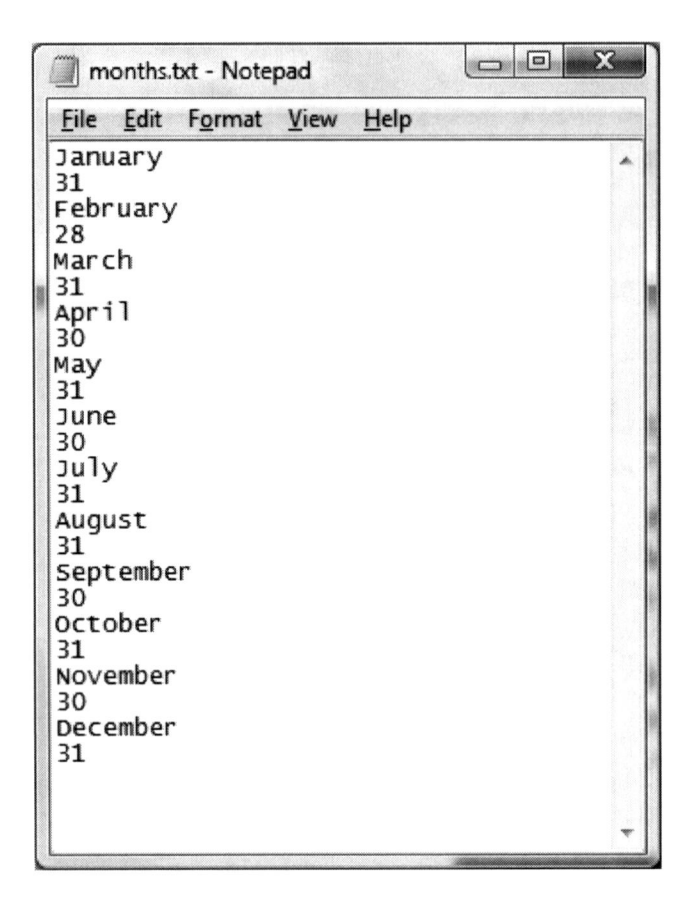

```
months.txt - Notepad
File  Edit  Format  View  Help
January
31
February
28
March
31
April
30
May
31
June
30
July
31
August
31
September
30
October
31
November
30
December
31
```

As expected, the file has 24 lines with names and number of days alternating.

Sequential File Input

To **read** content from a sequential file, we essentially reverse the write procedure. To get the **contents** of **linenumber** in **filename**, use:

```
contents = File.ReadLine(filename, linenumber)
```

Information is read from a sequential file in the same order it was written. To read it in properly, you need to know how the file is structured (e.g., the number of variables in each line and the order variables were written to the file).

If you developed the structure of the sequential file (say for a configuration file), you obviously know all of this information. And, if it is a file you generated from another source (Excel, Access), the information should be known. If the file is from an unknown source, you may have to do a little detective work. Open the file in a text editor and look at the data. See if you can figure out what is in the file.

Many times, you may know the order and type of variables in a sequential file, but the number of variables may vary. For example, you may export monthly sales data from an Excel spreadsheet. One month may have 30 lines, the next 31 lines, and February would have 28 or 29. In such a case, you can read from the file until you reach an end-of-file condition. This is checked by looking for a blank line.

Example 14-2. Sequential File Input

Write a program that reads the **months.txt** file created in **Example 14-1**. Have the input information display on separate lines in a text box control.

Small Basic Code:

```
'Guide to Small Basic, Example 14-2
GraphicsWindow.Show()
GraphicsWindow.Title = "Example 14-2"
GraphicsWindow.Width = 300
GraphicsWindow.Height = 200
'multi-line text box
GraphicsWindow.BrushColor = "Black"
GraphicsWindow.FontSize = 16
GraphicsWindow.FontBold = "false"
MonthsTextBox = Controls.AddMultiLineTextBox(10, 10)
Controls.SetSize(MonthsTextBox, 280, 180)
'read from file
DisplayText = ""
For I = 1 To 12
  Month = File.ReadLine(Program.Directory + "\months.txt", I * 2 - 1)
  Days = File.ReadLine(Program.Directory + "\months.txt", I * 2)
  DisplayText = DisplayText + Month + " has " + Days + " days." + Text.GetCharacter(13)
EndFor
Controls.SetTextBoxText(MonthsTextBox, DisplayText)
```

Saved as **Example 14-2** in **Guide to Small Basic\Programs\Chapter 14** folder. Notice how similar the read code is to the write code. In the **For** loop we construct the **DisplayText** variable for display in the text box (**MonthsTextBox**). The value Text.GetCharacter(13) is a 'carriage return' character used to start a new line.

Save and **Run** the program. The file will be opened, **DisplayText** constructed and shown in the text box control:

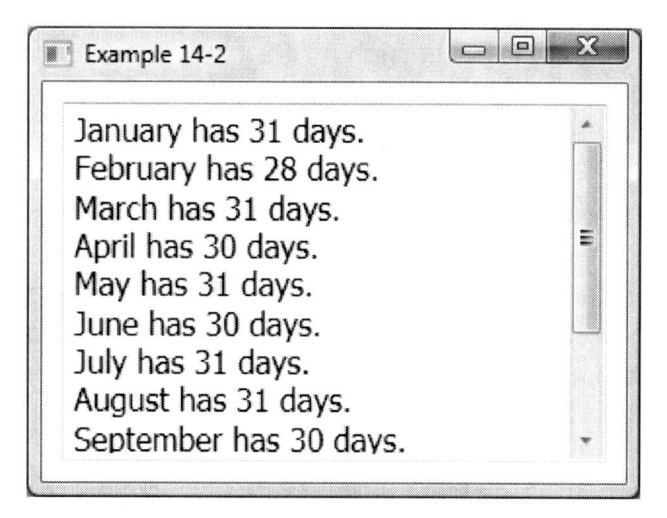

```
Example 14-2
January has 31 days.
February has 28 days.
March has 31 days.
April has 30 days.
May has 31 days.
June has 30 days.
July has 31 days.
August has 31 days.
September has 30 days.
```

This is the first time we've used a multi-line text box. Notice how it adds a scroll bar since there are more lines than can be displayed. Also, February doesn't always have 28 days - in a later chapter, we'll talk about how to check this.

CSV (Comma Separated Values) Files

One of the most common sequential file formats you will encounter is the **CSV** (comma separated values) file. In such a file, each line has one or more variables, each separated by a comma. Almost every application that has an export capability can export files in this format.

To read such a file and extract the individual variable values, we need to **parse** each line. We read in a single line as a long string. Then, we successively remove substrings from this longer line that represent each variable. To do this, we need to know how many variables are in a line and their location in the line. The location will be specified by the comma delimiter. If there are **N** variables in a line, there will be **N-1** commas.

The steps to extract variables from a line of comma-separated variables are:

1. Read line (**DataLine**) from **linenumber** of **filename** using:

   ```
   DataLine = File.ReadLine(filename, linenumber)
   ```

2. Find location of comma (**CL**) in **DataLine**:

   ```
   CL = Text.GetIndexOf(DataLine, ",")
   ```

3. If **CL <> 0**, extract **Variable** (get characters to left of comma):

   ```
   Variable = Text.GetSubText(DataLine, 1, CL - 1)
   ```

   Shorten **DataLine** (get characters to right of comma):

   ```
   DataLine = Text.GetSubTextToEnd(DataLine, CL + 1)
   ```

   Return to Step 2 to get next **Variable** from shortened **DataLine**.

4. If **CL = 0**, no commas remain so set **Variable** to **DataLine** (what's left of the original line after parsing out other variables):

   ```
   Variable = DataLine
   ```

You repeat the above steps for each data line in a **CSV** file to extract all the variables.

You may want to create your own **CSV** files. The process is simple. Decide what variables go on a particular line. Then, using the concatenation operator (+), form a string consisting of the variable values with commas between them. For example, if you have four variables (**Var1, Var2, Var3, Var4**), the **DataLine** you form is:

```
DataLine = Var1 + "," + Var2 +"," + Var3 + "," + Var4
```

Then, to write this line to **filename** at **linenumber**, use:

```
File.WriteLine(filename, linenumber, DataLine)
```

You repeat this process for every line needed in the **CSV** file.

Example 14-3. CSV Data Files

In the **Guide to Small Basic\Programs\Chapter 14** folder is a file entitled **mar95.csv**. Open this file using the Windows Notepad. You see:

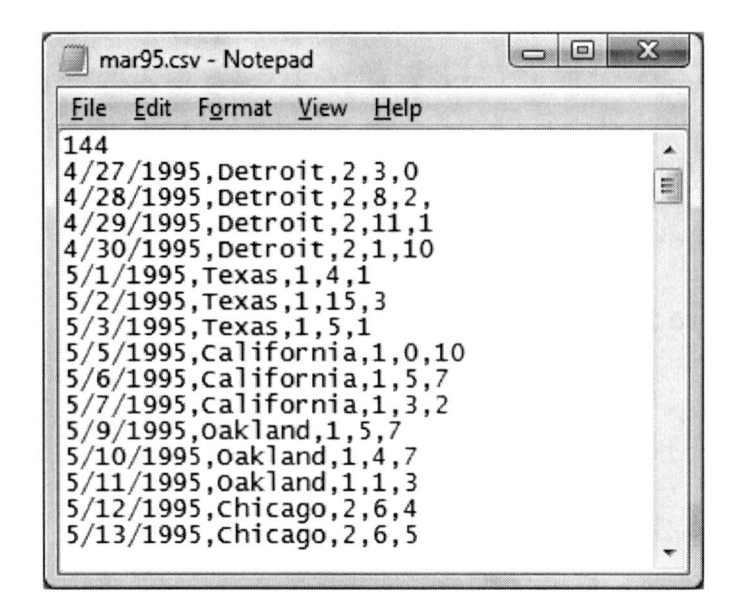

```
mar95.csv - Notepad
File  Edit  Format  View  Help
144
4/27/1995,Detroit,2,3,0
4/28/1995,Detroit,2,8,2,
4/29/1995,Detroit,2,11,1
4/30/1995,Detroit,2,1,10
5/1/1995,Texas,1,4,1
5/2/1995,Texas,1,15,3
5/3/1995,Texas,1,5,1
5/5/1995,California,1,0,10
5/6/1995,California,1,5,7
5/7/1995,California,1,3,2
5/9/1995,Oakland,1,5,7
5/10/1995,Oakland,1,4,7
5/11/1995,Oakland,1,1,3
5/12/1995,Chicago,2,6,4
5/13/1995,Chicago,2,6,5
```

This file chronicles the strike-shortened 1995 season of the Seattle Mariners baseball team, their most exciting year up until 2001. Not much has happened for the Mariners since then! (Our apologies to foreign readers who don't understand the game of baseball!) The first line tells how many lines are in the file. Each subsequent line represents a single game. There are five variables on each line:

Variable Number	Description
1	Date of Game
2	Opponent
3	(1-Away game, 2-Home game)
4	Mariners runs
5	Opponent runs

Write a program that reads this file, determines which team won each game and outputs to another **CSV** file the game number and current Mariners winning or losing streak (consecutive wins or losses). Use positive integers for wins, negative integers for losses. Also display the output in a text box control.

As an example, the corresponding output file for the lines displayed above would be:

    1,1 (a win)
    2,2 (a win)
    3,3 (a win)
    4,-1 (a loss)
    5,1 (a win)
    6,2 (a win)
    7,3 (a win)
    8,-1 (a loss)
    9,-2 (a loss)
    10,1 (a win)

There will be 144 lines in this output file. Load the resulting file in Excel (if you have it) and obtain a bar chart for the output data. Before starting, copy **mar95.csv** into your program folder.

Small Basic Code:

```
'Guide to Small Basic, Example 14-3
GraphicsWindow.Show()
GraphicsWindow.Title = "Example 14-3"
GraphicsWindow.Width = 300
GraphicsWindow.Height = 200
'multi-line text box
GraphicsWindow.BrushColor = "Black"
GraphicsWindow.FontSize = 16
GraphicsWindow.FontBold = "false"
ResultsTextBox = Controls.AddMultiLineTextBox(10, 10)
Controls.SetSize(ResultsTextBox, 280, 180)
'initialize Streak
Streak = 0
'read from file
NumberOfGames = File.ReadLine(Program.Directory + "\mar95.csv", 1)
For I = 1 To NumberOfGames
  DataLine = File.ReadLine(Program.Directory + "\mar95.csv", I + 1)
  NextVariable()
  GameDate = Variable
  NextVariable()
  Opponent = Variable
  NextVariable()
  HomeAway = Variable
```

```
    NextVariable()
    MarRuns = Variable
    NextVariable()
    OppRuns = Variable
    'See who won
    If (MarRuns > OppRuns) Then
      'Mariners win - extend existing streak or start new one
      If (Streak > 0) Then
        Streak = Streak + 1
      Else
        Streak = 1
      EndIf
    Else
      'Mariners lose - extend existing streak or start new one
      If (Streak < 0) Then
        Streak = Streak - 1
      Else
        Streak = -1
      EndIf
    EndIf
    'Write DataLine to file and append to text box as check
    DataLine = I + "," + Streak
    File.WriteLine(Program.Directory + "\streak.csv", I, DataLine)
    CurrentText = Controls.GetTextBoxText(ResultsTextBox)
    Controls.SetTextBoxText(ResultsTextBox, CurrentText + DataLine + Text.GetCharacter(13))
EndFor

Sub NextVariable
  'Look for comma in DataLine
  CL = Text.GetIndexOf(DataLine, ",")
  If (CL <> 0) Then
    'parse out variable
    Variable = Text.GetSubText(DataLine, 1, CL - 1)
    'shorten line
    DataLine = Text.GetSubTextToEnd(DataLine, CL + 1)
  Else
    'one variable remains
    Variable = DataLine
  EndIf
EndSub
```

Saved as **Example 14-3** in **Guide to Small Basic\Programs\Chapter 14** folder.

The code goes through each line in **mar95.csv**, extracting five variables from each (really only needing the two team scores). To do this, it uses the subroutine **NextVariable** which implements all of the steps outlined earlier to parse a comma separated line of variables. With the scores, the code determines which team wins and adjust the win or loss **Streak** value accordingly. The game number (**For** loop index **I**) and **Streak** are then written to the **streak.csv** file one line at a time. The values are also displayed in the text box control.

Save and **Run** the program. Here's the results in the text box:

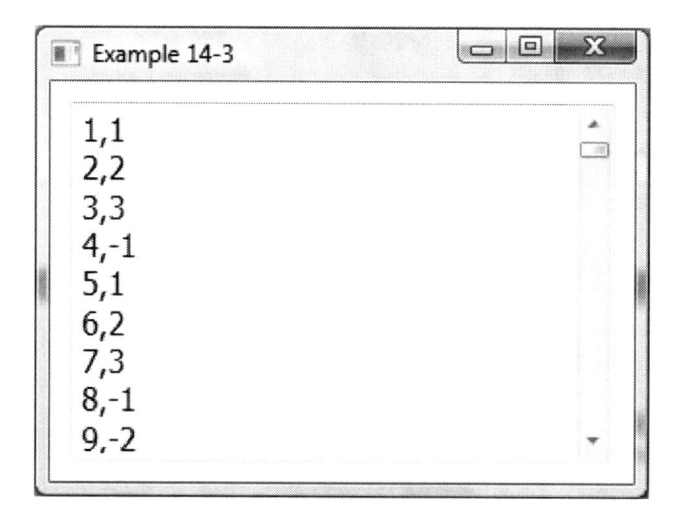

```
Example 14-3
1,1
2,2
3,3
4,-1
5,1
6,2
7,3
8,-1
9,-2
```

Open **streak.csv** (in your program folder) in Excel. Here's what I see:

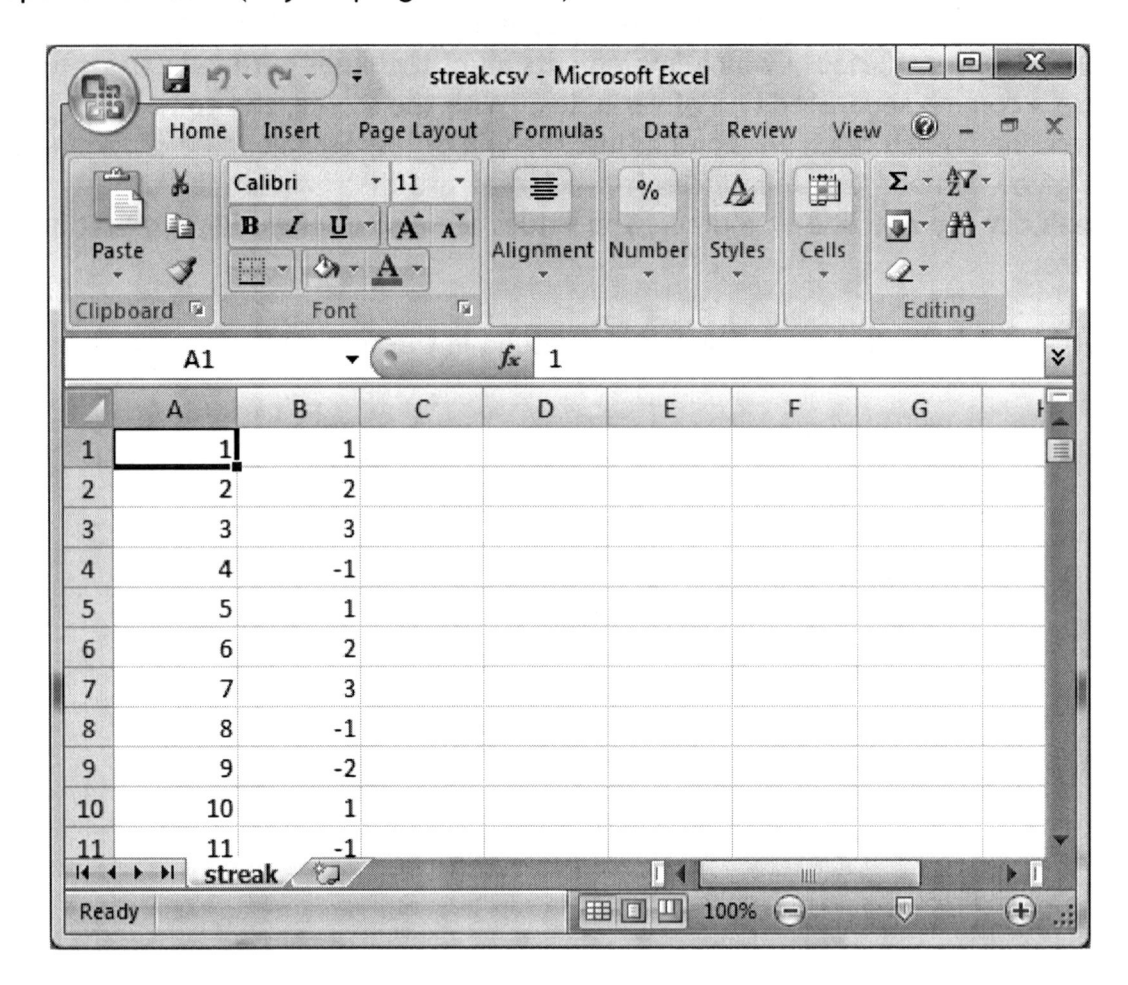

Try plotting the data as a bar chart in Excel. Here's my little plot:

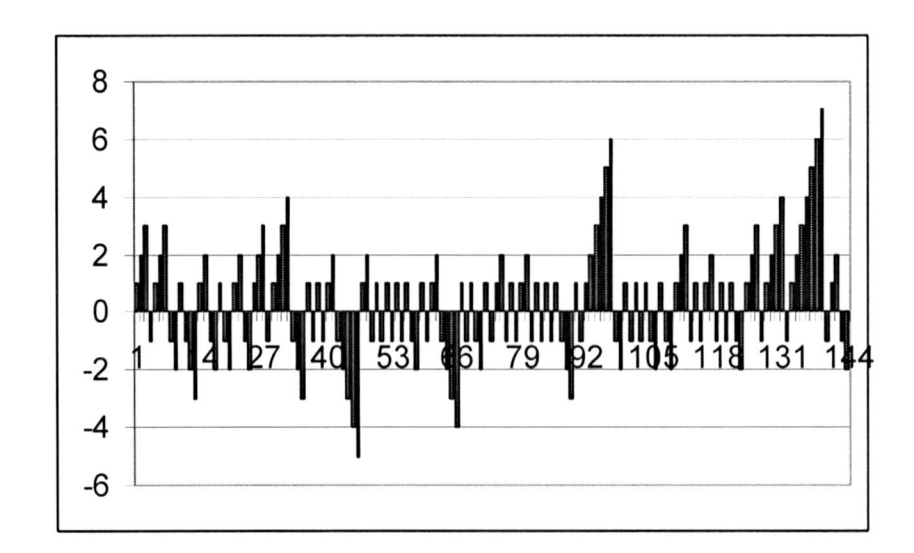

Writing and Reading Text Using Sequential Files

In many applications, we would like to be able to save text information and retrieve it for later reference. This information could be a **text file** created by an application or the contents of a Small Basic **text box** control. . Writing and reading text using sequential files involves some functions we have already seen and a couple of new ones.

To **write** a sequential text file, we simply write each line of the file using the **File** object **WriteLine** method. To write **textline** to **linenumber** of **filename**, use:

```
File.WriteLine(filename, linenumber, textline)
```

This assumes you have somehow generated the string **textline**. How you generate this data depends on your particular application. The **WriteLine** method should be in a loop that encompasses all lines of the file. You must know the number of lines in your file, beforehand. A typical code segment to accomplish this task is:

```
For I = 1 To NumberLines
  'need code here to generate string data textline
  File.WriteContents(filename, I, textline)
EndFor
```

If we want to write the contents of a text box named **ExampleTextBox** to a file named **filename**, we only need one line of code:

```
File.WriteContents(filename,
Controls.GetTextBoxText(ExampleTextBox))
```

The text is now saved in the file for later retrieval.

To **read** the contents of a previously-saved text file, we read each individual line with the **ReadLine** method. To retrieve **textline** from **linenumber** of **filename**, use:

```
textline = File.ReadLine(filename, linenumber)
```

This line is usually placed in a loop structure that is repeated until all lines of the file are read in. We can check for a blank line to detect an end-of-file condition, if you don't know, beforehand, how many lines are in the file. A typical code segment to accomplish this task is:

```
NextLine:
textline = File.ReadLine(filename, linenumber)
If (textline <> "") Then
  'do something with textline here
  Goto NextLine
EndIf
```

This code reads text lines from the sequential file **filename** until the end-of-file is reached. You could put a counter in the loop to count lines if you like.

To place the contents of a sequential file (**filename**) into a text box control (**ExampleTextBox**), use:

```
Controls.SetTextBoxText(File.ReadContents(filename))
```

Configuration Files

In the introduction to this chapter, we discussed one possible application for a sequential file - an **initialization** or **configuration file**. These files are used to save user selected options from one execution of an application to the next. With such files, the user avoids the headache of re-establishing desired values each time an application is run.

Every Windows application uses configuration files. For example, Microsoft Word remembers your favorite page settings, what font you like to use, what toolbars you want displayed, and many other options. How does it do this? When you start Word, it opens and reads the configuration file (or files) and sets your choices. When you exit Word, the configuration files are written back to disk, making note of any changes you may have made while running Word.

You can add the same capability to Small Basic applications. How do you decide what your configuration file will contain and how it will be formatted? That is completely up to you, the application designer. Typical information stored in a **configuration** file includes: current dates and times, selected colors, font name, font style, font size, and selected options. You decide what is important in your application. You develop variables to save information and read and write these variables from and to the sequential configuration file. There is usually one variable for each option being saved.

Once you've decided on values to save and the format of your file, how do you proceed? A first step is to create an initial file using a text editor. If the number of variables being saved is relatively short, I suggest putting one variable on each line of the file. Save your configuration file in your program folder. Configuration files will always be kept in the program path. And, the usual three letter file extension for a configuration file is **ini** (for initialization).

Once you have developed the configuration file, you need to write code to fit this framework:

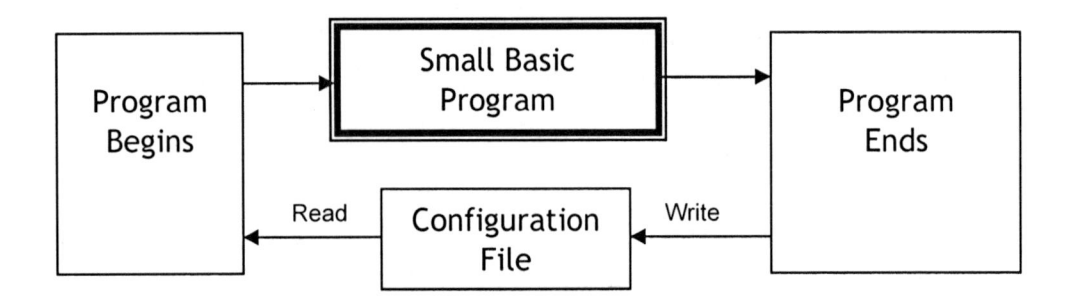

```
Program          Small Basic              Program
Begins  ──────▶  Program      ──────▶     Ends
   ▲                                         │
   │      Read   Configuration    Write      │
   └─────────────    File      ◀─────────────┘
```

When your application begins, read the configuration file and use the variables to establish the respective options. Establishing options involves things like setting fonts, establishing colors, simulating click events on button controls, and setting properties.

When your program ends (usually by clicking a button that says **Stop** or **Exit** or **End**), examine all options to be saved, establish respective variables to represent these options, and write the configuration file. Sometimes, as in the example to follow, you need multiple configuration files. This usually happens when you are saving variables and text information. You can use one file for all your variables, but usually will need individual files for each piece of text information (usually text box controls contents) you need to save.

Example 14-4. Configuration Files

Write a program with a text box control and a button control to stop the program. When the window is clicked, randomly change the graphics window background color. Use configuration files to save the last window color and any text in the text box control.

Small Basic Code:

```
'Guide to Small Basic, Example 14-4
InitializeProgram()

Sub InitializeProgram
  GraphicsWindow.Show()
  GraphicsWindow.Title = "Example 14-4"
  GraphicsWindow.Width = 400
  GraphicsWindow.Height = 300
  'multi-line text box
  GraphicsWindow.BrushColor = "Black"
  GraphicsWindow.FontSize = 16
  GraphicsWindow.FontBold = "false"
  ExampleTextBox = Controls.AddMultiLineTextBox(60, 40)
  Controls.SetSize(ExampleTextBox, 280, 180)
  'button
  ColorButton = Controls.AddButton("Exit", 180, 240)
  Controls.ButtonClicked = ButtonClickedSub
  GraphicsWindow.MouseDown = MouseDownSub
  'read configuration files
  Red = File.ReadLine(Program.Directory + "\colors.ini", 1)
  Green = File.ReadLine(Program.Directory + "\colors.ini", 2)
  Blue = File.ReadLine(Program.Directory + "\colors.ini", 3)
  GraphicsWindow.BackgroundColor = GraphicsWindow.GetColorFromRGB(Red, Green, Blue)
  Controls.SetTextBoxText(ExampleTextBox, File.ReadContents(Program.Directory + "\text.ini"))
EndSub

Sub MouseDownSub
  Red = Math.GetRandomNumber(256) - 1
  Green = Math.GetRandomNumber(256) - 1
  Blue = Math.GetRandomNumber(256) - 1
  GraphicsWindow.BackgroundColor = GraphicsWindow.GetColorFromRGB(Red, Green, Blue)
EndSub
```

```
Sub ButtonClickedSub
  'write configuration files
  File.WriteLine(Program.Directory + "\colors.ini", 1, Red)
  File.WriteLine(Program.Directory + "\colors.ini", 2, Green)
  File.WriteLine(Program.Directory + "\colors.ini", 3, Blue)
  File.WriteContents(Program.Directory + "\text.ini",
Controls.GetTextBoxText(ExampleTextBox))
  Program.End()
EndSub
```

Saved as **Example 14-4** in **Guide to Small Basic\Programs\Chapter 14** folder.

Two configuration files are used here. The file **colors.ini** holds the three color components for the screen color. The file **text.ini** holds text displayed in the text box control. When the program starts, both files are read and used to establish initial conditions. When the program ends (click **Exit** button), the values are written back to their respective files and the program is ended using **Program.End()**.

Save and **Run** the program. The first time you run the program, you will see a dark window and a blank text box control:

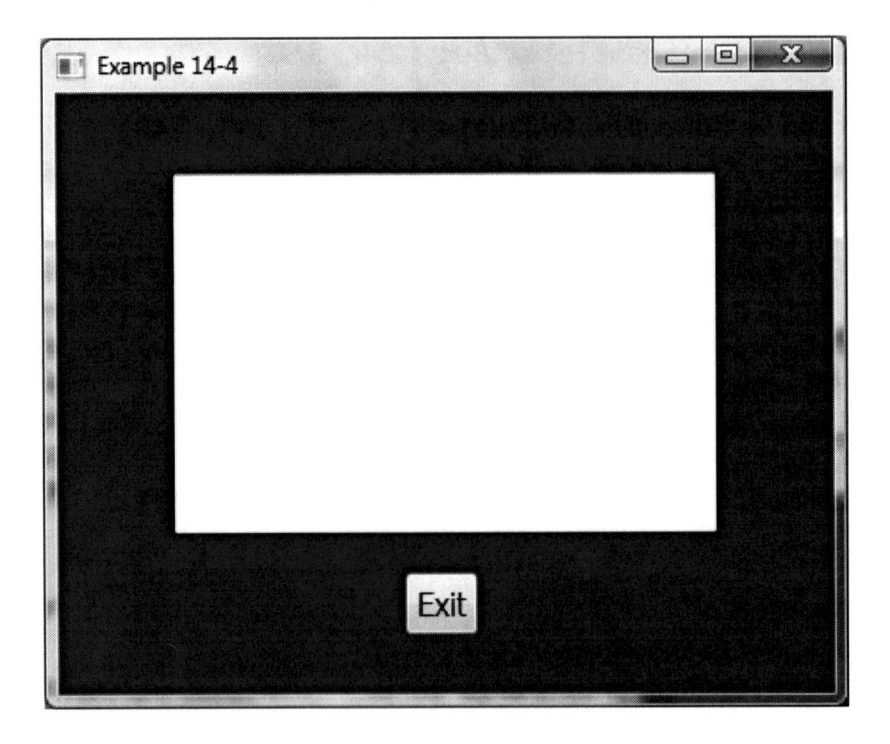

This happens because neither file exists so zeroes are assumed for **Red**, **Green** and **Blue** and blank is assumed for text.

Click the window (outside the text box) to see the screen change color. Type some text in the text box. Here's my window:

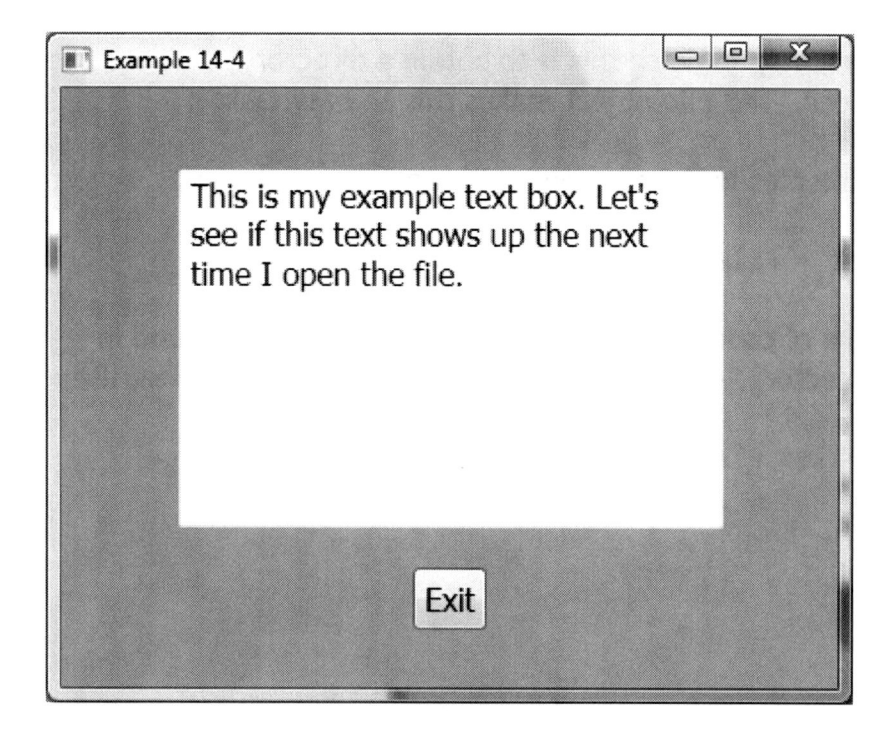

Click **Exit**. **Run** the program again and you should see the same values as the initial conditions:

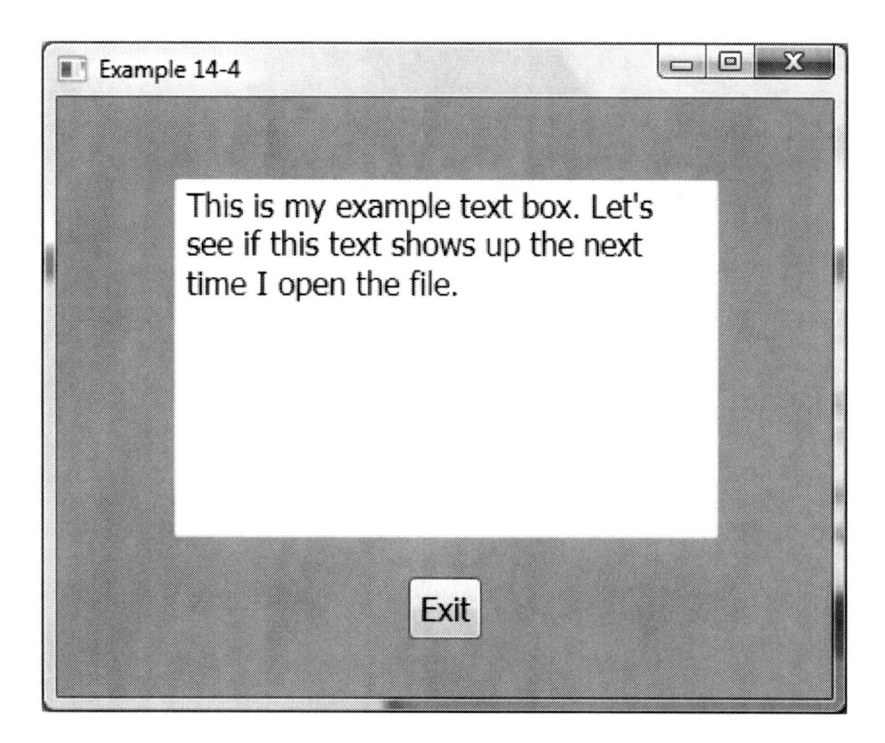

File Directory

Many times, you would like to know if a particular file exists in your program folder. A first step in doing this is to obtain a directory of all the files in your program folder. The **File** object makes this an easy task.

To find all the files in the program directory, use:

```
AllFiles = File.GetFiles(Program.Directory)
```

After this line of code, **AllFiles** is an array of all the files found in **Program.Directory**. To know how many files have been found, use:

```
NumberFiles = Array.GetItemCount(AllFiles)
```

Example 14-5. File Directory

Write a program that lists all the files in your program directory in a multi-line text box control.

Small Basic

```
'Guide to Small Basic, Example 14-5
GraphicsWindow.Show()
GraphicsWindow.Title = "Example 14-5"
GraphicsWindow.Width = 600
GraphicsWindow.Height = 200
'multi-line text box
GraphicsWindow.BrushColor = "Black"
GraphicsWindow.FontSize = 16
GraphicsWindow.FontBold = "false"
FilesTextBox = Controls.AddMultiLineTextBox(20, 20)
Controls.SetSize(FilesTextBox, 560, 160)
'get files
AllFiles = File.GetFiles(Program.Directory)
NumberFiles = Array.GetItemCount(AllFiles)
FilesText = ""
For I = 1 To NumberFiles
  'add next file
  FilesText = FilesText + AllFiles[I] + Text.GetCharacter(13)
EndFor
Controls.SetTextBoxText(FilesTextBox, FilesText)
```

Save and **Run** the program. All the files in **Program.Directory** are listed:

```
Example 14-5
C:\Guide to Small Basic\Programs\Chapter 14\colors.ini
C:\Guide to Small Basic\Programs\Chapter 14\Example 14-1.exe
C:\Guide to Small Basic\Programs\Chapter 14\Example 14-1.pdb
C:\Guide to Small Basic\Programs\Chapter 14\Example 14-1.sb
C:\Guide to Small Basic\Programs\Chapter 14\Example 14-2.exe
C:\Guide to Small Basic\Programs\Chapter 14\Example 14-2.pdb
C:\Guide to Small Basic\Programs\Chapter 14\Example 14-2.sb
C:\Guide to Small Basic\Programs\Chapter 14\Example 14-3.exe
```

Notice each file is listed with its complete path. It is possible to strip off the path information (using **Text** methods) leaving only the file name. Let's do that.

The length of the **Program.Directory** is given by:

```
Text.GetLength(Program.Directory)
```

Now, since **Program.Directory** does not include the last slash (\), the program name starts two characters past the last character in **Program.Directory**. Hence, if we strip off everything two characters to the right of the given length, we are left with the program name. The **GetSubTextToEnd** method does this "stripping". Make the shaded modifications to the **For** loop in the code:

```
For I = 1 To NumberFiles
  'add next file
  FileName = Text.GetSubTextToEnd(AllFiles[I], Text.GetLength(Program.Directory) + 2))
  FilesText = FilesText + FileName + Text.GetCharacter(13)
EndFor
```

Save and Run the program again. Only the file names should appear:

```
Example 14-5
colors.ini
Example 14-1.exe
Example 14-1.pdb
Example 14-1.sb
Example 14-2.exe
Example 14-2.pdb
Example 14-2.sb
Example 14-3.exe
```

This modified version is saved as **Example 14-5** in **Guide to Small Basic\Programs\Chapter 14** folder.

Locating Files

Once you have a directory of files, a next step is to find a particular file. Perhaps, you want to view a text file or see a photo. Once found, you can use the file as needed.

The usual way to select a certain file is based on the file **extension**. The extension is the part of the file name after the dot (.). For example, photo files usually have **jpg** extensions, data files have **csv** extensions, configuration files have **ini** files and Small Basic files have **sb** extensions.

To locate a certain type of file, we go through the list provided by the directory methods and save files with a particular extension or extensions. To see if a particular **filename** has a particular **extension**, we use:

```
Text.IsSubText(filename, extension)
```

If this returns **"true"**, the file is of the desired type.

Once you have found the file of interest, you develop some type of code for file selection. We do that in the example that follows.

File Object   14-31

Example 14-6. Locating Files

Write a program with a single text box and single button. With each click of the button control, display a file of a certain type (I choose to use Small Basic files with **sb** extensions).

Small Basic Code:

```
'Guide to Small Basic, Example 14-6
InitializeProgram()

Sub InitializeProgram
  GraphicsWindow.Show()
  GraphicsWindow.Title = "Example 14-6"
  GraphicsWindow.Width = 520
  GraphicsWindow.Height = 150
  'text box
  GraphicsWindow.BrushColor = "Black"
  GraphicsWindow.FontSize = 14
  GraphicsWindow.FontBold = "false"
  FileTextBox = Controls.AddTextBox(10, 40)
  Controls.SetSize(FileTextBox, 500, 30)
  'button
  NextButton = Controls.AddButton("Next File", 60, 80)
  Controls.ButtonClicked = ButtonClickedSub
  'get .sb files
  AllFiles = File.GetFiles(Program.Directory)
  NumberFiles = Array.GetItemCount(AllFiles)
  NumberSBFiles = 0
  For I = 1 To NumberFiles
    'check for sb extension
    If (Text.IsSubText(AllFiles[I], ".sb")) Then
      NumberSBFiles = NumberSBFiles + 1
      SBFiles[NumberSBFiles] = AllFiles[I]
    EndIf
  EndFor
  FileIndex = 1
  Controls.SetTextBoxText(FileTextBox, SBFiles[FileIndex])
EndSub

Sub ButtonClickedSub
  FileIndex = FileIndex + 1
  If (FileIndex > NumberSBFiles) Then
    FileIndex = 1
  EndIf
```

```
  Controls.SetTextBoxText(FileTextBox, SBFiles[FileIndex])
EndSub
```

Saved as **Example 14-6** in **Guide to Small Basic\Programs\Chapter 14** folder.

This repeats code from **Example 14-5**, getting all the files in the directory (array **AllFiles**). It goes through that array and stores files (complete path) with **sb** extension in new array **SBFiles**. With each click of the button control, a new **sb** file is displayed. Note this code won't work if no **sb** files are found.

Save and **Run** the program. The first file with an **sb** extension will be seen in the text box control:

[Example 14-6 window showing: C:\Guide to Small Basic\Programs\Chapter 14\Example 14-1.sb with a "Next File" button]

With each click of **Next File**, another file will be listed. Once the end of the list is reached, it starts over again at the beginning.

Once a file is in the text window (knowing its **FileIndex**), you could have another button that, once clicked, does something with the file. It could display its contents, play the sound (if a **wav** file) or display the image (if an image file).

Chapter Review

After completing this chapter, you should understand:

- ➢ Use of the **File** object.
- ➢ What a sequential file is.
- ➢ How to read/write variables and text with sequential files.
- ➢ How to work with **CSV** files.
- ➢ How to use configuration files.
- ➢ How to locate specific files in a directory.

We have completed our overview of the Small Basic objects. Use these chapters as a reference. The next several chapters look at a variety of more advanced Small Basic programming topics.

This page intentionally not left blank.

15. Debugging a Small Basic Program

Preview

As you begin building more elaborate Small Basic programs, you will undoubtedly encounter errors in your code. In this chapter, we look at handling errors in projects, using the Small Basic debugger.

You will see this chapter currently ends here. The Small Basic debugger is a planned addition to Small Basic Version 1.0. When the Small Basic debugger is released, we will provide this chapter to you.

This page intentionally not left blank.

16. Input Validation

Preview

In this chapter, we examine validating user input (dates and numbers) before processing it with Small Basic code.

Text Box Input Validation

The text box is a useful control for obtaining some kind of input from a user. As a programmer, we need to insure any inputs received from the user are properly formatted. As an example, say we need the user to type a date in the form **Month/Day/Year**, but one of the slashes or one of three values is omitted. What if the date is properly formatted, but the **Month** number is 22? Or, what if a text entry with all capitals is needed, but the user uses lower case? Or what if a numeric entry is needed, but the user types his name in the text box instead? Each of these cases could cause problems with further processing.

We need some kind of **input validation** procedure. We will look at two of the above mentioned cases here: **date validation** and **numeric validation**. You can use the frameworks for these two cases to build code for any particular validation situation you encounter.

The steps for both **date** and **numeric** validation are similar:

- Get **value** to validate.
- Call validation subroutine.
- In subroutine, determine if **value** is valid.
- If valid, set **IsValid** flag to "true" and return from subroutine.
- If not valid, inform user why. Set **IsValid** flag to "false". Return from subroutine.
- Make decisions based on **IsValid** flag.

To inform a user of problems with validation, we will use the **GraphicsWindow ShowMessage** method. This method lets you display a small message box to your user. It can be used to display error messages, describe potential problems or just to show the result of some computation. The user responds by clicking an **OK** button in the message box

To use the **ShowMessage** method, you decide what the **Text** of the message should be and what **Title** you desire for the box. Then, to display the message box in code, you use:

```
GraphicsWindow.ShowMessage(Text, Title)
```

As an example, if you use this code:

```
GraphicsWindow.Show()
GraphicsWindow.ShowMessage("Quick Message for You", "Hey You!!")
```

The resulting message box is:

You will find a lot of uses for this message boxes you progress in Small Basic.

Date Validation

A common text box entry is a **date**. We look at how to validate a date typed in the format:

Month/Day/Year

That is, each numeric value separated by a slash ("/"). This is the "American way" to specify a date – apologies to our users who normally write it as Day/Month/Year. You can modify the code here if desired.

Before using such an entry, we need to validate it. There are many steps to this validation process. To validate an entered date, we perform the following initial steps:

> - Check for first slash. If no slash, declare invalid.
> - Obtain **Month** (number to left of slash).
> - Check for second slash. If no slash, declare invalid.
> - Obtain **Day** (number to left of second slash).
> - Obtain **Year** (number to right of second slash).

If we successfully extract **Month**, **Day** and **Year**, there are still validation steps:

> - Make sure **Month** is between 1 and 12.
> - Make sure **Day** is between 1 and the maximum number of days in the selected month.

We're almost done, but we must confront the "February problem." In "normal" years, February has 28 days. In a leap years, there are 29 days in February. So, one last validation step is performed. If we are in a leap year (**Year** is evenly divisible by 4) and **Month** is 2, we need to make sure **Day** is not greater than 29 (rather than the usual 28). That's a lot of work for one little month!

An entered date must satisfy all of these validation steps to be declared valid. Let's do an example, building a general purpose subroutine for date validation.

Example 16-1. Date Validation

Write a program with a single text box and single button. Enter a date (in proper or improper format) in the text box. Click the button to validate the entered date.

Small Basic Code:

```
'Guide to Small Basic, Example 16-1
InitializeProgram()

Sub InitializeProgram
  GraphicsWindow.Show()
  GraphicsWindow.Title = "Example 16-1"
  GraphicsWindow.Width = 220
  GraphicsWindow.Height = 150
  'text box
  GraphicsWindow.BrushColor = "Black"
  GraphicsWindow.FontSize = 18
  GraphicsWindow.FontBold = "false"
  DateTextBox = Controls.AddTextBox(10, 40)
  Controls.SetSize(DateTextBox, 200, 30)
  'button
  GraphicsWindow.FontSize = 14
  ValidateButton = Controls.AddButton("Validate Date", 60, 80)
  Controls.ButtonClicked = ButtonClickedSub
EndSub

Sub ButtonClickedSub
  DateToValidate = Controls.GetTextBoxText(DateTextBox)
  ValidateDate()
  If (DateIsValid) Then
    GraphicsWindow.ShowMessage("Date is properly formatted.", "Valid Date")
  EndIf
EndSub

Sub ValidateDate
  'days in each month
  MonthDays[1] = 31
  MonthDays[2] = 28
  MonthDays[3] = 31
  MonthDays[4] = 30
  MonthDays[5] = 31
  MonthDays[6] = 30
```

```
MonthDays[7] = 31
MonthDays[8] = 31
MonthDays[9] = 30
MonthDays[10] = 31
MonthDays[11] = 30
MonthDays[12] = 31
'store DateToValidate in temporary string
DV = DateToValidate
DateIsValid = "true"
'find first slash and  month
SL = Text.GetIndexOf(DV, "/")
If (SL = 0) Then
   GraphicsWindow.ShowMessage("Invalid format for date - must be Month/Day/Year", "Invalid Date")
   DateIsValid = "false"
   Goto ExitValidateDate
EndIf
Month = Text.GetSubText(DV, 1, SL - 1)
'find next slash and  day
DV = Text.GetSubTextToEnd(DV, SL + 1)
SL = Text.GetIndexOf(DV, "/")
If (SL = 0) Then
   GraphicsWindow.ShowMessage("Invalid format for date - must be Month/Day/Year", "Invalid Date")
   DateIsValid = "false"
   Goto ExitValidateDate
EndIf
Day = Text.GetSubText(DV, 1, SL - 1)
'find  year
Year = Text.GetSubTextToEnd(DV, SL + 1)
'maximum days in month (check for leap year if february)
If (Month = 2 And Math.Remainder(Year, 4) = 0) Then
   MaxDays = 29
Else
   MaxDays = MonthDays[Month]
EndIf
If (Month < 1 Or Month > 12) Then
   GraphicsWindow.ShowMessage("Month number must be 1 to 12", "Invalid Month")
   DateIsValid = "false"
 ElseIf (Day < 1 Or Day > MaxDays) Then
   GraphicsWindow.ShowMessage("Day number must be 1 to " + MaxDays, "Invalid Day")
   DateIsValid = "false"
 ElseIf (Year < 1901) Then
```

```
    GraphicsWindow.ShowMessage("Year must be greater than 1900",
"Invalid Year")
      DateIsValid = "false"
  EndIf
  ExitValidateDate:
EndSub
```

Saved as **Example 16-1** in **Guide to Small Basic\Programs\Chapter 16** folder.

The **InitializeProgram** subroutine sets up a text box for entry and a button to validate the entered date. The date validation is in the subroutine **ValidateDate**. You provide the subroutine with **DateToValidate**. It goes through the listed validation steps. If any part of the date is invalid, a message box is displayed, telling the user the problem. The **DateIsValid** flag is "**false**" for invalid dates, "**true**" for valid dates. A user looks at this flag to see if the entered date is valid. If it is valid, you can use the determined values of **Month**, **Day** and **Year**.

We have added one more step to the validation process. We make sure the year is greater than 1900. Why? It has to do with leap years. We check for leap years to see how many days February can have. Our code says a leap year is a year that is evenly divisible by four. This is true except for most "century" years, those divisible by 100. Even though a century year is divisible by four, it is only a leap year if it is also divisible by 400. So 1900 is not a leap year, 2000 is. As written, our code would think 1900 (and 1700 and 1800) is a leap year, which is not true. You can modify the code to check for these odd leap year cases if you like. As written, the **ValidateDate** subroutine works for any year from 1901 to 2099 (before the next century year that is not a leap year).

Save and **Run** the program. You see:

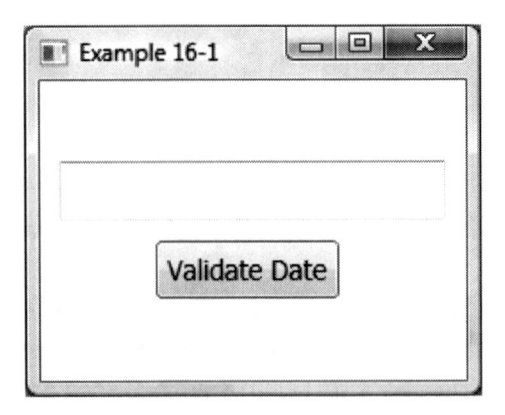

Type a date in the text box and click **Validate Date**. I tried my birthday:

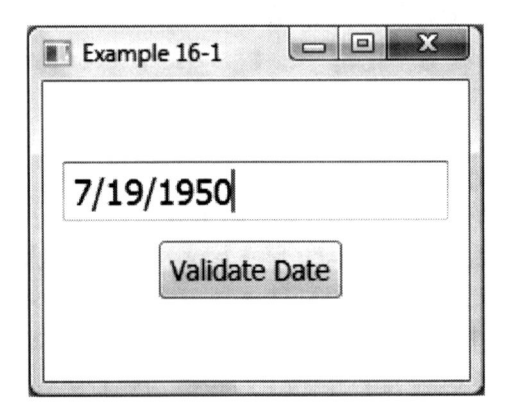

This is valid, so I get this message box:

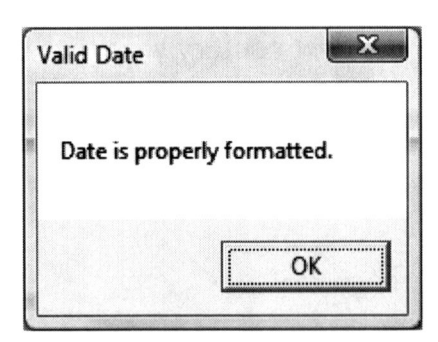

Input Validation 16-9

Try an invalid date. Here's what I see when I try to enter 2/29/1959 (a non-leap year):

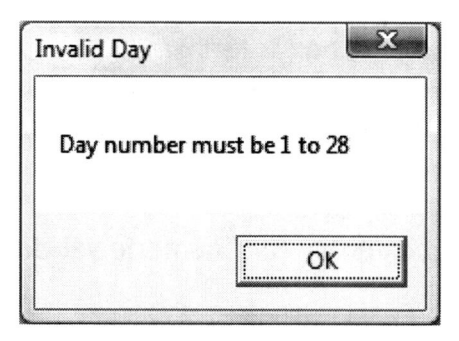

Invalid Day

Day number must be 1 to 28

[OK]

Or, 113/2010 (missing a slash):

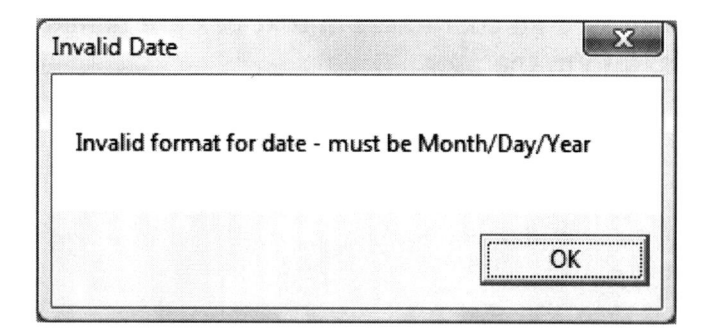

Invalid Date

Invalid format for date - must be Month/Day/Year

[OK]

The **ValidateDate** subroutine can be used anywhere you need validation of input dates. Recall, if it returns **DateIsValid** as "**true**", it also has valid values for **Month**, **Day** and **Year**.

Numeric Validation

Another common task is to input a number in a text box to be used for some further calculations. If the text box is left empty or contains non-numeric characters, error could be introduced in the calculations. Like the **ValidateDate** subroutine in **Example 16-1**, we can build a **ValidateNumber** subroutine to check for valid numeric entries.

The steps to check a text box entry for "numeric validity" are:

- Check to see if entry is blank. If so, inform user.
- If not blank, check for only one decimal point. If multiple decimals, inform the user.
- Check to make sure all characters in text box are numeric (numerals). If not numeric, inform the user.
- If none of above errors found, entry is valid numeric entry.

Example 16-2. Numeric Validation

Write a program with a single text box and single button. Type something in the text box. Click the button to see if the text box contents are "numerically valid".

Small Basic Code:

```
'Guide to Small Basic, Example 16-2
InitializeProgram()

Sub InitializeProgram
  GraphicsWindow.Show()
  GraphicsWindow.Title = "Example 16-2"
  GraphicsWindow.Width = 220
  GraphicsWindow.Height = 150
  'text box
  GraphicsWindow.BrushColor = "Black"
  GraphicsWindow.FontSize = 18
  GraphicsWindow.FontBold = "false"
  NumberTextBox = Controls.AddTextBox(10, 40)
  Controls.SetSize(NumberTextBox, 200, 30)
  'button
  GraphicsWindow.FontSize = 14
  ValidateButton = Controls.AddButton("Validate Number", 60, 80)
  Controls.ButtonClicked = ButtonClickedSub
EndSub

Sub ButtonClickedSub
  NumberToValidate = Controls.GetTextBoxText(NumberTextBox)
  ValidateNumber()
  If (NumberIsValid) Then
    GraphicsWindow.ShowMessage("Entry is properly formatted.", "Valid Number")
  EndIf
EndSub

Sub ValidateNumber
  'sees if NumberToValidate has only digits and a single decimal and is not blank
  NumberIsValid = "true"
  If (NumberToValidate = "") Then
    GraphicsWindow.ShowMessage("Entry is blank", "Invalid Number")
    NumberIsValid = "false"
    Goto ExitValidateNumber
```

```
    EndIf
    DecimalCount = 0
    For I = 1 To Text.GetLength(NumberToValidate)
      CC = Text.GetCharacterCode(Text.GetSubText(NumberToValidate, I, 1))
      If (CC = Text.GetCharacterCode(".")) Then
        DecimalCount = DecimalCount + 1
        If (DecimalCount > 1) Then
          GraphicsWindow.ShowMessage("Multiple decimal points", "Invalid Number")
          NumberIsValid = "false"
          Goto ExitValidateNumber
        EndIf
      ElseIf (CC < Text.GetCharacterCode("0") Or CC > Text.GetCharacterCode("9")) Then
        GraphicsWindow.ShowMessage("Only 0 through 9 allowed", "Invalid Number")
        NumberIsValid = "false"
        Goto ExitValidateNumber
      EndIf
    EndFor
ExitValidateNumber:
EndSub
```

Saved as **Example 16-2** in **Guide to Small Basic\Programs\Chapter 16** folder.

The **InitializeProgram** subroutine sets up a text box for entry and a button to validate the entered number. The numeric validation is in the subroutine **ValidateNumber**. You provide the subroutine with **NumberToValidate**. It goes through the listed validation steps. If any part of the number is invalid, a message box is displayed, telling the user the problem. The **NumberIsValid** flag is **"false"** for invalid numbers, **"true"** for valid numbers. A user looks at this flag to see if the entered number is valid.

Save and **Run** the program. You see:

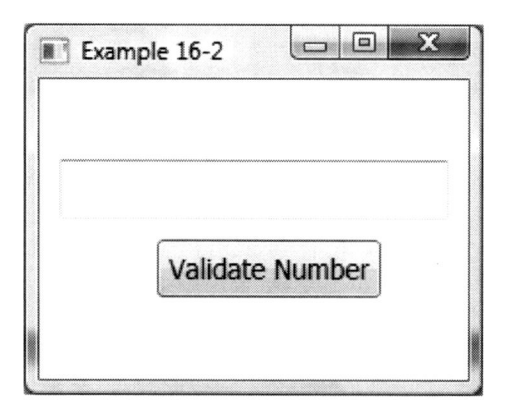

Click **Validate Number** with no entry. You should see:

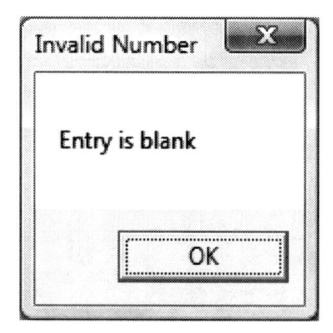

Type in numbers with two decimals, non-numeric entries to make sure the validation works.

Try a valid number like this:

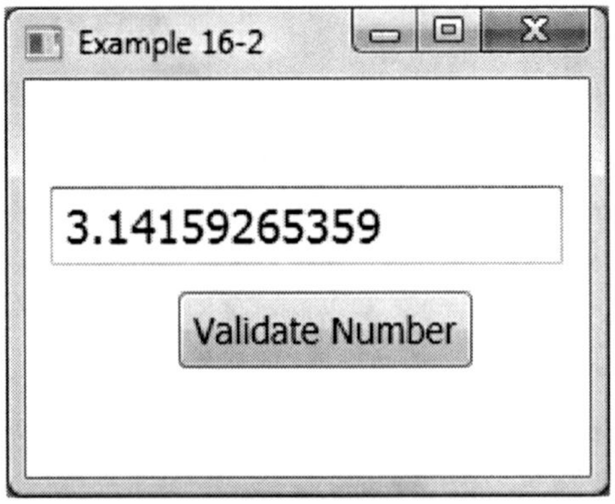
Example 16-2
3.14159265359
Validate Number

Click **Validate Number** and you see:

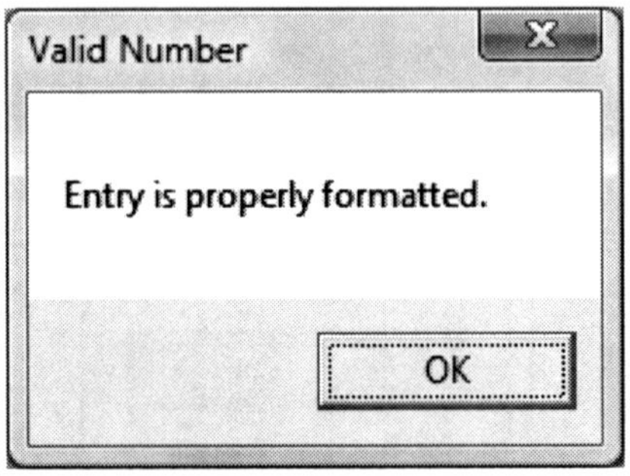
Valid Number
Entry is properly formatted.
OK

The **ValidateNumber** subroutine can be used anywhere you need numeric validation of text box entries.

Chapter Review

After completing this chapter, you should understand:

- The idea of input validation.
- How to validate dates entered in a text box control.
- How to validate numbers entered in a text box control.

This page intentionally not left blank.

17. Date Arithmetic

Preview

A common practice in computer programming is to have the ability to subtract two dates. In this chapter, we develop Small Basic code to accomplish this task.

Subtracting Dates

There are occasions in programming where you need to know the difference between two dates. You may need to know how many days elapsed since a product was ordered. You might want to know how many days someone has been alive. You may need to compute a daily average of some quantity.

Many computer programming languages have the ability to do date mathematics, such as subtracting two dates. Small Basic does not have such an ability, but we can do it anyway. Assume with have two dates, **Date1** and **Date2**, in the form:

Month/Day/Year

Here are the steps to find the number of days between **Date1** and **Date2**:

- Make sure **Date1** and **Date2** are valid dates (use the **ValidateDate** subroutine from the previous chapter). Extract the **Month**, **Day** and **Year** from each date.
- Define a reference date that represents 'day one'. In this program, we use January 1, 1901. This is the same 'reference' used in **ValidateDate**. We discussed ways to adjust this in the previous chapter.
- For **Date1**, determine how many days have elapsed since day one. Define that to be **ElapsedDays1**.
- For **Date2**, determine how many days have elapsed since day one. Subtract that number (**ElapsedDays2**) from **ElapsedDays1** and assign the result to **NumberDays.**

Notice **NumberDays** will be positive if **Date1** is after **Date2**, otherwise it will be negative.

So, the question is, given a particular date (**Month**, **Day**, **Year**, results available following a call to **ValidateDate**), how many days have elapsed (**ElapsedDays**) since day one? This subroutine, **ComputeElapsedDays**, does just that:

```
Sub ComputeElapsedDays
  'number of days in each month
  MonthDays[1] = 31
  MonthDays[2] = 28
  MonthDays[3] = 31
  MonthDays[4] = 30
  MonthDays[5] = 31
  MonthDays[6] = 30
  MonthDays[7] = 31
  MonthDays[8] = 31
  MonthDays[9] = 30
  MonthDays[10] = 31
  MonthDays[11] = 30
  MonthDays[12] = 31
  'January 1, 1901 is Day 1
  BaseYear = 1901
  ElapsedDays = 0
  'Difference in years
  DeltaY = Year - BaseYear
  If (DeltaY > 0) Then
    'move to January 1 of current year
    For J = BaseYear To Year - 1
      'leap year?
      If (Math.Remainder(J, 4) = 0) Then
        ElapsedDays = ElapsedDays + 366
      Else
        ElapsedDays = ElapsedDays + 365
      EndIf
    EndFor
  EndIf
  'Difference in months
  DeltaM = Month - 1
  If (DeltaM > 0) Then
    'move to current month
    For J = 1 To Month - 1
      'if february, leap year?
      If (J = 2) Then
        If (Math.Remainder(YY, 4) = 0) Then
          ElapsedDays = ElapsedDays + 29
        Else
          ElapsedDays = ElapsedDays + 28
```

```
            EndIf
        Else
            ElapsedDays = ElapsedDays + MonthDays[J]
        EndIf
    EndFor
  EndIf
  'difference in days
  ElapsedDays = ElapsedDays + Days - 1
EndSub
```

The steps are straightforward. We first set up an array (**MonthDays**) with the number of days in each month. Yes, this is the same array we have in the **ValidateDate** subroutine in the previous chapter. But, we need to keep this repeated code here in case **ComputeElapsedDays** is used without **ValidateDate**.

ElapsedDays is initialized to zero. We check to see how many years have elapsed (**DeltaY**). For each elapsed year, we add 365 days for a normal year and 366 days for a leap year (years evenly divisible by 4). We then check to see how many months have elapsed (**DeltaM**). For each elapsed month, we add the appropriate number of days. Note special consideration for February in leap years. Lastly, we add in the number of days that have elapsed since the first of the month (**DD - 1**). The resulting total is **ElapsedDays**. Like **ValidateDate**, this routine will work for any year between 1901 and 2099.

Date Arithmetic   17-5

Example 17-1. Subtracting Dates

Write a program with a two text boxes, a **Shapes** object displaying text and a single button control. Enter a date in each text box. Click the button and display the difference (in days) between the two dates in the **Shapes** object.

Small Basic Code:

```
'Guide to Small Basic, Example 17-1
InitializeProgram()

Sub InitializeProgram
  GraphicsWindow.Show()
  GraphicsWindow.Title = "Example 17-1"
  GraphicsWindow.Width = 220
  GraphicsWindow.Height = 170
  'text boxes
  GraphicsWindow.BrushColor = "Black"
  GraphicsWindow.FontSize = 18
  GraphicsWindow.FontBold = "false"
  Date1TextBox = Controls.AddTextBox(10, 10)
  Controls.SetSize(Date1TextBox, 200, 30)
  Date2TextBox = Controls.AddTextBox(10, 50)
  Controls.SetSize(Date2TextBox, 200, 30)
  'shapes object
  GraphicsWindow.BrushColor = "Yellow"
  GraphicsWindow.FillRectangle(10, 130, 200, 30)
  GraphicsWindow.BrushColor = "Blue"
  DaysDisplay = Shapes.AddText("0 Days")
  Shapes.Move(DaysDisplay, 70, 135)
  'button
  GraphicsWindow.BrushColor = "Black"
  GraphicsWindow.FontSize = 14
  ValidateButton = Controls.AddButton("Compute Difference", 40, 90)
  Controls.ButtonClicked = ButtonClickedSub
EndSub

Sub ButtonClickedSub
  'do Date1 then Date2
  DateToValidate = Controls.GetTextBoxText(Date1TextBox)
  ValidateDate()
  If (DateIsValid) Then
    'compute elapsed days
    ComputeElapsedDays()
```

```
    ElapsedDays1 = ElapsedDays
  EndIf
  DateToValidate = Controls.GetTextBoxText(Date2TextBox)
  ValidateDate()
  If (DateIsValid) Then
    'compute elapsed days
    ComputeElapsedDays()
    ElapsedDays2 = ElapsedDays
  EndIf
  Shapes.SetText(DaysDisplay, (ElapsedDays1 - ElapsedDays2) + "
Days")
EndSub

Sub ValidateDate
  'days in each month
  MonthDays[1] = 31
  MonthDays[2] = 28
  MonthDays[3] = 31
  MonthDays[4] = 30
  MonthDays[5] = 31
  MonthDays[6] = 30
  MonthDays[7] = 31
  MonthDays[8] = 31
  MonthDays[9] = 30
  MonthDays[10] = 31
  MonthDays[11] = 30
  MonthDays[12] = 31
  'store DateToValidate in temporary string
  DV = DateToValidate
  DateIsValid = "true"
  'find first slash and  month
  SL = Text.GetIndexOf(DV, "/")
  If (SL = 0) Then
    GraphicsWindow.ShowMessage("Invalid format for date - must be
Month/Day/Year", "Invalid Date")
    DateIsValid = "false"
    Goto ExitValidateDate
  EndIf
  Month = Text.GetSubText(DV, 1, SL - 1)
  'find next slash and  day
  DV = Text.GetSubTextToEnd(DV, SL + 1)
  SL = Text.GetIndexOf(DV, "/")
  If (SL = 0) Then
    GraphicsWindow.ShowMessage("Invalid format for date - must be
Month/Day/Year", "Invalid Date")
    DateIsValid = "false"
```

Date Arithmetic

```
      Goto ExitValidateDate
    EndIf
    Day = Text.GetSubText(DV, 1, SL - 1)
    'find year
    Year = Text.GetSubTextToEnd(DV, SL + 1)
    'maximum days in month (check for leap year if february)
    If (Month = 2 And Math.Remainder(Year, 4) = 0) Then
      MaxDays = 29
    Else
      MaxDays = MonthDays[Month]
    EndIf
    If (Month < 1 Or Month > 12) Then
      GraphicsWindow.ShowMessage("Month number must be 1 to 12",
"Invalid Month")
      DateIsValid = "false"
    ElseIf (Day < 1 Or Day > MaxDays) Then
      GraphicsWindow.ShowMessage("Day number must be 1 to " +
MaxDays, "Invalid Day")
      DateIsValid = "false"
    ElseIf (Year < 1901) Then
      GraphicsWindow.ShowMessage("Year must be greater than 1900",
"Invalid Year")
      DateIsValid = "false"
    EndIf
    ExitValidateDate:
EndSub

Sub ComputeElapsedDays
    'number of days in each month
    MonthDays[1] = 31
    MonthDays[2] = 28
    MonthDays[3] = 31
    MonthDays[4] = 30
    MonthDays[5] = 31
    MonthDays[6] = 30
    MonthDays[7] = 31
    MonthDays[8] = 31
    MonthDays[9] = 30
    MonthDays[10] = 31
    MonthDays[11] = 30
    MonthDays[12] = 31
    'January 1, 1901 is Day 1
    BaseYear = 1901
    ElapsedDays = 0
    'Difference in years
    DeltaY = Year - BaseYear
```

```
  If (DeltaY > 0) Then
    'move to January 1 of current year
    For J = BaseYear To Year - 1
      'leap year?
      If (Math.Remainder(J, 4) = 0) Then
        ElapsedDays = ElapsedDays + 366
      Else
        ElapsedDays = ElapsedDays + 365
      EndIf
    EndFor
  EndIf
  'Difference in months
  DeltaM = Month - 1
  If (DeltaM > 0) Then
    'move to current month
    For J = 1 To Month - 1
      'if february, leap year?
      If (J = 2) Then
        If (Math.Remainder(Year, 4) = 0) Then
          ElapsedDays = ElapsedDays + 29
        Else
          ElapsedDays = ElapsedDays + 28
        EndIf
      Else
        ElapsedDays = ElapsedDays + MonthDays[J]
      EndIf
    EndFor
  EndIf
  'difference in days
  ElapsedDays = ElapsedDays + Day - 1
EndSub
```

Saved as **Example 17-1** in **Guide to Small Basic\Programs\Chapter 17** folder.

Most of this code is the **ValidateDate** (from the previoius chapter) and **ComputeElapsedDays** subroutines. In **ButtonClickedSub**, each date is read from the text boxes and validated. Then, **ElapsedDays** is computed for each date and the difference displayed in **DaysDisplay**.

Save and **Run** the program. You see:

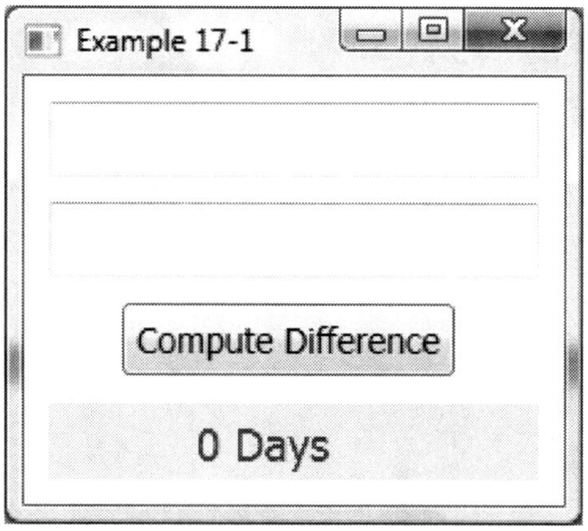
Example 17-1
Compute Difference
0 Days

Enter two dates (after 1901) and click **Compute Difference.** Here's what I see when I enter today's date and my birthday:

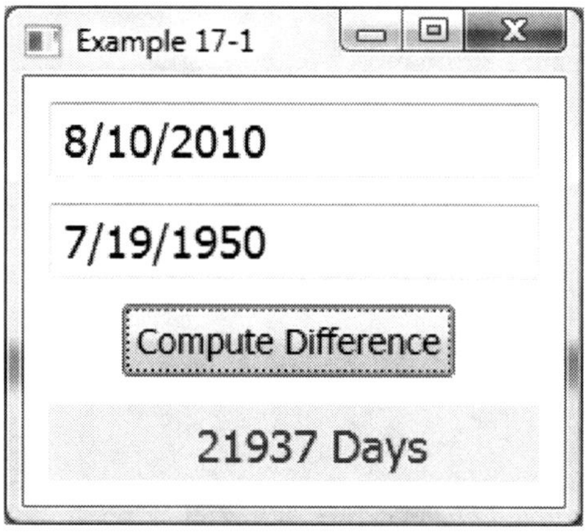
Example 17-1
8/10/2010
7/19/1950
Compute Difference
21937 Days

Chapter Review

After completing this chapter, you should understand:

- The idea of input validation.
- How to validate dates entered in a text box control.
- How to validate numbers entered in a text box control.

18. Shuffling Integers

Preview

In this chapter, we develop a general subroutine for shuffling (randomizing) N integers. We use this routine to shuffle and display a deck of common playing cards. We build a simple poker game.

Shuffling Integers

In many games, we have the need to randomly sort a sequence of integers. For example, to shuffle a deck of cards, we sort the integers from 1 to 52. To randomly sort the state names in a states/capitals game, we would randomize the values from 1 to 50. To randomly sort 4 multiple choice answers, we would randomize the numbers 1, 2, 3, 4. Because of its close connection with a deck of cards, we call this a shuffling routine.

Usually when we need a computer version of something we can do without a computer, it is fairly easy to write down the steps taken and duplicate them in code. When we shuffle a deck of cards, we separate the deck in two parts, then interleaf the cards as we fan each part, making that familiar shuffling noise. I don't know how you could write code to do this. We'll take another approach which is hard or tedious to do off the computer, but is easy to do on a computer.

We perform what is called a "one card shuffle." Say you have a deck of N cards (normally 52). In a one card shuffle, you pull a single card (at random) out of the deck and lay it aside on a pile. Repeat this N times and the cards are shuffled. Try it! I think you see this idea is simple, but doing a one card shuffle with a real deck of cards would be awfully time-consuming. We'll use the idea of a one card shuffle here, with a slight twist. Rather than lay the selected card on a pile, we will swap it with the bottom card in the stack of cards remaining to be shuffled. This takes the selected card out of the deck and replaces it with the remaining bottom card. The result is the same as if we lay it aside.

Here's how the shuffle works with N numbers:

- Start with a list of N consecutive integers.
- Randomly pick one item from the list. Swap that item with the last item. You now have one fewer items in the list to be sorted (called the remaining list), or N is now N - 1.
- Randomly pick one item from the remaining list. Swap it with the item on the bottom of the remaining list. Again, your remaining list now has one fewer items.
- Repeatedly remove one item from the remaining list and swap it with the item on the bottom of the remaining list until you have run out of items. When done, the list will have been replaced with the original list in random order.

The code to do a one card shuffle, or sort **NumberIntegers** integers, is placed in a subroutine named **ShuffleIntegers**. The code computes an array (**ShuffledArray**) containing the randomly sorted integers. The code is:

```
Sub ShuffleIntegers
  'Randomly shuffles NumberIntegers integers and puts results in SortedArray
  'Order all elements initially
  For I = 1 To NumberIntegers
    ShuffledArray[I] = I
  EndFor
  'J is the number of integers remaining
  For J = NumberIntegers To 2 Step -1
    I = Math.GetRandomNumber(J)
    Temp = ShuffledArray[J]
    ShuffledArray[J] = ShuffledArray[I]
    ShuffledArray[I] = Temp
  EndFor
EndSub
```

You should be able to see each step of the shuffle procedure.

This subroutine is general (shuffling **NumberIntegers** integers) and can be used in other projects requiring random lists of integers. We'll use it in Example 8-2 to play Video Poker. I've used it to randomize the letters of the alphabet, scramble words in spelling games, randomize answers in multiple choice tests, and even playback compact disc songs in random order (yes, you can build a CD player with Small Basic).

18-4   The Developer's Reference Guide to Small Basic

Example 18-1. Random Integers

Write a program with a button and a multi-line text box. When the button is clicked, display 25 random integers in the text box.

Small Basic Code:

```
'Guide to Small Basic, Example 18-1
InitializeProgram()

Sub InitializeProgram
  GraphicsWindow.Show()
  GraphicsWindow.Title = "Example 18-1"
  GraphicsWindow.Width = 200
  GraphicsWindow.Height = 300
  'text box
  GraphicsWindow.BrushColor = "Black"
  GraphicsWindow.FontSize = 14
  GraphicsWindow.FontBold = "false"
  NumberTextBox = Controls.AddMultiLineTextBox(10, 10)
  Controls.SetSize(NumberTextBox, 180, 240)
  'button
  NextButton = Controls.AddButton("Randomize", 60, 260)
  Controls.ButtonClicked = ButtonClickedSub
EndSub

Sub ButtonClickedSub
  NumberIntegers = 25
  ShuffleIntegers()
  ShuffledList = ""
  For I = 1 To NumberIntegers
    ShuffledList = Text.Append(ShuffledList, ShuffledArray[I] + Text.GetCharacter(13))
  EndFor
  Controls.SetTextBoxText(NumberTextBox, ShuffledList)
EndSub

Sub ShuffleIntegers
  'Randomly shuffles NumberIntegers integers and puts results in SortedArray
  'Order all elements initially
  For I = 1 To NumberIntegers
    ShuffledArray[I] = I
  EndFor
  'J is the number of integers remaining
```

```
  For J = NumberIntegers To 2 Step -1
    I = Math.GetRandomNumber(J)
    Temp = ShuffledArray[J]
    ShuffledArray[J] = ShuffledArray[I]
    ShuffledArray[I] = Temp
  EndFor
EndSub
```

Saved as **Example 18-1** in **Guide to Small Basic\Programs\Chapter 18** folder.

When the button is clicked, the **ShuffleIntegers** routine is called (using **NumberIntegers = 25**). The elements of the resulting **ShuffledArray** are displayed on individual lines in the text box control (**NumberTextBox**).

Save and **Run** the program. Click **Randomize**. You see (yours will be different since the numbers are random):

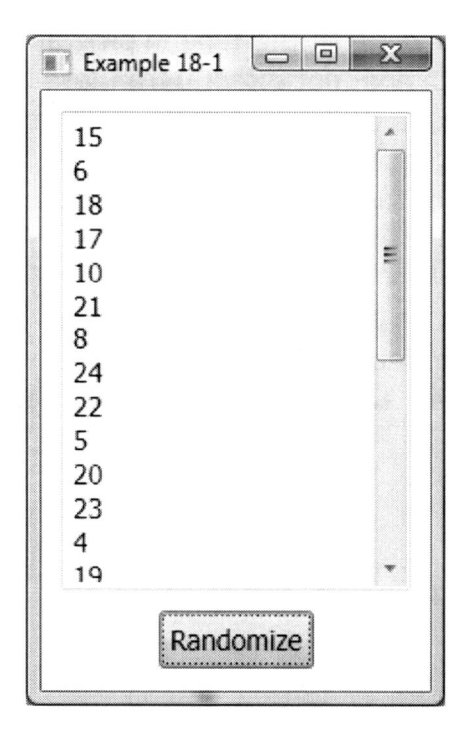

Scroll through the list to see all the values. Click **Randomize** again and you get a different list. You will get different results with each click of the button.

Displaying Playing Cards

As mentioned, a common use for a shuffling routine is to shuffle a deck of cards. In this case, we use the **ShuffleIntegers** routine with **NumberIntegers = 52**. Once we have shuffled a deck of cards, we would also like to use the resulting array of integers (**ShuffledArray**) to define and display the cards. With the ability to display cards, there are many card games you can program: Blackjack, Crazy Eights, War, Gin, Poker.

Defining a card consists of answering two questions: what is the card suit and what is the card value? The four suits are Hearts, Diamonds, Clubs, and Spades. The thirteen card values are: Ace (A), 2, 3, 4, 5, 6, 7, 8, 9, 10, Jack (J), Queen (Q), King (K). As noted, we will use integers from 1 to 52 to represent the cards. How do we translate that card number to a card suit and value? (Notice the distinction between card **number** and card **value** - card number ranges from 1 to 52, card value can only range from Ace to King.) We need to develop some type of translation rule. This is done all the time in programming. If the number you compute with or work with does not directly translate to information you need, you need to make up rules to do the translation. For example, the numbers 1 to 12 are used to represent the months of the year. But, these numbers tell us nothing about the names of the month - we need a rule to translate each number to a month name.

We know we need 13 of each card suit. Hence, an easy rule to decide suit is: cards numbered 1 - 13 are Hearts, cards numbered 14 - 26 are Diamonds, cards numbered 27 - 39 are Clubs, and cards numbered 40 - 52 are Spades.

For card values, lower numbers should represent lower cards. A rule that does this for each number in each card suit is:

Card Numbers

Hearts	Diamonds	Clubs	Spades	Card Value
1	14	27	40	A
2	15	28	41	2
3	16	29	42	3
4	17	30	43	4
5	18	31	44	5
6	19	32	45	6
7	20	33	46	7
8	21	34	47	8
9	22	35	48	9
10	23	36	49	10
11	24	37	50	J
12	25	38	51	Q
13	26	39	52	K

As examples, notice card number 12 is a Queen of Hearts. Card number 31 is a 5 of Clubs. These card numbers will be used to establish an image file associated with the card.

We will use 52 different image files to display cards. As mentioned, a card number is used to establish the image file that represents the corresponding card. In the **Guide to Small Basic\Programs\CardGraphics** folder are 52 graphics files (**gif** files) that represent the 52 playing cards (these images were found on the Internet). The files are named **card01.gif** to **card52.gif**. And, yes, the file numbers (the last two digits in the name) correspond to the card numbers we've assigned. So **card12.gif** is a Queen of Hearts and **card31.gif** is a 5 of Clubs. Open the files in a graphics program if you like. So, once we know a card number, we know which file is used to display that card.

Two approaches can be taken to display cards in a program. The first is that whenever a card must be displayed, we could load the appropriate file into an image using the **ImageList.LoadImage** method. Then, it could be displayed in the graphics window. In this approach, every time a card is needed, the program would have to find the file and load it from disk. This approach would require multiple accesses to disk files, slowing down the program.

The second approach (and the one we use) is to preload all image files (still using **ImageList.LoadImage** method) into an array of images. Then, when a card must be displayed, we can draw the image using the appropriate array element. This is a much faster approach and only requires opening the image files one time. The preloading of images is done when we initialize the program window. As always, we assume the image files are in your program folder (**Program.Directory**).

Example 18-2. Displaying Playing Cards

Write a program with a single button. With each click of the button, cycle through a deck of unshuffled playing cards. Remember to copy the card images from **Guide to Small Basic\Programs\Card Graphics** to your program folder.

Small Basic Code:

```
'Guide to Small Basic, Example 18-2
InitializeProgram()

Sub InitializeProgram
  GraphicsWindow.Show()
  GraphicsWindow.Title = "Example 18-2"
  GraphicsWindow.Width = 200
  GraphicsWindow.Height = 300
  GraphicsWindow.BackgroundColor = "Blue"
  'button
  NextButton = Controls.AddButton("Randomize", 60, 260)
  Controls.ButtonClicked = ButtonClickedSub
  'preload images
  For CardNumber = 1 To 52
    ImageFile = Program.Directory + "\card"
    If (CardNumber < 10) Then
      ImageFile = ImageFile + Text.Append("0", CardNumber) +".gif"
    Else
      ImageFile = ImageFile + CardNumber +".gif"
    EndIf
    CardImage[CardNumber] = ImageList.LoadImage(ImageFile)
  EndFor
  CardNumber = 0
EndSub

Sub ButtonClickedSub
  CardNumber = CardNumber + 1
  If (CardNumber > 52) Then
    CardNumber = 1
  EndIf
  'display cardnumber
  GraphicsWindow.DrawResizedImage(CardImage[CardNumber], 10, 10, 180, 240)
EndSub
```

18-10 The Developer's Reference Guide to Small Basic

Saved as **Example 18-2** in **Guide to Small Basic\Programs\Chapter 18** folder. The card images are loaded in the **CardImage** array. Notice the code to form the corresponding file name. With each click of the button, a new card is displayed.

Save and **Run** the program. Click **Next Card**. You will see the Ace of Hearts (**CardNumber = 1**):

Keep clicking to see all the cards. When you reach the end of the deck (**CardNumber = 52**), the deck starts over.

Example 18-3. Video Poker

In the game, you are given five cards from a shuffled deck of cards. You decide which cards you want to discard in hopes of improving your hand. The game gives you the requested cards. This final hand decides your winnings. This example is intended to be a fun card game. If you or a family member feels you have a problem with gambling, we recommend you contact http://www.gamblersanonymous.org/.

Build a program that simulates the dealing of the initial hand, the discarding of cards and the receipt of additional cards. The logic to decide winnings is very difficult to program so we won't ask you to do that. We do discuss the logic at the end of this example.

Small Basic Code:

```
'Guide to Small Basic, Example 18-3
InitializeProgram()

Sub InitializeProgram
  GraphicsWindow.Show()
  GraphicsWindow.Width = 490
  GraphicsWindow.Height = 220
  GraphicsWindow.BackgroundColor = GraphicsWindow.GetColorFromRGB(192, 192, 255)
  GraphicsWindow.Title = "Example 18-3"
  'buttons
  GraphicsWindow.BrushColor = "Black"
  GraphicsWindow.FontSize = 16
  GraphicsWindow.FontBold = "false"
  DealButton = Controls.AddButton("Deal Cards", 10, 170)
  AddCardsButton = Controls.AddButton("Add Cards", 10, 170)
  Controls.HideControl(AddCardsButton)
  'load card images
  For CardNumber = 1 To 52
    ImageFile = Program.Directory + "\card"
    If (CardNumber < 10) Then
      ImageFile = ImageFile + Text.Append("0", CardNumber) +".gif"
    Else
      ImageFile = ImageFile + CardNumber +".gif"
    EndIf
    CardImage[CardNumber] = ImageList.LoadImage(ImageFile)
  EndFor
  'Shuffle cards
```

```smallbasic
  NumberIntegers = 52
  ShuffleIntegers()
  CardIndex = 1
  CanDiscard = "false"
  Controls.ButtonClicked = ButtonClickedSub
  GraphicsWindow.MouseDown = MouseDownSub
EndSub

Sub ShuffleIntegers
  'Randomly shuffles NumberIntegers integers and puts results in SortedArray
  'Order all elements initially
  For I = 1 To NumberIntegers
    ShuffledArray[I] = I
  EndFor
  'J is the number of integers remaining
  For J = NumberIntegers To 2 Step -1
    I = Math.GetRandomNumber(J)
    Temp = ShuffledArray[J]
    ShuffledArray[J] = ShuffledArray[I]
    ShuffledArray[I] = Temp
  EndFor
EndSub

Sub ButtonClickedSub
  B = Controls.LastClickedButton
  If (B = DealButton) Then
    DealButtonClicked()
  ElseIf (B = AddCardsButton) Then
    AddCardsButtonClicked()
  EndIf
EndSub

Sub DealButtonClicked
  'reshuffle?
  If (CardIndex > 40) Then
    ShuffleIntegers()
    CardIndex = 1
  EndIf
  'draw next five cards
  For I = 1 To 5
GraphicsWindow.DrawResizedImage(CardImage[ShuffledArray[CardIndex]], 10 + (I - 1) * 95, 40, 90, 120)
    CardIndex = CardIndex + 1
    Discard[I] = 0
```

```
    EndFor
    Controls.HideControl(DealButton)
    Controls.ShowControl(AddCardsButton)
    GraphicsWindow.BrushColor = "Black"
    GraphicsWindow.FontSize = 18
    GraphicsWindow.FontBold = "false"
    GraphicsWindow.DrawText(10, 10, "Click on Cards to Discard - Then Click Add Cards")
    CanDiscard = "true"
EndSub

Sub MouseDownSub
  'get discards
  X = GraphicsWindow.MouseX
  Y = GraphicsWindow.MouseY
  GraphicsWindow.BrushColor = GraphicsWindow.BackgroundColor
  If (CanDiscard And (Y > 40 And Y < 160)) Then
    For I = 1 To 5
      If (X > 10 + (I - 1) * 95 And X < 100 + (I - 1) * 95) Then
        Discard[I] = 1
        GraphicsWindow.FillRectangle(10 + (I - 1) * 95, 40, 90, 120)
      EndIf
    EndFor
  EndIf
EndSub

Sub AddCardsButtonClicked
  'clear message
  GraphicsWindow.BrushColor = GraphicsWindow.BackgroundColor
  GraphicsWindow.FillRectangle(10, 10, 400, 20)
  Controls.ShowControl(DealButton)
  Controls.HideControl(AddCardsButton)
  'add card?
  For I = 1 To 5
    If (Discard[I] <> 0) Then
      GraphicsWindow.DrawResizedImage(CardImage[ShuffledArray[CardIndex]], 10 + (I - 1) * 95, 40, 90, 120)
      CardIndex = CardIndex + 1
    EndIf
  EndFor
  CanDiscard = "false"
EndSub
```

Saved as **Example 18-3** in **Guide to Small Basic\Programs\Chapter 18** folder. This is a pretty long program. Let's explain what each subroutine does.

InitializeProgram – sets up the interface, loads the card images, shuffles the cards and initializes variables.
ShuffleIntegers – shuffles the cards.
ButtonClickedSub – determines which subroutine to call (**DealButtonClicked** or **AddCardsButtonClicked**) based on clicked button.
DealButtonClicked – checks for reshuffle, displays next five cards in deck, swaps buttons and display discard message to user.
MouseDownSub – determines which of the five cards is clicked and 'discards' that card.
AddCardsButtonClicked – adds cards in spaces left open by discarded cards, swaps button controls to be ready for next deal.

Save and **Run** the program. Click **Deal Cards**. You will see five cards. Here's my screen:

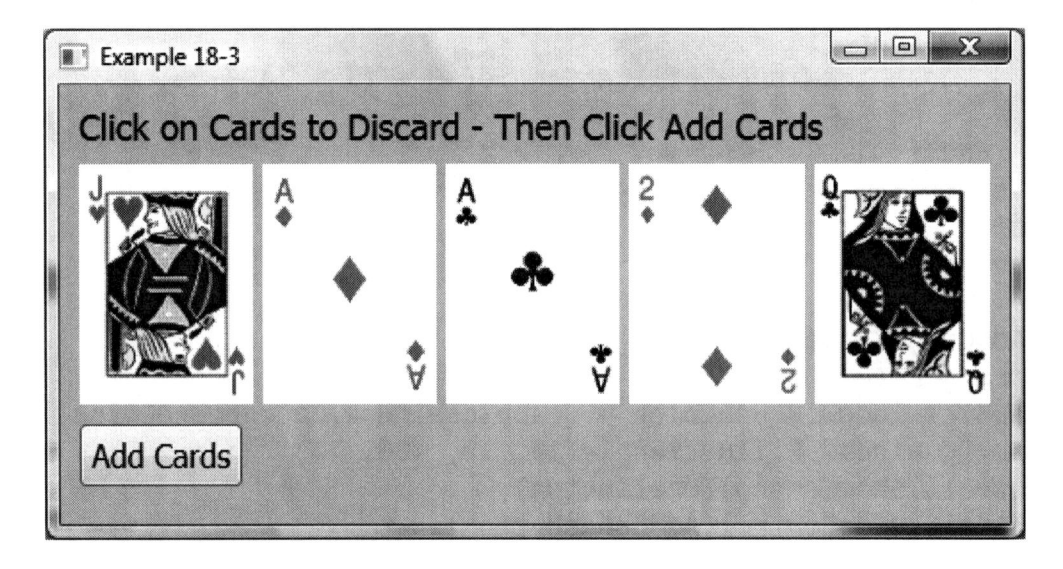

At this point, you decide which cards to discard. I will keep my pair of aces, so I click on the other three cards.

After discarding, my screen is:

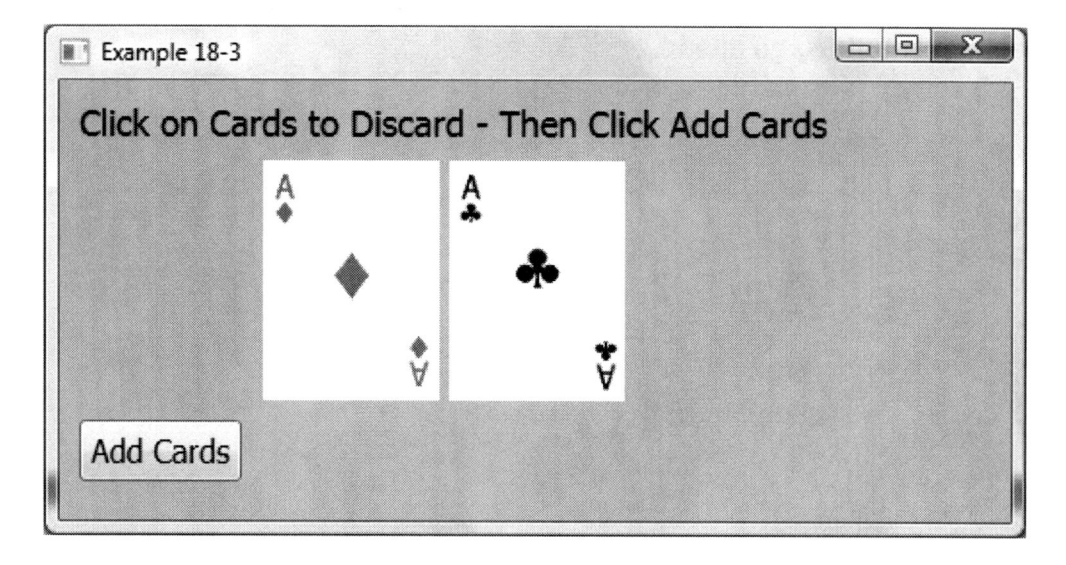

I click **Add Cards** to see the newly added cards:

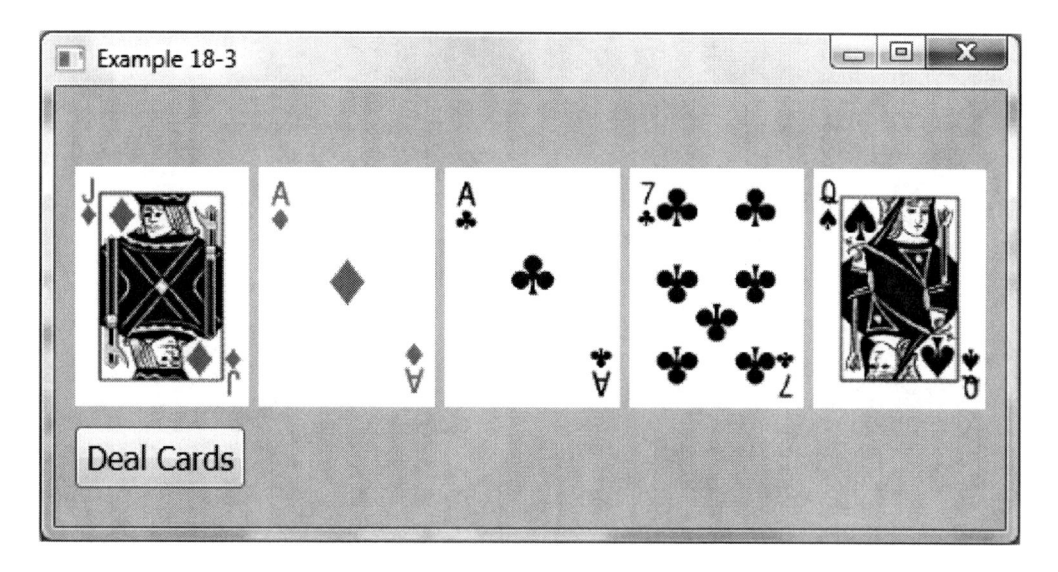

I didn't get much help – I still just have a pair of Aces.

After getting new cards following the discard, you can determine your winnings. The logic to detect different hands is fairly complex and we won't do it here. If you feel adventurous, go ahead.

Chapter Review

After completing this chapter, you should understand:

- How to shuffle a list of integers.
- How to display a playing card given an index from 1 to 52.
- How to program a fairly complex card game.

This page intentionally not left blank.

19. Line, Bar and Pie Charts

Preview

In this chapter, we develop subroutines you can use in Small Basic programs for data display. Subroutines for line, bar and pie charts are provided.

Line Charts and Bar Charts

Two useful data display tools are **line charts** and **bar charts**. Line charts are used to plot Cartesian pairs of data (x, y) generated using some function, supplied in code or read from a sequential file. They are useful for seeing trends in data. As an example, you could plot your weight while following a diet and exercise regime. And, here is a line chart of yearly attendance at the Seattle Mariners baseball games from 1991 to 2000:

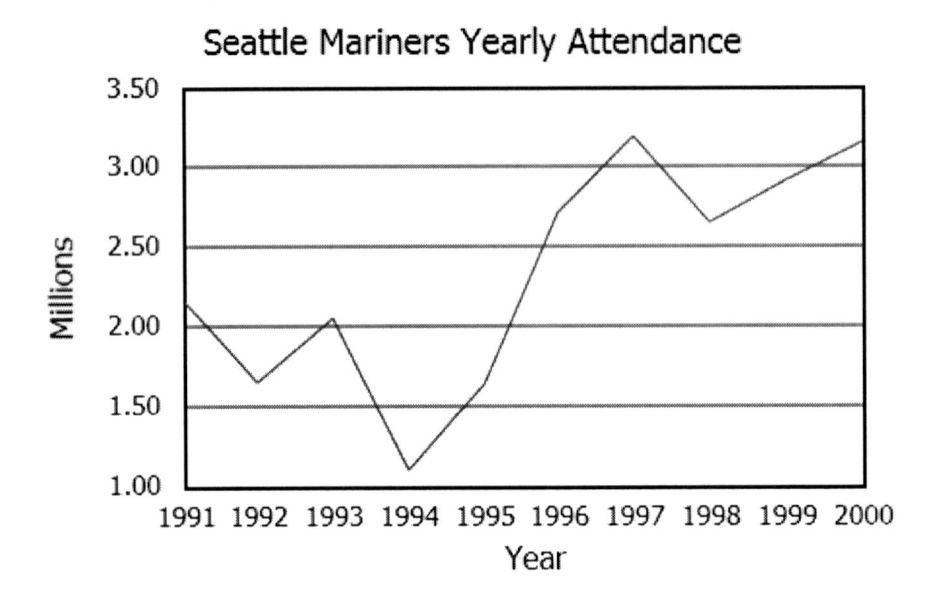

You can see there was increased interest in the team after the 1995. Using examples in this chapter, we build a program that draws this plot.

The **GraphicsWindow DrawLine** method can be used to create line charts. The steps for generating such a chart are simple:

- Generate **N** Cartesian pairs of data to be plotted. Store the horizontal values in an array **X**, the corresponding vertical values in an array **Y**.
- Loop through all **N** points, connecting consecutive points using the **DrawLine** method.

Bar charts plot values as horizontal or vertical bars (referenced to some base value, many times zero). They can also be used to see trends and to compare values, like pie charts. Here's a vertical bar chart of the same attendance data in the line chart above (the base value is 1 million):

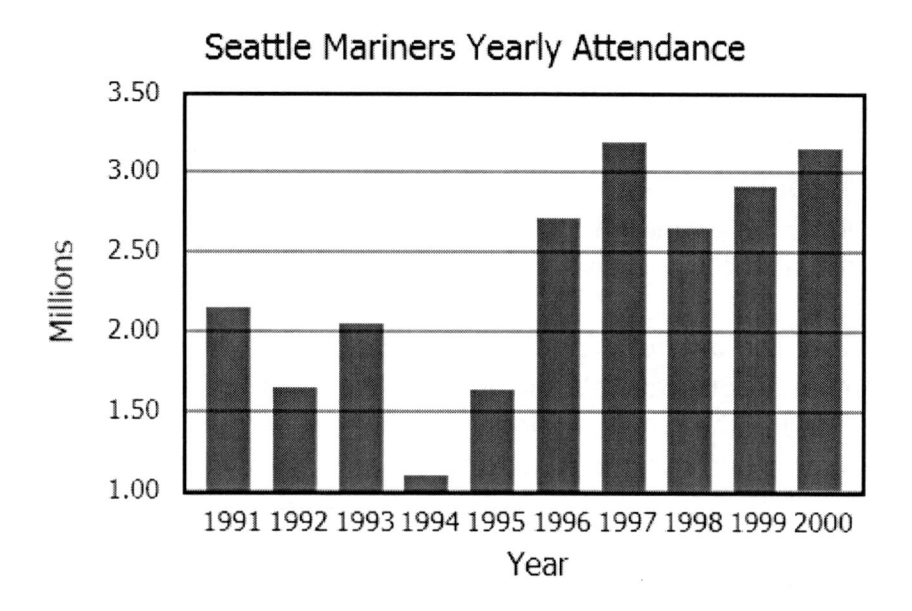

Seattle Mariners Yearly Attendance

The increase in attendance after 1995 is very pronounced. And, here's a bar chart (base value of zero) of Seattle's monthly rainfall (again, note how big the 'winter' bars are):

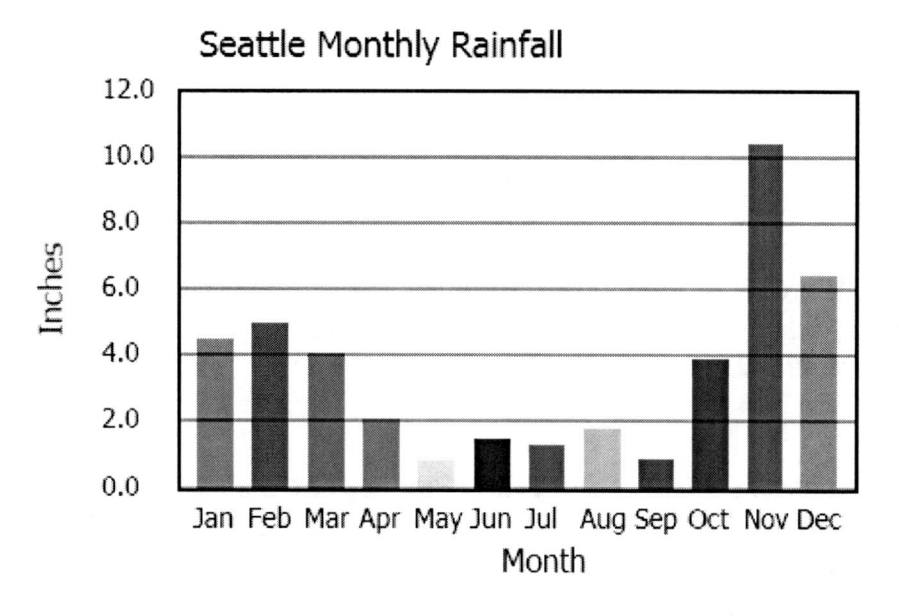

Seattle Monthly Rainfall

Both of these plots will be drawn using Small Basic in this chapter's examples.

The **GraphicsWindow FillRectangle** method can be used for bar charts. The steps for generating a vertical bar chart:

> - Generate **N** pieces of data to be plotted. Store this data in an array **Y**.
> - Determine the width of each bar, using width of the plot area as a guide. I usually allow some space between each bar.
> - Select a base value (the value at the bottom of the bar). This is often zero.
> - For each bar, determine horizontal position based on bar width and current bar being drawn. Draw each bar (pick a unique, identifying color, if desired) using **FillRectangle**. The bar height begins at the base value and ends at the respective **Y** value.

At this point, we could write code to implement general subroutines for drawing line and bar charts. But, there's a problem. And, that problem relates to the **coordinates** used in the graphics window. Let me illustrate. Say we wanted to draw a very simple line chart in a rectangular area, **PlotWidth** pixels wide and **PlotHeight** pixels high, located at (**PlotLeft**, **PlotTop**) in the graphics window. The line is described by the four Cartesian pairs:

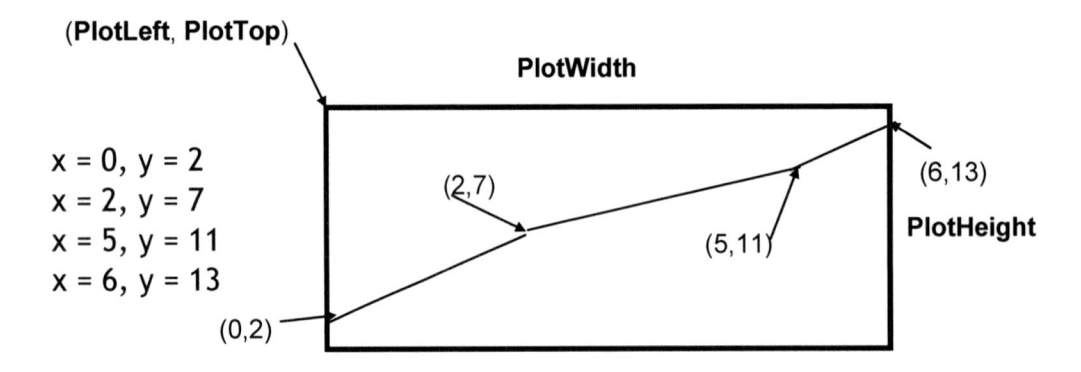

(PlotLeft, PlotTop)

PlotWidth

x = 0, y = 2
x = 2, y = 7
x = 5, y = 11
x = 6, y = 13

(2,7)
(5,11)
(6,13)
PlotHeight
(0,2)

In this plot, the data origin is at (0, 0) in the lower left corner. The horizontal axis value (x) begins at 0 and reaches a maximum of 6. The vertical axis value (y) has a minimum value of 2, a maximum of 13. And, y increases in an upward direction.

The plot area has an origin of (**PlotLeft**, **PlotTop**) at the upper left corner. The maximum x value is **PlotWidth - 1**, the maximum y value is **PlotHeight -1** and y increases in a downward direction. Hence, to plot our data, we need to first compute where each (x, y) pair in our 'data-coordinates' fits within the dimensions of the plot area. This is a straightforward coordinate conversion computation.

Line, Bar and Pie Charts

Coordinate Conversions

Drawing in the plot area is done in pixels. Data for plotting line and bar charts is usually in some physically meaningful units (inches, degrees, dollars) we'll call **data coordinates**. In order to draw a line or bar chart, we need to be able to convert from data coordinates to plot area coordinates (pixels). We will do each axis (horizontal and vertical) separately.

The horizontal (**XPlot** axis) in the plot area is **PlotWidth** pixels wide. The far left pixel is at **XPlot = PlotLeft** and the far right is at **XPlot = PlotLeft + PlotWidth - 1**. Xplot increases from left to right:

PlotLeft **XPlot** **PlotLeft + PlotWidth - 1**

Assume the horizontal data (**XData** axis) in our data coordinates runs from a minimum, **XMin**, at the left to a maximum, **XMmax,** at the right. Thus, the first pixel on the horizontal axis of our data coordinates will be **XMmin** and the last will be **XMmax**:

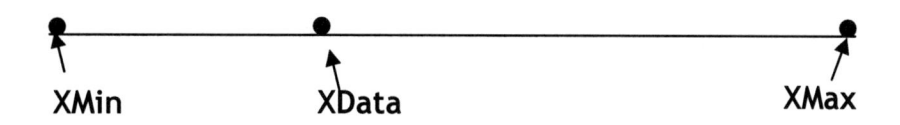

XMin **XData** **XMax**

With these two depictions, we can compute the **XPlot** value corresponding to a given **XData** value using simple **proportions**, dividing the distance from some point on the axis to the minimum value by the total distance. The process is also called **linear interpolation**. These proportions show:

$$\frac{XData - XMin}{XMax - XMin} = \frac{XPlot - PlotLeft}{PlotLeft + PlotWidth - 1 - PlotLeft}$$

Solving this for **XPlot** yields the desired conversion from a user value on the horizontal axis (**XData**) to a pixel value for plotting:

   XPlot = PlotLeft + (XData - XMin)(PlotWidth - 1)/(XMax - XMin)

You can see this is correct at each extreme value. When **XData = XMin**, **XPlot = PlotLeft**. When **XData = XMax**, **XPlot = PlotLeft + PlotWidth - 1**.

Now, we find the corresponding conversion for the vertical axis. We'll place the two axes side-by-side for easy comparison:

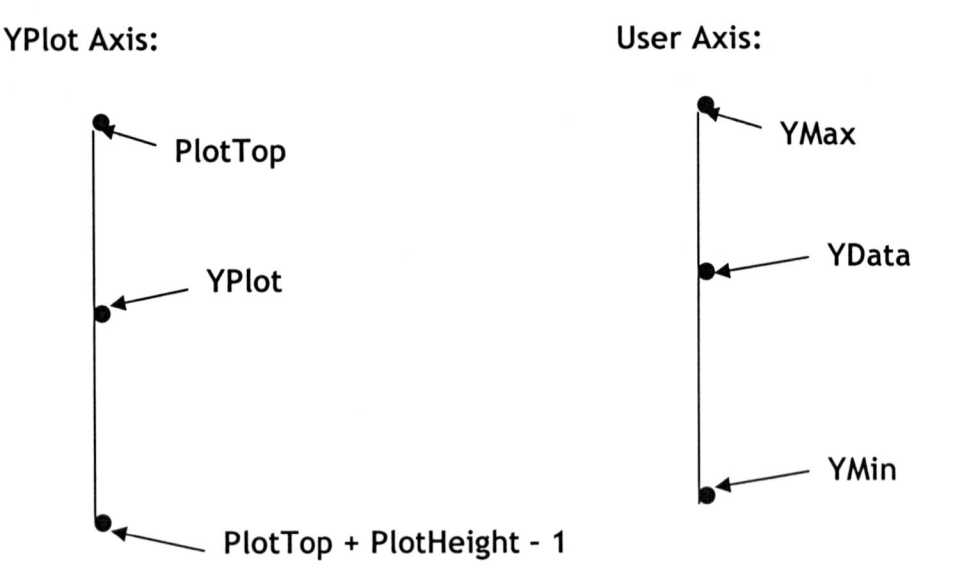

YPlot Axis: PlotTop ... YPlot ... PlotTop + PlotHeight - 1

User Axis: YMax ... YData ... YMin

The vertical (**YPlot** axis) in pixels is **PlotHeight** pixels high. The topmost pixel is at **YPlot** = **PlotTop** and the bottom is at **YPlot** = **PlotTop + PlotHeight - 1**. YPlot increases from top to bottom. The vertical data (**YData** axis) in our data coordinates, runs from a minimum, **YMin**, at the bottom, to a maximum, **YMax**, at the top. Thus, the top pixel on the vertical axis of our data coordinates will be **YMax** and the bottom will be **YMin** (note our user axis increases up, rather than down).

With these two depictions, we can compute the **YPlot** value corresponding to a given **YData** value using linear interpolation. The computations show:

$$\frac{YData - YMin}{YMax - YMin} = \frac{YPlot - (PlotTop + PlotHeight - 1)}{PlotTop - (PlotTop + PlotHeight - 1)}$$

Solving this for **YPlot** yields the desired conversion from a data value on the vertical axis (**YData**) to a pixel value for plotting (this requires a bit algebra, but it's straightforward):

YPlot = PlotTop + (YMax - YData)(PlotHeight - 1)/(YMax - YMin)

Again, check the extremes. When **YData** = **YMin**, YPlot = PlotTop + PlotHeight - 1. When **YData** = **YMax**, YPlot = PlotTop. It looks good.

Whenever we plot real, physical data, we will need coordinate conversions. In these notes, we use two subroutines (**XDataToXPlot** and **YDataToYPlot**) to do the conversions. To do the conversions, each subroutine requires values for **PlotLeft**, **PlotTop**, **PlotWidth** and **PlotHeight**. These define the plot area in the graphics window.

XDataToXPlot requires **XMin** and **XMax** (the extreme values for the X data values). For each point to convert, supply the subroutine with the x value to convert **XData**. The subroutine computes the corresponding plot value **XPlot**.

Similarly, **YDataToYPlot** requires **YMin** and **YMax** (the extreme values for the Y data values). For each point to convert, supply the subroutine with the y value to convert **YData**. The subroutine computes the corresponding plot value **YPlot**. After calling both subroutines using the Cartesian pair (**XData**, **YData**), we have the corresponding (**XPlot**, **YPlot**).

The Small Basic subroutines **XDataToXPlot** and **YDataToYPlot** simply use the derived conversion equations:

```
Sub XDataToXPlot
  'converts XData to XPlot
  XPlot = PlotLeft + (XData - XMin) * (PlotWidth - 1) / (XMax - XMin)
EndSub

Sub YDataToYPlot
  'converts YData to YPlot
  YPlot = PlotTop + (Ymax - YData) * (PlotHeight - 1) / (Ymax - YMin)
EndSub
```

Drawing a Line Chart

With the ability to transform coordinates, we can now develop general line and bar chart subroutines. The modified steps to create a line chart are:

> Generate **N** Cartesian pairs of data to be plotted. Store the horizontal values in an array **X**, the corresponding vertical values in an array **Y**.
> Loop through all **N** points to determine the minimum and maximum **X** and **Y** values.
> Again, loop through all **N** points. For each point, convert the **X** and **Y** values to pixel values, then connect the current point with the previous point using the **DrawLine** method.

We use two subroutines to do these steps. The subroutine **FindMinMax** will find the minimum and maximum values. It requires the number of points to plot, **NPoints**, **XValue**, the array of horizontal values, and **YValue** the array of vertical values:

```
Sub FindMinMax
  'find minimums and maximums
  XMin = XValue[1]
  XMax = XValue[1]
  YMin = YValue[1]
  Ymax = YValue[1]
  For I = 2 To NPoints
    XMin = Math.Min(XMin, XValue[I])
    XMax = Math.Max(XMax, XValue[I])
    YMin = Math.Min(YMin, YValue[I])
    Ymax = Math.Max(Ymax, YValue[I])
  EndFor
EndSub
```

We keep this process separate from the plot code in case we want to change the minimum and maximum values (we will see why we would want to do this soon).

Line, Bar and Pie Charts

Next, the subroutine **LineChart** draws a line chart in the graphics window:

```
Sub LineChart
  'Constructs a  line chart - pairs of (x,y) coordinates
  'NPoints - number of points to plot
  'XValue - array of x points
  'YValue - array of y points
  If (NPoints < 2) Then
    Goto ExitLineChart
  EndIf
  'plot the pairs -  get first point
  XData = XValue[1]
  YData = YValue[1]
  XDataToXPlot()
  YDataToYPlot()
  XPrevious = XPlot
  YPrevious = YPlot
  GraphicsWindow.PenColor = LineColor
  GraphicsWindow.PenWidth = 1
  For I = 2 To NPoints
    'connect subsequent points to previous
    XData = XValue[I]
    YData = YValue[I]
    XDataToXPlot()
    YDataToYPlot()
    GraphicsWindow.DrawLine(XPrevious, YPrevious, XPlot, YPlot)
    XPrevious = XPlot
    YPrevious = YPlot
  EndFor
ExitLineChart:
EndSub
```

It uses the results from **FindMinMax** and the coordinate conversion subroutines **XDataToXPlot** and **YDataToYPlot**. The subroutine requires location and size of plot area (**PlotLeft, PlotTop, PlotWidth, PlotHeight**), **NPoints, XValue** and **YValue** arrays, and **LineColor**, the color of the line to be plotted.

19-10 The Developer's Reference Guide to Small Basic

Example 19-1. Mariners Attendance Line Chart

Write a program that plots the Seattle Mariners attendance data in a line chart. Use the **LineChart**, **FindMinMax**, **XDataToXPlot** and **YDataToYPlot** subroutines. The data you need is:

XValue (the year)	YValue (attendance in millions)
1991	2.15
1992	1.65
1993	2.05
1994	1.1
1995	1.64
1996	2.72
1997	3.19
1998	2.65
1999	2.92
2000	3.15

Small Basic Code:

```
'Guide to Small Basic, Example 19-1
InitializeProgram()

Sub InitializeProgram
  GraphicsWindow.Show()
  GraphicsWindow.Width = 500
  GraphicsWindow.Height = 300
  GraphicsWindow.Title = "Example 19-1"
  'Mariners data
  NPoints = 10
  XValue[1] = 1991
  XValue[2] = 1992
  XValue[3] = 1993
  XValue[4] = 1994
  XValue[5] = 1995
  XValue[6] = 1996
  XValue[7] = 1997
  XValue[8] = 1998
  XValue[9] = 1999
  XValue[10] = 2000
  YValue[1] = 2.15
  YValue[2] = 1.65
  YValue[3] = 2.05
  YValue[4] = 1.1
```

```
  YValue[5] = 1.64
  YValue[6] = 2.72
  YValue[7] = 3.19
  YValue[8] = 2.65
  YValue[9] = 2.92
  YValue[10] = 3.15
  LineColor = "Blue"
  'plot area
  PlotLeft = 100
  PlotTop = 50
  PlotWidth = 350
  PlotHeight = 200
  GraphicsWindow.PenColor = "Black"
  GraphicsWindow.DrawRectangle(PlotLeft, PlotTop, PlotWidth, PlotHeight)
  FindMinMax()
  LineChart()
EndSub
```

We have not shown the code from **FindMinMax**, **XDataToXPlot**, **YDataToYPlot** or **LineChart**, but they need to be in your program. Saved as **Example 19-1** in **Guide to Small Basic\Programs\Chapter 19** folder.

Most of the code is setting up the arrays (**XValue** and **YValue**) of data to plot. Once these arrays are defined, we define the location and size of the plot area and draw an empty rectangle. A call to **FindMinMax**, then **LineChart** does the plotting.

Save and **Run** the program. You will see the data plotted as a blue line in the black rectangular plot area:

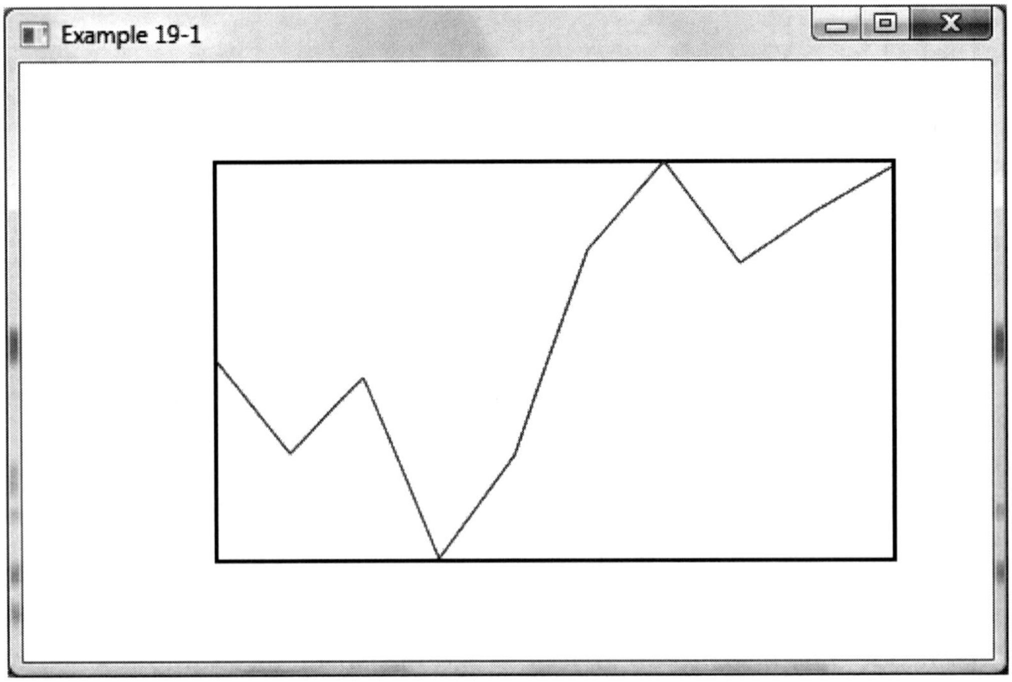

This is a good first step, but needs a bit of improvement. First, let's label the axes so we know the range of data values.

Axis Labeling

In a line chart, the x and y axes are usually labeled with numbers indicating the data range of each. You are shown the minimum and maximum values along with intermediate, evenly spaced values. And, there may be grid lines drawn at these intermediate values.

For the Mariners attendance data, we would like to see labels like this:

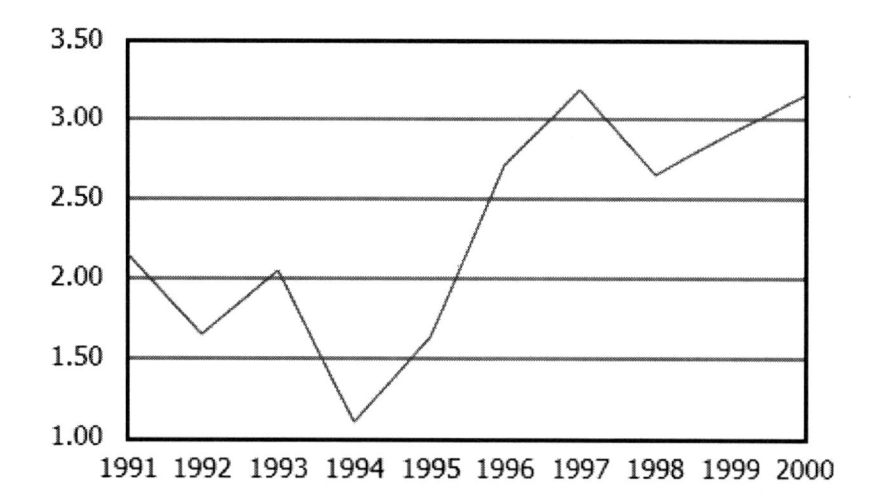

Note for the attendance axis (vertical), the minimum value is 1.0, the maximum value is 3.5, with intermediate values every 0.5. Grid lines are drawn. For the year axis (horizontal), the minimum is 1991, the maximum 2000, with all values displayed. There are no grid lines for these values.

If you look at the actual attendance data, you will see the minimum value is 1.1 and the maximum value is 3.19 (the **YMin** and **YMax** values found in **FindMinMax**). So, how do we come up with the nicely spaced values (0.5 to 3.5) shown in the plot above - we need another subroutine. This is the reason we the **FindMinMax** subroutine separate from the plotting. We may want to overwrite the actual minimums and maximums to get nice looking axis labels.

Here's a subroutine (**FindAxisSpacing**) based on code I first found in the early 1980's to compute nicely spaced values for plot axes (I don't know how this works, but it does):

```
Sub FindAxisSpacing
  'provide AxisMin and AxisMax
  'computes new AxisMin, AxisMax, IntervalSpacing, NumberIntervals
  Eps = 0.025
  If (AxisMin = AxisMax) Then
    AxisMin = 0.9 * AxisMax
  EndIf
  ATemp = Math.Abs(AxisMin)
  If Math.Abs(AxisMin) < Math.Abs(AxisMax) Then
    ATemp = Math.Abs(AxisMax)
  EndIf
  Scale = Math.Power(10, Math.Floor(Math.Log(ATemp) / Math.Log(10) / 10.0))
  NextScale:
  Scale = Scale * 10
  MinA = AxisMin / Scale
  MaxA = AxisMax / Scale
  DTemp = (MaxA - MinA) / 4.5
  JTemp = DTemp * Eps
  ETemp = Math.Floor((Math.Log(DTemp) / Math.Log(10)))
  FTemp = DTemp / Math.Power(10, ETemp)
  VTemp = 10
  If FTemp < Math.SquareRoot(2) Then
    VTemp = 1
  ElseIf FTemp < Math.SquareRoot(10) Then
    VTemp = 2
  ElseIf FTemp < Math.SquareRoot(50) Then
    VTemp = 5
  EndIf
  Delta = VTemp * Math.Power(10, ETemp)
  GTemp = Math.Floor(MinA / Delta)
  If Math.Abs(GTemp + 1 - MinA / Delta) < JTemp Then
    GTemp = GTemp + 1
  EndIf
  MinP = Delta * GTemp
  HTemp = Math.Floor(MaxA / Delta) + 1
  If Math.Abs(MaxA / Delta + 1 - HTemp) < JTemp Then
    HTemp = HTemp - 1
  EndIf
  MaxP = Delta * HTemp
  NumberIntervals = HTemp - GTemp
```

```
  If (Math.Abs(MaxP) >= 10 Or Math.Abs(MinP) >= 10) Then
    Goto NextScale
  EndIf
  AxisMin = MinP * Scale
  AxisMax = MaxP * Scale
  AxisSpacing = Delta * Scale
EndSub
```

You provide this subroutine with minimum (**AxisMin**) and maximum (**AxisMax**) axis values, based on the data to plot. It computes new values for **AxisMin** and **AxisMax** to give "nice" labeling. It also computes **NumberIntervals** (the number of intervals between **AxisMin** and **AxisMax**) and the spacing for each interval (**AxisSpacing**). You should see that the results satisfy this relation:

AxisSpacing = (AxisMax - AxisMin) / NumberIntervals

Once we have this nice axis spacing information, we can add axis labels and grid lines (if we want). We will do the vertical axis first, then the horizontal axis.

If there are **NumberIntervals** intervals along the vertical axis, we need **NumberIntervals + 1** labels. The process is easy. Start with the lowest value (**AxisMin**). Write that value (using **DrawText** method) next to the lower left corner of the plot area. Then, "march up" the axis, writing a new value (you add **AxisSpacing** to the previous value). For values other than **AxisMin** and **AxisMax**, you can optionally draw a grid line. Each value is positioned horizontally to the left of the plot area. It is positioned vertically by converting the data coordinate into a plot coordinate with a little "upward" adjustment to center the value appropriately. Here is a subroutine (**LabelYAxis**) to do the vertical axis labeling. It is called once values for **AxisMin**, **AxisMax**, **AxisSpacing** and **NumberIntervals** are available. If **DrawYGrid** is "true", grid lines will be drawn.

```
Sub LabelYAxis
   GraphicsWindow.BrushColor = "Black"
   GraphicsWindow.FontSize = 14
   GraphicsWindow.FontBold = "false"
   GraphicsWindow.PenColor = "Black"
   GraphicsWindow.PenWidth = 1
   YData = AxisMin
   For I = 1 To NumberIntervals + 1
     'get y position
     YDataToYPlot()
     GraphicsWindow.DrawText(PlotLeft - 40, YPlot - 10, YData)
     If (DrawYGrid And I > 1 And I < NumberIntervals + 1) Then
        GraphicsWindow.DrawLine(PlotLeft, YPlot, PlotLeft + PlotWidth, YPlot)
     EndIf
     YData = YData + AxisSpacing
   EndFor
EndSub
```

The label (**YData**) is drawn with this line of code:

```
GraphicsWindow.DrawText(PlotLeft - 40, YPlot - 10, YData)
```

You may need to adjust the subtracted values (40 and 10) to "fine tune" label locations.

Line, Bar and Pie Charts   19-17

Example 19-2. Y Axis Labeling

Modify **Example 19-1** so that the vertical axis (attendance values) is labeled and has grid lines.

Make sure to add the **FindAxisSpacing** and **LabelYAxis** subroutines to your program. We will not repeat that code here.

Small Basic Code (changes to **InitializeProgram** are shaded; we have left out lines defining the data arrays):

```
Sub InitializeProgram
  GraphicsWindow.Show()
  GraphicsWindow.Width = 500
  GraphicsWindow.Height = 300
  GraphicsWindow.Title = "Example 19-2"
  'Mariners data
     .
     .
     .
  'plot area
  PlotLeft = 100
  PlotTop = 50
  PlotWidth = 350
  PlotHeight = 200
  GraphicsWindow.PenColor = "Black"
  GraphicsWindow.DrawRectangle(PlotLeft, PlotTop, PlotWidth, PlotHeight)
  FindMinMax()
  'compute spacing on y axis
  AxisMin = YMin
  AxisMax = YMax
  FindAxisSpacing()
  YMin = AxisMin
  YMax = AxisMax
  LineChart()
  DrawYGrid = "true"
  LabelYAxis()
EndSub
```

Saved as **Example 19-2** in **Guide to Small Basic\Programs\Chapter 19** folder.

Note the process is to use the original **YMin** and **YMax** to compute axis spacing information. Then **YMin** and **YMax** are replaced by **AxisMin** and **AxisMax** (from **FindAxisSpacing**) before labeling and drawing the line chart.

Save and **Run** the program. The y axis of the plot is now nicely labeled:

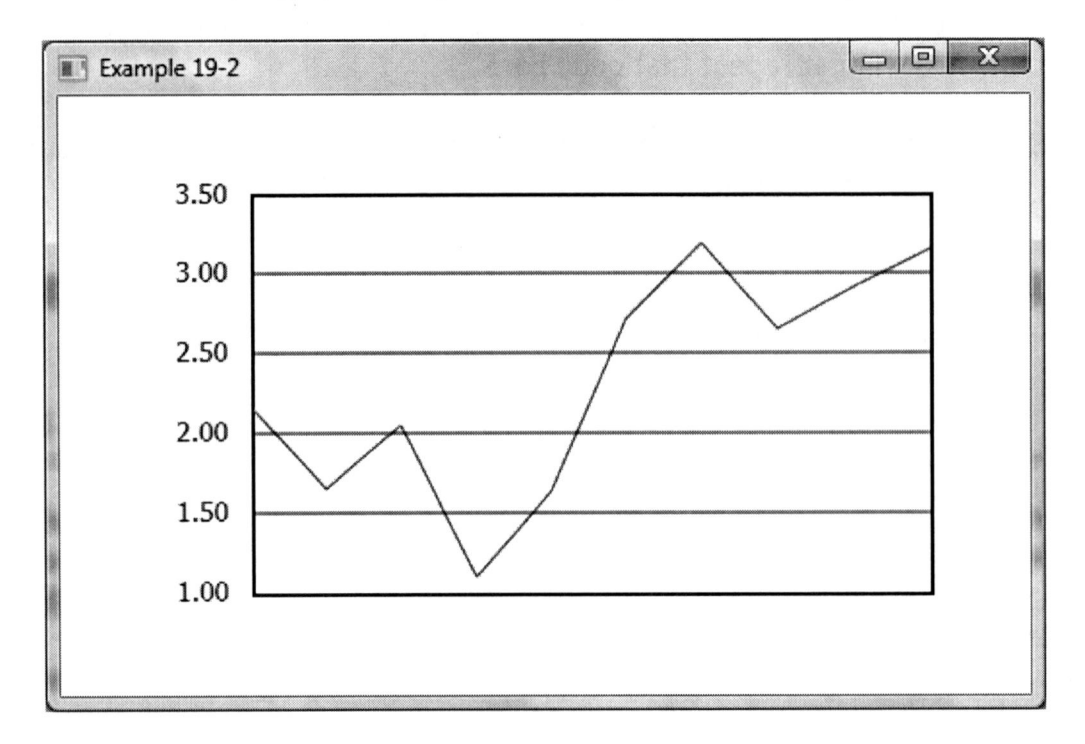

Example 19-3. X Axis Labeling

Modify **Example 19-2** so that the horizontal axis (years) is labeled and has no grid lines. Here is a subroutine (**LabelXAxis**) to do x axis labeling (it is very similar to **LabelYAxis**). The steps should be easy to follow.

```
Sub LabelXAxis
  GraphicsWindow.BrushColor = "Black"
  GraphicsWindow.FontSize = 14
  GraphicsWindow.FontBold = "false"
  GraphicsWindow.PenColor = "Black"
  GraphicsWindow.PenWidth = 1
  XData = AxisMin
  For I = 1 To NumberIntervals + 1
    'get x position
    XDataYToXPlot()
    GraphicsWindow.DrawText(XPlot - 15, PlotTop + PlotHeight + 5, XData)
    If (DrawXGrid And I > 1 And I < NumberIntervals + 1) Then
      GraphicsWindow.DrawLine(XPlot, PlotTop, XPlot, PlotTop + PlotHeight)
    EndIf
    XData = XData + AxisSpacing
  EndFor
EndSub
```

Add this subroutine to your program. The label (**XData**) is drawn in this line:

```
GraphicsWindow.DrawText(XPlot - 15, PlotTop + PlotHeight + 5, XData)
```

Like **LabelYAxis**, you may need to change the location adjustments (-15 and 5).

Small Basic Code (changes to **InitializeProgram** are shaded; again, we have left out lines defining the data arrays):

```
Sub InitializeProgram
  GraphicsWindow.Show()
  GraphicsWindow.Width = 500
  GraphicsWindow.Height = 300
  GraphicsWindow.Title = "Example 19-3"
  'Mariners data
      .
      .
  'plot area
  PlotLeft = 100
  PlotTop = 50
  PlotWidth = 350
  PlotHeight = 200
  GraphicsWindow.PenColor = "Black"
  GraphicsWindow.DrawRectangle(PlotLeft, PlotTop, PlotWidth, PlotHeight)
  FindMinMax()
  'compute spacing on y axis
  AxisMin = YMin
  AxisMax = YMax
  FindAxisSpacing()
  YMin = AxisMin
  YMax = AxisMax
  LineChart()
  DrawYGrid = "true"
  LabelYAxis()
  AxisMin = 1991
  AxisMax = 2000
  NumberIntervals = 9
  AxisSpacing = 1
  DrawXGrid = "false"
  LabelXAxis()
EndSub
```

Saved as **Example 19-3** in **Guide to Small Basic\Programs\Chapter 19** folder.

We take a different approach in labeling the x axis. If we use **FindAxisSpacing**, it will compute **AxisMin = 1990, AxisMax = 2000, NumberIntervals = 5, AxisSpacing = 2**. I'd rather see every year print out as a label and I have no value for 1990. So rather than use values computed by **FindAxisSpacing**, I just assign values I want to use: **AxisMin = 1991, AxisMax = 2000, NumberIntervals = 9, AxisSpacing = 1**. For each plot you draw, you should decide whether to use computed spacings or ones you desire.

Save and **Run** the program. Both axes now have nice labels:

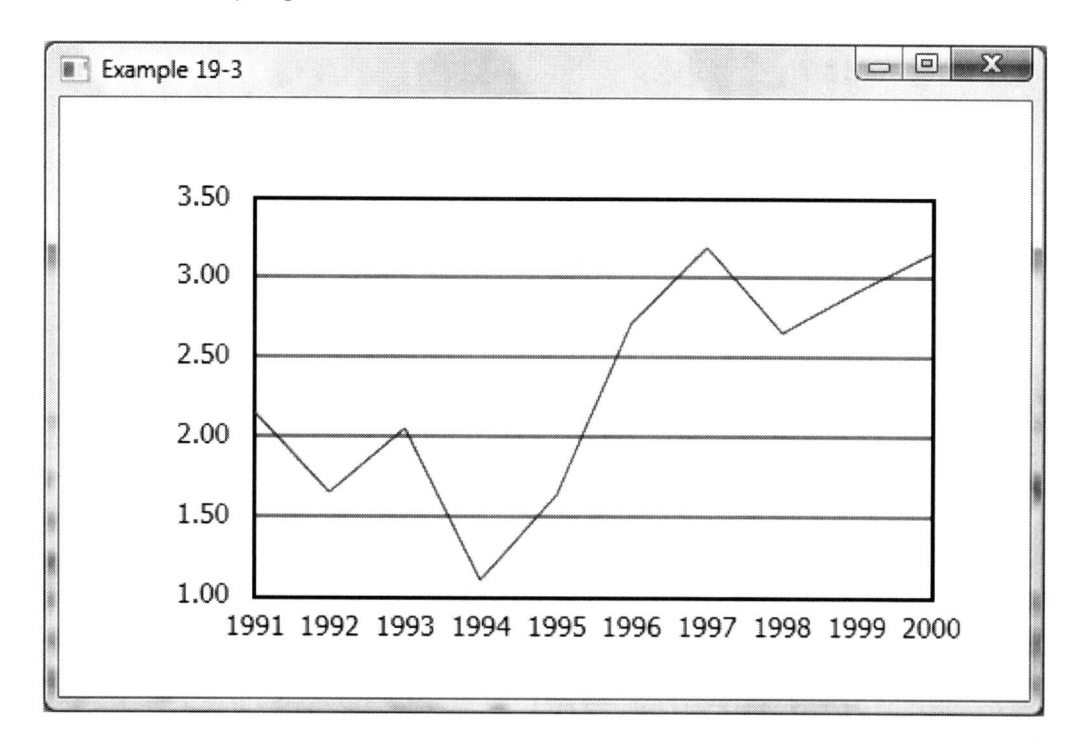

Plot Labeling

One last thing our plot needs is some text labeling. We will add a title to the plot and add text descriptions of both the x and y axis. We will use **Shapes** objects for these labels. This will allow us to rotate the y axis label.

One more subroutine does the task. The subroutine **AddPlotLabels** will place **PlotTitle** over the plot area, **PlotXLabel** under the x axis and a rotated **PlotYLabel** next to the y axis:

```
Sub AddPlotLabels
  'title
  GraphicsWindow.BrushColor = "Black"
  GraphicsWindow.FontSize = 18
  GraphicsWindow.FontBold = "false"
  TitleDisplay = Shapes.AddText(PlotTitle)
  Shapes.Move(TitleDisplay, PlotLeft + 10, PlotTop - 35)
  'x axis
  GraphicsWindow.FontSize = 16
  XAxisDisplay = Shapes.AddText(PlotXLabel)
  Shapes.Move(XAxisDisplay, PlotLeft + 0.5 * PlotWidth - 10,
PlotTop + PlotHeight + 25)
  'y axis
  GraphicsWindow.FontSize = 16
  YAxisDisplay = Shapes.AddText(PlotYLabel)
  Shapes.Move(YAxisDisplay, PlotLeft - 90, PlotTop + 0.5 *
PlotHeight - 10)
  Shapes.Rotate(YAxisDisplay, 270)
EndSub
```

Notice how we **Rotate** the y axis label so it appears vertically. And, like the x and y axis labeling subroutines, you may want to fine tune some of the positionings in the **Move** statements.

Example 19-4. Plot Labeling

Modify **Example 19-3** to add a title and axis labeling to the Mariners attendance plot. Be sure to add the **AddPlotLabels** subroutine to your program.

Small Basic Code (changes to **InitializeProgram** are shaded):

```
Sub InitializeProgram
  GraphicsWindow.Show()
  GraphicsWindow.Width = 500
  GraphicsWindow.Height = 300
  GraphicsWindow.Title = "Example 19-4"
  'Mariners data
  NPoints = 10
  XValue[1] = 1991
  XValue[2] = 1992
  XValue[3] = 1993
  XValue[4] = 1994
  XValue[5] = 1995
  XValue[6] = 1996
  XValue[7] = 1997
  XValue[8] = 1998
  XValue[9] = 1999
  XValue[10] = 2000
  YValue[1] = 2.15
  YValue[2] = 1.65
  YValue[3] = 2.05
  YValue[4] = 1.1
  YValue[5] = 1.64
  YValue[6] = 2.72
  YValue[7] = 3.19
  YValue[8] = 2.65
  YValue[9] = 2.92
  YValue[10] = 3.15
  LineColor = "Blue"
  'plot area
  PlotLeft = 100
  PlotTop = 50
  PlotWidth = 350
  PlotHeight = 200
  GraphicsWindow.PenColor = "Black"
  GraphicsWindow.DrawRectangle(PlotLeft, PlotTop, PlotWidth, PlotHeight)
  FindMinMax()
  'compute spacing on y axis
```

```
    AxisMin = YMin
    AxisMax = YMax
    FindAxisSpacing()
    YMin = AxisMin
    YMax = AxisMax
    LineChart()
    DrawYGrid = "true"
    LabelYAxis()
    AxisMin = 1991
    AxisMax = 2000
    NumberIntervals = 9
    AxisSpacing = 1
    DrawXGrid = "false"
    LabelXAxis()
    PlotTitle = "Seattle Mariners Yearly Attendance"
    PlotXLabel = "Year"
    PlotYLabel = "Millions"
    AddPlotLabels()
EndSub

Sub FindMinMax
    'find minimums and maximums
    XMin = XValue[1]
    XMax = XValue[1]
    YMin = YValue[1]
    Ymax = YValue[1]
    For I = 2 To NPoints
        XMin = Math.Min(XMin, XValue[I])
        XMax = Math.Max(XMax, XValue[I])
        YMin = Math.Min(YMin, YValue[I])
        Ymax = Math.Max(Ymax, YValue[I])
    EndFor
EndSub

Sub LineChart
    'Constructs a  line chart - pairs of (x,y) coordinates
    'NPoints - number of points to plot
    'XValue - array of x points
    'YValue - array of y points
    If (NPoints < 2) Then
        Goto ExitLineChart
    EndIf
    'plot the pairs -  get first point
    XData = XValue[1]
    YData = YValue[1]
    XDataToXPlot()
```

```
    YDataToYPlot()
    XPrevious = XPlot
    YPrevious = YPlot
    GraphicsWindow.PenColor = LineColor
    GraphicsWindow.PenWidth = 1
    For I = 2 To NPoints
      'connect subsequent points to previous
      XData = XValue[I]
      YData = YValue[I]
      XDataToXPlot()
      YDataToYPlot()
      GraphicsWindow.DrawLine(XPrevious, YPrevious, XPlot, YPlot)
      XPrevious = XPlot
      YPrevious = YPlot
    EndFor
ExitLineChart:
EndSub

Sub XDataToXPlot
  'converts XData to XPlot
  XPlot = PlotLeft + (XData - XMin) * (PlotWidth - 1) / (XMax - XMin)
EndSub

Sub YDataToYPlot
  'converts YData) to YPlot
  YPlot = PlotTop + (Ymax - YData) * (PlotHeight - 1) / (Ymax - YMin)
EndSub

Sub FindAxisSpacing
  'provide AxisMin and AxisMax
  'computes new AxisMin, AxisMax, IntervalSpacing, NumberIntervals
  Eps = 0.025
  If (AxisMin = AxisMax) Then
    AxisMin = 0.9 * AxisMax
  EndIf
  ATemp = Math.Abs(AxisMin)
  If Math.Abs(AxisMin) < Math.Abs(AxisMax) Then
    ATemp = Math.Abs(AxisMax)
  EndIf
  Scale = Math.Power(10, Math.Floor(Math.Log(ATemp) / Math.Log(10) / 10.0))
  NextScale:
  Scale = Scale * 10
  MinA = AxisMin / Scale
```

```
    MaxA = AxisMax / Scale
    DTemp = (MaxA - MinA) / 4.5
    JTemp = DTemp * Eps
    ETemp = Math.Floor((Math.Log(DTemp) / Math.Log(10)))
    FTemp = DTemp / Math.Power(10, ETemp)
    VTemp = 10
    If FTemp < Math.SquareRoot(2) Then
      VTemp = 1
    ElseIf FTemp < Math.SquareRoot(10) Then
      VTemp = 2
    ElseIf FTemp < Math.SquareRoot(50) Then
      VTemp = 5
    EndIf
    Delta = VTemp * Math.Power(10, ETemp)
    GTemp = Math.Floor(MinA / Delta)
    If Math.Abs(GTemp + 1 - MinA / Delta) < JTemp Then
      GTemp = GTemp + 1
    EndIf
    MinP = Delta * GTemp
    HTemp = Math.Floor(MaxA / Delta) + 1
    If Math.Abs(MaxA / Delta + 1 - HTemp) < JTemp Then
      HTemp = HTemp - 1
    EndIf
    MaxP = Delta * HTemp
    NumberIntervals = HTemp - GTemp
    If (Math.Abs(MaxP) >= 10 Or Math.Abs(MinP) >= 10) Then
      Goto NextScale
    EndIf
    AxisMin = MinP * Scale
    AxisSpacing = Delta * Scale
    AxisMax = AxisMin + NumberIntervals * AxisSpacing
EndSub

Sub LabelYAxis
    GraphicsWindow.BrushColor = "Black"
    GraphicsWindow.FontSize = 14
    GraphicsWindow.FontBold = "false"
    GraphicsWindow.PenColor = "Black"
    GraphicsWindow.PenWidth = 1
    YData = AxisMin
    For I = 1 To NumberIntervals + 1
      'get y position
      YDataToYPlot()
      GraphicsWindow.DrawText(PlotLeft - 40, YPlot - 10, YData)
      If (DrawYGrid And I > 1 And I < NumberIntervals + 1) Then
```

```
      GraphicsWindow.DrawLine(PlotLeft, YPlot, PlotLeft + PlotWidth, YPlot)
    EndIf
    YData = YData + AxisSpacing
  EndFor
EndSub

Sub LabelXAxis
  GraphicsWindow.BrushColor = "Black"
  GraphicsWindow.FontSize = 14
  GraphicsWindow.FontBold = "false"
  GraphicsWindow.PenColor = "Black"
  GraphicsWindow.PenWidth = 1
  XData = AxisMin
  For I = 1 To NumberIntervals + 1
    'get x position
    XDataToXPlot()
    GraphicsWindow.DrawText(XPlot - 15, PlotTop + PlotHeight + 5, XData)
    If (DrawXGrid And I > 1 And I < NumberIntervals + 1) Then
      GraphicsWindow.DrawLine(XPlot, PlotTop, XPlot, PlotTop + PlotHeight)
    EndIf
    XData = XData + AxisSpacing
  EndFor
EndSub

Sub AddPlotLabels
  'title
  GraphicsWindow.BrushColor = "Black"
  GraphicsWindow.FontSize = 18
  GraphicsWindow.FontBold = "false"
  TitleDisplay = Shapes.AddText(PlotTitle)
  Shapes.Move(TitleDisplay, PlotLeft + 10, PlotTop - 35)
  'x axis
  GraphicsWindow.FontSize = 16
  XAxisDisplay = Shapes.AddText(PlotXLabel)
  Shapes.Move(XAxisDisplay, PlotLeft + 0.5 * PlotWidth - 10, PlotTop + PlotHeight + 25)
  'y axis
  GraphicsWindow.FontSize = 16
  YAxisDisplay = Shapes.AddText(PlotYLabel)
  Shapes.Move(YAxisDisplay, PlotLeft - 90, PlotTop + 0.5 * PlotHeight - 10)
  Shapes.Rotate(YAxisDisplay, 270)
EndSub
```

Saved as **Example 19-4** in **Guide to Small Basic\Programs\Chapter 19** folder.

We have shown the entire line chart plotting program with all the subroutines. You can use this program as a framework for any line charts you might like to draw. Recall we don't use "automatic" calculations of spacings for the x axis labels. You might want to change this for other plots.

Save and **Run** the program to see the final plot:

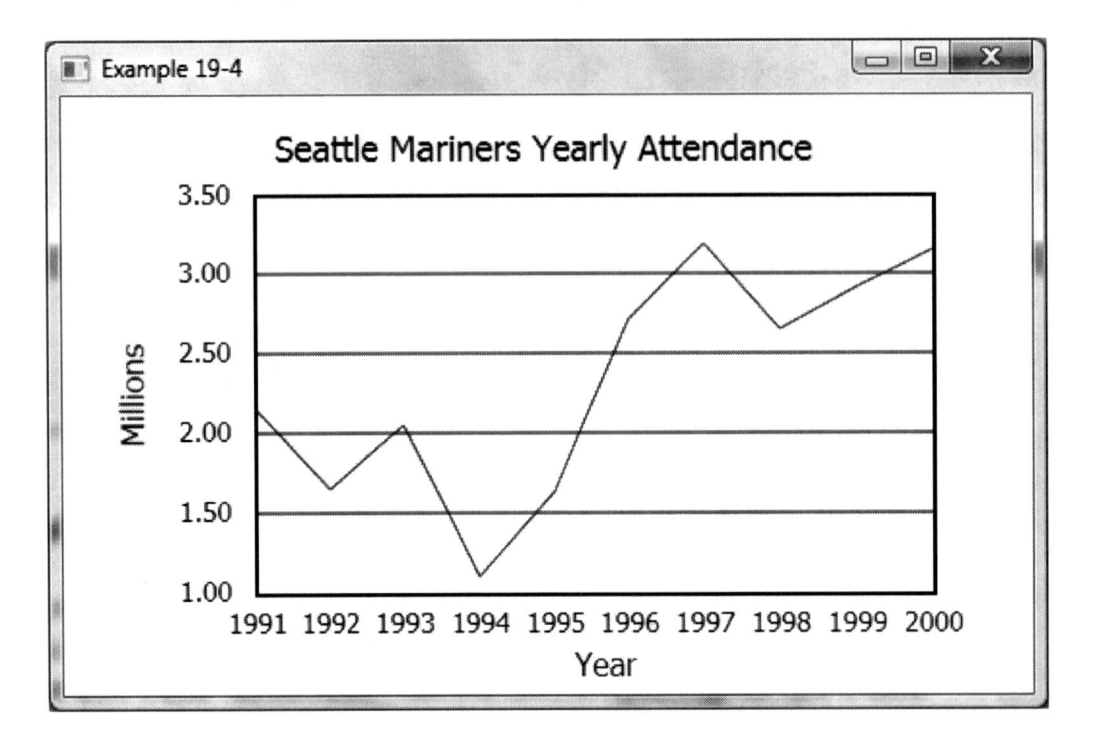

Drawing a Bar Chart

We can use many of the subroutines developed for a line chart to draw a bar chart.

The steps to create a bar chart are:

- Generate **N** pieces of data to be plotted. Store this data in an array **Y**.
- Determine the width of each bar, using width of the plot area as a guide. I allow some space between each bar.
- Loop through all **N** points to determine the minimum and maximum **Y** value. Adjust values for "nice spacing".
- Select a base value (the value at the bottom of the bar). This is often zero. Convert the base value to plot coordinates.
- For each bar, determine horizontal position based on bar width and current bar being drawn. Draw each bar (pick a unique, identifying color, if desired) using **FillRectangle**. The bar height begins at the base value and ends at the respective **Y** value (converted to plot coordinates).

The subroutine **FindMinMax** will find the minimum and maximum values. Recall it requires the number of points to plot, **NPoints**, **XValue**, the array of horizontal values, and **YValue** the array of vertical values. Here, we only want the extremes for the vertical values. We need to form a 'dummy' **XValue** array for the code to work properly.

The subroutine **BarChart** draws a bar chart in the graphics window:

```
Sub BarChart
  'Constructs a  bar chart
  'NPoints - number of bars to draw
  'YValue - array of bar values
  'BaseValue - base value for bars - convert to pixels
  YData = BaseValue
  YDataToYPlot()
  BasePlot = YPlot
  'Find bar width in pixels, use half bar-width as margins between bars
  BarWidth = 2 * PlotWidth / (3 * NPoints + 1)
  For I = 1 To NPoints
    GraphicsWindow.BrushColor = BarColor[I]
    YData = YValue[I]
    YDataToYPlot()
    'draw bars
    If (BasePlot > YPlot) Then
```

```
        GraphicsWindow.FillRectangle(PlotLeft + (1.5 * I - 1) *
BarWidth, YPlot, BarWidth, BasePlot - YPlot)
    Else
        GraphicsWindow.FillRectangle(PlotLeft + (1.5 * I - 1) *
BarWidth, BasePlot, BarWidth, YPlot - BasePlot)
    EndIf
  EndFor
  'Line at base
  GraphicsWindow.PenColor = "Black"
  GraphicsWindow.PenWidth = 1
  GraphicsWindow.DrawLine(PlotLeft, BasePlot, PlotLeft +
PlotWidth, BasePlot)
EndSub
```

It uses the coordinate conversion subroutine **YDataToYPlot** (which needs **YMin** and **YMax**). The subroutine also requires location and size of plot area (**PlotLeft, PlotTop, PlotWidth, PlotHeight**), **NPoints** and **YValue** arrays, **BaseValue**, the base value to draw bars to, and **BarColor**, an array (with **NPoints** elements) specifying the colors for each bar drawn.

In the subroutine, we compute **BarWidth** by assuming there will be one-half of a bar width between bars. So, if we have **N** bars (**BarWidth** wide), we will have **N + 1** gaps (one-half **BarWidth** wide). The total width is **PlotWidth**, so we see:

   N * BarWidth + (N + 1) * 0.5 * BarWidth = PlotWidth

Solving this little algebra equation gives us the relation in the code:

   BarWidth = 2 * PlotWidth / (3 * NPoints + 1)

We also use **BarWidth** to determine where to start drawing each bar.

Line, Bar and Pie Charts

Example 19-5. Mariners Attendance Bar Chart

Write a program that plots the Seattle Mariners attendance data in a bar chart. Use the **BarChart** subroutine. This is actually just a slight modification to **Example 19-4**. So, that's a good place to start.

Small Basic Code:

```
'Guide to Small Basic, Example 19-5
InitializeProgram()

Sub InitializeProgram
  GraphicsWindow.Show()
  GraphicsWindow.Width = 500
  GraphicsWindow.Height = 300
  GraphicsWindow.Title = "Example 19-5"
  'Mariners data
  NPoints = 10
  For I = 1 To NPoints
    'dummy array
    XValue[I] = I
    BarColor[I] = "Blue"
  EndFor
  YValue[1] = 2.15
  YValue[2] = 1.65
  YValue[3] = 2.05
  YValue[4] = 1.1
  YValue[5] = 1.64
  YValue[6] = 2.72
  YValue[7] = 3.19
  YValue[8] = 2.65
  YValue[9] = 2.92
  YValue[10] = 3.15
  'plot area
  PlotLeft = 100
  PlotTop = 50
  PlotWidth = 350
  PlotHeight = 200
  GraphicsWindow.PenColor = "Black"
  GraphicsWindow.DrawRectangle(PlotLeft, PlotTop, PlotWidth, PlotHeight)
  FindMinMax()
  'compute spacing on y axis
  AxisMin = YMin
  AxisMax = YMax
```

```
    FindAxisSpacing()
    YMin = AxisMin
    YMax = AxisMax
    BaseValue = AxisMin
    BarChart()
    DrawYGrid = "true"
    LabelYAxis()
    PlotTitle = "Seattle Mariners Yearly Attendance"
    PlotXLabel = "Year"
    PlotYLabel = "Millions"
    AddPlotLabels()
EndSub

Sub FindMinMax
    'find minimums and maximums
    XMin = XValue[1]
    XMax = XValue[1]
    YMin = YValue[1]
    Ymax = YValue[1]
    For I = 2 To NPoints
        XMin = Math.Min(XMin, XValue[I])
        XMax = Math.Max(XMax, XValue[I])
        YMin = Math.Min(YMin, YValue[I])
        Ymax = Math.Max(Ymax, YValue[I])
    EndFor
EndSub

Sub BarChart
    'Constructs a  bar chart
    'NPoints - number of bars to draw
    'YValue - array of bar values
    'BaseValue - base value for bars - convert to pixels
    YData = BaseValue
    YDataToYPlot()
    BasePlot = YPlot
    'Find bar width in pixels, use half bar-width as margins between bars
    BarWidth = 2 * PlotWidth / (3 * NPoints + 1)
    For I = 1 To NPoints
        GraphicsWindow.BrushColor = BarColor[I]
        YData = YValue[I]
        YDataToYPlot()
        'draw bars
        If (BasePlot > YPlot) Then
            GraphicsWindow.FillRectangle(PlotLeft + (1.5 * I - 1) * BarWidth, YPlot, BarWidth, BasePlot - YPlot)
```

```
    Else
      GraphicsWindow.FillRectangle(PlotLeft + (1.5 * I - 1) *
BarWidth, BasePlot, BarWidth, YPlot - BasePlot)
    EndIf
  EndFor
  'line at base
  GraphicsWindow.PenColor = "Black"
  GraphicsWindow.PenWidth = 1
  GraphicsWindow.DrawLine(PlotLeft, BasePlot, PlotLeft +
PlotWidth, BasePlot)
EndSub

Sub YDataToYPlot
  'converts YData) to YPlot
  YPlot = PlotTop + (Ymax - YData) * (PlotHeight - 1) / (Ymax -
YMin)
EndSub

Sub FindAxisSpacing
  'provide AxisMin and AxisMax
  'computes new AxisMin, AxisMax, IntervalSpacing, NumberIntervals
  Eps = 0.025
  If (AxisMin = AxisMax) Then
    AxisMin = 0.9 * AxisMax
  EndIf
  ATemp = Math.Abs(AxisMin)
  If Math.Abs(AxisMin) < Math.Abs(AxisMax) Then
    ATemp = Math.Abs(AxisMax)
  EndIf
  Scale = Math.Power(10, Math.Floor(Math.Log(ATemp) / Math.Log(10)
/ 10.0))
  NextScale:
  Scale = Scale * 10
  MinA = AxisMin / Scale
  MaxA = AxisMax / Scale
  DTemp = (MaxA - MinA) / 4.5
  JTemp = DTemp * Eps
  ETemp = Math.Floor((Math.Log(DTemp) / Math.Log(10)))
  FTemp = DTemp / Math.Power(10, ETemp)
  VTemp = 10
  If FTemp < Math.SquareRoot(2) Then
    VTemp = 1
  ElseIf FTemp < Math.SquareRoot(10) Then
    VTemp = 2
  ElseIf FTemp < Math.SquareRoot(50) Then
    VTemp = 5
```

```
    EndIf
    Delta = VTemp * Math.Power(10, ETemp)
    GTemp = Math.Floor(MinA / Delta)
    If Math.Abs(GTemp + 1 - MinA / Delta) < JTemp Then
      GTemp = GTemp + 1
    EndIf
    MinP = Delta * GTemp
    HTemp = Math.Floor(MaxA / Delta) + 1
    If Math.Abs(MaxA / Delta + 1 - HTemp) < JTemp Then
      HTemp = HTemp - 1
    EndIf
    MaxP = Delta * HTemp
    NumberIntervals = HTemp - GTemp
    If (Math.Abs(MaxP) >= 10 Or Math.Abs(MinP) >= 10) Then
      Goto NextScale
    EndIf
    AxisMin = MinP * Scale
    AxisSpacing = Delta * Scale
    AxisMax = AxisMin + NumberIntervals * AxisSpacing
EndSub

Sub LabelYAxis
    GraphicsWindow.BrushColor = "Black"
    GraphicsWindow.FontSize = 14
    GraphicsWindow.FontBold = "false"
    GraphicsWindow.PenColor = "Black"
    GraphicsWindow.PenWidth = 1
    YData = AxisMin
    For I = 1 To NumberIntervals + 1
      'get y position
      YDataToYPlot()
      GraphicsWindow.DrawText(PlotLeft - 40, YPlot - 10, YData)
      If (DrawYGrid And I > 1 And I < NumberIntervals + 1) Then
        GraphicsWindow.DrawLine(PlotLeft, YPlot, PlotLeft + PlotWidth, YPlot)
      EndIf
      YData = YData + AxisSpacing
    EndFor
EndSub

Sub AddPlotLabels
    'title
    GraphicsWindow.BrushColor = "Black"
    GraphicsWindow.FontSize = 18
    GraphicsWindow.FontBold = "false"
    TitleDisplay = Shapes.AddText(PlotTitle)
```

```
  Shapes.Move(TitleDisplay, PlotLeft + 10, PlotTop - 35)
  'x axis
  GraphicsWindow.FontSize = 16
  XAxisDisplay = Shapes.AddText(PlotXLabel)
  Shapes.Move(XAxisDisplay, PlotLeft + 0.5 * PlotWidth - 10,
PlotTop + PlotHeight + 25)
  'y axis
  GraphicsWindow.FontSize = 16
  YAxisDisplay = Shapes.AddText(PlotYLabel)
  Shapes.Move(YAxisDisplay, PlotLeft - 90, PlotTop + 0.5 *
PlotHeight - 10)
  Shapes.Rotate(YAxisDisplay, 270)
EndSub
```

Saved as **Example 19-5** in **Guide to Small Basic\Programs\Chapter 19** folder.

As mentioned, you should see that this is very similar to **Example 19-4**. The needed subroutines are: **FindMinMax, BarChart, YDataToYPlot, FindAxisSpacing, LabelYAxis** and **AddPlotLabels**. We see it has the same subroutines as **Example 19-4**, excluding **XDataToXPlot** and **LabelXAxis**. We don't need **XDataToXPlot** since we never need to convert any x values to plot coordinates (the bars have know even spacing). And we don't use **LabelXAxis** because we need a different way of labeling the axis for a bar chart (it may not necessarily be numeric labeling). All these subroutines make quick work of building a bar chart program.

In **InitializeProgram**, we fill a dummy **XValue** array (just needed so **FindMinMax** doesn't fail) and we setup a color array for the bars (**BarColor**). We set all the bars to blue. The only other changes (compared to **Example 19-4**) are to remove the code adjusting the x axis and to replace the call to **LineChart** with a call to **BarChart**.

Save and **Run** the program. The bar chart will appear in nearly complete form:

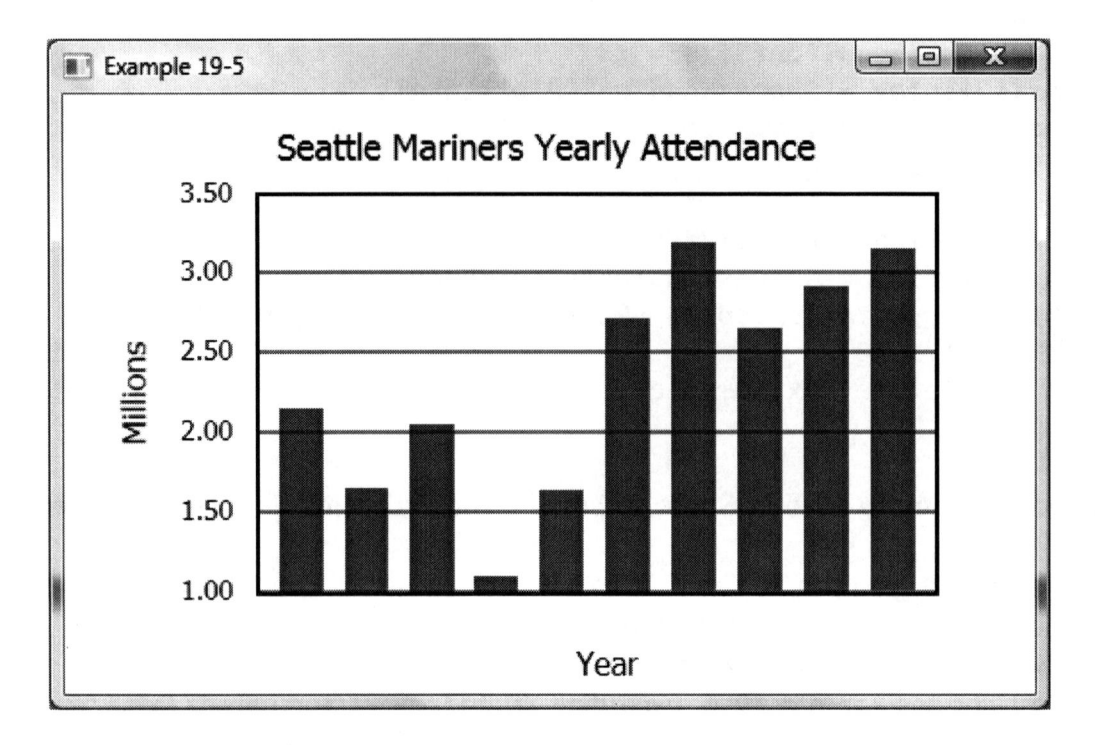

The only thing missing is label information for the x axis.

Bar Chart X Axis Labeling

In a line chart, the horizontal value (x axis) is usually described by numeric data. Hence, using the **LabelXAxis** subroutine (with specified limits and intervals) fits that type of chart.

In a bar chart, we usually want a label under each bar and that label may not be numeric. It could be text such as months of the year, days of the week, a person's name. Hence, we take a different approach to labeling the x axis of a bar chart. For each bar, we have an array element **XLabel** with a text description of that bar. We then draw that text under the corresponding bar. It is suggested that the labels be kept fairly short so they fit under the plot.

This subroutine **LabelBarChartXAxis** adds the elements of **XLabel** to a plot:

```
Sub LabelBarChartXAxis
  GraphicsWindow.BrushColor = "Black"
  GraphicsWindow.FontSize = 14
  GraphicsWindow.FontBold = "false"
  For I = 1 To NPoints
    GraphicsWindow.DrawText(PlotLeft + (1.5 * I - 1) * BarWidth - 2, PlotTop + PlotHeight + 5, XLabel[I])
  EndFor
EndSub
```

This subroutine requires some plot area specifics (**PlotLeft**, **PlotWidth**), the number of bars, **NPoints**. The labels are drawn in the line:

```
GraphicsWindow.DrawText(PlotLeft + (1.5 * I - 1) * BarWidth - 2, PlotTop + PlotHeight + 5, XLabel[I])
```

You may need to adjust the numeric values here for your specific labels.

Example 19-6. Bar Chart X Axis Labeling

Modify **Example 19-5** to add x axis labeling to the bar chart. As a first step, add **LabelBarChartXAxis** subroutine to the program.

Small Basic Code (modifications are only in **InitializeProgram**; changes are shaded):

```
Sub InitializeProgram
  GraphicsWindow.Show()
  GraphicsWindow.Width = 500
  GraphicsWindow.Height = 300
  GraphicsWindow.Title = "Example 19-6"
  'Mariners data
  NPoints = 10
  For I = 1 To NPoints
    'dummy array
    XValue[I] = I
    BarColor[I] = "Blue"
  EndFor
  YValue[1] = 2.15
  YValue[2] = 1.65
  YValue[3] = 2.05
  YValue[4] = 1.1
  YValue[5] = 1.64
  YValue[6] = 2.72
  YValue[7] = 3.19
  YValue[8] = 2.65
  YValue[9] = 2.92
  YValue[10] = 3.15
  'x axis labels
  XLabel[1] = "1991"
  XLabel[2] = "1992"
  XLabel[3] = "1993"
  XLabel[4] = "1994"
  XLabel[5] = "1995""
  XLabel[6] = "1996"
  XLabel[7] = "1997"
  XLabel[8] = "1998"
  XLabel[9] = "1999"
  XLabel[10] = "2000"
  'plot area
  PlotLeft = 100
  PlotTop = 50
  PlotWidth = 350
```

```
    PlotHeight = 200
    GraphicsWindow.PenColor = "Black"
    GraphicsWindow.DrawRectangle(PlotLeft, PlotTop, PlotWidth, PlotHeight)
    FindMinMax()
    'compute spacing on y axis
    AxisMin = YMin
    AxisMax = YMax
    FindAxisSpacing()
    YMin = AxisMin
    YMax = AxisMax
    BaseValue = AxisMin
    BarChart()
    DrawYGrid = "true"
    LabelYAxis()
    LabelBarChartXAxis()
    PlotTitle = "Seattle Mariners Yearly Attendance"
    PlotXLabel = "Year"
    PlotYLabel = "Millions"
    AddPlotLabels()
EndSub
```

Saved as **Example 19-6** in **Guide to Small Basic\Programs\Chapter 19** folder. We added labeling for the x axis and called the labeling subroutine **(LabelBarChartXAxis)**.

Save and **Run** the program. The bar chart will appear in nearly complete form:

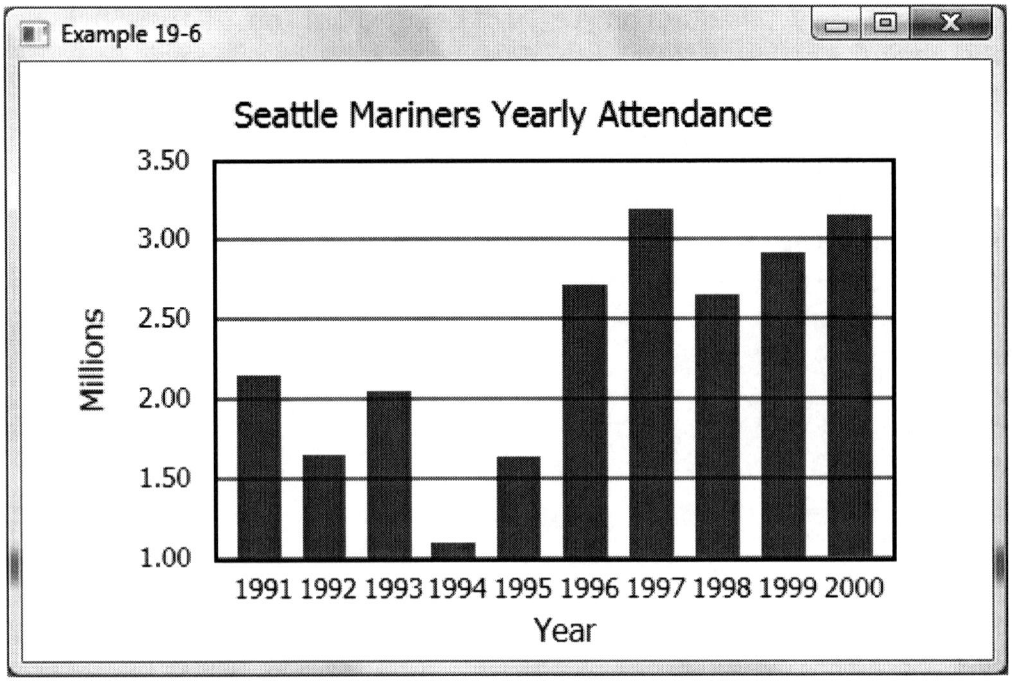
Example 19-6
Seattle Mariners Yearly Attendance
3.50
3.00
2.50
2.00
1.50
1.00
Millions
1991 1992 1993 1994 1995 1996 1997 1998 1999 2000
Year

Example 19-6 is a complete bar chart plotting program. With changes only to **InitializeProgram**, you can draw other bar charts. We do that in the next example.

Example 19-7. Seattle Rainfall Bar Chart

Modify the **InitializeProgram** subroutine in **Example 19-6** to draw a bar chart of the monthly rainfall in Seattle. Use a different color for each of the 12 bars. The data you need is:

Month	Amount
Jan	4.5
Feb	5.0
Mar	4.1
Apr	2.1
May	0.8
Jun	1.5
Jul	1.3
Aug	1.8
Sep	0.9
Oct	3.9
Nov	10.4
Dec	6.4

Small Basic Code (modifications to **InitializeProgram** are shaded):

```
Sub InitializeProgram
  GraphicsWindow.Show()
  GraphicsWindow.Width = 500
  GraphicsWindow.Height = 300
  GraphicsWindow.Title = "Example 19-7"
  'Rainfall data
  NPoints = 12
  For I = 1 To NPoints
    'dummy array
    XValue[I] = I
  EndFor
  YValue[1] = 4.5
  YValue[2] = 5.0
  YValue[3] = 4.1
  YValue[4] = 2.1
  YValue[5] = 0.8
  YValue[6] = 1.5
  YValue[7] = 1.3
  YValue[8] = 1.8
  YValue[9] = 0.9
  YValue[10] = 3.9
  YValue[11] = 10.4
```

```
YValue[12] = 6.4
'x axis labels
XLabel[1] = "Jan"
XLabel[2] = "Feb"
XLabel[3] = "Mar"
XLabel[4] = "Apr"
XLabel[5] = "May""
XLabel[6] = "Jun"
XLabel[7] = "Jul"
XLabel[8] = "Aug"
XLabel[9] = "Sep"
XLabel[10] = "Oct"
XLabel[11] = "Nov"
XLabel[12] = "Dec"
'colors
BarColor[1] = "Red"
BarColor[2] = "Blue"
BarColor[3] = "Green"
BarColor[4] = "Magenta"
BarColor[5] = "Yellow"
BarColor[6] = "Black"
BarColor[7] = "Brown"
BarColor[8] = "Cyan"
BarColor[9] = "DarkRed"
BarColor[10] = "DarkBlue"
BarColor[11] = "DarkGreen"
BarColor[12] = "CornflowerBlue"
'plot area
PlotLeft = 100
PlotTop = 50
PlotWidth = 350
PlotHeight = 200
GraphicsWindow.PenColor = "Black"
GraphicsWindow.DrawRectangle(PlotLeft, PlotTop, PlotWidth, PlotHeight)
FindMinMax()
'compute spacing on y axis
AxisMin = YMin
AxisMax = YMax
FindAxisSpacing()
YMin = AxisMin
YMax = AxisMax
BaseValue = AxisMin
BarChart()
DrawYGrid = "true"
LabelYAxis()
```

```
  LabelBarChartXAxis()
  PlotTitle = "Seattle Monthly Rainfall"
  PlotXLabel = "Month"
  PlotYLabel = "Inches"
  AddPlotLabels()
EndSub
```

Saved as **Example 19-7** in **Guide to Small Basic\Programs\Chapter 19** folder.

Save and **Run** the program and you see::

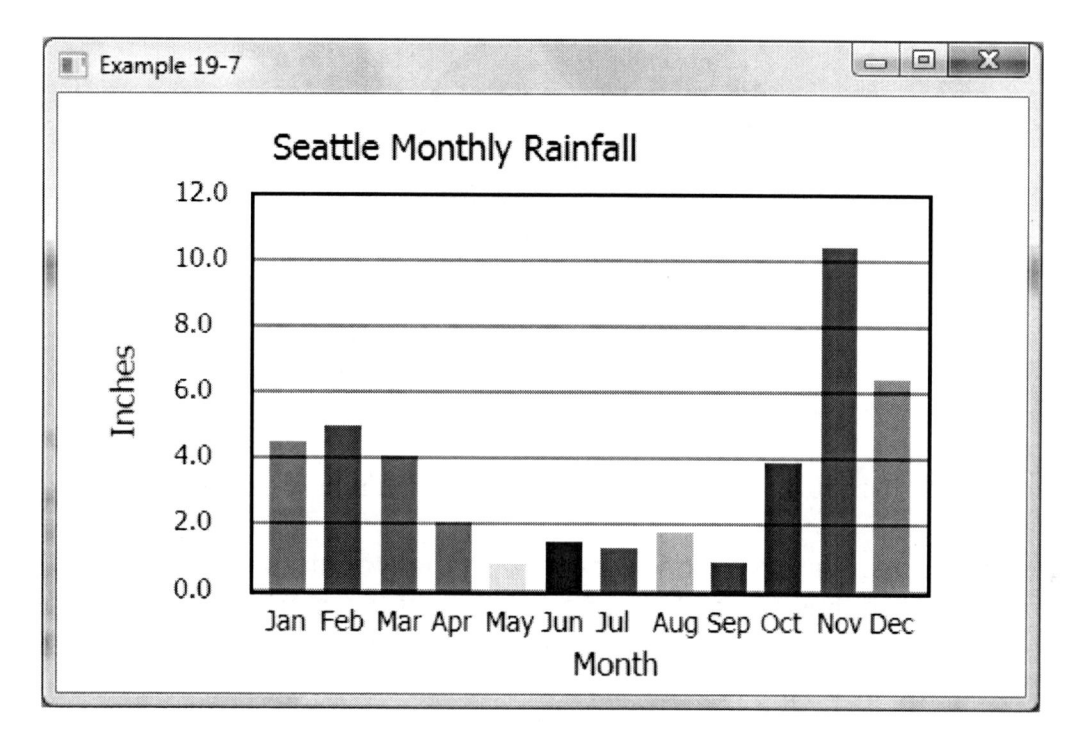

The winter months are very large!

Pie Charts

Another common chart is the **pie chart.** Pie charts are used to compare values of like information or to show what makes up a particular quantity. For example, a pie chart could illustrate what categories your monthly expenses fit into. Or, here is a pie chart of the Seattle rainfall data we just plotted in a bar chart. There are 12 segments, one for each month:

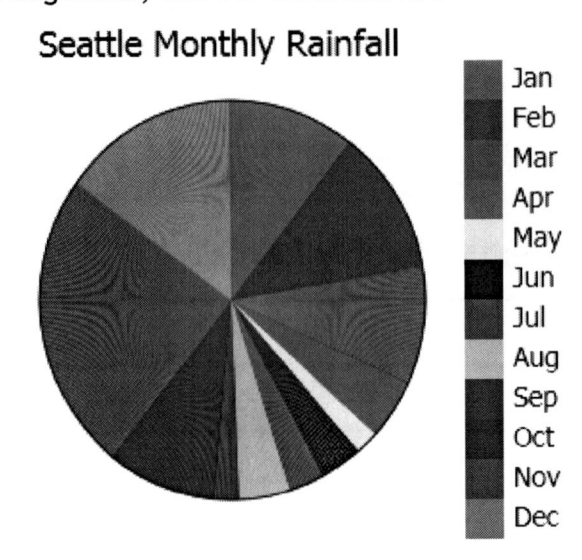

We will build this chart with Small Basic in the remaining examples.

A pie chart is built within a circle (drawn with the graphics window **DrawEllipse** method). Let's discuss a bit of circle geometry. If you start at the top of the circle and move around its edge in a clockwise direction, you sweep through 360 degrees in one rotation. To draw a pie chart, each segment will be defined by a **StartAngle** (zero degrees at the top of the circle) and a **SweepAngle.** If you sum the **SweepAngle** values for all the pie segments, you will get 360 degrees.

The steps for getting angle values and drawing a pie chart are straightforward. Assume you have **N** pieces of data (monthly rainfall, categorized expenditures, seasonal air traffic, or various income sources). Follow these steps to create a pie chart:

> ➢ Generate **N** pieces of data to be plotted. Store this data in an array **Y**.
> ➢ Sum the **N** elements of the **Y** array to obtain a total value.
> ➢ Divide each **Y** element by the computed total to obtain the proportional contributions of each.
> ➢ Multiply each proportion by 360 degrees - the resulting value will be the **SweepAngle** for that segment.
> ➢ Draw each pie segment (use a unique, identifying color). Initialize the **StartAngle** at zero. After drawing each segment, the next **StartAngle** will be the previous value incremented by the current **SweepAngle**.

This all sounds fairly easy except for one particular step. How do you draw a pie segment, given a **StartAngle**, a **SweepAngle** and a color? There is no Small Basic graphics method to draw a filled circle segment, only filled, full circles. We'll use a little bit of trigonometry (and the Small Basic **FillTriangle** method) to solve this problem. You can skip the math if you want and just grab the subroutine that does this task.

Look at this diagram:

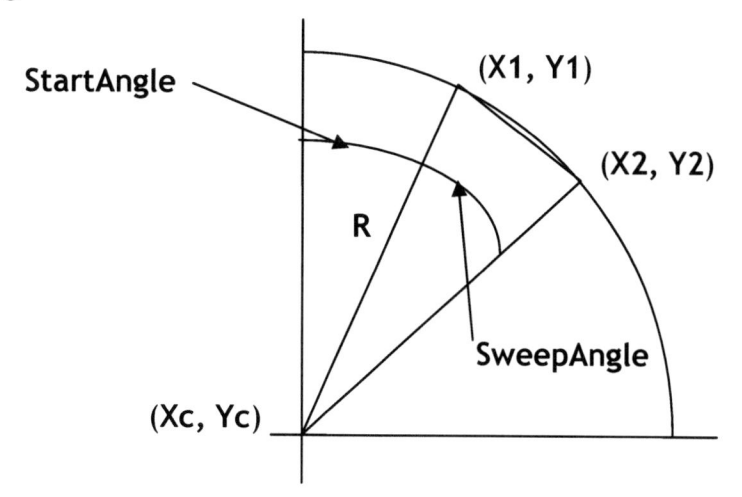

Here we have a circle segment from a circle of radius **R**. The circle is centered at (**Xc**, **Yc**) in the graphics window. The line connecting (**Xc**, **Yc**) to (**X1**, **Y1**) is at an angle **StartAngle**, from the vertical. The line connecting (**Xc**, **Yc**) to (**X2**, **Y2**) is at an angle **StartAngle** + **SweepAngle**. If we fill the triangle defined by (**Xc**, **Yc**), (**X1**, **Y1**) and (**X2**, **Y2**), we get an approximation to a filled circle segment. Just what we need for our pie chart!

Equations for the points on the circle are:

> X1 = Xc + R * Sin(StartAngle)
> Y1 = Yc - R * Cos(StartAngle)
> X2 = Xc + R * Sin(StartAngle + SweepAngle)
> Y2 = Yc - R * Cos(StartAngle + SweepAngle)

where **Sin** and **Cos** are trigonometric functions.

For big angles, "pie" segments drawn as triangles will look more like triangles than circular segments. To solve this problem, we will draw a segment **SweepAngle** in size one degree at a time. This will give us a pretty nice looking pie segment. This subroutine **DrawPieSegment** does the job:

```
Sub DrawPieSegment
  'converts degrees to radians
  DegToRad = Math.Pi / 180
  'draws segment from StartAngle, through SweepAngle, in
SegmentColor
  For I = StartAngle To StartAngle + SweepAngle - 1
    X1 = XCircle + RCircle * Math.Sin(I * DegToRad)
    Y1 = YCircle - RCircle * Math.Cos(I * DegToRad)
    X2 = XCircle + RCircle * Math.Sin((I + 1) * DegToRad)
    Y2 = YCircle - RCircle * Math.Cos((I + 1) * DegToRad)
    GraphicsWindow.BrushColor = SegmentColor
    GraphicsWindow.FillTriangle(XCircle, YCircle, X1, Y1, X2, Y2)
  EndFor
EndSub
```

You give this subroutine a circle radius in pixels (**RCircle**) and the location of the circle center in the graphics window (**XCircle, YCircle**). Also, provide a **StartAngle** and **SweepAngle** (both in degrees) and a color **SegmentColor**. Call **DrawPieSegment** and the corresponding segment will be drawn.

Example 19-8. Drawing a Pie Segment

Build a program that draws a pie segment in the graphics window.

Small Basic Code:

```
'Guide to Small Basic, Example 19-8
InitializeProgram()

Sub InitializeProgram
  GraphicsWindow.Show()
  GraphicsWindow.Width = 300
  GraphicsWindow.Height = 300
  GraphicsWindow.Title = "Example 19-8"
  RCircle = 100
  XCircle = 150
  YCircle = 150
  StartAngle = 45
  SweepAngle = 60
  SegmentColor = "Red"
  DrawPieSegment()
  GraphicsWindow.PenColor = "Black"
  GraphicsWindow.PenWidth = 1
  GraphicsWindow.DrawEllipse(XCircle - RCircle, YCircle - RCircle, 2 * RCircle, 2 * RCircle)
EndSub

Sub DrawPieSegment
  'converts degrees to radians
  DegToRad = Math.Pi / 180
  'draws segment from StartAngle, through SweepAngle, in SegmentColor
  For I = StartAngle To StartAngle + SweepAngle - 1
    X1 = XCircle + RCircle * Math.Sin(I * DegToRad)
    Y1 = YCircle - RCircle * Math.Cos(I * DegToRad)
    X2 = XCircle + RCircle * Math.Sin((I + 1) * DegToRad)
    Y2 = YCircle - RCircle * Math.Cos((I + 1) * DegToRad)
    GraphicsWindow.BrushColor = SegmentColor
    GraphicsWindow.FillTriangle(XCircle, YCircle, X1, Y1, X2, Y2)
  EndFor
EndSub
```

19-48   The Developer's Reference Guide to Small Basic

Saved as **Example 19-8** in **Guide to Small Basic\Programs\Chapter 19** folder. The program sets values for a pie segment and draws it using **DrawPieSegment**.

Save and **Run** the program and you see a red segment from 45 degrees (**StartAngle**) to 105 degrees (**SweepAngle = 60**).

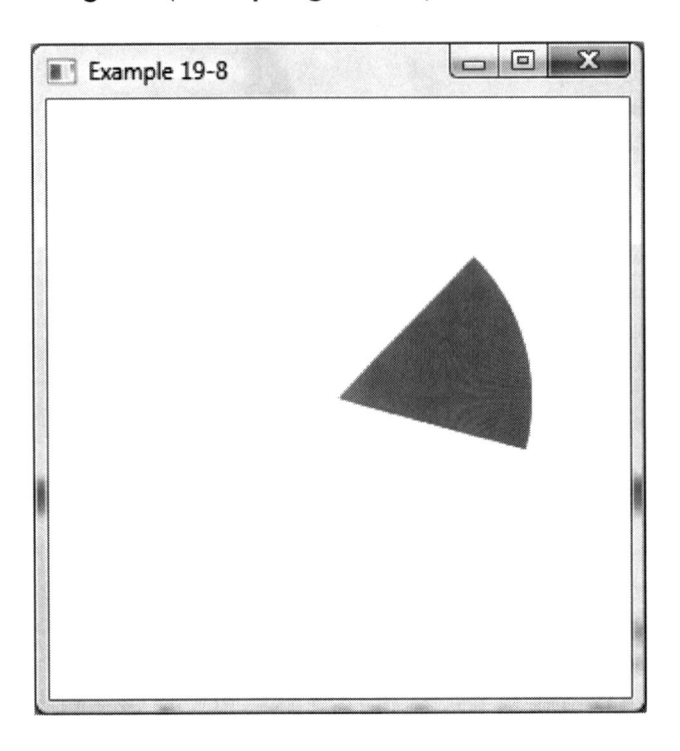

Drawing a Pie Chart

With the ability to draw a pie segment, we can draw a pie chart. Here are the modified steps outlined earlier:

- Generate **N** pieces of data to be plotted. Store this data in an array **Y**.
- Sum the **N** elements of the **Y** array to obtain a total value.
- Divide each **Y** element by the computed total to obtain the proportional contributions of each.
- Multiply each proportion by 360 degrees – the resulting value will be the **SweepAngle** for that segment.
- Use **DrawPieSegment** to draw each segment. Use a different color for each segment.
- Once all segments are drawn, enclose the pie chart in a circle.

The subroutine **PieChart** implements these steps and draws a pie chart in the graphics window:

```
Sub PieChart
  'find sum of values
  Sum = 0
  For I = 1 To NPoints
    Sum = Sum + YValue[I]
  EndFor
  'for each slice determine SweepAngle and draw using PieColor
  StartAngle = 0
  For I = 1 To NPoints
    SegmentColor = PieColor[I]
    SweepAngle = 360 * YValue[I] / Sum
    DrawPieSegment()
    StartAngle = StartAngle + SweepAngle
  EndFor
  GraphicsWindow.PenColor = "Black"
  GraphicsWindow.PenWidth = 1
  GraphicsWindow.DrawEllipse(XCircle - RCircle, YCircle - RCircle, 2 * RCircle, 2 * RCircle)
EndSub
```

The subroutine requires location and size of the pie chart circle (**XCircle**, **YCircle**, **RCircle**). It also needs the number of points (**NPoints**), the y values (**YValue**), and corresponding segment colors (**PieColor** array).

Example 19-9. Seattle Rainfall Pie Chart

Write a program to draw a pie chart of the monthly rainfall in Seattle. Use a different color for each of the 12 segments. The data you need is (same data used for bar chart example):

Month	Amount
Jan	4.5
Feb	5.0
Mar	4.1
Apr	2.1
May	0.8
Jun	1.5
Jul	1.3
Aug	1.8
Sep	0.9
Oct	3.9
Nov	10.4
Dec	6.4

Make sure to add the **DrawPieSegment** and **PieChart** subroutine to your program.

Small Basic Code (we don't show **DrawPieSegment** or **PieChart**):

```
'Guide to Small Basic, Example 19-9
InitializeProgram()

Sub InitializeProgram
  GraphicsWindow.Show()
  GraphicsWindow.Width = 300
  GraphicsWindow.Height = 300
  GraphicsWindow.Title = "Example 19-9"
  'rainfall data
  NPoints = 12
  YValue[1] = 4.5
  YValue[2] = 5.0
  YValue[3] = 4.1
  YValue[4] = 2.1
  YValue[5] = 0.8
  YValue[6] = 1.5
  YValue[7] = 1.3
  YValue[8] = 1.8
  YValue[9] = 0.9
  YValue[10] = 3.9
```

```
    YValue[11] = 10.4
    YValue[12] = 6.4
    'colors
    PieColor[1] = "Red"
    PieColor[2] = "Blue"
    PieColor[3] = "Green"
    PieColor[4] = "Magenta"
    PieColor[5] = "Yellow"
    PieColor[6] = "Black"
    PieColor[7] = "Brown"
    PieColor[8] = "Cyan"
    PieColor[9] = "DarkRed"
    PieColor[10] = "DarkBlue"
    PieColor[11] = "DarkGreen"
    PieColor[12] = "CornflowerBlue"
    'circle location
    RCircle = 100
    XCircle = 150
    YCircle = 150
    PieChart()
EndSub
```

Saved as **Example 19-9** in **Guide to Small Basic\Programs\Chapter 19** folder. The **InitializeProgram** subroutine establishes the rainfall values in the **YValue** array and sets colors in the **PieColor** array. It uses the same circle in previous examples, then calls **PieChart**.

Save and **Run** the program and you see::

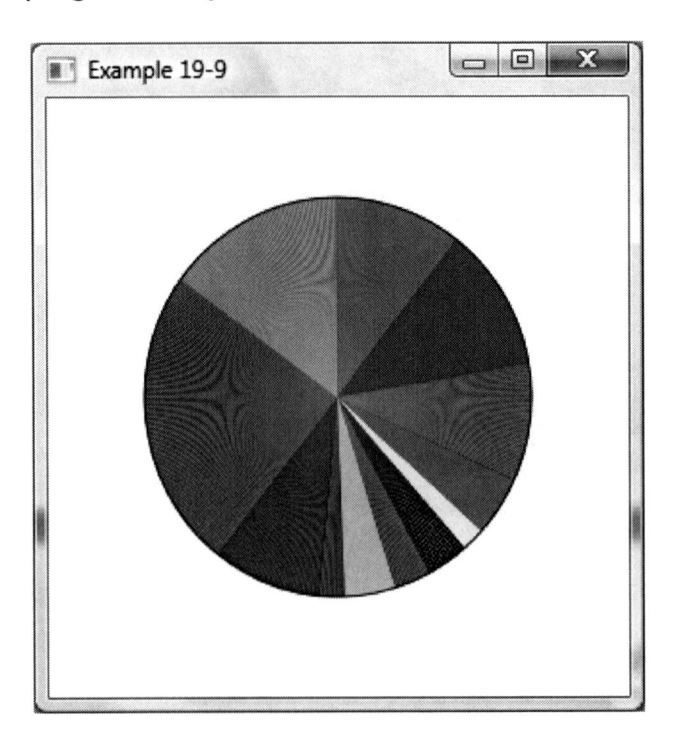

[Example 19-9 pie chart]

Let's add some labeling and we're done.

Pie Chart Labeling

The pie chart needs some text labeling to complete it. It needs a title - we will use a **Shapes** text object similar to that used for line and bar charts. And, it needs a legend.

The legends will consist of small color boxes, one for each pie segment. Next to the colored box will be some indication of what the correspondingly colored pie segment represents. These, too, will be **Shapes** text objects. You can use some text description, perhaps the **YValue** element or the percentage represented by that pie segment. You decide.

The subroutine **AddPieChartLabels** adds the needed title (**PlotTitle**) and legends including label (**SegmentLabel** array):

```
Sub AddPieChartLabels
  'title
  GraphicsWindow.BrushColor = "Black"
  GraphicsWindow.FontSize = 18
  GraphicsWindow.FontBold = "false"
  TitleDisplay = Shapes.AddText(PlotTitle)
  Shapes.Move(TitleDisplay, XCircle - RCircle, YCircle - RCircle - 40)
  'legends
  GraphicsWindow.FontSize = 14
  For I =1 To NPoints
    GraphicsWindow.BrushColor = PieColor[I]
    GraphicsWindow.FillRectangle(XCircle + RCircle + 20, YCircle - RCircle - 20 + (I - 1) *20, 20, 20)
    GraphicsWindow.BrushColor = "Black"
    GraphicsWindow.DrawText(XCircle + RCircle + 45, YCircle - RCircle - 20 + (I - 1) * 20, SegmentLabel[I])
  EndFor
EndSub
```

19-54   The Developer's Reference Guide to Small Basic

Example 19-10. Pie Chart Labeling

Add labeling and legends to the pie chart drawn in **Example 19-9**. Remember to include the **AddPieChartLabels** subroutine to your program.

Small Basic Code (changes to **InitializeProgram** are shaded):

```
Sub InitializeProgram
  GraphicsWindow.Show()
  GraphicsWindow.Width = 400
  GraphicsWindow.Height = 300
  GraphicsWindow.Title = "Example 19-10"
  'rainfall data
  NPoints = 12
  YValue[1] = 4.5
  YValue[2] = 5.0
  YValue[3] = 4.1
  YValue[4] = 2.1
  YValue[5] = 0.8
  YValue[6] = 1.5
  YValue[7] = 1.3
  YValue[8] = 1.8
  YValue[9] = 0.9
  YValue[10] = 3.9
  YValue[11] = 10.4
  YValue[12] = 6.4
  'colors
  PieColor[1] = "Red"
  PieColor[2] = "Blue"
  PieColor[3] = "Green"
  PieColor[4] = "Magenta"
  PieColor[5] = "Yellow"
  PieColor[6] = "Black"
  PieColor[7] = "Brown"
  PieColor[8] = "Cyan"
  PieColor[9] = "DarkRed"
  PieColor[10] = "DarkBlue"
  PieColor[11] = "DarkGreen"
  PieColor[12] = "CornflowerBlue"
  'circle location
  RCircle = 100
  XCircle = 150
  YCircle = 150
  PieChart()
  PlotTitle = "Seattle Monthly Rainfall"
```

```
  'segment labels
  SegmentLabel[1] = "Jan"
  SegmentLabel[2] = "Feb"
  SegmentLabel[3] = "Mar"
  SegmentLabel[4] = "Apr"
  SegmentLabel[5] = "May"""
  SegmentLabel[6] = "Jun"
  SegmentLabel[7] = "Jul"
  SegmentLabel[8] = "Aug"
  SegmentLabel[9] = "Sep"
  SegmentLabel[10] = "Oct"
  SegmentLabel[11] = "Nov"
  SegmentLabel[12] = "Dec"
  AddPieChartLabels()
EndSub

Sub PieChart
  'find sum of values
  Sum = 0
  For I = 1 To NPoints
    Sum = Sum + YValue[I]
  EndFor
  'for each slice determine SweepAngle and draw using PieColor
  StartAngle = 0
  For I = 1 To NPoints
    SegmentColor = PieColor[I]
    SweepAngle = 360 * YValue[I] / Sum
    DrawPieSegment()
    StartAngle = StartAngle + SweepAngle
  EndFor
  GraphicsWindow.PenColor = "Black"
  GraphicsWindow.PenWidth = 1
  GraphicsWindow.DrawEllipse(XCircle - RCircle, YCircle - RCircle, 2 * RCircle, 2 * RCircle)
EndSub

Sub DrawPieSegment
  'converts degrees to radians
  DegToRad = Math.Pi / 180
  'draws segment from StartAngle, through SweepAngle, in SegmentColor
  For AValue = StartAngle To StartAngle + SweepAngle
    X1 = XCircle + RCircle * Math.Sin(AValue * DegToRad)
    Y1 = YCircle - RCircle * Math.Cos(AValue * DegToRad)
    X2 = XCircle + RCircle * Math.Sin((AValue + 1) * DegToRad)
    Y2 = YCircle - RCircle * Math.Cos((AValue + 1) * DegToRad)
```

```
      GraphicsWindow.BrushColor = SegmentColor
      GraphicsWindow.FillTriangle(XCircle, YCircle, X1, Y1, X2, Y2)
  EndFor
EndSub

Sub AddPieChartLabels
  'title
  GraphicsWindow.BrushColor = "Black"
  GraphicsWindow.FontSize = 18
  GraphicsWindow.FontBold = "false"
  TitleDisplay = Shapes.AddText(PlotTitle)
  Shapes.Move(TitleDisplay, XCircle - RCircle, YCircle - RCircle - 40)
  'Legends
  GraphicsWindow.FontSize = 14
  For I =1 To NPoints
    GraphicsWindow.BrushColor = PieColor[I]
    GraphicsWindow.FillRectangle(XCircle + RCircle + 20, YCircle - RCircle - 20 + (I - 1) *20, 20, 20)
    GraphicsWindow.BrushColor = "Black"
    GraphicsWindow.DrawText(XCircle + RCircle + 45, YCircle - RCircle - 20 + (I - 1) * 20, SegmentLabel[I])
  EndFor
EndSub
```

Saved as **Example 19-10** in **Guide to Small Basic\Programs\Chapter 19** folder.

We have shown the entire pie chart plotting program with all the subroutines. You can use this program as a framework for any pie charts you might like to draw. You should only have to change code in the **InitializeProgram** subroutine.

Save and **Run** the program. You will see the final pie chart for Seattle rainfall:

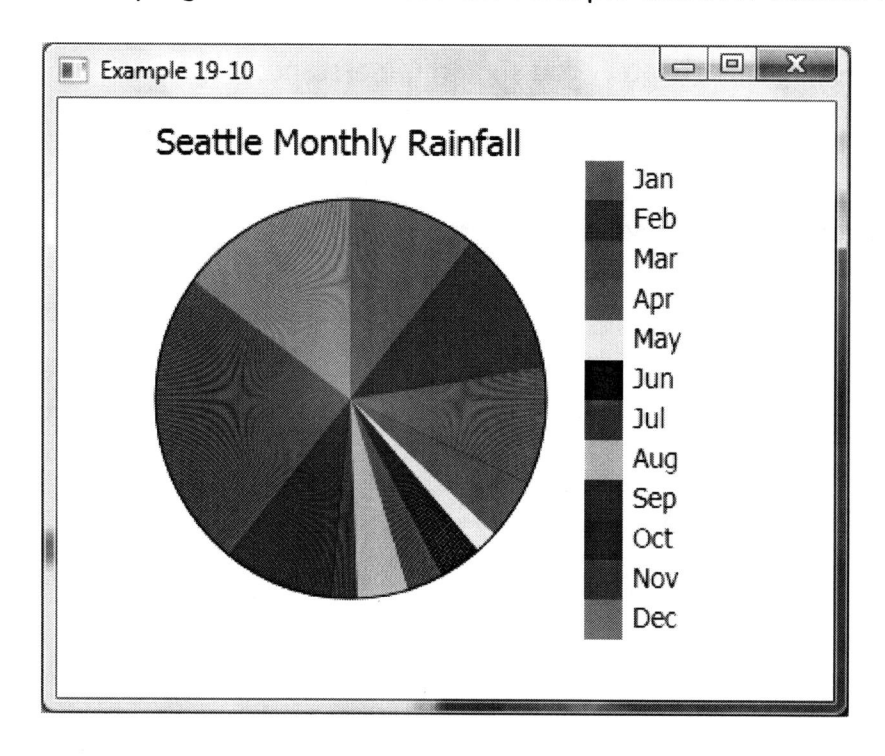

Chapter Review

After completing this chapter, you should understand:

- How to draw and label a line chart.
- How to draw and label a bar chart.
- How to draw and label a pie chart.

20. Animation

Preview

In this chapter, we learn skills to build animated games using Small Basic. We discuss animation, collision detection and sounds. We build a version of the first commercial video game ever - Pong!

Animation with Small Basic

Programming animated games in Small Basic requires a specific set of skills. We need to know how to create a **Shapes** object hosting a graphic image, how to move (animate) that image and how to see if one image collides with another image. We also want to add sounds to our games. We will discuss all these new skills. We start with **animation**.

Animation is fairly simple with Small Basic. We create a **Shapes** object holding an image. Then, using the **Shapes Move** method, we give the image an appearance of motion. Though we only use images here, animation can be done with any **Shapes** object - rectangles, ellipses, lines, triangles, ...

The first step to create a **Shapes** object is to load an image from a graphics file. This is done with:

```
MyImage = ImageList.LoadImage(FileName)
```

where **FileName** is a complete path to the graphics file. We usually keep the graphics files in the program folder. With this, the **Shapes** object displaying the image (**MyShape**) is created using:

```
MyShape = Shapes.AddImage(MyImage)
```

Once created, we position the **Shapes** object at (**X, Y**) using the **Move** method:

```
Shapes.Move(MyShape, X, Y)
```

This statement will remove **MyShape** at its previous location in the graphics window (if any) and move it to (**X, Y**). By periodically (using a **Timer** object) changing the value of (**X, Y**) and moving the shape to that new location we obtain a nice smooth animated motion. It really is that easy.

Animation 20-3

Two other **Shapes** methods useful in animation are the **HideShape** and **ShowShape** methods. To remove a shape (**MyShape**) from the graphics window, use:

```
Shapes.HideShape(MyShape)
```

Then, to make a hidden shape reappear, use:

```
Shapes.ShowShape(MyShape)
```

One question you may have is why not use the **Shapes** object **Animate** method to do animation? Recall that method is:

```
Shapes.Animate(MyShape, X, Y, Duration)
```

This is similar to the **Move** method, moving **MyShape** from its current position to a new position (**X, Y**), taking **Duration** milliseconds to do the move. This method does a nice smooth animation, but the problem is no other events can be recognized in a Small Basic program during the movement.

The incremental motion of the **Move** method, in conjunction with the **Timer** object makes the tasks of determining if shapes collide, if the user makes some choice or other things occur in your program much easier. The **Animate** method provides a smooth, nice animation, but it is best used when no user interaction is expected.

Example 20-1. Dropping Ball

Write a program with a single button control that starts and stops a **Timer** object. Have the program animate a ball dropping from the top of the graphics window to the bottom. In the **Guide to Small Basic\Programs\Chapter 20** folder is a graphic we will use for this example:

ball.gif

Copy this file to your program's folder.

Small Basic Code:

```
'Guide to Small Basic, Example 20-1
InitializeProgram()

Sub InitializeProgram
  GraphicsWindow.Show()
  GraphicsWindow.Title = "Example 20-1"
  GraphicsWindow.Width = 250
  GraphicsWindow.Height = 400
  'ball graphic
  BallImage = ImageList.LoadImage(Program.Directory + "\ball.gif")
  BallW = ImageList.GetWidthOfImage(BallImage)
  BallH = ImageList.GetHeightOfImage(BallImage)
  Ball = Shapes.AddImage(BallImage)
  BallX = 50
  BallY = 0
  BallYSpeed = 10
  Shapes.Move(Ball, BallX, BallY)
  'button
  GraphicsWindow.BrushColor = "Black"
  GraphicsWindow.FontSize = 16
  GraphicsWindow.FontBold = "false"
  TimerButton = Controls.AddButton("Start", 190, 10)
  Controls.ButtonClicked = ButtonClickedSub
  Timer.Interval = 100
  Timer.Tick = TickSub
  Timer.Pause()
EndSub
```

```
Sub ButtonClickedSub
  If (Controls.GetButtonCaption(TimerButton) = "Start") Then
    Controls.SetButtonCaption(TimerButton, "Stop")
    Timer.Resume()
  Else
    Controls.SetButtonCaption(TimerButton, "Start")
    Timer.Pause()
  EndIf
EndSub

Sub TickSub
  BallY = BallY + BallYSpeed
  Shapes.Move(Ball, BallX, BallY)
EndSub
```

Saved as **Example 20-1** in **Guide to Small Basic\Programs\Chapter 20** folder.

In **InitializeProgram**, we create the **Ball Shapes** object using the image (**ball.gif**) and find its width (**BallW**) and height (**BallH**). We initialize the location (**BallX, BallY**) at the top of the window. A speed value (**BallYSpeed**) is set. A button (**TimerButton**) is used to start and stop the **Timer** object that controls the animation.

In the **TickSub** subroutine, the vertical position of the ball (**BallY**) is increased by **BalllYSpeed** each time the event is executed (every 0.1 seconds). The ball is moving down. Since the window height is 400 pixels and the **BallYSpeed** is 10, It should take 40 executions of this routine, or about 4 seconds, for the ball to reach the bottom.

Save and **Run** the program. Click the button to start/stop the timer. Watch the ball drop:

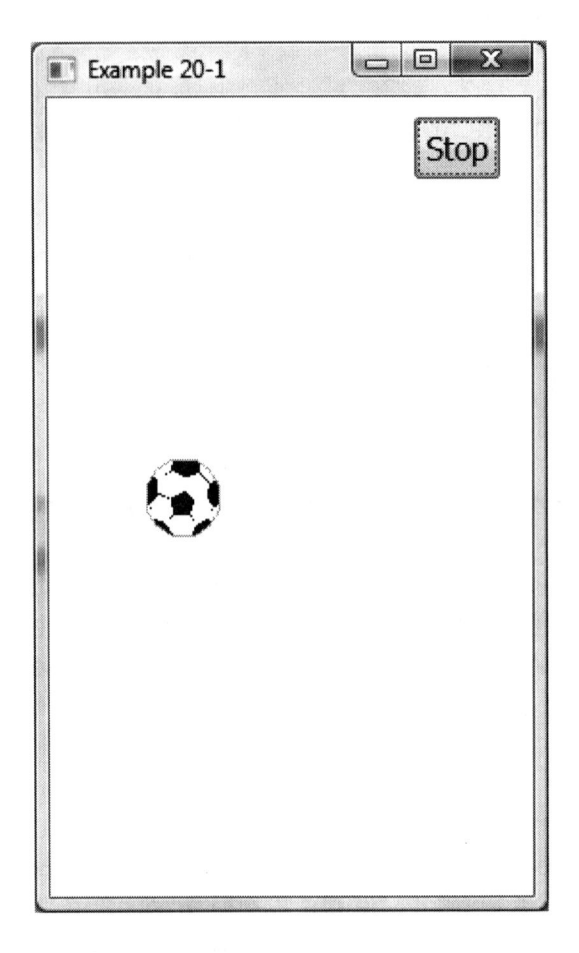

Pretty easy, wasn't it? How long does it take the ball to reach the bottom? What happens when it reaches the bottom? It just keeps on going down through the window and out through the bottom of your computer monitor to who knows where! We need to be able to detect this disappearance and do something about it. We'll look at two ways to handle this. First, we'll make the ball reappear at the top of the window, or scroll. Then, we'll make it bounce. Stop the program. Make sure you have saved it. We'll be modifying it several times as we build new examples.

Border Crossing

When shapes are moving in a window, we need to know when they move out of the window across a border. Such information is often needed in video type games. We just saw this need with the dropping ball example. When a **border crossing** happens, we can either ignore that shape or perhaps make it "scroll" around to other side of the window. How do we decide if a image has disappeared? It's basically a case of comparing various positions and dimensions.

We need to detect whether a shape has completely moved across one of four window borders (top, bottom, left, right). Each of these detections can be developed using this diagram of a shape (**MyShape**) within a graphics window:

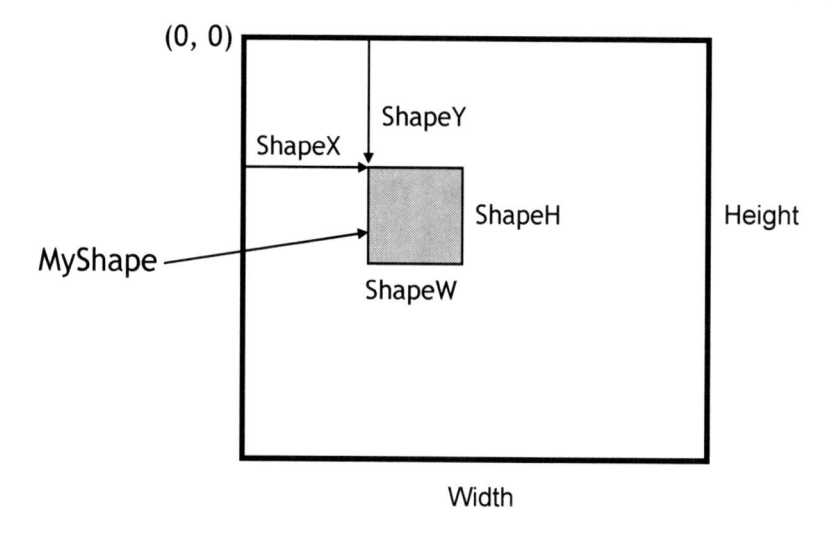

Notice the shape is located at (**ShapeX**, **ShapeY**), is **ShapeW** pixels wide and **ShapeH** pixels high.

If the shape is moving down, it completely crosses the graphics window bottom border when its top (**ShapeY**) is lower than the bottom border. The bottom of the graphics window is **GraphicsWindow.Height**. Small Basic code for a bottom border crossing is:

```
If (ShapeY > GraphicsWindow.Height) Then
  'Code for bottom border crossing
EndIf
```

If the shape is moving up, the window top border is completely crossed when the bottom of the shape (**ShapeY + ShapeH**) becomes less than 0. In Small Basic, this is detected with:

```
If (ShapeY + ShapeH < 0) Then
   'Code for top border crossing
EndIf
```

If the shape is moving to the left, the window left border is completely crossed when shape right side (**ShapeX + ShapeW**) becomes less than 0. In Small Basic, this is detected with:

```
If (ShapeX + ShapeW < 0) Then
   'Code for left border crossing
EndIf
```

If the shape is moving to the right, it completely crosses the window right border when its left side (**ShapeX**) passes the border. The right side of the panel is **GraphicsWindow.Width**. Small Basic code for a right border crossing is:

```
If (ShapeX > GraphicsWindow.Width) Then
   'Code for right border crossing
EndIf
```

Example 20-2. Scrolling Ball

Modify **Example 20-1** so the ball magically reappears at the top of the window once it crosses the graphics window bottom border. We say the ball is scrolling.

Small Basic Code (modifications are shaded):

```
'Guide to Small Basic, Example 20-2
InitializeProgram()

Sub InitializeProgram
  GraphicsWindow.Show()
  GraphicsWindow.Title = "Example 20-2"
  GraphicsWindow.Width = 250
  GraphicsWindow.Height = 400
  'ball graphic
  BallImage = ImageList.LoadImage(Program.Directory + "\ball.gif")
  BallW = ImageList.GetWidthOfImage(BallImage)
  BallH = ImageList.GetHeightOfImage(BallImage)
  Ball = Shapes.AddImage(BallImage)
  BallX = 50
  BallY = 0
  BallYSpeed = 10
  Shapes.Move(Ball, BallX, BallY)
  'button
  GraphicsWindow.BrushColor = "Black"
  GraphicsWindow.FontSize = 16
  GraphicsWindow.FontBold = "false"
  TimerButton = Controls.AddButton("Start", 190, 10)
  Controls.ButtonClicked = ButtonClickedSub
  Timer.Interval = 100
  Timer.Tick = TickSub
  Timer.Pause()
EndSub

Sub ButtonClickedSub
  If (Controls.GetButtonCaption(TimerButton) = "Start") Then
    Controls.SetButtonCaption(TimerButton, "Stop")
    Timer.Resume()
  Else
    Controls.SetButtonCaption(TimerButton, "Start")
    Timer.Pause()
  EndIf
EndSub
```

```
Sub TickSub
  BallY = BallY + BallYSpeed
  Shapes.Move(Ball, BallX, BallY)
  If (BallY > GraphicsWindow.Height) Then
    BallY = -BallH
  EndIf
EndSub
```

Saved as **Example 20-2** in **Guide to Small Basic\Programs\Chapter 20** folder.

The only change to the previous code is a few added lines in **TickSub**. We added the bottom border crossing logic. Notice when the shape crosses the border, we reset its **BallY** value so it is repositioned just off the top of the window.

Save and **Run** the project. Watch the ball scroll. Here it is just reappearing from the top:

Pretty easy, wasn't it?

Border Intersection

What if, in the dropping ball example, instead of scrolling, we want the ball to bounce back up when it reaches the bottom border? This is another common animation task - detecting the initiation of **border intersections**. Such intersections are used to change the direction of moving images, that is, make them bounce. How do we detect border intersections?

The same diagram used for border crossings can be used here. Checking to see if a shape has intersected a graphics window border is like checking for a border crossing, except the shape has not moved quite as far. For top and bottom checks, the shape movement is less by an amount equal to its height value (**ShapeH**). For left and right checks, the shape movement is less by an amount equal to its width value (**ShapeW**). Look back at that diagram and you should see these code segments accomplish the respective border intersection directions:

```
If (ShapeY + ShapeH > GraphicsWindow.Height) Then
  'Code for bottom border intersection
EndIf

If (ShapeY < 0) Then
  'Code for top border intersection
EndIf

If (ShapeX < 0) Then
  'Code for left border intersection
EndIf

If (ShapeX + ShapeW > GraphicsWindow.Width) Then
  'Code for right border intersection
EndIf
```

20-12   The Developer's Reference Guide to Small Basic

Example 20-3. Bouncing Ball

Modify **Example 20-2** so the ball bounces back up once it reaches the graphics window bottom border.

Small Basic Code (modifications are shaded):

```
'Guide to Small Basic, Example 20-3
InitializeProgram()

Sub InitializeProgram
  GraphicsWindow.Show()
  GraphicsWindow.Title = "Example 20-3"
  GraphicsWindow.Width = 250
  GraphicsWindow.Height = 400
  'ball graphic
  BallImage = ImageList.LoadImage(Program.Directory + "\ball.gif")
  BallW = ImageList.GetWidthOfImage(BallImage)
  BallH = ImageList.GetHeightOfImage(BallImage)
  Ball = Shapes.AddImage(BallImage)
  BallX = 50
  BallY = 0
  BallYSpeed = 10
  Shapes.Move(Ball, BallX, BallY)
  'button
  GraphicsWindow.BrushColor = "Black"
  GraphicsWindow.FontSize = 16
  GraphicsWindow.FontBold = "false"
  TimerButton = Controls.AddButton("Start", 190, 10)
  Controls.ButtonClicked = ButtonClickedSub
  Timer.Interval = 100
  Timer.Tick = TickSub
  Timer.Pause()
EndSub

Sub ButtonClickedSub
  If (Controls.GetButtonCaption(TimerButton) = "Start") Then
    Controls.SetButtonCaption(TimerButton, "Stop")
    Timer.Resume()
  Else
    Controls.SetButtonCaption(TimerButton, "Start")
    Timer.Pause()
  EndIf
EndSub
```

```
Sub TickSub
  BallY = BallY + BallYSpeed
  Shapes.Move(Ball, BallX, BallY)
  If (BallY + BallH > GraphicsWindow.Height) Then
    BallY = GraphicsWindow.Height - BallH
    BallYSpeed = -BallYSpeed
  EndIf
EndSub
```

In **TickSub**, we have replaced the code in the existing **If/EndIf** structure with code for a bottom border intersection. Notice when an intersection is detected, the ball is repositioned (by resetting **BallY**) at the bottom of the window (**GraphicsWindow.Height - BallH**) and the sign on **BallYSpeed** is changed by multiplying the current value by -1. This reverses the ball direction.

Save and **Run** the project. Now when the ball reaches the bottom of the window, it reverses direction and heads back up. We've made the ball bounce! But, once it reaches the top, it's gone again! Let's fix that.

Add top border intersection detection, so the **TickSub** subroutine is now (changes are shaded):

```
Sub TickSub
  BallY = BallY + BallYSpeed
  Shapes.Move(Ball, BallX, BallY)
  If (BallY + BallH > GraphicsWindow.Height) Then
    BallY = GraphicsWindow.Height - BallH
    BallYSpeed = -BallYSpeed
  ElseIf (BallY < 0) Then
    BallY = 0
    BallYSpeed = -BallYSpeed
  EndIf
EndSub
```

In the top intersection code (the **ElseIf** portion), we reset **BallY** to 0 (the top of the window) and reverse the sign on **BallYSpeed**.

Save and **Run** the program again. The ball will now bounce up and down until you stop it. Here's the ball heading back down after a top bounce:

The code we've developed here for checking and resetting **Shapes** objects positions is a common task in Small Basic. As you develop your programming skills, you should make sure you are comfortable with what all these properties and dimensions mean and how they interact. As an example, do you see how we could compute **BallX** so the ball is centered in the graphics window? In the bouncing ball example, change the line in **InitializeProgram** that sets **BallX** to **50** with this line:

```
BallX = 0.5 * (GraphicsWindow.Width - BallW)
```

Save and **Run** the project. The bouncing ball is now in the middle of the window:

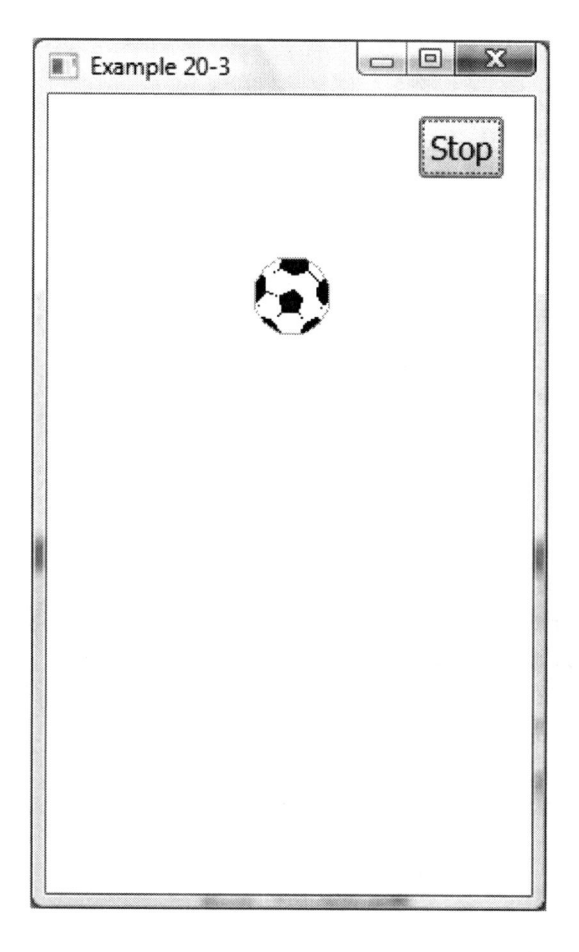

This final version of the program is saved as **Example 20-3** in **Guide to Small Basic\Programs\Chapter 20** folder.

Example 20-4. Bouncing Ball With Sound

Modify **Example 20-3** so with each bounce of the ball, a sound plays. Recall we looked at playing sounds in Chapter 13. A bouncing sound (**bounce.wav**) is included in the **Guide to Small Basic\Programs\Chapter 20** folder. Copy this file to your program folder.

Small Basic Code (modifications are shaded):

```
'Guide to Small Basic, Example 20-4
InitializeProgram()

Sub InitializeProgram
  GraphicsWindow.Show()
  GraphicsWindow.Title = "Example 20-4"
  GraphicsWindow.Width = 250
  GraphicsWindow.Height = 400
  'ball graphic
  BallImage = ImageList.LoadImage(Program.Directory + "\ball.gif")
  BallW = ImageList.GetWidthOfImage(BallImage)
  BallH = ImageList.GetHeightOfImage(BallImage)
  Ball = Shapes.AddImage(BallImage)
  BallX = 0.5 * (GraphicsWindow.Width - BallW)
  BallY = 0
  BallYSpeed = 10
  Shapes.Move(Ball, BallX, BallY)
  'button
  GraphicsWindow.BrushColor = "Black"
  GraphicsWindow.FontSize = 16
  GraphicsWindow.FontBold = "false"
  TimerButton = Controls.AddButton("Start", 190, 10)
  Controls.ButtonClicked = ButtonClickedSub
  Timer.Interval = 100
  Timer.Tick = TickSub
  Timer.Pause()
EndSub

Sub ButtonClickedSub
  If (Controls.GetButtonCaption(TimerButton) = "Start") Then
    Controls.SetButtonCaption(TimerButton, "Stop")
    Timer.Resume()
  Else
    Controls.SetButtonCaption(TimerButton, "Start")
    Timer.Pause()
  EndIf
```

```
EndSub

Sub TickSub
  BallY = BallY + BallYSpeed
  Shapes.Move(Ball, BallX, BallY)
  If (BallY + BallH > GraphicsWindow.Height) Then
    BallY = GraphicsWindow.Height - BallH
    BallYSpeed = -BallYSpeed
    Sound.Stop(Program.Directory + "\bounce.wav")
    Sound.Play(Program.Directory + "\bounce.wav")
  ElseIf (BallY < 0) Then
    BallY = 0
    BallYSpeed = -BallYSpeed
    Sound.Stop(Program.Directory + "\bounce.wav")
    Sound.Play(Program.Directory + "\bounce.wav")
  EndIf
EndSub
```

Saved as **Example 20-4** in **Guide to Small Basic\Programs\Chapter 20** folder.

The shaded code plays the bounce sound. We stop the sound first, in case it is still playing from a previous call to the **Play** method.

Save and **Run** the project. Now with each bounce of the ball you hear a little bong sound.

20-18   The Developer's Reference Guide to Small Basic

Example 20-5. Two Bouncing Balls

Write a program with a single button control that starts and stops a **Timer** object. Have the program animate two randomly moving balls within the graphics window. Have the balls bounce of the sides of the window. With each bounce, play the bounce (**bounce.wav**) sound. Use the same graphic (**ball.gif**) used for previous examples.

Small Basic Code:

```
'Guide to Small Basic, Example 20-5
InitializeProgram()

Sub InitializeProgram
  GraphicsWindow.Show()
  GraphicsWindow.Title = "Example 20-5"
  GraphicsWindow.Width = 600
  GraphicsWindow.Height = 400
  'ball graphic
  BallImage = ImageList.LoadImage(Program.Directory + "\ball.gif")
  BallW = ImageList.GetWidthOfImage(BallImage)
  BallH = ImageList.GetHeightOfImage(BallImage)
  Ball[1] = Shapes.AddImage(BallImage)
  Ball[2] = Shapes.AddImage(BallImage)
  Shapes.HideShape(Ball[1])
  Shapes.HideShape(Ball[2])
  'button
  GraphicsWindow.BrushColor = "Black"
  GraphicsWindow.FontSize = 16
  GraphicsWindow.FontBold = "false"
  TimerButton = Controls.AddButton("Start", 280, 360)
  Controls.ButtonClicked = ButtonClickedSub
  Timer.Interval = 100
  Timer.Tick = TickSub
  Timer.Pause()
EndSub

Sub ButtonClickedSub
  If (Controls.GetButtonCaption(TimerButton) = "Start") Then
    Controls.SetButtonCaption(TimerButton, "Stop")
    For I = 1 To 2
      BallX[I] = Math.GetRandomNumber(GraphicsWindow.Width - BallW) - 1
      BallY[I] = Math.GetRandomNumber(GraphicsWindow.Height - BallH) - 1
```

```
      BallXSpeed[I] = 21 - Math.GetRandomNumber(41)
      BallYSpeed[I] = 21 - Math.GetRandomNumber(41)
      Shapes.Move(Ball[I], BallX[I], BallY[I])
      Shapes.ShowShape(Ball[I])
    EndFor
    Timer.Resume()
  Else
    Controls.SetButtonCaption(TimerButton, "Start")
    Shapes.HideShape(Ball[1])
    Shapes.HideShape(Ball[2])
    Timer.Pause()
  EndIf
EndSub

Sub TickSub
  For I = 1 To 2
    BallX[I] = BallX[I] + BallXSpeed[I]
    BallY[I] = BallY[I] + BallYSpeed[I]
    Shapes.Move(Ball[I], BallX[I], BallY[I])
    If (BallY[I] + BallH > GraphicsWindow.Height) Then
      'top bounce?
      BallY[I] = GraphicsWindow.Height - BallH
      BallYSpeed[I] = -BallYSpeed[I]
      Sound.Stop(Program.Directory + "\bounce.wav")
      Sound.Play(Program.Directory + "\bounce.wav")
    ElseIf (BallY[I] < 0) Then
      'bottom bounce?
      BallY[I] = 0
      BallYSpeed[I] = -BallYSpeed[I]
      Sound.Stop(Program.Directory + "\bounce.wav")
      Sound.Play(Program.Directory + "\bounce.wav")
    ElseIf (BallX[I] < 0) Then
      'left bounce?
      BallX[I] = 0
      BallXSpeed[I] = -BallXSpeed[I]
      Sound.Stop(Program.Directory + "\bounce.wav")
      Sound.Play(Program.Directory + "\bounce.wav")
    ElseIf (BallX[I] + BallW > GraphicsWindow.Width) Then
      'right bounce?
      BallX[I] = GraphicsWindow.Width - BallW
      BallXSpeed[I] = -BallXSpeed[I]
      Sound.Stop(Program.Directory + "\bounce.wav")
      Sound.Play(Program.Directory + "\bounce.wav")
    EndIf
  EndFor
EndSub
```

Saved as **Example 20-5** in **Guide to Small Basic\Programs\Chapter 20** folder.

In **InitializeProgram**, we create two **Shapes** objects (**Ball** array) using the image (**ball.gif**). The balls are hidden. In the **ButtonClickedSub** subroutine, when the button caption is **Start**, we randomly place the two **Ball** shapes in the window using **BallX** and **BallY** arrays. Speeds in horizontal direction (**BallXSpeed** and **BallYSpeed** arrays) are randomly set between -20 and 20. Once values are set, the two balls are displayed using the **ShowShape** method and the timer is started. In the **ButtonClickedSub** subroutine, when the button caption is **Stop**, we stop the timer and hide the balls.

In the **TickSub** subroutine, the position of the each ball is changed by their speed values in each direction. Bounces along each of the four borders are checked. If there is a bounce, the corresponding speed is multiplied by -1 (changing the direction) and a sound is played.

Save and **Run** the project. Click **Start**. Two balls will appear and start moving in a diagonal direction. With each bounce, the ball will change direction and a bounce will be heard. Here's a run I made:

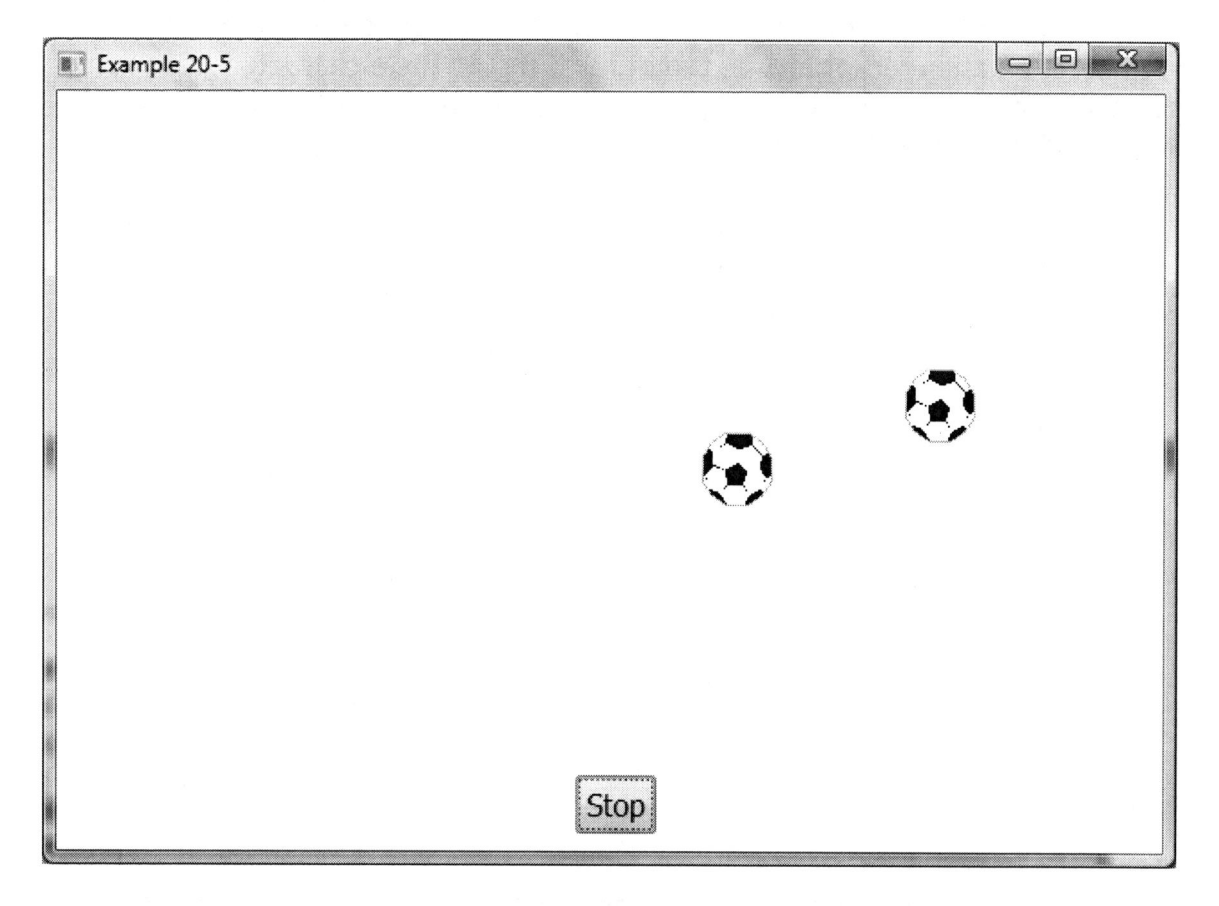

You've now seen how to do lots of things with animations. You can make images move, make them disappear and reappear, and make them bounce. And you can play sounds. Do you have some ideas of simple video games you would like to build? You still need one more skill – collision detection - which is discussed next.

Collision Detection

Another requirement in animation is to determine if two images (represented by **Shapes** objects) have collided. This is needed in games to see if a ball hits a paddle, if an alien rocket hits its target, or if a cute little character grabs some reward. Or, in the two ball example just created, we might like something to happen if the two balls hit each other.

Each **Shapes** object is a rectangle, so the **collision detection** problem is to see if two rectangles collide, or overlap. This check is done using each shape's position and dimensions. Here are two shapes (**Shape[1]** and **Shape[2]**) in a window:

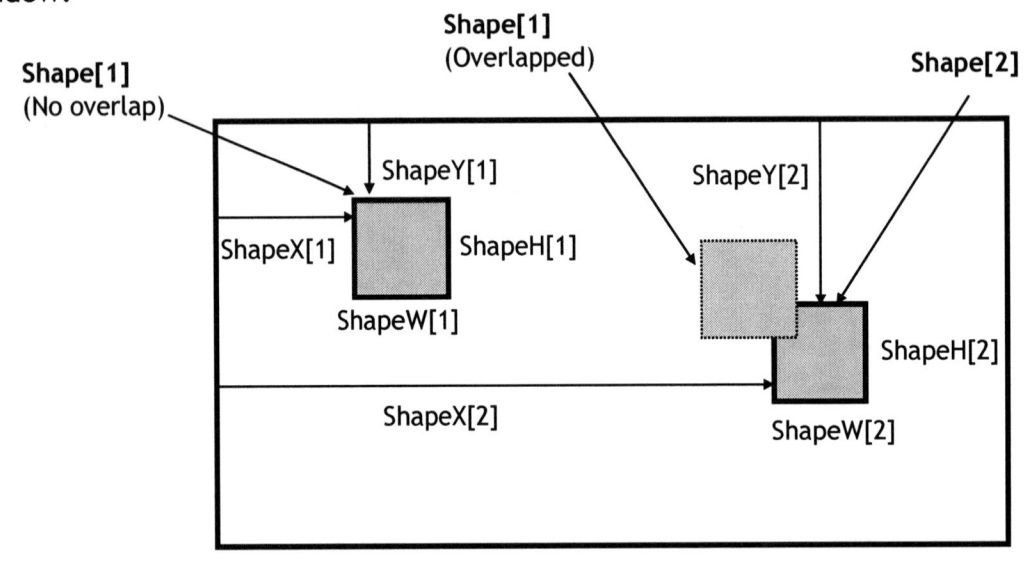

Shape[1] is positioned at (**ShapeX[1]**, **ShapeY[1]**), is **ShapeW[1]** wide and **ShapeH[1]** high. Similarly, **Shape[2]** is positioned at (**ShapeX[2]**, **ShapeY[2]**), is **ShapeW[2]** wide and **ShapeH[2]** high.

Looking at this diagram, you should see there are four requirements for the two shapes to overlap:

1. The right side of Shape[1] (**ShapeX[1] + ShapeW[1]**) must be "farther right" than the left side of Shape[2] (**ShapeX[2]**)
2. The left side of Shape[1] (**ShapeX[1]**) must be "farther left" than the right side of Shape[2] (**ShapeX[2] + ShapeW[2]**)
3. The bottom of Shape[1] (**ShapeY[1] + ShapeH[1]**) must be "farther down" than the top of Shape[2] (**ShapeY[2]**)
4. The top of Shape[1] (**ShapeY[1]**) must be "farther up" than the bottom of Shape[2] (**ShapeY[2] + ShapeH[2]**)

All four of these requirements must be met for a collision.

The Small Basic code to check if these shapes overlap is:

```
If (ShapeX[1] + ShapeW[1] > ShapeX[2]) Then
  If (ShapeX[1] < ShapeX[2] + ShapeW[2]) Then
    If (ShapeY[1] + ShapeH[1] > ShapeY[2]) Then
      If (ShapeY[1] < ShapeY[2] + ShapeH[2]) Then
        ' Small Basic code for overlap, or collision
      EndIf
    EndIf
  EndIf
EndIf
```

This code checks the four conditions for overlap using four "nested" **If** structures. The Small Basic code for a collision is executed only if all four conditions are found to be **"true"**.

We will use this subroutine (**CheckCollision**) to check for collisions between two shapes:

```
Sub CheckCollision
  Collision = "false"
  If (ShapeX[1] + ShapeW[1] > ShapeX[2]) Then
    If (ShapeX[1] < ShapeX[2] + ShapeW[2]) Then
      If (ShapeY[1] + ShapeH[1] > ShapeY[2]) Then
        If (ShapeY[1] < ShapeY[2] + ShapeH[2]) Then
          Collision = "true"
        EndIf
      EndIf
    EndIf
  EndIf
EndSub
```

To use this, you provide locations for two shapes in the **ShapeX** and **ShapeY** arrays. You also provide the shape dimensions in the **ShapeW** and **ShapeH** arrays. The subroutine determines a value for **Collision** ("**true**" if the shapes collided, "**false**" if not).

Animation

Example 20-6. Two Colliding Balls

Modify **Example 20-5** so that when the two bouncing balls collide, a little explosion graphic appears and a collide sound is heard. In the **Guide to Small Basic\Programs\Chapter 20** are a collision sound file (**collide.wav**) and a collision graphic:

collide.gif

Copy both of these files to your program folder.

Small Basic Code (modifications are shaded):

```
'Guide to Small Basic, Example 20-6
InitializeProgram()

Sub InitializeProgram
  GraphicsWindow.Show()
  GraphicsWindow.Title = "Example 20-6"
  GraphicsWindow.Width = 600
  GraphicsWindow.Height = 400
  'ball graphic
  BallImage = ImageList.LoadImage(Program.Directory + "\ball.gif")
  BallW = ImageList.GetWidthOfImage(BallImage)
  BallH = ImageList.GetHeightOfImage(BallImage)
  Ball[1] = Shapes.AddImage(BallImage)
  Ball[2] = Shapes.AddImage(BallImage)
  Shapes.HideShape(Ball[1])
  Shapes.HideShape(Ball[2])
  'collision graphic
  CollideImage = ImageList.LoadImage(Program.Directory + "\collide.gif")
  Collide = Shapes.AddImage(CollideImage)
  Shapes.HideShape(Collide)
  'button
  GraphicsWindow.BrushColor = "Black"
  GraphicsWindow.FontSize = 16
  GraphicsWindow.FontBold = "false"
  TimerButton = Controls.AddButton("Start", 280, 360)
  Controls.ButtonClicked = ButtonClickedSub
  Timer.Interval = 100
  Timer.Tick = TickSub
```

```
    Timer.Pause()
EndSub

Sub ButtonClickedSub
  If (Controls.GetButtonCaption(TimerButton) = "Start") Then
    Controls.SetButtonCaption(TimerButton, "Stop")
    Shapes.HideShape(Collide)
    For I = 1 To 2
      BallX[I] = Math.GetRandomNumber(GraphicsWindow.Width - BallW) - 1
      BallY[I] = Math.GetRandomNumber(GraphicsWindow.Height - BallH) - 1
      BallXSpeed[I] = 21 - Math.GetRandomNumber(41)
      BallYSpeed[I] = 21 - Math.GetRandomNumber(41)
      Shapes.Move(Ball[I], BallX[I], BallY[I])
      Shapes.ShowShape(Ball[I])
    EndFor
    Timer.Resume()
  Else
    Controls.SetButtonCaption(TimerButton, "Start")
    Shapes.HideShape(Ball[1])
    Shapes.HideShape(Ball[2])
    Timer.Pause()
  EndIf
EndSub

Sub TickSub
  For I = 1 To 2
    BallX[I] = BallX[I] + BallXSpeed[I]
    BallY[I] = BallY[I] + BallYSpeed[I]
    Shapes.Move(Ball[I], BallX[I], BallY[I])
    If (BallY[I] + BallH > GraphicsWindow.Height) Then
      'top bounce?
      BallY[I] = GraphicsWindow.Height - BallH
      BallYSpeed[I] = -BallYSpeed[I]
      Sound.Stop(Program.Directory + "\bounce.wav")
      Sound.Play(Program.Directory + "\bounce.wav")
    ElseIf (BallY[I] < 0) Then
      'bottom bounce?
      BallY[I] = 0
      BallYSpeed[I] = -BallYSpeed[I]
      Sound.Stop(Program.Directory + "\bounce.wav")
      Sound.Play(Program.Directory + "\bounce.wav")
    ElseIf (BallX[I] < 0) Then
      'left bounce?
      BallX[I] = 0
```

```
      BallXSpeed[I] = -BallXSpeed[I]
      Sound.Stop(Program.Directory + "\bounce.wav")
      Sound.Play(Program.Directory + "\bounce.wav")
    ElseIf (BallX[I] + BallW > GraphicsWindow.Width) Then
      'right bounce?
      BallX[I] = GraphicsWindow.Width - BallW
      BallXSpeed[I] = -BallXSpeed[I]
      Sound.Stop(Program.Directory + "\bounce.wav")
      Sound.Play(Program.Directory + "\bounce.wav")
    EndIf
  EndFor
  'check for collision
  ShapeX[1] = BallX[1]
  ShapeY[1] = BallY[1]
  ShapeW[1] = BallW
  ShapeH[1] = BallH
  ShapeX[2] = BallX[2]
  ShapeY[2] = BallY[2]
  ShapeW[2] = BallW
  ShapeH[2] = BallH
  CheckCollision()
  If (Collision) Then
    'display collide graphic and play sound
    Shapes.HideShape(Ball[1])
    Shapes.HideShape(Ball[2])
    Shapes.Move(Collide, 0.5 * (BallX[1] + BallX[2]), 0.5 *
(BallY[1] + BallY[2]))
    Shapes.ShowShape(Collide)
    Sound.Stop(Program.Directory + "\collide.wav")
    Sound.Play(Program.Directory + "\collide.wav")
    ButtonClickedSub()
  EndIf
EndSub

Sub CheckCollision
  Collision = "false"
  If (ShapeX[1] + ShapeW[1] > ShapeX[2]) Then
    If (ShapeX[1] < ShapeX[2] + ShapeW[2]) Then
      If (ShapeY[1] + ShapeH[1] > ShapeY[2]) Then
        If (ShapeY[1] < ShapeY[2] + ShapeH[2]) Then
          Collision = "true"
        EndIf
      EndIf
    EndIf
  EndIf
EndSub
```

Saved as **Example 20-6** in **Guide to Small Basic\Programs\Chapter 20** folder.

We added the **CheckCollision** subroutine. In **InitializeProgram**, we create the **Collide Shapes** object using the image (**collide.gif**). It is hidden. In the **ButtonClickedSub** subroutine, we added a line to hide the **Collide** object when the button caption is **Start**. This erases the image if it is displayed from a previous run.

In the **TickSub** subroutine, after moving the balls, we use the **CheckCollision** subroutine to see if the two balls overlap. If they do, the balls are removed from window, the collision graphic is displayed (at the average position of the balls) and the collide sound (**collide.wav**) is played. Lastly, a call to the **ButtonClickedSub** subroutine stops the timer and resets the button caption to **Start**.

Save and **Run** the project. Click **Start**. Two balls will appear and start moving around. When they collide, you will see this (and hear a cute collision sound):

Example 20-7. Bouncing Ball with Paddle

Let's build a little video game. Modify **Example 20-4** (the vertical bouncing ball program):

- Make the ball fall diagonally (add a **BallXSpeed** variable).
- Add a paddle (use a **Shapes** rectangle) at the bottom (moved with the left and right arrow keys).
- If the ball collides with the paddle, have it bounce back up.
- If the ball misses the paddle, have it go off screen and play a miss sound, then start a new ball.

Small Basic Code (modifications to **Example 20-4** are shaded):

```
'Guide to Small Basic, Example 20-7
InitializeProgram()

Sub InitializeProgram
  GraphicsWindow.Show()
  GraphicsWindow.Title = "Example 20-7"
  GraphicsWindow.Width = 250
  GraphicsWindow.Height = 400
  'ball graphic
  BallImage = ImageList.LoadImage(Program.Directory + "\ball.gif")
  BallW = ImageList.GetWidthOfImage(BallImage)
  BallH = ImageList.GetHeightOfImage(BallImage)
  Ball = Shapes.AddImage(BallImage)
  BallX = 0.5 * (GraphicsWindow.Width - BallW)
  BallY = 0
  BallXSpeed = 5
  BallYSpeed = 10
  Shapes.Move(Ball, BallX, BallY)
  'paddle
  GraphicsWindow.PenWidth = 2
  GraphicsWindow.PenColor = "Black"
  GraphicsWindow.BrushColor = "Red"
  PaddleW = 40
  PaddleH = 20
  Paddle = Shapes.AddRectangle(PaddleW, PaddleH)
  PaddleX = 100
  PaddleY = 380
  Shapes.Move(Paddle, PaddleX, PaddleY)
  'button
  GraphicsWindow.BrushColor = "Black"
  GraphicsWindow.FontSize = 16
```

```
  GraphicsWindow.FontBold = "false"
  TimerButton = Controls.AddButton("Start", 190, 10)
  Controls.ButtonClicked = ButtonClickedSub
  Timer.Interval = 100
  Timer.Tick = TickSub
  Timer.Pause()
  GraphicsWindow.KeyDown = KeyDownSub
EndSub

Sub ButtonClickedSub
  If (Controls.GetButtonCaption(TimerButton) = "Start") Then
    Controls.SetButtonCaption(TimerButton, "Stop")
    Timer.Resume()
  Else
    Controls.SetButtonCaption(TimerButton, "Start")
    Timer.Pause()
  EndIf
EndSub

Sub TickSub
  BallX = BallX + BallXSpeed
  BallY = BallY + BallYSpeed
  Shapes.Move(Ball, BallX, BallY)
  If (BallX < 0) Then
    BallX = 0
    BallXSpeed = -BallXSpeed
    Sound.Stop(Program.Directory + "\bounce.wav")
    Sound.Play(Program.Directory + "\bounce.wav")
  ElseIf (BallX + BallW > GraphicsWindow.Width) Then
    BallX = GraphicsWindow.Width - BallW
    BallXSpeed = -BallXSpeed
    Sound.Stop(Program.Directory + "\bounce.wav")
    Sound.Play(Program.Directory + "\bounce.wav")
  ElseIf (BallY + BallH > GraphicsWindow.Height) Then
    BallY = 0
    Sound.Stop(Program.Directory + "\missed.wav")
    Sound.Play(Program.Directory + "\missed.wav")
  ElseIf (BallY < 0) Then
    BallY = 0
    BallYSpeed = -BallYSpeed
    Sound.Stop(Program.Directory + "\bounce.wav")
    Sound.Play(Program.Directory + "\bounce.wav")
  EndIf
  'check for collision with paddle
  ShapeX[1] = BallX
  ShapeY[1] = BallY
```

```
    ShapeW[1] = BallW
    ShapeH[1] = BallH
    ShapeX[2] = PaddleX
    ShapeY[2] = PaddleY
    ShapeW[2] = PaddleW
    ShapeH[2] = PaddleH
    CheckCollision()
    If (Collision) Then
        BallYSpeed = -BallYSpeed
    EndIf
EndSub

Sub CheckCollision
    Collision = "false"
    If (ShapeX[1] + ShapeW[1] > ShapeX[2]) Then
        If (ShapeX[1] < ShapeX[2] + ShapeW[2]) Then
            If (ShapeY[1] + ShapeH[1] > ShapeY[2]) Then
                If (ShapeY[1] < ShapeY[2] + ShapeH[2]) Then
                    Collision = "true"
                EndIf
            EndIf
        EndIf
    EndIf
EndSub

Sub KeyDownSub
    K = GraphicsWindow.LastKey
    If (K = "Left") Then
        PaddleX = PaddleX - 3
    ElseIf (K = "Right") Then
        PaddleX = PaddleX + 3
    EndIf
    Shapes.Move(Paddle, PaddleX, PaddleY)
EndSub
```

Saved as **Example 20-7** in **Guide to Small Basic\Programs\Chapter 20** folder.

In **InitializeProgram**, we established a horizontal speed (**BallXSpeed**) and created a **Paddle Shapes** object. We add a line to indicated the **KeyDownSub** subroutine will be called when a key is pressed (used to move the paddle). The **KeyDownSub** is added. It uses the left and right arrow keys to move the paddle rectangle.

In the **TickSub** subroutine, we add bounce detection on the vertical sides of the window. We also change the logic when the ball reaches the bottom of the window. In this case, we play a "miss" sound and start a new ball, rather than bounce. After moving the ball, we use the **CheckCollision** subroutine to see if the ball hits the paddle. If it does, we reverse the **BallYSpeed** and play a bounce sound.

Save and **Run** the project. The paddle will appear at the bottom of the window. Try moving it with the arrow keys:

Click **Start**. The ball will begin moving diagonally. Keep the ball bouncing by moving the paddle under it as it reaches the bottom. Here's the middle of my game:

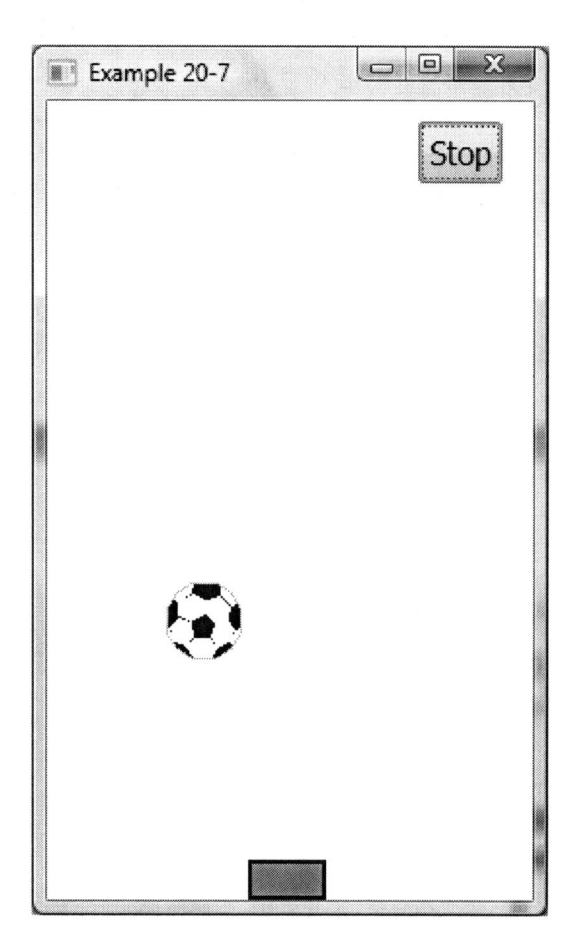

20-34 The Developer's Reference Guide to Small Basic

Example 20-8. The Original Video Game - Pong!

In the early 1970's, Nolan Bushnell began the video game revolution with Atari's Pong game -- a very simple Ping-Pong kind of game. In this example, we list the code where we try to replicate this game using Small Basic. In the game, a ball bounces from one end of a court to another, bouncing off sidewalls. Players try to deflect the ball at each end using a controllable paddle. In this program, the A and Z keys move the paddle on the left. The M and K keys move the paddle on the right.

In the **Guide to Small Basic\Programs\Chapter 20** folder are four sound files (**cheering.wav, missed.wav, paddle.wav, wallhit.wav**). Copy these files into your program folder.

Small Basic Code:

```
'Guide to Small Basic, Example 20-8
InitializeProgram()

Sub InitializeProgram
  GraphicsWindow.Show()
  GraphicsWindow.Title = "Example 20-8"
  GraphicsWindow.Width = 600
  GraphicsWindow.Height = 400
  GraphicsWindow.BackgroundColor =
GraphicsWindow.GetColorFromRGB(48, 48, 48)
  'ball graphic
  BallW = 20
  BallH = 20
  GraphicsWindow.BrushColor = "White"
  GraphicsWindow.PenColor = "White"
  Ball = Shapes.AddEllipse(BallW, BallH)
  Shapes.HideShape(Ball)
  'paddles
  PaddleW = 10
  PaddleH = 50
  Paddle[1] = Shapes.AddRectangle(PaddleW, PaddleH)
  Paddle[2] = Shapes.AddRectangle(PaddleW, PaddleH)
  PaddleX[1] = 20
  PaddleY[1] = 175
  PaddleX[2] = 570
  PaddleY[2] = 175
  Shapes.Move(Paddle[1], PaddleX[1], PaddleY[1])
  Shapes.Move(Paddle[2], PaddleX[2], PaddleY[2])
```

```
  'button
  GraphicsWindow.BrushColor = "Black"
  GraphicsWindow.FontSize = 16
  GraphicsWindow.FontBold = "false"
  TimerButton = Controls.AddButton("Start", 280, 360)
  Controls.ButtonClicked = ButtonClickedSub
  Timer.Interval = 100
  Timer.Tick = TickSub
  Timer.Pause()
  GraphicsWindow.KeyDown = KeyDownSub
  SpeedMax = 20
  'scores
  GraphicsWindow.BrushColor = "White"
  GraphicsWindow.FontSize = 48
  ScoreDisplay[1] = Shapes.AddText("0")
  Shapes.Move(ScoreDisplay[1], 120, 10)
  ScoreDisplay[2] = Shapes.AddText("0")
  Shapes.Move(ScoreDisplay[2], 450, 10)
EndSub

Sub ButtonClickedSub
  Controls.HideControl(TimerButton)
  'get ball started randomly
  If (Math.GetRandomNumber(2) = 1) Then
    BallX = PaddleX[1] + PaddleW
    BallXSpeed = SpeedMax
  Else
    BallX = PaddleX[2] - BallW
    BallXSpeed = -SpeedMax
  EndIf
  BallY = 0.5 * (GraphicsWindow.Height - 0.5 * PaddleH)
  BallYSpeed = 0
  Shapes.Move(Ball, BallX, BallY)
  Shapes.ShowShape(Ball)
  Score[1] = 0
  Score[2] = 0
  UpdateScore()
  Timer.Resume()
EndSub

Sub TickSub
  BallX = BallX + BallXSpeed
  BallY = BallY + BallYSpeed
  Shapes.Move(Ball, BallX, BallY)
  'wall hit?
  If (BallY + BallH > GraphicsWindow.Height) Then
```

```
    BallY = GraphicsWindow.Height - BallH
    BallYSpeed = -BallYSpeed
    Sound.Stop(Program.Directory + "\wallhit.wav")
    Sound.Play(Program.Directory + "\wallhit.wav")
    Goto ExitTickSub
  ElseIf (BallY < 0) Then
    BallY = 0
    BallYSpeed = -BallYSpeed
    Sound.Stop(Program.Directory + "\wallhit.wav")
    Sound.Play(Program.Directory + "\wallhit.wav")
    Goto ExitTickSub
  EndIf
  'check for collision with paddle
  For I = 1 To 2
    ShapeX[1] = BallX
    ShapeY[1] = BallY
    ShapeW[1] = BallW
    ShapeH[1] = BallH
    ShapeX[2] = PaddleX[I]
    ShapeY[2] = PaddleY[I]
    ShapeW[2] = PaddleW
    ShapeH[2] = PaddleH
    CheckCollision()
    If (Collision) Then
      Sound.Stop(Program.Directory + "\bounce.wav")
      Sound.Play(Program.Directory + "\bounce.wav")
      BallXSpeed = -BallXSpeed
      'set BallYSpeed based on where ball hits paddle
      BallCenter = BallY + 0.5 * BallH
      If (BallCenter < PaddleY[I] + 0.2 * PaddleH) Then
        BallYSpeed = -SpeedMax
      ElseIf (BallCenter < PaddleY[I] + 0.4 * PaddleH) Then
        BallYSpeed = -0.5 * SpeedMax
      ElseIf (BallCenter < PaddleY[I] + 0.6 * PaddleH) Then
        BallYSpeed = 0
      ElseIf (BallCenter < PaddleY[I] + 0.8 * PaddleH) Then
        BallYSpeed = 0.5 * SpeedMax
      Else
        BallYSpeed = SpeedMax
      EndIf
      Goto ExitTickSub
    EndIf
  EndFor
  'off ends?
  If (BallX < 0) Then
    'point for player 2
```

```
      Score[2] = Score[2] + 1
      Sound.Stop(Program.Directory + "\missed.wav")
      Sound.Play(Program.Directory + "\missed.wav")
      BallX = PaddleX[2] - BallW
      BallXSpeed = -SpeedMax
      BallY = 0.5 * (GraphicsWindow.Height - 0.5 * PaddleH)
      BallYSpeed = 0
      Shapes.Move(Ball, BallX, BallY)
      Goto ExitTickSub
    ElseIf (BallX + BallW > GraphicsWindow.Width) Then
      'point for player 1
      Score[1] = Score[1] + 1
      Sound.Stop(Program.Directory + "\missed.wav")
      Sound.Play(Program.Directory + "\missed.wav")
      BallX = PaddleX[1] + PaddleW
      BallXSpeed = SpeedMax
      BallY = 0.5 * (GraphicsWindow.Height - 0.5 * PaddleH)
      BallYSpeed = 0
      Shapes.Move(Ball, BallX, BallY)
    EndIf
  ExitTickSub:
    UpdateScore()
EndSub

Sub CheckCollision
  Collision = "false"
  If (ShapeX[1] + ShapeW[1] > ShapeX[2]) Then
    If (ShapeX[1] < ShapeX[2] + ShapeW[2]) Then
      If (ShapeY[1] + ShapeH[1] > ShapeY[2]) Then
        If (ShapeY[1] < ShapeY[2] + ShapeH[2]) Then
          Collision = "true"
        EndIf
      EndIf
    EndIf
  EndIf
EndSub

Sub KeyDownSub
  K = GraphicsWindow.LastKey
  If (K = "A") Then
    PaddleY[1] = PaddleY[1] - 10
    Shapes.Move(Paddle[1], PaddleX[1], PaddleY[1])
  ElseIf (K = "Z") Then
    PaddleY[1] = PaddleY[1] + 10
    Shapes.Move(Paddle[1], PaddleX[1], PaddleY[1])
  ElseIf (K = "K") Then
```

```
      PaddleY[2] = PaddleY[2] - 10
      Shapes.Move(Paddle[2], PaddleX[2], PaddleY[2])
    ElseIf (K = "M") Then
      PaddleY[2] = PaddleY[2] + 10
      Shapes.Move(Paddle[2], PaddleX[2], PaddleY[2])
    EndIf
EndSub

Sub UpdateScore
    Shapes.SetText(ScoreDisplay[1], Score[1])
    Shapes.SetText(ScoreDisplay[2], Score[2])
    If (Score[1] = 11 Or Score[2] = 11) Then
      Timer.Pause()
      Shapes.HideShape(Ball)
      Sound.PlayAndWait(Program.Directory + "\cheering.wav")
      Controls.ShowControl(TimerButton)
    EndIf
EndSub
```

Saved as **Example 20-8** in **Guide to Small Basic\Programs\Chapter 20** folder.

This program uses all the animation skills developed in this chapter. The code should look familiar and straightforward to follow. Note the use of **Shapes** text objects to keep track of the score.

Animation 20-39

Here is what the running program looks like in the middle of a game. Recall, the **A** and **Z** keys move the paddle on the left. The **M** and **K** keys move the paddle on the right:

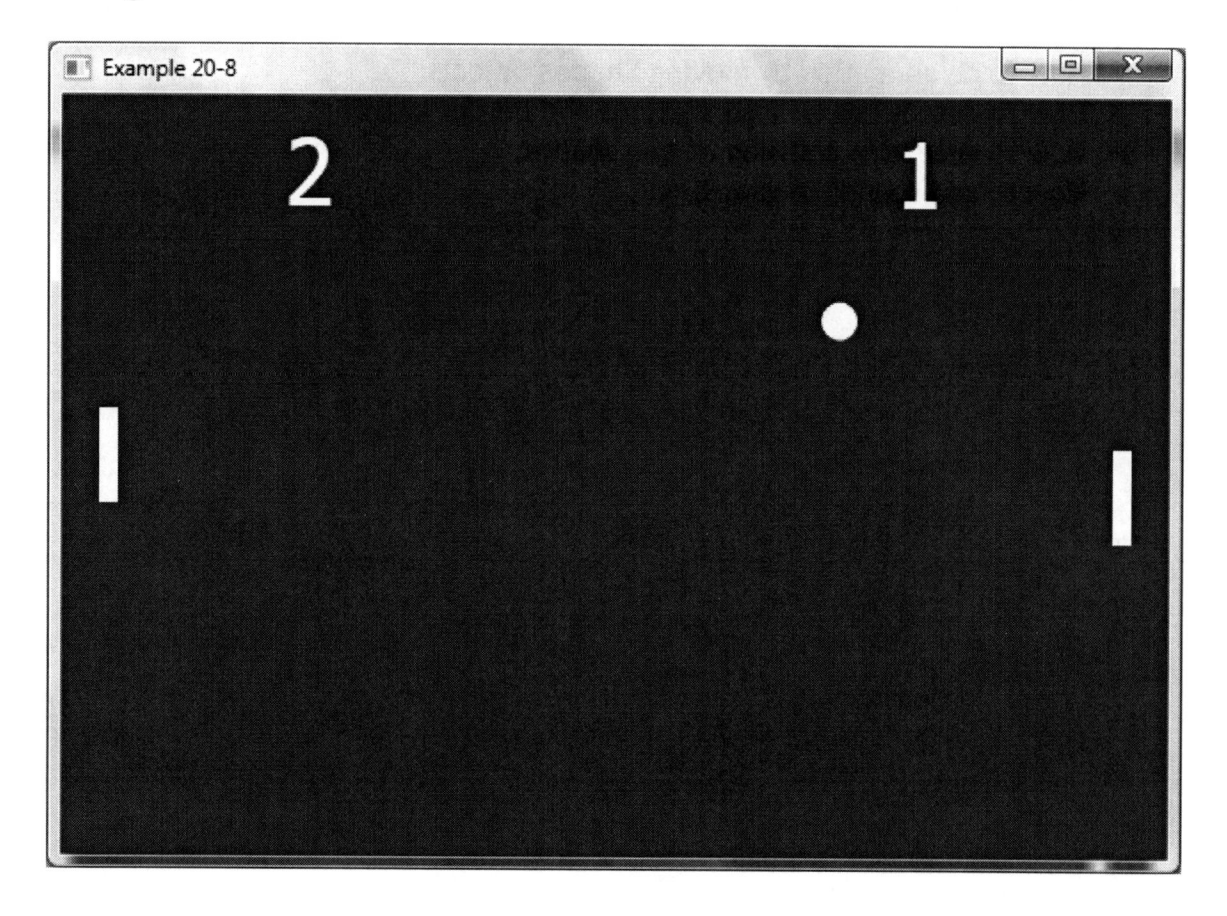

Class Review

After completing this class, you should understand:

- How to do animation by moving **Shapes** objects.
- How to detect border intersections and border crossings.
- How to detection collision of two shapes.
- How to add sounds to games.

21. Check Box and Radio Button Controls

Preview

In this chapter, we build subroutines that give your Small Basic programs two basic sets of controls that are used for selections. Check box controls are used to select any number of items from a list. Radio button controls allow selection of just one item from a list.

Check Box Controls

Windows applications feature many 'point and click' controls that let the user make a choice simply by clicking with the mouse. These controls are attractive, familiar and minimize the possibility of errors in an application. One such control included with Small Basic is the **button** control.

The **check box** control provides a way to make choices from a list of potential candidates. Some, all, or none of the choices in a group may be selected. Check boxes are used in all Windows applications. Examples of their use would be to turn options on and off in an application or to select from a 'shopping' list. Here is a group of check boxes that allow the selection of text formatting choices:

Text Formatting
- ☐ Bold
- ☐ Italic
- ☐ Underline
- ☐ Strikethrough

Clicking an empty box will place a check mark in that box. Clicking a box with a check mark will remove the mark. In our example, if you want **Bold** and **Underline** text, you check those boxes and see:

Text Formatting
- ☑ Bold
- ☐ Italic
- ☑ Underline
- ☐ Strikethrough

Small Basic does not offer a check box control. So, you ask, why talk about it? The answer is we can use Small Basic objects to build groups of check boxes. In these notes, we provide subroutines that create check box groups and subroutines that tell you when a particular check box is clicked.

Check Box and Radio Button Controls 21-3

The first subroutine is **CreateCheckBoxGroup**:

```
Sub CreateCheckBoxGroup
  NumberCheckBoxGroups = CBGroupNumber
  NumberCheckBoxes[CBGroupNumber] = CBNumberBoxes
  'draw backing
  GraphicsWindow.BrushColor = CBBackColor
  GraphicsWindow.FillRectangle(CBLeft, CBTop, CBWidth, CBHeight)
  'add title (optional)
  If (CBTitle <> "") Then
    GraphicsWindow.BrushColor = CBForeColor
    GraphicsWindow.FontSize = 16
    GraphicsWindow.FontBold = "true"
    GraphicsWindow.DrawText(CBLeft + 5, CBTop + 5, CBTitle)
    TopOffset = 10
  Else
    TopOffset = -10
  EndIf
  'create and add check boxes
  For I = 1 To CBNumberBoxes
    GraphicsWindow.PenColor = "White"
    GraphicsWindow.BrushColor = "White"
    CheckBox[CBGroupNumber][I] = Shapes.AddRectangle(15, 15)
    Shapes.Move(CheckBox[CBGroupNumber][I], CBLeft + 5, CBTop + TopOffset + I * 20)
    CheckBoxChecked[CBGroupNumber][I] = CBChecked[I]
    If (CBChecked[I]) Then
      ClickedGroup = CBGroupNumber
      ClickedBox = I
      MarkCheckBox()
    EndIf
    GraphicsWindow.BrushColor = CBForeColor
    GraphicsWindow.FontSize = 14
    GraphicsWindow.FontBold = "false"
    CheckBoxText[CBGroupNumber][I] = CBText[I]
    TextShape = Shapes.AddText(CBText[I])
    Shapes.Move(TextShape, CBLeft + 25, CBTop + TopOffset + I * 20)
  EndFor
EndSub
```

This code uses **Shapes** rectangle objects for the check boxes. Look through the code to see how it works.

21-4 The Developer's Reference Guide to Small Basic

This subroutine also requires **MarkCheckBox**:

```
Sub MarkCheckBox
  CheckBoxChecked[ClickedGroup][ClickedBox] = "true"
  CBL = Shapes.GetLeft(CheckBox[ClickedGroup][ClickedBox])
  CBT = Shapes.GetTop(CheckBox[ClickedGroup][ClickedBox])
  GraphicsWindow.PenColor = "Black"
  GraphicsWindow.PenWidth = 1
  CheckMark1[ClickedGroup][ClickedBox] = Shapes.AddLine(CBL + 3, CBT + 8, CBL + 7, CBT + 12)
  CheckMark2[ClickedGroup][ClickedBox] = Shapes.AddLine(CBL + 7, CBT + 12, CBL + 12, CBT + 3)
EndSub
```

When an empty check box is clicked, this subroutine is called to place a check mark in the corresponding box.

These two subroutines are used to create the initial configuration for a group of check boxes. The variables to set before calling **CreateCheckBoxGroup** are:

CBGroupNumber	Identifying number for check box group (starts at 1).
CBBackColor	Background color of rectangle surrounding check box group.
CBForeColor	Foreground color of text in check box group.
CBLeft	Left position of group rectangle in graphics window.
CBWidth	Width of group rectangle.
CBHeight	Height of group rectangle.
CBTitle	Title for check box group (optional).
CBNumberBoxes	Number of check boxes in group.
CBText	Array of captions for each check box.
CBChecked	Array of initial configuration for each check box ("true" if initially checked, else "false")

When **CreateCheckBoxGroup** is called after setting these variables, it creates two two-dimensional arrays of interest:

CheckBoxText[GroupNumber][BoxNumber]
Caption of check box **BoxNumber** in group **GroupNumber**.

CheckBoxChecked[GroupNumber][BoxNumber]
Value of check box **BoxNumber** in group **GroupNumber** ("true" if initially checked, else "false")

We examine these two arrays to make decisions in our Small Basic programs.

Check Box and Radio Button Controls

Example 21-1. Create Check Box Group

Write a program that uses the **CreateCheckBoxGroup** and **MarkCheckBox** subroutines to set up a group of check boxes for text formatting. This is the example shown earlier.

Small Basic Code:

```
'Guide to Small Basic, Example 21-1
InitializeProgram()

Sub InitializeProgram
  GraphicsWindow.Show()
  GraphicsWindow.Title = "Example 21-1"
  GraphicsWindow.Width = 400
  GraphicsWindow.Height = 200
  CBGroupNumber = 1
  CBBackColor = "SkyBlue"
  CBForeColor = "Black"
  CBLeft = 20
  CBTop = 20
  CBWidth = 160
  CBHeight = 120
  CBTitle = "Text Formatting"
  CBNumberBoxes = 4
  CBText[1] = "Bold"
  CBText[2] = "Italic"
  CBText[3] = "Underline"
  CBText[4] = "Strikethrough"
  CBChecked[1] = "false"
  CBChecked[2] = "false"
  CBChecked[3] = "false"
  CBChecked[4] = "false"
  CreateCheckBoxGroup()
EndSub
```

We have not shown the code from **CreateCheckBoxGroup** or **MarkCheckBox**, but they need to be in your program. Saved as **Example 21-1** in **Guide to Small Basic\Programs\Chapter 21** folder.

In **InitializeProgram**, we size the graphics window. We then set each of the needed variables and call the subroutine to create the check box group box.

Save and **Run** the program. The check box group will appear.

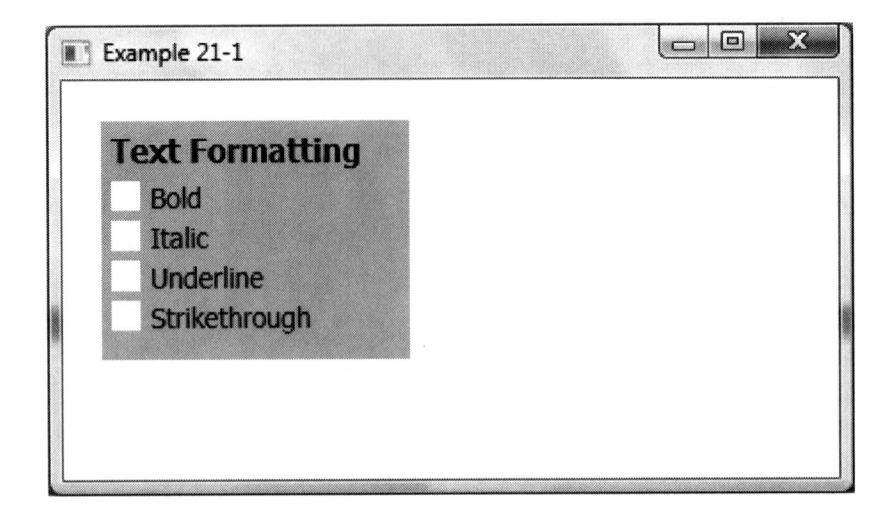

If you click a check box, nothing happens. Let's fix that.

Check Box and Radio Button Controls 21-7

Clicking a Check Box

If you click an empty check box, you want to draw a check mark in the selected box. If you click a check box with a check mark in it, you want to clear that check mark.

To accomplish this, we need to do two things. First, we need to add code to recognize the graphics window **MouseDown** event. We use:

```
GraphicsWindow.MouseDown = MouseDownSub
```

Second, in the **MouseDownSub**, we need to see if a check box has been selected. This subroutine (**CheckBoxClick**) does the task:

```
Sub CheckBoxClick
  CheckBoxClicked = "false"
  X = GraphicsWindow.MouseX
  Y = GraphicsWindow.MouseY
  For I = 1 to NumberCheckBoxGroups
    For J = 1 to NumberCheckBoxes[I]
      CBL = Shapes.GetLeft(CheckBox[I][J])
      CBT = Shapes.GetTop(CheckBox[I][J])
      If (X > CBL And X < CBL + 15 And Y > CBT And Y < CBT + 15) Then
        CheckBoxClicked = "true"
        ClickedGroup = I
        ClickedBox = J
        'change checked status
        If (CheckBoxChecked[I][J]) Then
          CheckBoxChecked[I][J] = "false"
          Shapes.Remove(CheckMark1[I][J])
          Shapes.Remove(CheckMark2[I][J])
        Else
          MarkCheckBox()
        EndIf
      EndIf
    EndFor
  EndFor
EndSub
```

After calling this subroutine, if **CheckBoxClicked** is "true", check box **ClickedBox** in group **ClickedGroup** has been clicked. The variable **CheckBoxChecked[ClickedGroup][ClickedBox]** tells you whether the box is checked ("true") or not checked ("false"). You can use this value to make further program decisions.

Check Box and Radio Button Controls   21-9

Example 21-2. Clicking Check Boxes

Modify **Example 21-1** to recognize clicking on the check boxes (using the **CheckBoxClick** subroutine). Display the status of each click using a **Shapes** text object.

Small Basic Code (modifications are shaded):

```
'Guide to Small Basic, Example 21-2
InitializeProgram()

Sub InitializeProgram
  GraphicsWindow.Show()
  GraphicsWindow.Title = "Example 21-2"
  GraphicsWindow.Width = 400
  GraphicsWindow.Height = 200
  CBGroupNumber = 1
  CBBackColor = "SkyBlue"
  CBForeColor = "Black"
  CBLeft = 20
  CBTop = 20
  CBWidth = 160
  CBHeight = 120
  CBTitle = "Text Formatting"
  CBNumberBoxes = 4
  CBText[1] = "Bold"
  CBText[2] = "Italic"
  CBText[3] = "Underline"
  CBText[4] = "Strikethrough"
  CBChecked[1] = "false"
  CBChecked[2] = "false"
  CBChecked[3] = "false"
  CBChecked[4] = "false"
  CreateCheckBoxGroup()
  'status text box
  Status = Shapes.AddText("No box clicked.")
  Shapes.Move(Status, 200, 20)
  GraphicsWindow.MouseDown = MouseDownSub
EndSub

Sub MouseDownSub
  CheckBoxClick()
  If (CheckBoxClicked) Then
    CRLF = Text.GetCharacter(13)
    StatusMessage = "A check box was clicked." + CRLF
```

```
    StatusMessage = StatusMessage + "It is Box " + ClickedBox + " in Group " + ClickedGroup + CRLF
    StatusMessage = StatusMessage + "Checked property is " + CheckBoxChecked[ClickedGroup][ClickedBox]
    Shapes.SetText(Status, StatusMessage)
  EndIf
EndSub
```

We have not shown the code from **CheckBoxClick**, but it needs to be in your program. Saved as **Example 21-2** in **Guide to Small Basic\Programs\Chapter 21** folder.

Save and **Run** the program. The check box group will appear with initial status displayed:

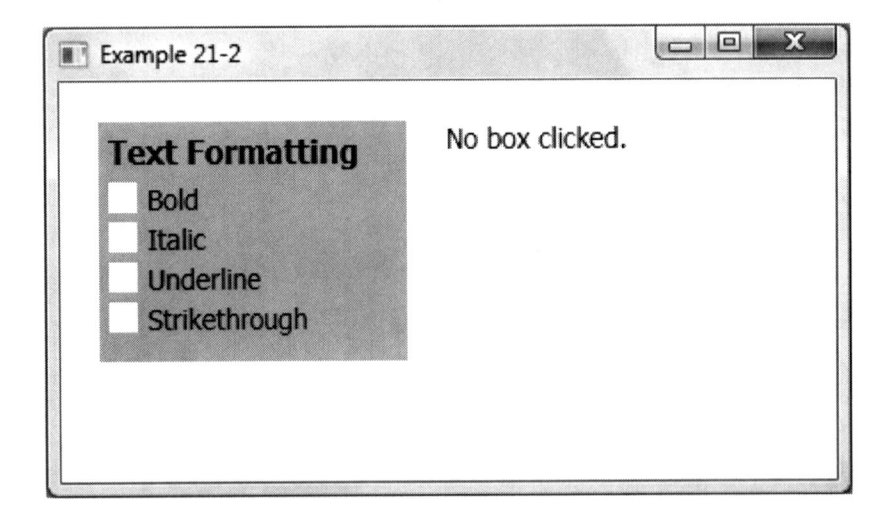

Click the check box next to **Bold**. You will see:

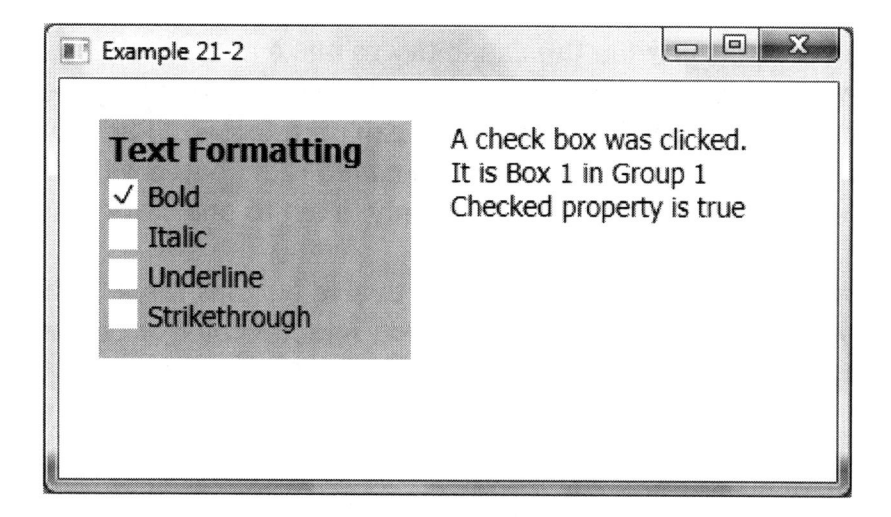

[Screenshot of Example 21-2 window showing Text Formatting group with Bold checked, Italic, Underline, Strikethrough unchecked. Message reads: "A check box was clicked. It is Box 1 in Group 1. Checked property is true"]

The message tells you a check box was clicked. It tells you which button in which group and displays the current value for its "checked" property. Try other buttons. See how the check marks appear and disappear with each click. See how the status changes.

The three subroutines we have provided (**CreateCheckBoxGroup**, **MarkCheckBox** and **CheckBoxClick**) can be used to add check boxes to your Small Basic programs. Though our example only uses one group of check boxes, it is very easy to use multiple groups. Just make sure each group has a unique, sequential value for the **CBGroupNumber** variable before creating the check box group.

Radio Button Controls

Radio button controls provide the capability to make a "mutually exclusive" choice among a group of potential candidate choices. This simply means, radio buttons work as a group, only one of which can be selected. Radio buttons are seen in all Windows applications. They are called radio buttons because they work like a tuner on a car radio – you can only listen to one station at a time!

Examples for radio button groups would be twelve buttons for selection of a month in a year, a group of buttons to let you select a color or buttons to select the difficulty in a game. Here is a group of radio buttons that allow the selection of the graphics window background color (**Red** is currently selected):

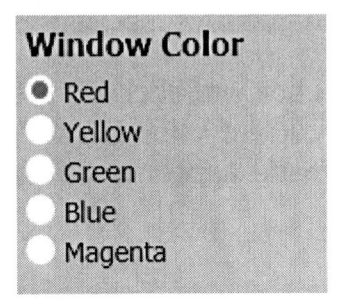

Clicking an empty radio button will mark that button and 'unmark' all other buttons in the group. In our example, if you want a **Green** window, you click that button and see:

Like check box controls, Small Basic does not offer a radio button control. So, like check boxes, we provide subroutines that create radio button groups and subroutines that tell you when a particular radio button is clicked.

The first subroutine is **CreateRadioButtonGroup**:

```
Sub CreateRadioButtonGroup
  NumberRadioButtonGroups = RBGroupNumber
  NumberRadioButtons[RBGroupNumber] = RBNumberButtons
  'draw backing
  GraphicsWindow.BrushColor = RBBackColor
  GraphicsWindow.FillRectangle(RBLeft, RBTop, RBWidth, RBHeight)
  'add title (optional)
  If (RBTitle <> "") Then
    GraphicsWindow.BrushColor = RBForeColor
    GraphicsWindow.FontSize = 16
    GraphicsWindow.FontBold = "true"
    GraphicsWindow.DrawText(RBLeft + 5, RBTop + 5, RBTitle)
    TopOffset = 10
  Else
    TopOffset = -10
  EndIf
  'create and add radio buttons
  For I = 1 To RBNumberButtons
    GraphicsWindow.PenColor = "White"
    GraphicsWindow.BrushColor = "White"
    RadioButton[RBGroupNumber][I] = Shapes.AddEllipse(15, 15)
    Shapes.Move(RadioButton[RBGroupNumber][I], RBLeft + 5, RBTop + TopOffset + I * 20)
    RadioButtonChecked[RBGroupNumber][I] = RBChecked[I]
    GraphicsWindow.BrushColor = RBForeColor
    GraphicsWindow.FontSize = 14
    GraphicsWindow.FontBold = "false"
    RadioButtonText[RBGroupNumber][I] = RBText[I]
    TextShape = Shapes.AddText(RBText[I])
    Shapes.Move(TextShape, RBLeft + 25, RBTop + TopOffset + I * 20)
  EndFor
  'create marker
  GraphicsWindow.PenColor = "SlateGray"
  GraphicsWindow.BrushColor = "SlateGray"
  Marker[RBGroupNumber] = Shapes.AddEllipse(9, 9)
  'position marker
  For I = 1 To RBNumberButtons
    If (RBChecked[I]) Then
      ClickedGroup = RBGroupNumber
      ClickedButton = I
      MarkRadioButton()
    EndIf
  EndFor
```

EndSub

This code uses **Shapes** ellipse objects for the radio buttons (**RadioButton**) and the group marker (**Marker**). Look through the code to see how it works.

This subroutine also requires **MarkRadioButton**:

```
Sub MarkRadioButton
    'move marker to selected button
    RadioButtonChecked[ClickedGroup][ClickedButton] = "true"
    RBL = Shapes.GetLeft(RadioButton[ClickedGroup][ClickedButton])
    RBT = Shapes.GetTop(RadioButton[ClickedGroup][ClickedButton])
    Shapes.Move(Marker[ClickedGroup], RBL + 3, RBT + 3)
    Shapes.ShowShape(Marker[ClickedGroup])
EndSub
```

When a radio button is clicked, this subroutine is called to mark that button and remove marks from all other buttons in the group.

These two subroutines are used to create the initial configuration for a group of radio buttons. The variables to set before calling **CreateRadioButtonGroup** are:

RBGroupNumber	Identifying number for radio button group (starts at 1).
RBBackColor	Background color of rectangle surrounding radio button group.
RBForeColor	Foreground color of text in radio button group.
RBLeft	Left position of group rectangle in graphics window.
RBWidth	Width of group rectangle.
RBHeight	Height of group rectangle.
RBTitle	Title for radio button group (optional).
RBNumberButtons	Number of radio buttons in group.
RBText	Array of captions for each radio button.
RBChecked	Array of initial configuration for each radio button (one button is "true", all others are "false")

When **CreateRadioButtonGroup** is called after setting these variables, it creates two two-dimensional arrays of interest:

RadioButtonText[GroupNumber][ButtonNumber]
Caption of radio button **ButtonNumber** in group **GroupNumber**.

RadioButtonChecked[GroupNumber][ButtonNumber]
Value of radio button **ButtonNumber** in group **GroupNumber** ("true" if initially checked, else "false")

We examine these two arrays to make decisions in our Small Basic programs.

21-16   The Developer's Reference Guide to Small Basic

Example 21-3. Create Radio Button Group

Write a program that uses the **CreateRadioButtonGroup** and **MarkRadioButton** subroutines to set up a group of radio buttons for setting the color of the graphics window. This is the example shown earlier.

Small Basic Code:

```
'Guide to Small Basic, Example 21-3
InitializeProgram()

Sub InitializeProgram
  GraphicsWindow.Show()
  GraphicsWindow.Title = "Example 21-3"
  GraphicsWindow.Width = 500
  GraphicsWindow.Height = 200
  RBGroupNumber = 1
  RBBackColor = "LightGray"
  RBForeColor = "Black"
  RBLeft = 20
  RBTop = 20
  RBWidth = 160
  RBHeight = 140
  RBTitle = "Window Color"
  RBNumberButtons = 5
  RBText[1] = "Red"
  RBText[2] = "Yellow"
  RBText[3] = "Green"
  RBText[4] = "Blue"
  RBText[5] = "Magenta"
  RBChecked[1] = "true"
  RBChecked[2] = "false"
  RBChecked[3] = "false"
  RBChecked[4] = "false"
  RBChecked[5] = "false"
  CreateRadioButtonGroup()
  'set default color
  For I = 1 To RBNumberButtons
    If (RBChecked[I]) Then
      GraphicsWindow.BackgroundColor = RBText[I]
    EndIf
  EndFor
EndSub
```

Check Box and Radio Button Controls   21-17

We have not shown the code from **CreateRadioButtonGroup** or **MarkRadioButton**, but they need to be in your program. Saved as **Example 21-3** in **Guide to Small Basic\Programs\Chapter 21** folder.

In **InitializeProgram**, we size the graphics window. We then set each of the needed variables and call the subroutine to create the radio button group. After creating the radio buttons, we cycle through each button to set the initial window color (Red - the first button).

Save and **Run** the program. The radio button group will appear and the window will be red:

If you click a radio button, nothing happens. Let's fix that.

Clicking a Radio Button

If you click an empty radio button, you want to draw a filled circle in the selected button and clear any previous selection. Like the check box, to accomplish this, we need to do two things. First, we need to add code to recognize the graphics window **MouseDown** event. We use:

```
GraphicsWindow.MouseDown = MouseDownSub
```

Second, in the **MouseDownSub**, we need to see if a radio button has been selected. This subroutine (**RadioButtonClick**) does the task:

```
Sub RadioButtonClick
  RadioButtonClicked = "false"
  X = GraphicsWindow.MouseX
  Y = GraphicsWindow.MouseY
  For I = 1 to NumberRadioButtonGroups
    For J = 1 to NumberRadioButtons[I]
      RBL = Shapes.GetLeft(RadioButton[I][J])
      RBT = Shapes.GetTop(RadioButton[I][J])
      If (X > RBL And X < RBL + 15 And Y > RBT And Y < RBT + 15) Then
        RadioButtonClicked = "true"
        ClickedGroup = I
        ClickedButton = J
        'change checked status
        MarkRadioButton()
      EndIf
    EndFor
  EndFor
EndSub
```

After calling this subroutine, if **RadioButtonClicked** is "true", radio button **ClickedButton** in group **ClickedGroup** has been clicked. The variable **RadioButtonChecked[ClickedGroup][ClickedButton]** tells you whether the button is checked ("true") or not checked ("false"). You can use this value to make further program decisions.

Example 21-4. Clicking Radio Buttons

Modify **Example 21-3** to recognize clicking on the radio buttons (using the **RadioButtonClick** subroutine). Change the graphics window color accordingly.

Small Basic Code (modifications are shaded):

```
'Guide to Small Basic, Example 21-4
InitializeProgram()

Sub InitializeProgram
  GraphicsWindow.Show()
  GraphicsWindow.Title = "Example 21-4"
  GraphicsWindow.Width = 500
  GraphicsWindow.Height = 200
  RBGroupNumber = 1
  RBBackColor = "Gray"
  RBForeColor = "White"
  RBLeft = 20
  RBTop = 20
  RBWidth = 160
  RBHeight = 140
  RBTitle = "Window Color"
  RBNumberButtons = 5
  RBText[1] = "Red"
  RBText[2] = "Yellow"
  RBText[3] = "Green"
  RBText[4] = "Blue"
  RBText[5] = "Magenta"
  RBChecked[1] = "true"
  RBChecked[2] = "false"
  RBChecked[3] = "false"
  RBChecked[4] = "false"
  RBChecked[5] = "false"
  CreateRadioButtonGroup()
  'set default color
  For I = 1 To RBNumberButtons
    If (RBChecked[I]) Then
      GraphicsWindow.BackgroundColor = RBText[I]
    EndIf
  EndFor
  GraphicsWindow.MouseDown = MouseDownSub
EndSub

Sub MouseDownSub
```

```
  RadioButtonClick()
  If (RadioButtonClicked) Then
    GraphicsWindow.BackgroundColor =
RadioButtonText[ClickedGroup][ClickedButton]
  EndIf
EndSub
```

We have not shown the code from **RadioButtonClick**, but it needs to be in your program. Saved as **Example 21-4** in **Guide to Small Basic\Programs\Chapter 21** folder.

Save and **Run** the program. The radio button group will appear with initial status displayed:

Click the check box next to **Green**. You will see:

```
Example 21-4
    Window Color
      ○ Red
      ○ Yellow
      ● Green
      ○ Blue
      ○ Magenta
```

The window color has changed. Try other buttons. See how the marks and screen color change with each click.

The three subroutines we have provided (**CreateRadioButtonGroup**, **MarkRadioButton** and **RadioButtonClick**) can be used to add radio buttons to your Small Basic programs. Though our example only uses one group of radio buttons, it is very easy to use multiple groups. Just make sure each group has a unique, sequential value for the **RBGroupNumber** variable before creating the radio button group. In the next example, we will use multiple radio button groups.

Example 21-5. Pizza Ordering

Build a program where a pizza order can be entered by simply clicking on check boxes and radio buttons. Have three groups of radio buttons – one to select size, one for thick or thin crust and one for eat in or take out. Use a group of check boxes for toppings. Display the finished pizza contents in a message box.

Small Basic Code:

```
'Guide to Small Basic, Example 21-5
InitializeProgram()

Sub InitializeProgram
  GraphicsWindow.Show()
  GraphicsWindow.Title = "Example 21-5"
  GraphicsWindow.Width = 290
  GraphicsWindow.Height = 280
  'size radio button group
  RBGroupNumber = 1
  RBBackColor = "Blue"
  RBForeColor = "White"
  RBLeft = 10
  RBTop = 10
  RBWidth = 100
  RBHeight = 100
  RBTitle = "Size"
  RBNumberButtons = 3
  RBText[1] = "Small"
  RBText[2] = "Medium"
  RBText[3] = "Large"
  RBChecked[1] = "true"
  RBChecked[2] = "false"
  RBChecked[3] = "false"
  CreateRadioButtonGroup()
  'set default size
  PizzaSize = "Small"
  'crust type radio button group
  RBGroupNumber = 2
  RBLeft = 10
  RBTop = 120
  RBHeight = 80
  RBTitle = "Crust"
  RBNumberButtons = 2
  RBText[1] = "Thin Crust"
  RBText[2] = "Thick Crust"
```

```
RBChecked[1] = "true"
RBChecked[2] = "false"
CreateRadioButtonGroup()
'set default size
PizzaCrust = "Thin Crust"
'where radio button group
RBGroupNumber = 3
RBLeft = 10
RBTop = 210
RBHeight = 60
RBTitle = ""
RBNumberButtons = 2
RBText[1] = "Eat In"
RBText[2] = "Take Out"
RBChecked[1] = "true"
RBChecked[2] = "false"
CreateRadioButtonGroup()
'set default where
PizzaWhere = "Eat In"
'toppings check box group
CBGroupNumber = 1
CBBackColor = "DarkRed"
CBForeColor = "White"
CBLeft = 120
CBTop = 10
CBWidth = 160
CBHeight = 160
CBTitle = "Toppings"
CBNumberBoxes = 6
CBText[1] = "Extra Cheese"
CBText[2] = "Mushrooms"
CBText[3] = "Green Peppers"
CBText[4] = "Onions"
CBText[5] = "Black Olives"
CBText[6] = "Tomatoes"
CBChecked[1] = "false"
CBChecked[2] = "false"
CBChecked[3] = "false"
CBChecked[4] = "false"
CBChecked[5] = "false"
CBChecked[6] = "false"
CreateCheckBoxGroup()
'build button
GraphicsWindow.BrushColor = "Black"
GraphicsWindow.FontSize = 16
BuildButton = Controls.AddButton("Build Pizza", 150, 180)
```

```
    GraphicsWindow.MouseDown = MouseDownSub
    Controls.ButtonClicked = ButtonClickedSub
EndSub

Sub MouseDownSub
  RadioButtonClick()
  If (RadioButtonClicked) Then
    'radio button clicked
    If (ClickedGroup = 1) Then
      PizzaSize = RadioButtonText[1][ClickedButton]
    ElseIf (ClickedGroup = 2) Then
      PizzaCrust = RadioButtonText[2][ClickedButton]
    Else
      PizzaWhere = RadioButtonText[3][ClickedButton]
    EndIf
  EndIf
  CheckBoxClick()
EndSub

Sub ButtonClickedSub
  'build button clicked
  CRLF = Text.GetCharacter(13)
  s = PizzaWhere + CRLF
  s = s + PizzaSize + " Pizza" + CRLF
  s = s + PizzaCrust + CRLF
  'Check each topping
  For I = 1 To 6
    If (CheckBoxChecked[1][I]) Then
      s = s + CheckBoxText[1][I] + CRLF
    EndIf
  EndFor
  GraphicsWindow.ShowMessage(s, "Your Pizza:")
EndSub
```

The code listing does not include the six subroutines needed for the check boxes and radio buttons: **CreateCheckBoxGroup**, **MarkCheckBox**, **CheckBoxClick**, **CreateRadioButtonGroup**, **MarkRadioButton** or **RadioButtonClick**, but they need to be in your program. Saved as **Example 21-5** in **Guide to Small Basic\Programs\Chapter 21** folder.

In **InitializeProgram**, three different radio button groups and a single check box group are set up. Values for three variables (**PizzaSize**, **PizzaCrust**, **PizzaWhere**) are set based on initial choices in the radio button groups. These values are changed in **MouseDownSub** whenever a radio button click is detected.

When the **Build Pizza** button is clicked (**ButtonClickedSub**), we describe the pizza using the above variables and add any selected toppings. The code then displays the pizza order in a message box.

Save and **Run** the program. Here's the initial window:

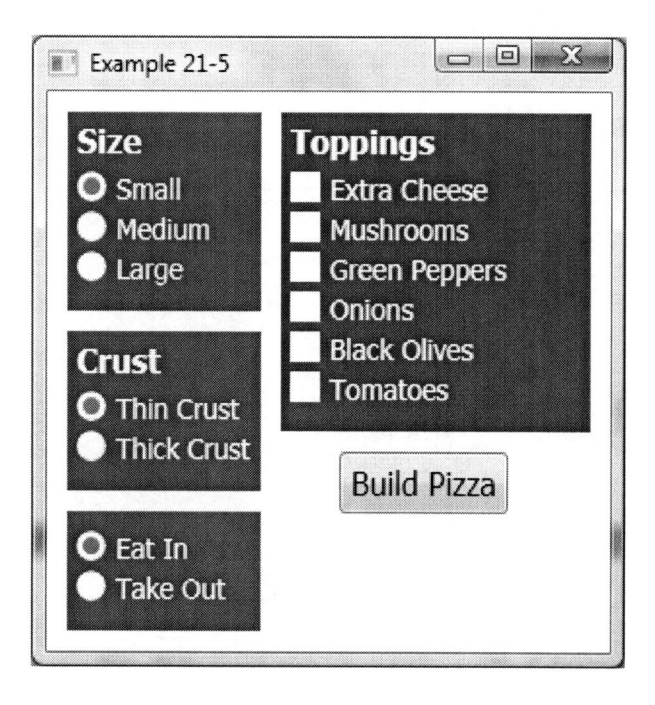

I change the size and crust and add some toppings:

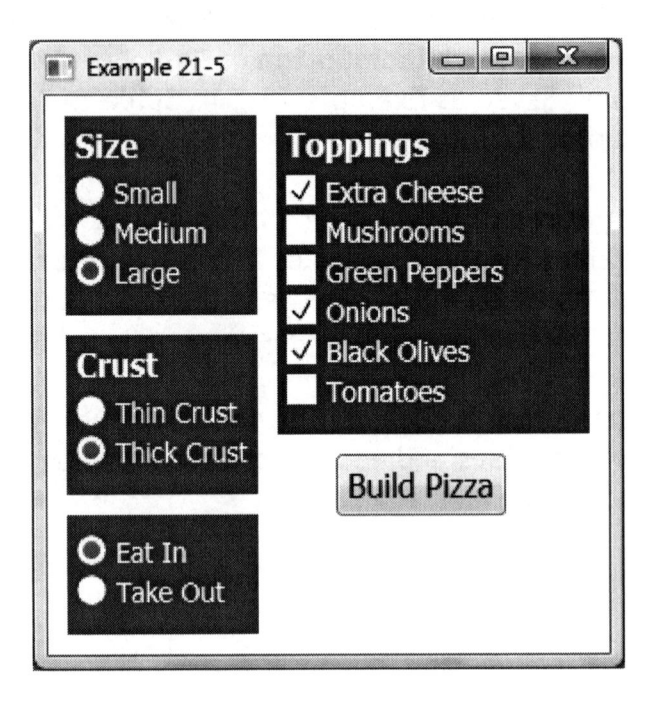

Then, when I click **Build Pizza**, I see:

Class Review

After completing this class, you should understand:

- How to do add check box groups to a Small Basic program.
- How to detect clicking on check boxes and interpreting the results.
- How to do add radio button groups to a Small Basic program.
- How to detect clicking on radio buttons and interpreting the results.

This page intentionally not left blank.

22. Turtle Graphics

Preview

In this chapter, we look at drawing graphics using the Small Basic **Turtle** object. It is a fun way for kids to learn programming.

Turtle Object

The **Turtle** object provides an easy way to draw in the graphics window. A neat thing about turtle graphics is that even younger children can grasp the ideas. There is no need to understand coordinate systems or even to know any Small Basic programming. Turtle graphics can be done without ever knowing about an (X, Y) coordinate pair. There is a need to understand angles. Kids need to know that there are 360 degrees in a circle.

Turtle Properties:

Angle
Gets or sets the current angle of the turtle. While setting, this will turn the turtle instantly to the new angle. When **Angle** is 0 (default value), turtle is pointing up. **Angle** is measured clockwise.

Speed
Specifies how fast the turtle should move. Valid values are 1 to 10. Default value is 5. If **Speed** is set to 10, the turtle moves and rotates instantly.

X
Gets or sets the X location of the turtle. While setting, this will move the turtle instantly to the new location. Initial value is 320.

Y
Gets or sets the Y location of the turtle. While setting, this will move the turtle instantly to the new location. Initial value is 240.

Turtle Graphics

Turtle Methods:

`Hide()`
Hides the turtle and disables interaction with it.

`Move(distance)`
Moves the turtle the specified **distance** at the current angle. If the pen is down, it will draw a line (using the current pen) as it moves.

`MoveTo(x, y)`
Turns and moves the turtle to the specified point (**x, y**). If the pen is down, it will draw a line (using the current pen) as it moves.

`PenDown()`
Sets the pen down to enable the turtle to draw as it moves.

`PenUp()`
Lifts the pen up to stop drawing as the turtle moves.

`Show()`
Shows the turtle to enable interaction with it.

`Turn(angle)`
Turns the turtle by the specified **angle**. Angle is in degrees and can be either positive or negative. If the angle is positive, the turtle turns to the right. If negative, the turtle turns to the left.

`TurnLeft()`
Turns the turtle 90 degrees to the left (counterclockwise).

`TurnRight()`
Turns the turtle 90 degrees to the right (clockwise).

Example 22-1. Draw a Square

Write a program that draws a red square using the turtle.

Small Basic Code:

```
'Guide to Small Basic, Example 22-1
GraphicsWindow.Show()
GraphicsWindow.Title = "Example 22-1"
'show turtle
Turtle.Show()
'draw square
GraphicsWindow.PenColor = "Red"
For I = 1 To 4
  Turtle.Move(150)
  Turtle.TurnRight()
EndFor
```

Saved as **Example 22-1** in **Guide to Small Basic\Programs\Chapter 22** folder.

The program simply does four left turns, drawing a line of 150 pixels between each turn.

Save and **Run** the program. The turtle will appear and draw the four sides of the square:

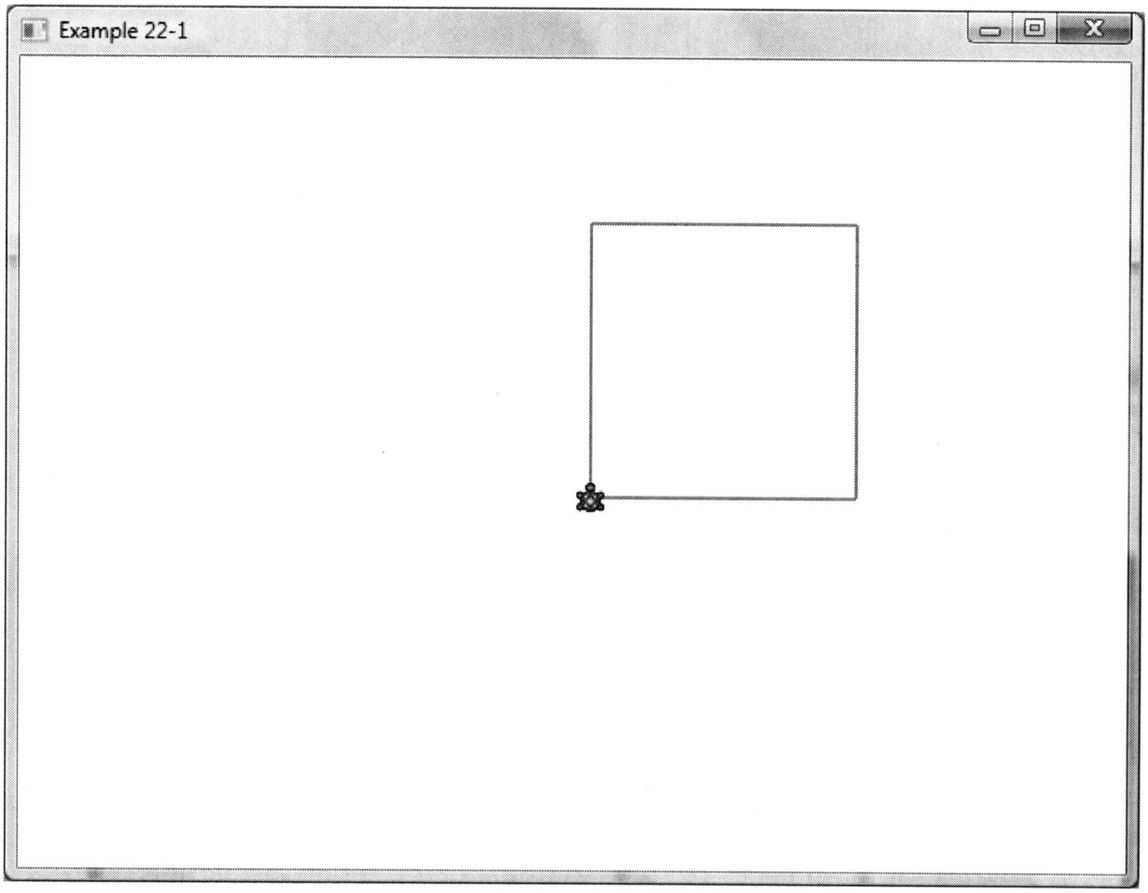

You could speed up the drawing process by changing the turtle **Speed** property.

Example 22-2. Draw a Polygon

Write a program that draws a blue polygon (**NSides** sides) using the turtle.

Small Basic Code:

```
'Guide to Small Basic, Example 22-2
GraphicsWindow.Show()
GraphicsWindow.Title = "Example 22-2"
'show turtle
Turtle.Show()
'you can change these numbers
NSides = 3
Perimeter = 600
GraphicsWindow.PenColor = "Blue"
'draw polygon
Side = Perimeter / NSides
Angle = 360 / NSides
For I = 1 To NSides
  Turtle.Move(Side)
  Turtle.Turn(Angle)
EndFor
```

Saved as **Example 22-2** in **Guide to Small Basic\Programs\Chapter 22** folder.

You set values for the number of sides (**NSides**) and the polygon perimeter (**Perimeter**). The given values will draw a triangle (**NSides** = 3) with a **Perimeter** of 600 pixels (200 pixels per side).

Save and **Run** the program. The turtle will appear and draw the three sides of a triangle:

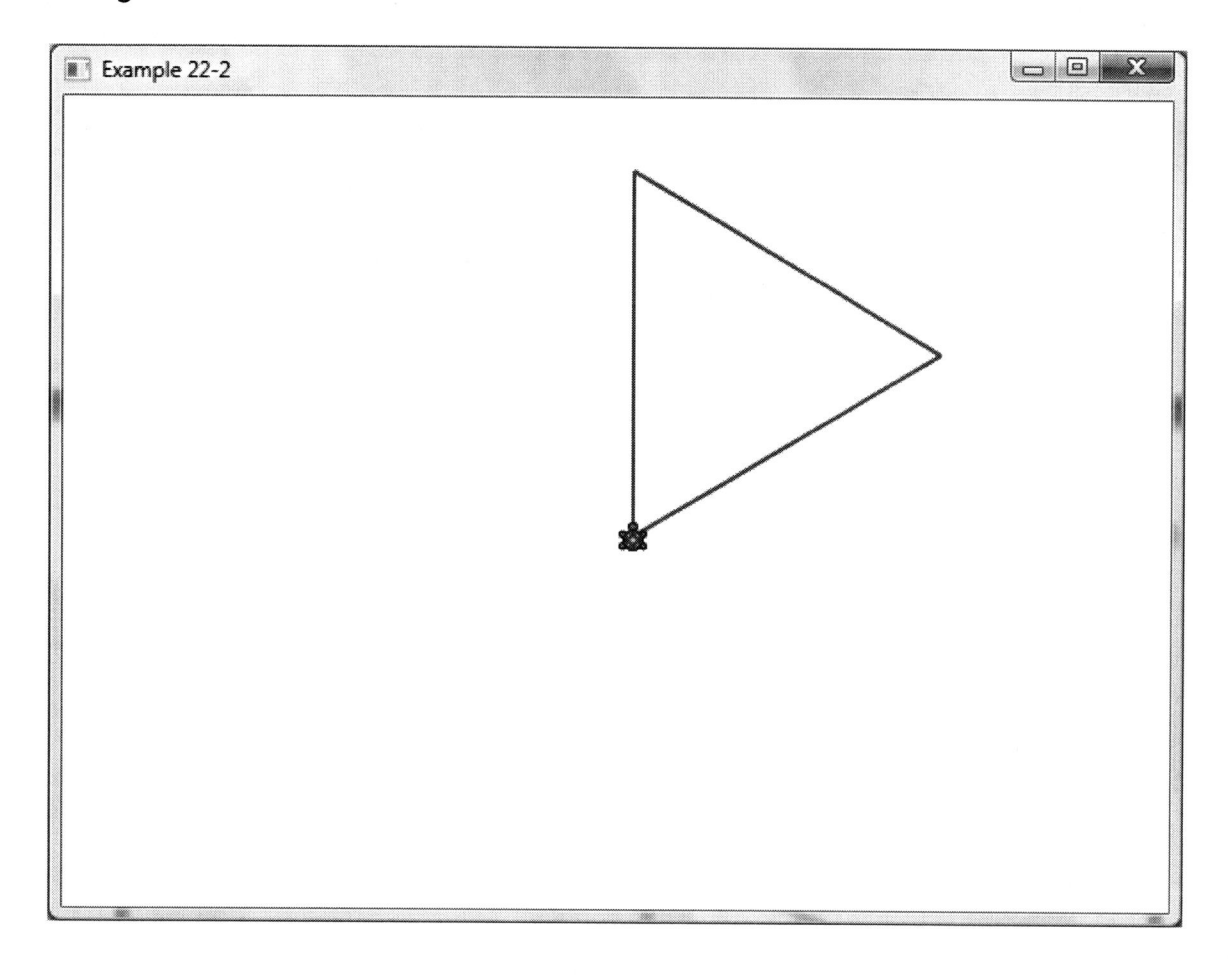

Change **NSides** to 8 to see an octagon (looks like a stop sign):

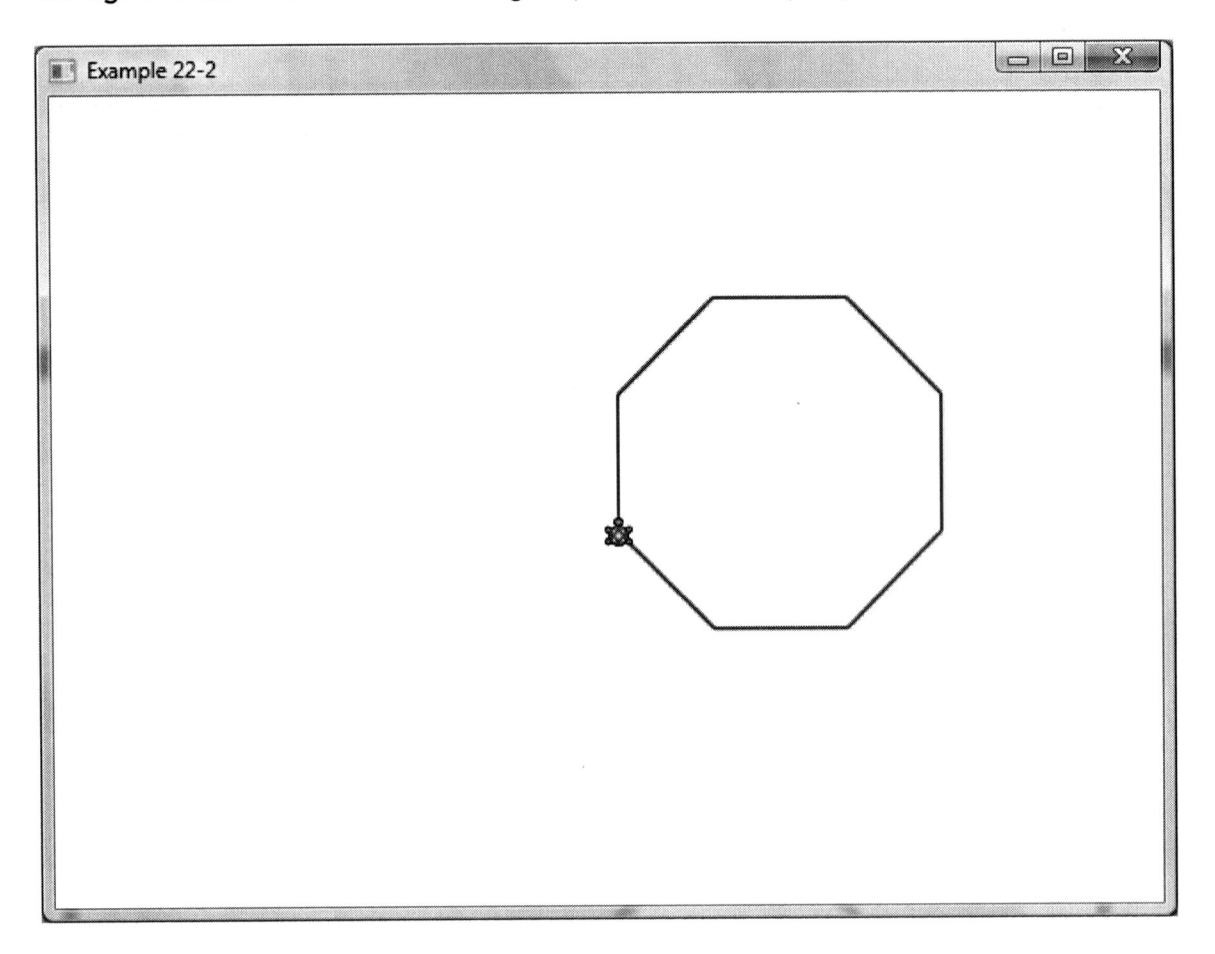

Change **NSides** to 30. Look at the result:

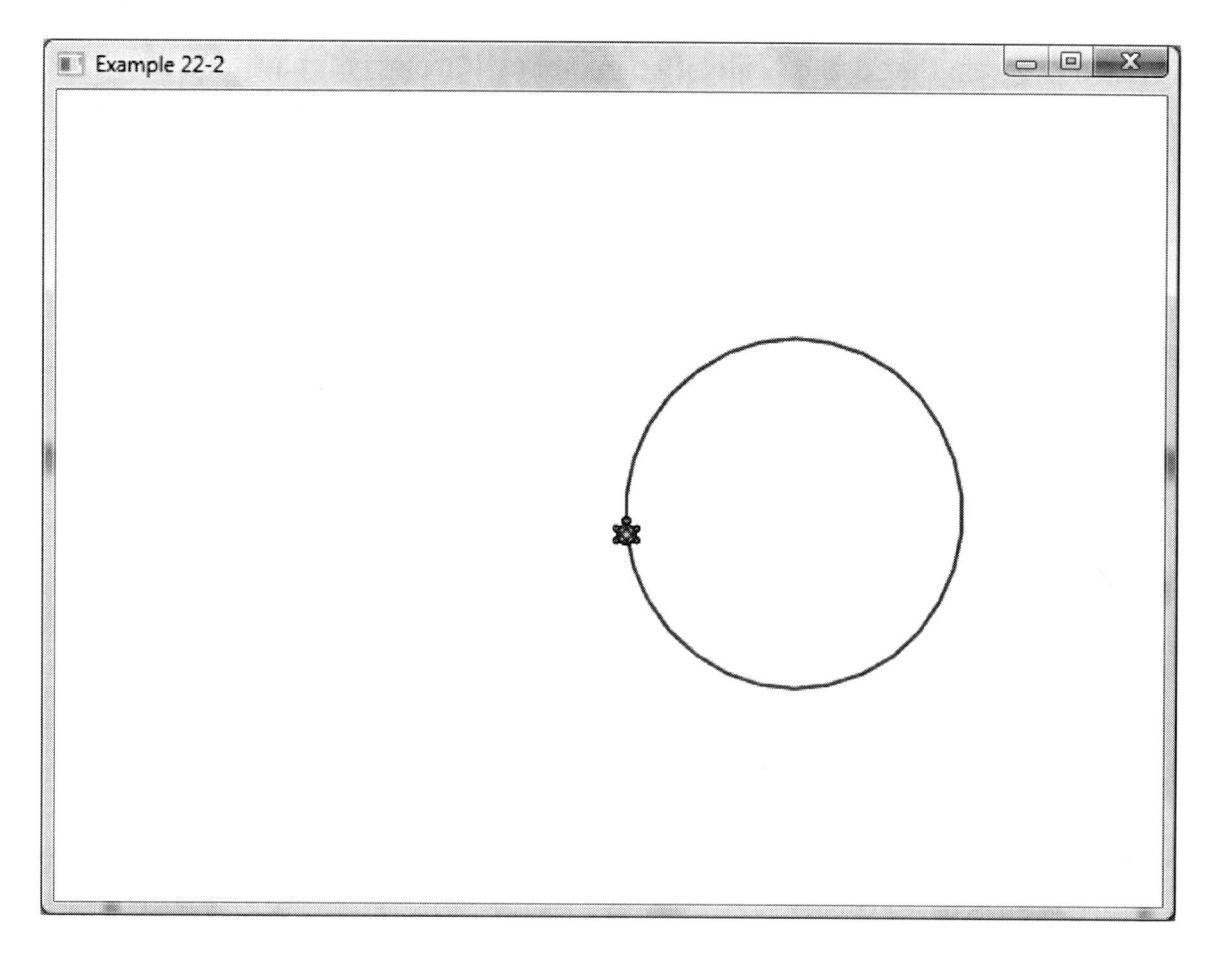

A polygon with many sides looks like a circle!

Example 22-3. Draw Multi-Colored Circles

Write a program that draws a specified number (**NCircles**) of multi-colored circles using the turtle. After each circle is drawn, turn the turtle a bit so the circles overlap.

Small Basic Code:

```
'Guide to Small Basic, Example 22-3
GraphicsWindow.Show()
GraphicsWindow.Title = "Example 22-3"
'show turtle
Turtle.Show()
Turtle.Speed = 10
'you can change these numbers
NSides = 30
Perimeter = 600
NCircles = 50
GraphicsWindow.PenColor = "Blue"
'draw polygon
Side = Perimeter / NSides
Angle = 360 / NSides
For J = 1 To NCircles
  GraphicsWindow.PenColor = GraphicsWindow.GetRandomColor()
  For I = 1 To NSides
    Turtle.Move(Side)
    Turtle.Turn(Angle)
  EndFor
  Turtle.Turn(360 / NCircles)
EndFor
```

Saved as **Example 22-3** in **Guide to Small Basic\Programs\Chapter 22** folder.

This is a slight modification to the previous example. We fix **NSides** at 30 to approximate a circle. We draw **NCircles**, each with a random color. After each circle is drawn, we turn the turtle **360 / NCircles** degrees to get circles that overlap evenly. We use a **Speed** of 10 to make things go faster.

Save and **Run** the program. Sit back and watch the turtle do this beautiful drawing:

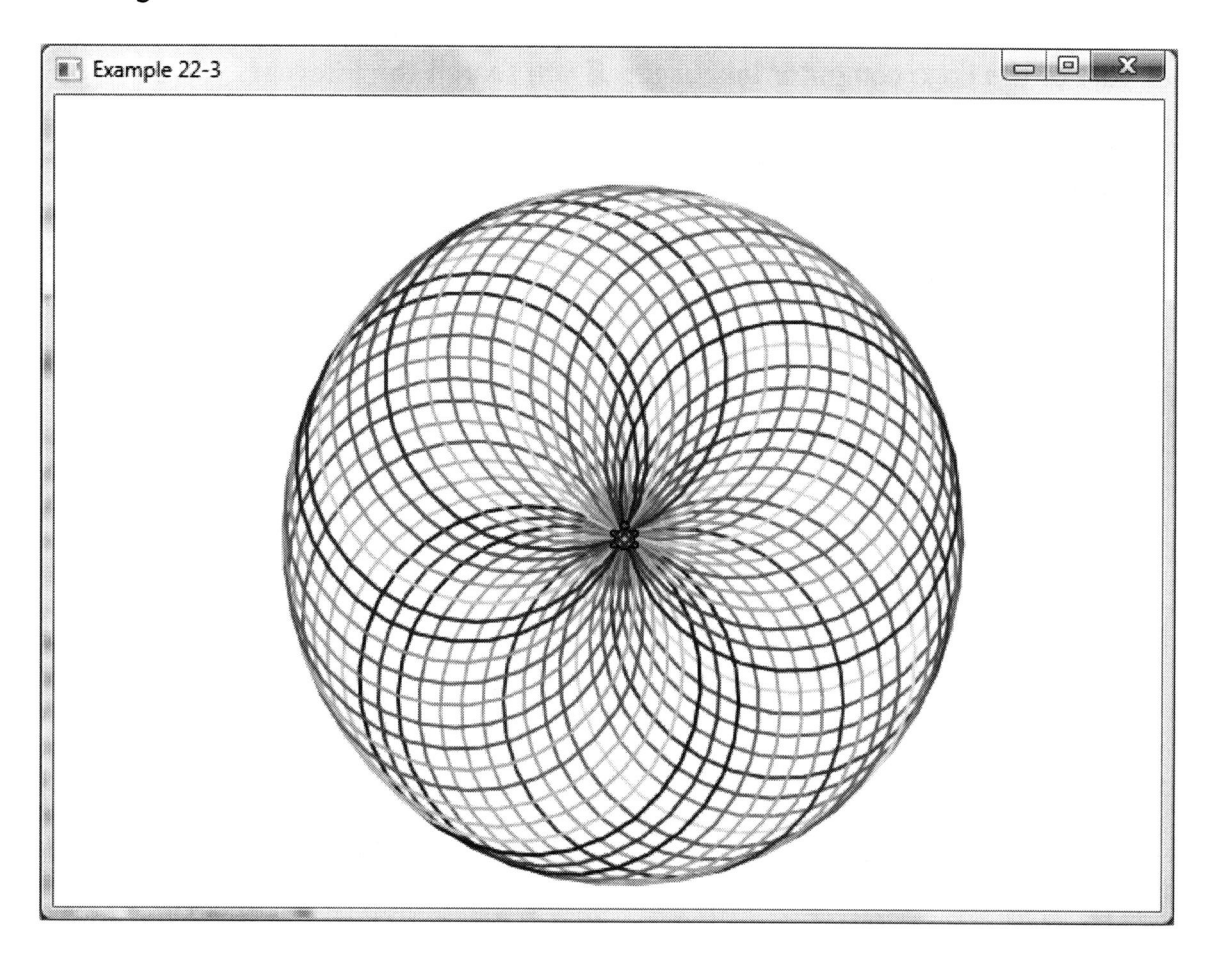

Other Turtle Graphics

Turtle graphics have been around for many years. The turtle was originally used as part of the Logo computer language. If you search the Internet, you can find lots of examples.

There are some pretty neat things out there. You may need to do a little translation between other turtle languages and the Small Basic equivalents. Let's look at a few examples.

Turtle Graphics

Example 22-4. Draw a Flower

Here's an example from the Internet that draws a little flower.

Small Basic Code:

```
'Guide to Small Basic, Example 22-4
GraphicsWindow.Show()
GraphicsWindow.Title = "Example 22-4"
'show turtle
Turtle.Show()
'move down a bit
Turtle.Speed = 10
Turtle.PenUp()
Turtle.Turn(180)
Turtle.Move(50)
Turtle.Turn(180)
'ground
Turtle.PenDown()
GraphicsWindow.PenColor = "Orange"
Turtle.Turn(90)
Turtle.Move(150)
Turtle.Turn(180)
Turtle.Move(300)
Turtle.Turn(180)
Turtle.Move(150)
Turtle.Turn(-90)
'draw plant body
GraphicsWindow.PenColor = "Green"
Turtle.Turn(-10)
For I =1 To 3
  Turtle.Move(100)
  Turtle.Turn(180)
  Turtle.Move(100)
  Turtle.Turn(190)
EndFor
'Draw stem
Turtle.Turn(-20)
Turtle.Move(120)
'Draw flower petals
GraphicsWindow.PenColor = "Red"
Turtle.Turn(-90)
For I =1 To 10
  Turtle.Move(20)
  For J =1 To 10
```

```
    Turtle.Turn(20)
    Turtle.Move(2)
  EndFor
  Turtle.Move(20)
EndFor
'flower center
GraphicsWindow.PenWidth = 3
GraphicsWindow.PenColor = "Yellow"
Turtle.PenUp()
Turtle.Move(-2)
Turtle.PenDown()
For I =1 To 18
  Turtle.Move(1)
  Turtle.Turn(20)
EndFor
'get turtle out of way
Turtle.PenUp()
Turtle.Move(100)
```

Saved as **Example 22-4** in **Guide to Small Basic\Programs\Chapter 22** folder.

Save and **Run** the program. Here's the result:

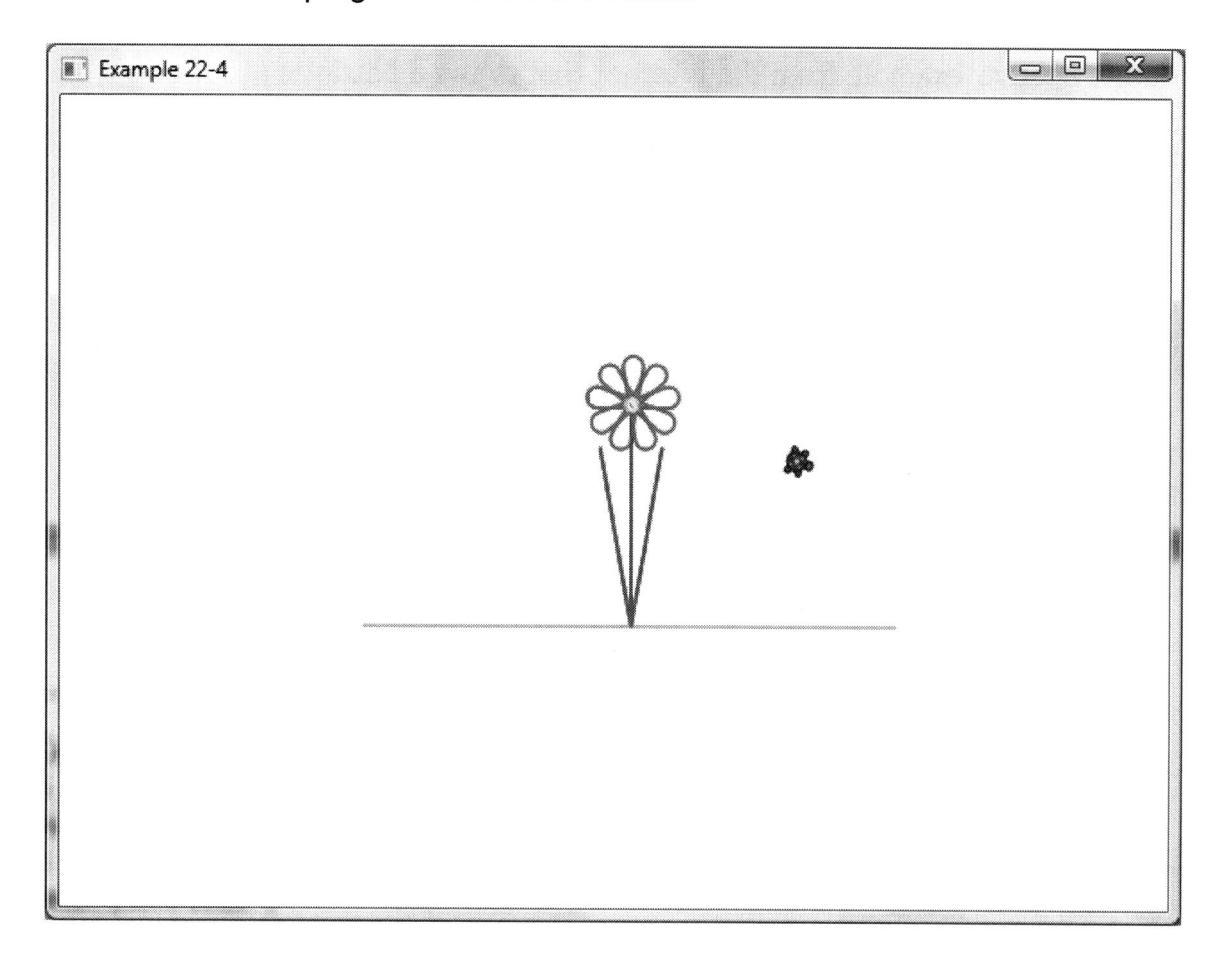

Example 22-5. Draw a Pinwheel

Here's another example from the Internet that draws a patriotic pinwheel.

Small Basic Code:

```
'Guide to Small Basic, Example 22-5
GraphicsWindow.Show()
GraphicsWindow.Title = "Example 22-5"
GraphicsWindow.BackgroundColor = "Black"
'show turtle
Turtle.Show()
Turtle.Speed = 10
For I = 1 To 10
  For J = 1 To 18
    If (Math.Remainder(J, 3) = 0) Then
      GraphicsWindow.PenColor = "Red"
    EndIf
    If (Math.Remainder(J, 3) = 1) Then
      GraphicsWindow.PenColor = "White"
    EndIf
    If (Math.Remainder(J, 3) = 2) Then
      GraphicsWindow.PenColor = "Blue"
    EndIf
    For K =1 To 2
      Turtle.Move(200)
      Turtle.Turn(200)
    EndFor
  EndFor
  Turtle.Turn(36)
EndFor
```

Saved as **Example 22-5** in **Guide to Small Basic\Programs\Chapter 22** folder.

Save and **Run** the program. Here's the result:

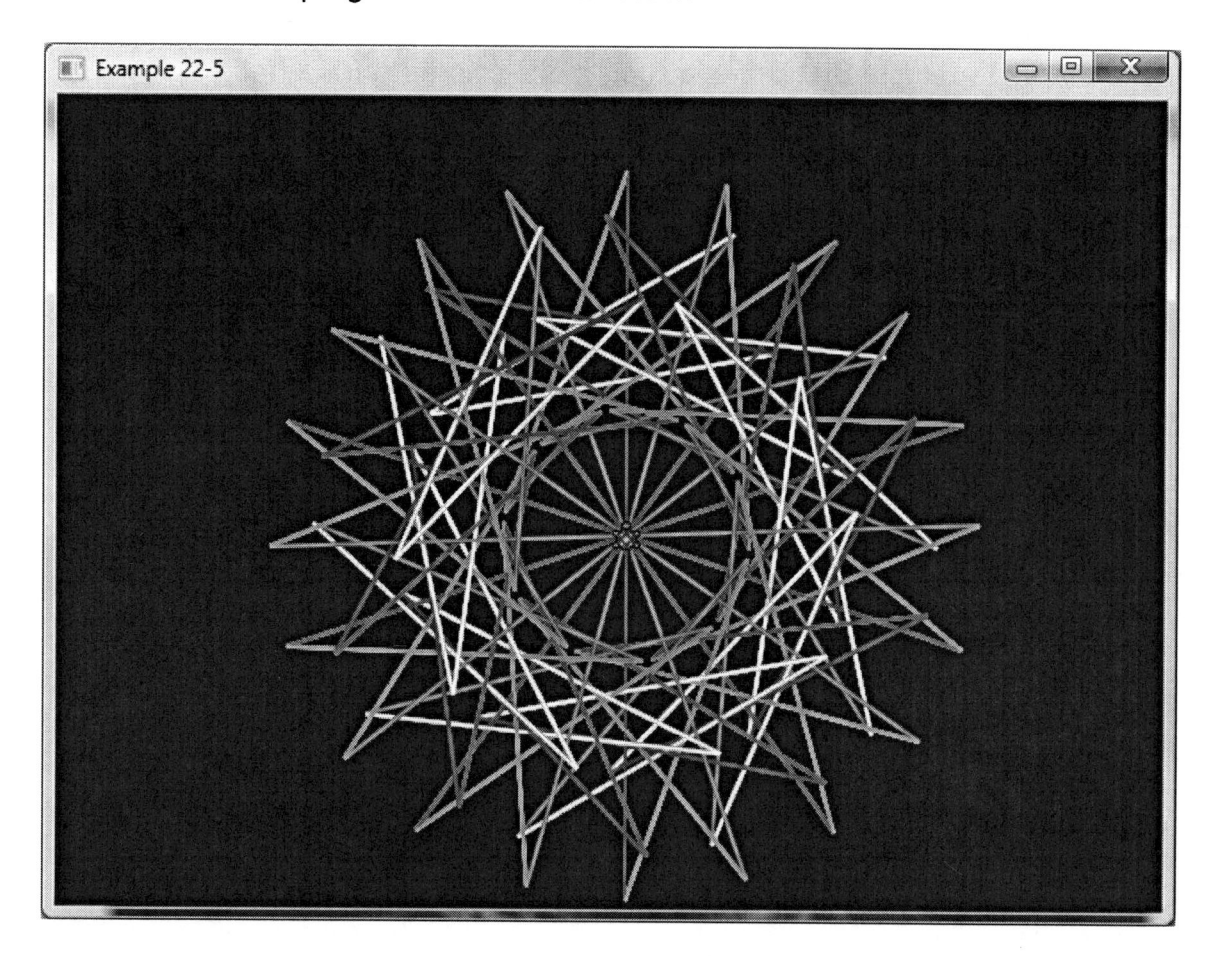

Pretty neat, huh?

Example 22-6. Draw a Spiral Effect

Here's a final example that draws a cool, multi-colored spiral effect.

Small Basic Code:

```
'Guide to Small Basic, Example 22-6
GraphicsWindow.Show()
GraphicsWindow.Title = "Example 22-6"
'show turtle
Turtle.Show()
D = 0.01
A = 89.5
X = 0.01
S = 250
Turtle.Turn(90)
Turtle.Speed = 10
For I = 1 To S
  GraphicsWindow.PenColor = GraphicsWindow.GetRandomColor()
  Turtle.Move(D * 0.5 * GraphicsWindow.Width)
  Turtle.Turn(A)
  D = D + X
EndFor
```

Saved as **Example 22-6** in **Guide to Small Basic\Programs\Chapter 22** folder.

Save and **Run** the program. It's quite hypnotizing:

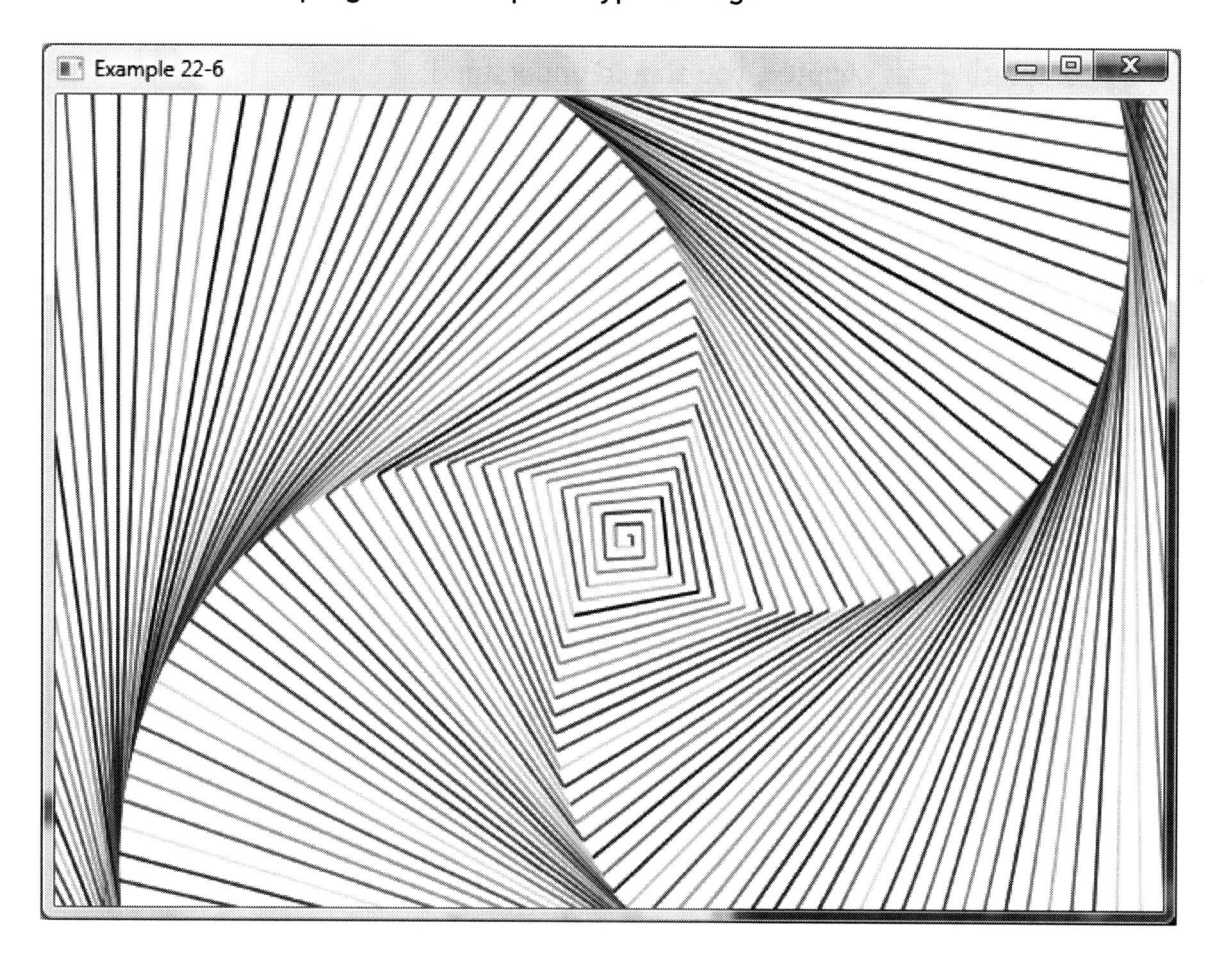

Chapter Review

After completing this chapter, you should understand:

- Use of the **Turtle** object.
- How the turtle **properties** and **methods** work.
- How to draw a polygon with the turtle.
- How to find other turtle graphics programs.

23. Flickr Photos

Preview

In this chapter, we look at displaying photos available on the **Flickr** website.

Flickr Class

The **Flickr** class provides access to photos saved on the **Flickr** photo services web site. To use this class, your computer must be connected to the Internet.

Flickr Methods:

```
GetPictureOfMoment()
```
Get the URL of the **Flickr** picture of the moment. Returns the URL.

```
GetRandomPicture(tag)
```
Get the URL of a random **Flickr** picture with the given **tag**. Returns the URL.

Example 23-1. Picture of the Moment

Write a program that randomly displays a **Flickr** photo of the moment every five seconds.

Small Basic Code:

```
'Guide to Small Basic, Example 23-1
GraphicsWindow.Show()
GraphicsWindow.Title = "Example 23-1"
GraphicsWindow.Show()
GraphicsWindow.Width = 600
GraphicsWindow.Height = 400
GetPhoto:
Photo = Flickr.GetPictureOfMoment()
GraphicsWindow.DrawResizedImage(Photo, 0, 0, 600, 400)
Program.Delay(5000)
Goto GetPhoto
```

Saved as **Example 23-1** in **Guide to Small Basic\Programs\Chapter 23** folder.

Save and **Run** the program. The initial photo will take some time to display, while the Internet site is accessed. Here is what I got:

Then, every five seconds, a new random photo will appear.

Here's my next photo:

Example 23-2. Tagged Picture

Write a program that displays a tagged **Flickr** photo.

Small Basic Code:

```
'Guide to Small Basic, Example 23-2
InitializeProgram()

Sub InitializeProgram
  GraphicsWindow.Show()
  GraphicsWindow.Title = "Example 23-2"
  GraphicsWindow.Show()
  GraphicsWindow.Width = 600
  GraphicsWindow.Height = 400
  GraphicsWindow.FontSize = 14
  GraphicsWindow.FontBold = "false"
  TagTextBox = Controls.AddTextBox(10, 10)
  ShowPhotoButton = Controls.AddButton("Show Photo", 10, 40)
  Controls.ButtonClicked = ButtonClickedSub
EndSub

Sub ButtonClickedSub
  Tag = Controls.GetTextBoxText(TagTextBox)
  Photo = Flickr.GetRandomPicture(Tag)
  GraphicsWindow.DrawResizedImage(Photo, 0, 0, 600, 400)
EndSub
```

Saved as **Example 23-2** in **Guide to Small Basic\Programs\Chapter 23** folder.

Save and **Run** the program. Type a tag in the text box and click **Show Photo**. Again, the initial photo will take some time to display, while the Internet site is accessed. Here is what I got for **Seattle**:

That's our beautiful skyline with the Space Needle.

Click **Show Photo** again and you will see another Seattle photo (the Experience Music Project):

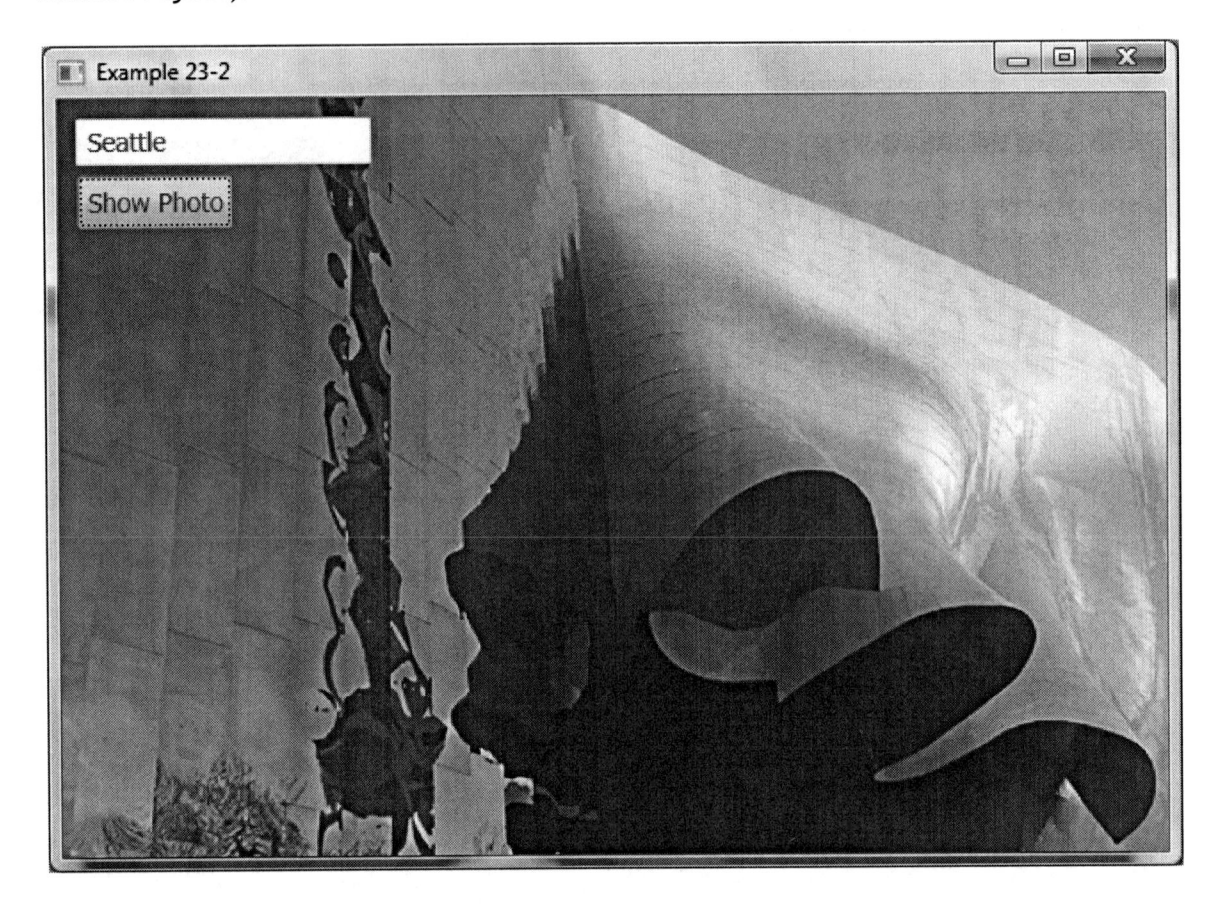

I changed the tag to **triathlon** and got:

Chapter Review

After completing this chapter, you should understand:

> - How to display random and tagged photos from the **Flickr** website.

24. Dictionary

Preview

In this chapter, we look at using an online dictionary to access definitions of words.

Dictionary Class

The **Dictionary** class provides access to an online dictionary. You can get definitions of words in English and French. I would bet future versions will support more languages. To use this class, your computer must be connected to the Internet.

Dictionary Methods:

```
GetDefinition(word)
```
Returns the definition of **word** in English.

```
GetDefinitionInFrench(word)
```
Returns the definition of **word** in French.

Dictionary

Example 24-1. Word Definition

Write a program that displays the definition of a word you input.

Small Basic Code:

```
'Guide to Small Basic, Example 24-1
InitializeProgram()

Sub InitializeProgram
  GraphicsWindow.Show()
  GraphicsWindow.Title = "Example 24-1"
  GraphicsWindow.Show()
  GraphicsWindow.Width = 320
  GraphicsWindow.Height = 290
  GraphicsWindow.BackgroundColor = "LightGray"
  GraphicsWindow.FontSize = 14
  GraphicsWindow.FontBold = "false"
  WordTextBox = Controls.AddTextBox(10, 10)
  DefineButton = Controls.AddButton("Define", 10, 40)
  DefinitionTextBox = Controls.AddMultiLineTextBox(10, 80)
  Controls.SetSize(DefinitionTextBox, 300, 200)
  Controls.ButtonClicked = ButtonClickedSub
EndSub

Sub ButtonClickedSub
  Word = Controls.GetTextBoxText(WordTextBox)
TextWindow.WriteLine(Word)
  Controls.SetTextBoxText(DefinitionTextBox,
Dictionary.GetDefinition(Word))
EndSub
```

Saved as **Example 24-1** in **Guide to Small Basic\Programs\Chapter 24** folder.

Save and **Run** the program. Type a word in the text box and click **Define**. The definition will appear in the multi-line text box (after some delay, while the Internet site is accessed). Here is what I got for **travel**:

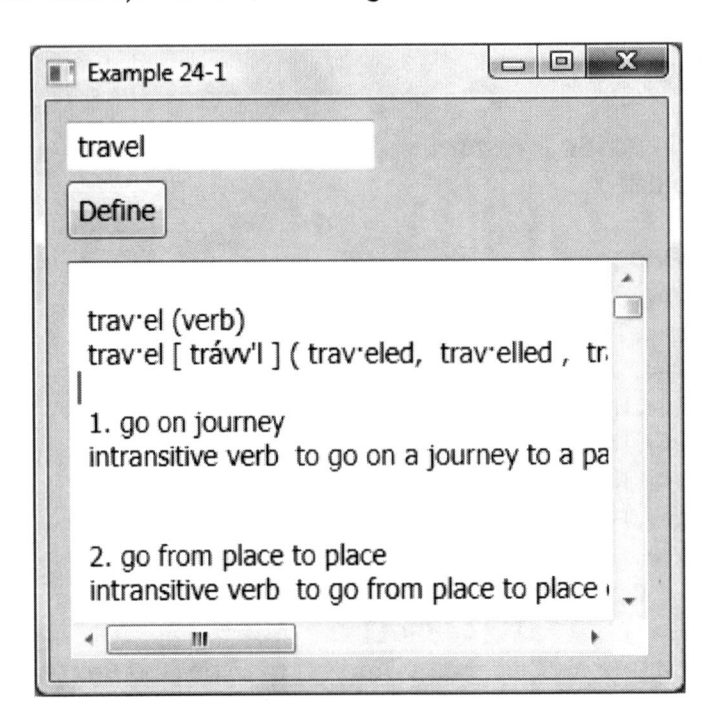

```
┌─ Example 24-1 ───────────────── □ ▣ X ┐
│                                        │
│  travel                                │
│  ┌──────┐                              │
│  │Define│                              │
│  └──────┘                              │
│  ┌──────────────────────────────────┐▲ │
│  │                                  │  │
│  │ trav·el (verb)                   │  │
│  │ trav·el [ tráv'l ] ( trav·eled,  │  │
│  │                       trav·elled, tr│
│  │ |                                │  │
│  │ 1. go on journey                 │  │
│  │ intransitive verb  to go on a journey to a pa│
│  │                                  │  │
│  │                                  │  │
│  │ 2. go from place to place        │  │
│  │ intransitive verb  to go from place to place│▼│
│  └──────────────────────────────────┘  │
└────────────────────────────────────────┘
```

Try other words. How about **smile**:

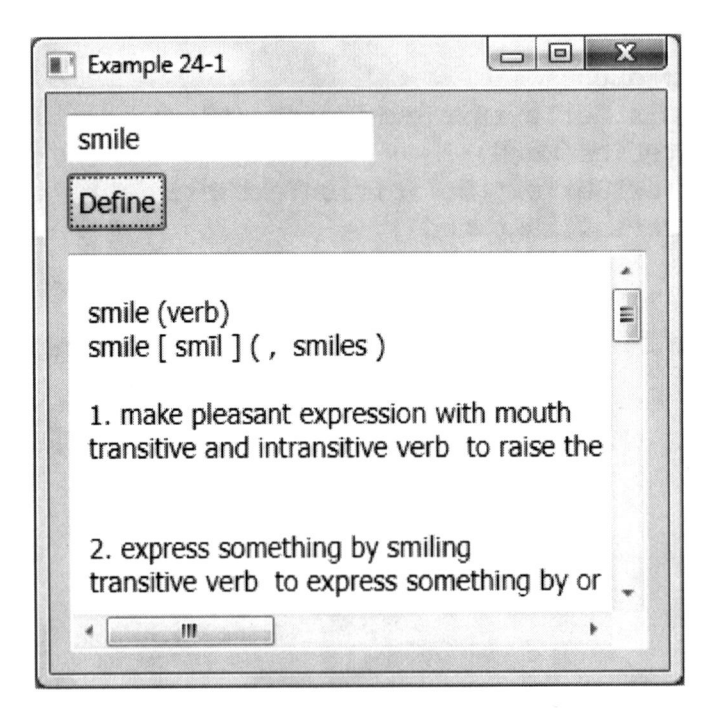

```
┌─ Example 24-1 ───────────────── □ ▣ X ┐
│                                        │
│  smile                                 │
│  ┌──────┐                              │
│  │Define│                              │
│  └──────┘                              │
│  ┌──────────────────────────────────┐▲ │
│  │ smile (verb)                     │≡ │
│  │ smile [ smīl ] ( , smiles )      │  │
│  │                                  │  │
│  │ 1. make pleasant expression with mouth│
│  │ transitive and intransitive verb  to raise the│
│  │                                  │  │
│  │                                  │  │
│  │ 2. express something by smiling  │  │
│  │ transitive verb  to express something by or│▼│
│  └──────────────────────────────────┘  │
└────────────────────────────────────────┘
```

If you like, try the French definition method. I don't know any French so I can't be of much help.

Chapter Review

After completing this chapter, you should understand:

> How to define words using the **Dictionary** class.

This page intentionally not left blank.

25. Sharing a Small Basic Program

Preview

In this chapter, we look at you can share your Small Basic programs with others. We also see how you can embed a Small Basic program in your own webpage.

Sharing a Program

I bet you're ready to show your friends and colleagues some of the programs you have built using Small Basic. Just give them a copy of your code, ask them to install Small Basic and learn how to open and run a program. Then, have them open your program and run it. I think you'll agree this might be asking a lot of your friends, colleagues, and, ultimately, your user base. We need to know how to run a program **without** Small Basic.

To run a program without Small Basic, you need to create an **executable** version of the program. So, how is an executable created? A little secret is that Small Basic builds an executable version of a program every time we run the program! This executable file is in the same folder you save your program in. Open the folder for any program you have built and you'll see a file with your program name of type **Program**.

For example, if I open the program folder for **Example 21-5** (the pizza order program):

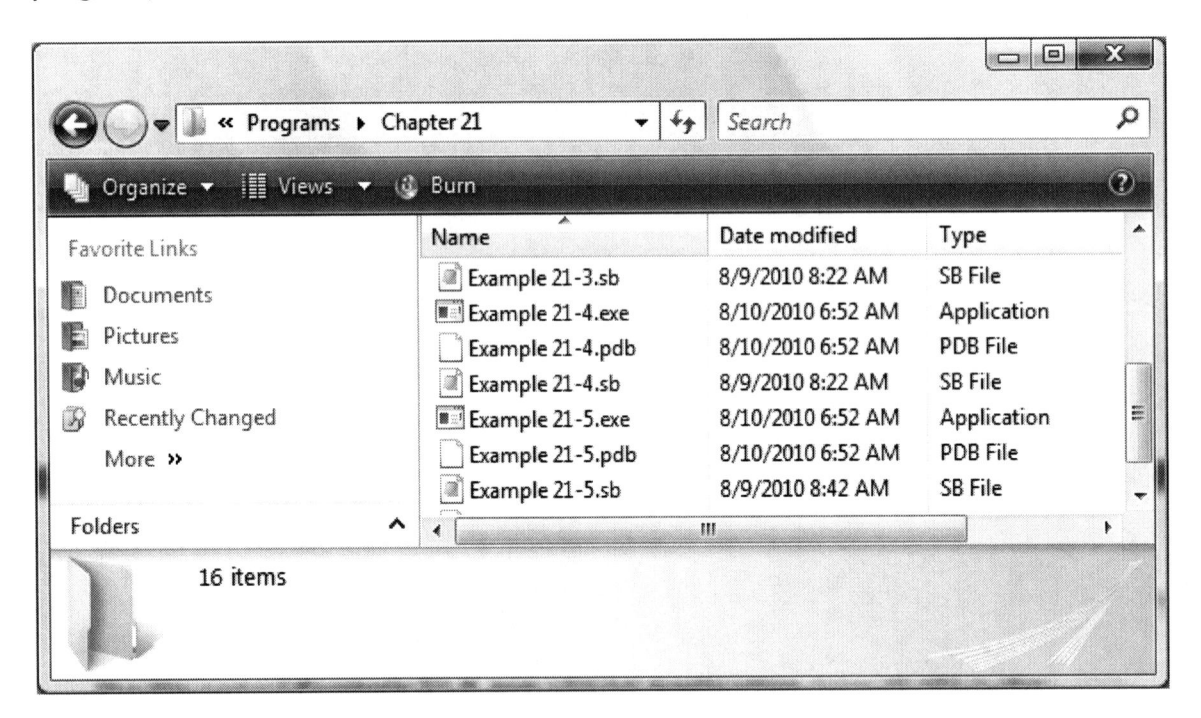

Name	Date modified	Type
Example 21-3.sb	8/9/2010 8:22 AM	SB File
Example 21-4.exe	8/10/2010 6:52 AM	Application
Example 21-4.pdb	8/10/2010 6:52 AM	PDB File
Example 21-4.sb	8/9/2010 8:22 AM	SB File
Example 21-5.exe	8/10/2010 6:52 AM	Application
Example 21-5.pdb	8/10/2010 6:52 AM	PDB File
Example 21-5.sb	8/9/2010 8:42 AM	SB File

16 items

The file named **Example 21-5.exe** of type **Application** (size 20 KB) is the executable version of the program. If I make sure Small Basic is not running and double-click this file, the following appears:

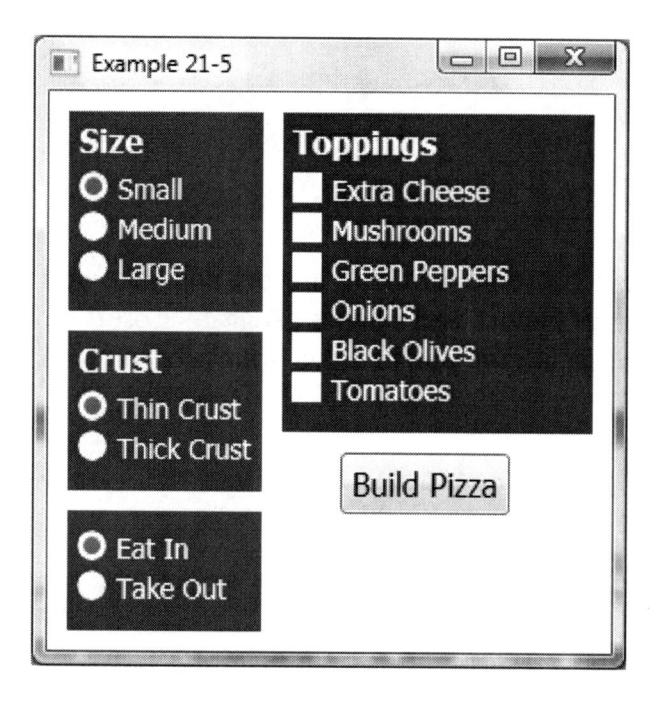

Voila! The **Pizza Order** program is running outside of the Small Basic development environment! Go ahead and try it if you like.

So distributing a Small Basic program is as simple as giving your user a copy of the executable file (and the **SmallBasicLibrary.dll** file in your program folder - this has some support code), having them place the files in a folder on their computer and double-clicking the executable file to run it? Maybe. This worked on my computer (and will work on yours) because I have a very important set of files known as the **.NET Framework** installed (they are installed when Small Basic is installed). Every Small Basic program needs the .NET Framework to be installed on the hosting computer.

The next question is: how do you know if your user has the .NET Framework installed on his or her computer? And, if they don't, how can you get it installed? These are difficult questions. So, in addition to our program's executable file, we also need to give a potential user the Microsoft .NET Framework files and inform them how to install and register these files on their computer. Things are getting complicated. Let's look at an easier and very flashy solution – letting users access and run your programs over the Internet!

Start Small Basic and take a look at the toolbar. There are two buttons there we haven't talked about yet. Between the buttons to open and save files and the ones for editing are buttons marked **Import** and **Publish**:

These are remarkable buttons. Clicking **Import** will take you to a Microsoft website where you can import and open a program stored on the Internet by you or other users. **Publish** allows you to store your programs on the Internet for others to use.

Make sure your computer is connected to the Internet. Go ahead and click **Import**. You should see:

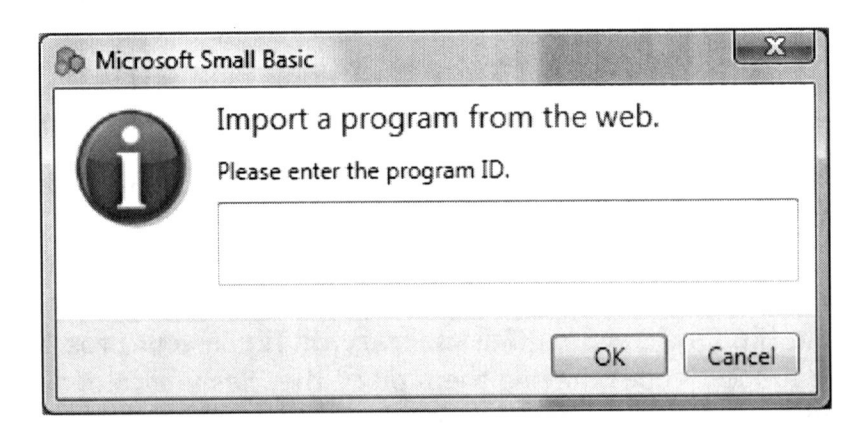

To import a program, you require a **Program ID**. How do you get such an ID? It is assigned when you **Publish** a program, so let's try that. Click the **Cancel** button for now.

Publishing a Program

When you publish a program, it will be available for all to see and use. And, for now, there is no way to "unpublish" a program. So, be careful what you publish. You may be leary about just giving your hard work away. For the example here, I will use a very simple two line program just to show how things work. You can decide what you want to publish.

Here is the program I will use:

```
GraphicsWindow.Show()
GraphicsWindow.DrawText(10, 10 , "I can publish!!")
```

Type in this code (or use some other program), then click **Publish**. You will see a message something like this:

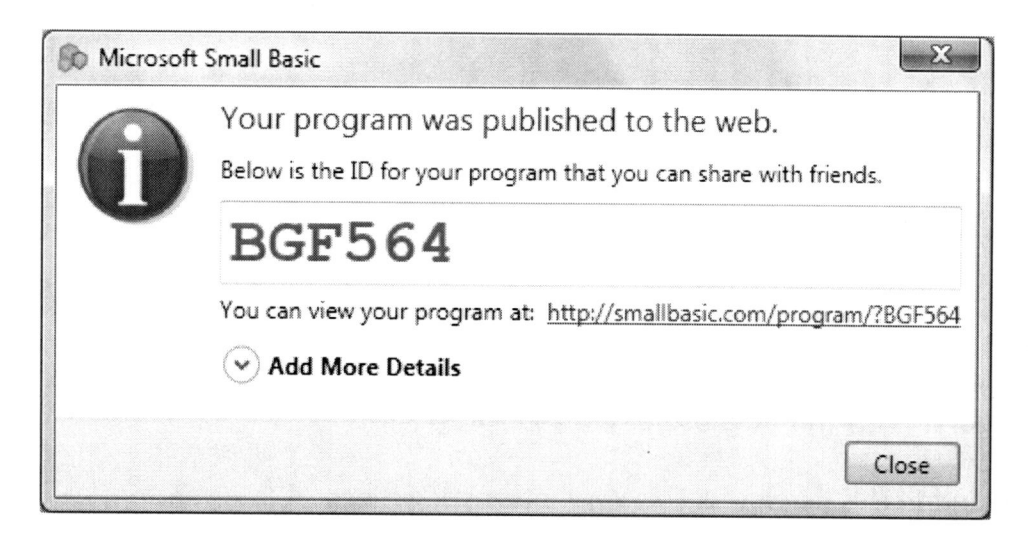

Your program is assigned a Program **ID** (remember we need this to import a program).

Click **Add More Details:**

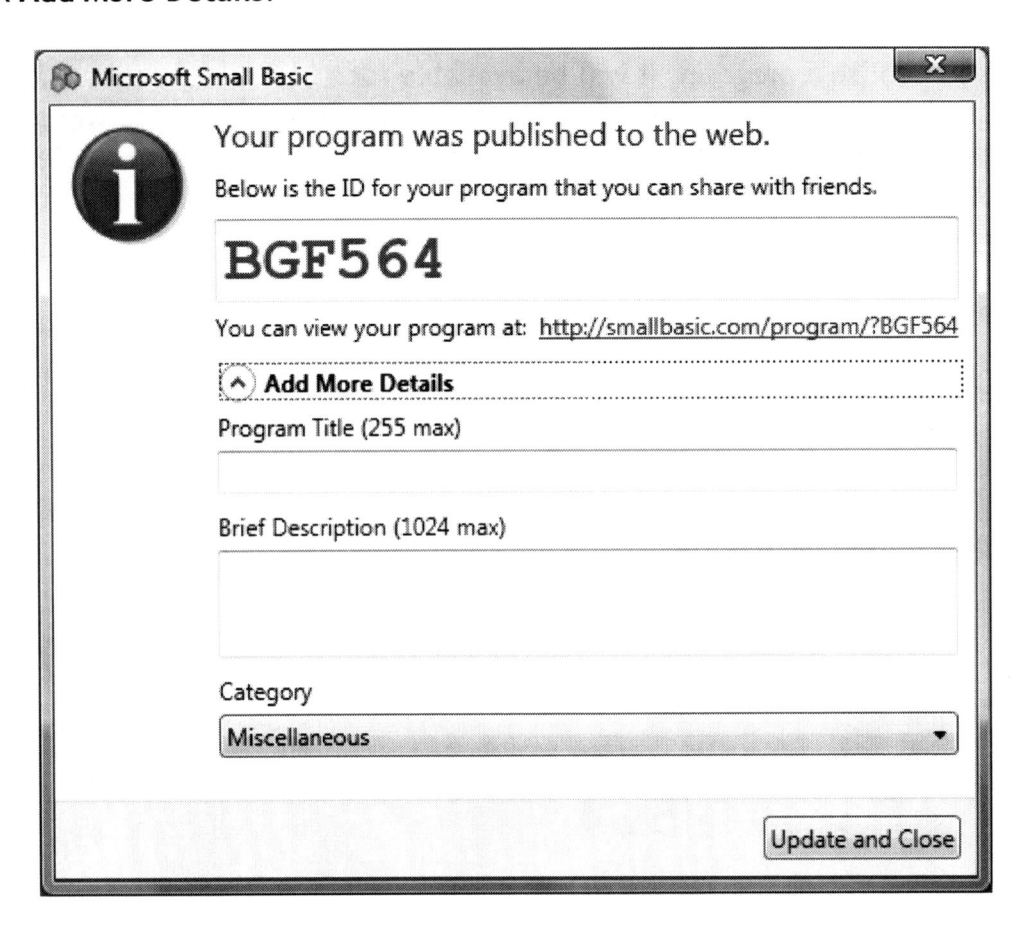

[Screenshot of Microsoft Small Basic dialog: "Your program was published to the web. Below is the ID for your program that you can share with friends. BGF564. You can view your program at: http://smallbasic.com/program/?BGF564. Add More Details. Program Title (255 max). Brief Description (1024 max). Category: Miscellaneous. Update and Close"]

Here, you can describe what your program is and what it does. You can provide a category. This will help users find your program

Also listed in this window is this very interesting piece of information:

You can view your program at: http://smallbasic.com/program/?BGF564

If you click this link (or give the link to others and let them click it), "magic" occurs.

Sharing a Small Basic Program   25-7

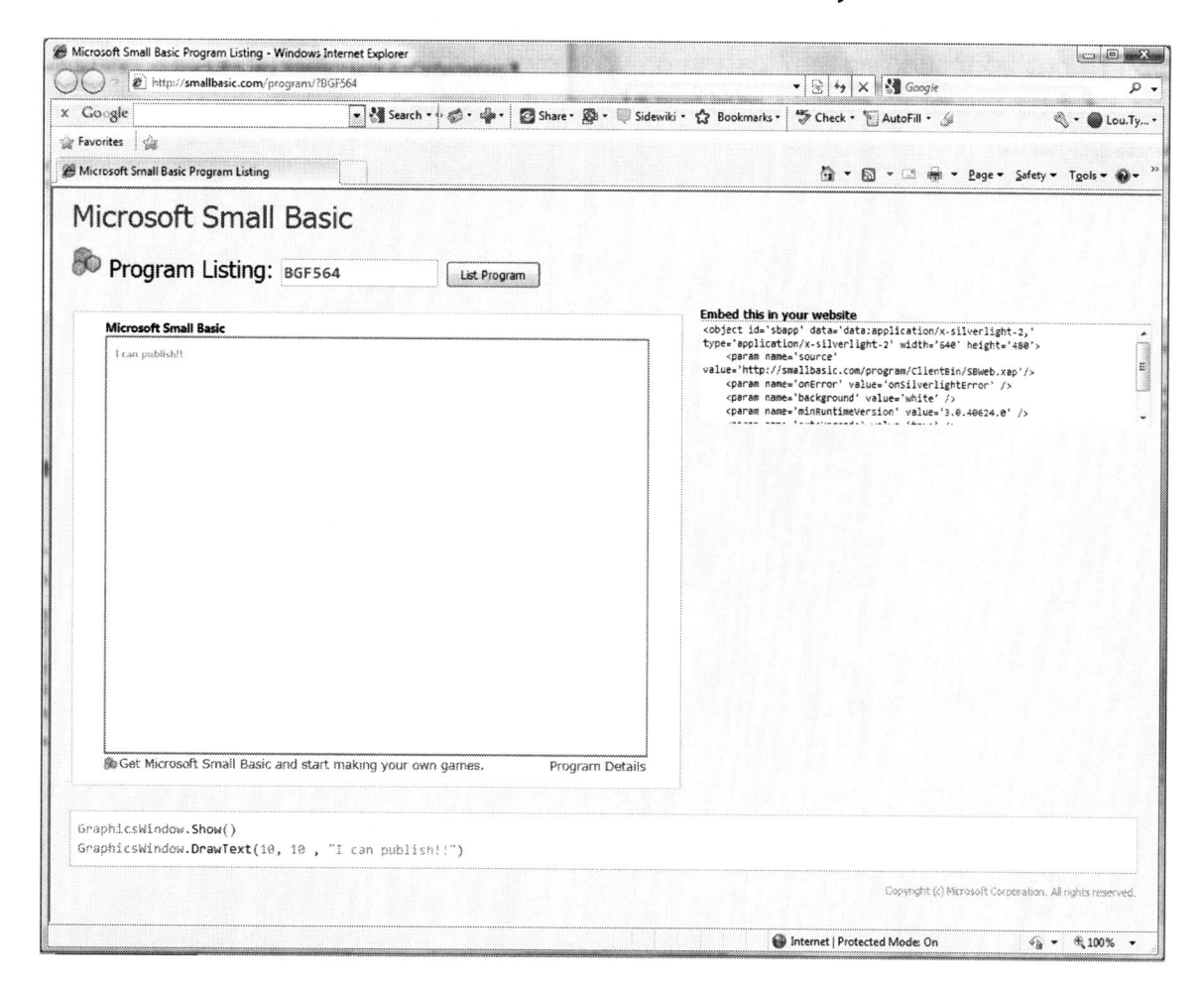

When I click the link, I am taken to this website hosted by Microsoft:

The running program is shown, along with a code listing.

I think you'll agree this pretty neat. To share your programs with other users, **Publish** them, then give them the program link given to you. If they click the link, they can run the program. Well, almost. To use this feature, a user's computer must have a Microsoft product called **Silverlight** installed on their computer. It can be downloaded from this website:

http://www.silverlight.net/

If a user attempts to access your Small Basic program via a provided link and they do not have the required **Silverlight** product, they will be taken through the installation steps.

Return to the website with your running program. In the upper right corner is a box marked **Embed this in your website.** In this box is some code that allows you to put your running application on your own website, if you have one. The steps to do this are beyond this discussion, but I wanted you to know such a step was possible.

Importing a Program

Before leaving, lets return to the **Import** button in Small Basic. Click it again and enter the program ID for your program (I used **BGF564**):

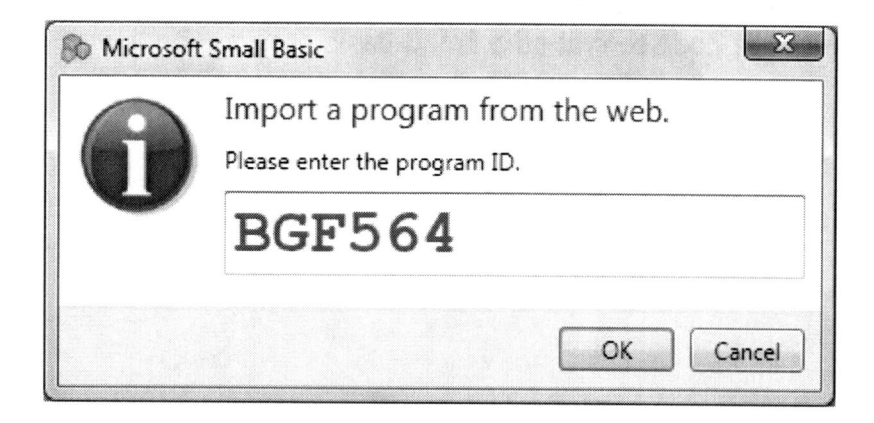

Click **OK**. The imported code will appear in your editor:

```
GraphicsWindow.Show()
GraphicsWindow.DrawText(10, 10 , "I can publish!!")
```

So, you have access to any code published to the Microsoft Small Basic library. I'm guessing this library will be growing very quickly.

Chapter Review

After completing this chapter, you should understand:

- ➤ How to publish a Small Basic program.
- ➤ Where to get code to embed a Small Basic program on a web page.
- ➤ How to import a Small Basic program.

Appendix I. Small Basic Colors

Color	Name	RGB Value
	AliceBlue	#F0F8FF
	AntiqueWhite	#FAEBD7
	Aqua	#00FFFF
	Aquamarine	#7FFFD4
	Azure	#F0FFFF
	Beige	#F5F5DC
	Bisque	#FFE4C4
	Black	#000000
	BlanchedAlmond	#FFEBCD
	Blue	#0000FF
	BlueViolet	#8A2BE2
	Brown	#A52A2A
	BurlyWood	#DEB887
	CadetBlue	#5F9EA0
	Chartreuse	#7FFF00
	Chocolate	#D2691E
	Coral	#FF7F50
	CornflowerBlue	#6495ED

	Cornsilk	#FFF8DC
	Crimson	#DC143C
	Cyan	#00FFFF
	DarkBlue	#00008B
	DarkCyan	#008B8B
	DarkGoldenrod	#B8860B
	DarkGray / DarkGrey[†]	#A9A9A9
	DarkGreen	#006400
	DarkKhaki	#BDB76B
	DarkMagenta	#8B008B
	DarkOliveGreen	#556B2F
	DarkOrange	#FF8C00
	DarkOrchid	#9932CC
	DarkRed	#8B0000
	DarkSalmon	#E9967A
	DarkSeaGreen	#8FBC8F
	DarkSlateBlue	#483D8B
	DarkSlateGray / DarkSlateGrey[†]	#2F4F4F
	DarkTurquoise	#00CED1
	DarkViolet	#9400D3
	DeepPink	#FF1493

Appendix I. Small Basic Colors

	DeepSkyBlue	#00BFFF
	DimGray / DimGrey[†]	#696969
	DodgerBlue	#1E90FF
	FireBrick	#B22222
	FloralWhite	#FFFAF0
	ForestGreen	#228B22
	Fuchsia	#FF00FF
	Gainsboro	#DCDCDC
	GhostWhite	#F8F8FF
	Gold	#FFD700
	Goldenrod	#DAA520
	Gray / Grey[†]	#808080
	Green	#008000
	GreenYellow	#ADFF2F
	Honeydew	#F0FFF0
	HotPink	#FF69B4
	IndianRed	#CD5C5C
	Indigo	#4B0082
	Ivory	#FFFFF0
	Khaki	#F0E68C
	Lavender	#E6E6FA

	LavenderBlush	#FFF0F5
	LawnGreen	#7CFC00
	LemonChiffon	#FFFACD
	LightBlue	#ADD8E6
	LightCoral	#F08080
	LightCyan	#E0FFFF
	LightGoldenrodYellow	#FAFAD2
	LightGreen	#90EE90
	LightGray[†] / LightGrey	#D3D3D3
	LightPink	#FFB6C1
	LightSalmon	#FFA07A
	LightSeaGreen	#20B2AA
	LightSkyBlue	#87CEFA
	LightSlateGray / LightSlateGrey[†]	#778899
	LightSteelBlue	#B0C4DE
	LightYellow	#FFFFE0
	Lime	#00FF00
	LimeGreen	#32CD32
	Linen	#FAF0E6
	Magenta	#FF00FF
	Maroon	#800000

Appendix I. Small Basic Colors

I-5

	MediumAquamarine	#66CDAA
	MediumBlue	#0000CD
	MediumOrchid	#BA55D3
	MediumPurple	#9370DB
	MediumSeaGreen	#3CB371
	MediumSlateBlue	#7B68EE
	MediumSpringGreen	#00FA9A
	MediumTurquoise	#48D1CC
	MediumVioletRed	#C71585
	MidnightBlue	#191970
	MintCream	#F5FFFA
	MistyRose	#FFE4E1
	Moccasin	#FFE4B5
	NavajoWhite	#FFDEAD
	Navy	#000080
	OldLace	#FDF5E6
	Olive	#808000
	OliveDrab	#6B8E23
	Orange	#FFA500
	OrangeRed	#FF4500
	Orchid	#DA70D6

	PaleGoldenrod	#EEE8AA
	PaleGreen	#98FB98
	PaleTurquoise	#AFEEEE
	PaleVioletRed	#DB7093
	PapayaWhip	#FFEFD5
	PeachPuff	#FFDAB9
	Peru	#CD853F
	Pink	#FFC0CB
	Plum	#DDA0DD
	PowderBlue	#B0E0E6
	Purple	#800080
	Red	#FF0000
	RosyBrown	#BC8F8F
	RoyalBlue	#4169E1
	SaddleBrown	#8B4513
	Salmon	#FA8072
	SandyBrown	#F4A460
	SeaGreen	#2E8B57
	Seashell	#FFF5EE
	Sienna	#A0522D
	Silver	#C0C0C0

Appendix I. Small Basic Colors

	SkyBlue	#87CEEB
	SlateBlue	#6A5ACD
	SlateGray / SlateGrey[†]	#708090
	Snow	#FFFAFA
	SpringGreen	#00FF7F
	SteelBlue	#4682B4
	Tan	#D2B48C
	Teal	#008080
	Thistle	#D8BFD8
	Tomato	#FF6347
	Turquoise	#40E0D0
	Violet	#EE82EE
	Wheat	#F5DEB3
	White	#FFFFFF
	WhiteSmoke	#F5F5F5
	Yellow	#FFFF00
	YellowGreen	#9ACD32

Other Small Basic Resources from BIBLEBYTE BOOKS

BIBLEBYTE BOOKS offers several Microsoft Small Basic Programming Tutorials which help introduce the Microsoft Small Basic Development Environment to kids and adults. The Small Basic Programming Tutorials are appropriate for Middle School students and early High School students. Beginning Small Basic programming adults will also find these tutorials fun and engaging as well.

Beginning Small Basic Programming Tutorial

The **Beginning Small Basic Programming Tutorial** is a self-study first semester **"beginner"** programming tutorial consisting of 11 chapters explaining (in simple, easy-to-follow terms) how to write Microsoft Small Basic programs. The last chapter of the tutorial shows you how four different Small Basic games would look in BASIC, Visual Basic, Visual C# and Java. This beginning level self-paced tutorial can be used at home or school. The tutorial is simple enough for kids yet engaging enough for beginning adults.

Computer Bible Games for Microsoft Small Basic

COMPUTER BIBLE GAMES FOR MICROSOFT SMALL BASIC is a self-study **"beginner"** programming tutorial for Christian Schools and Homeschools. This tutorial consists of 13 Chapters explaining (in simple, easy-to-follow terms) how to build Computer Bible Games in Small Basic. It covers the exact same material that is presented in the Beginning Small Basic Programming Tutorial above except that it also includes the Small Basic source code for the original Computer Bible Games and not the secular Small Basic Computer Games porting chapter. This special edition of the Beginning Small Basic Programming Tutorial is specifically designed for Christian Middle & High Schools as well as Christian Homeschools.

Programming Kid Games with Microsoft Small Basic

Programming Kid Games with Microsoft Small Basic is a self-study second semester **"intermediate"** level programming tutorial consisting of 10 chapters explaining (in simple, easy-to-follow terms) how to write kid video games in Microsoft Small Basic. Students will learn how to program the following Small Basic video games: Safecracker, Tic Tac Toe, Match Game, Pizza Delivery, Moon Landing, and Leap Frog. This intermediate level self-paced tutorial can be used at home or at school. You will learn about program design, using Small Basic objects (including v.09+ button controls), many elements of the Small Basic language, and how to debug and share finished programs. Game skills learned include handling multiple players, scoring, graphics, animation, and sounds.

David Ahl's "Small Basic" Computer Adventures

David Ahl's Small Basic Computer Adventures is a Microsoft Small Basic re-make of the classic *BASIC COMPUTER ADVENTURES* programming book originally written by David H. Ahl. This new book includes the following classic adventure simulations; Marco Polo, Westward Ho!, The Longest Automobile Race, The Orient Express, Amelia Earhart: Around the World Flight, Tour de France, Subway Scavenger, Hong Kong Hustle, and Voyage to Neptune. Learn how to program these classic computer simulations in Microsoft Small Basic. This "intermediate" level self-paced tutorial can be used at home or school. With the purchase of this Small Basic Computer Adventures E-Book, you and/or your students are eligible to participate in our first Small Basic Programming Competition scheduled to start January 1, 2011.

We also offer several other Beginning and Intermediate Level Computer Programming Tutorials for Microsoft Small Basic.

The Developer's Reference Guide to Microsoft Small Basic

While developing all the different Microsoft Small Basic tutorials below we found it necessary to write The Developer's Reference Guide to Microsoft Small Basic . The Developer's Reference Guide to Microsoft Small Basic is over 500 pages long and includes over 100 Small Basic programming examples for you to learn from and include in your own Microsoft Small Basic programs.

Basic Computer Games - Small Basic Edition

This book is a re-make of the classic BASIC COMPUTER GAMES book originally edited by David H. Ahl. It contains 100 of the original retro-games that started it all, now re-written in Microsoft Small Basic.

We also offer several other Beginning Level Computer Programming Tutorials for Microsoft Small Basic, Microsoft Visual Basic, Microsoft Visual C# and Oracle Java.

We also offer several Beginning Computer Programming Tutorials for Christian Schools and Homeschools. These Tutorials cover most of the same material that is found in our Beginning Programming Tutorials except that we have added several classic Computer Bible Games for your student to learn and develop.

We also offer several Advanced Math and Life Skills Honors Projects that allow students to develop a Dual Mode Stop Watch, Consumer Loan Assistant Calculator, Home Inventory Manager, a Two-Player Snow Ball Toss Game, Flash Card Math Quiz, and Multiple Choice Exam.